The Sappho Companion

The Sappho Companion

EDITED AND INTRODUCED BY

MARGARET REYNOLDS

palgrave

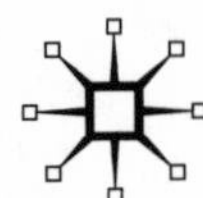

THE SAPPHO COMPANION

First published in paperback 2002 by PALGRAVE™
175 Fifth Avenue, New York, N.Y. 10010
Companies and representatives throughout the world.

PALGRAVE is the new global publishing imprint of St. Martin's Press LLC Scholarly and Reference Division and Palgrave Publishers Ltd. (formerly Macmillan Press Ltd.).

ISBN 0-312-29510-3

Library of Congress Cataloging-in-Publication Data available at the Library of Congress.

First published in Great Britain in 2000 by Chatto & Windus

First PALGRAVE paperback edition: June 2002
10 9 8 7 6 5 4 3 2 1

Printed in the United States of America.

For Jeanette Winterson,
with love

CONTENTS

come, my sacred tortoiseshell lyre
speak, and let my music
give you voice

Sappho, Fragment 118

BEFORE THE BEGINNING

. . . Orpheus, son of Apollo, was the most famous musician the world has ever known. Animals crowded round to hear his song and even the lion lay down tamely at his feet. Mountains would heave their rocky foundations and move towards the sound; trees would bend and pull up their roots to follow his music.

When his wife Eurydice died, Orpheus pursued her into Hades and so charmed the god of death with the music of his lyre that his prayer was granted and Eurydice was restored to life. But Orpheus forgot the one condition – that he should not look back as they made their way up and out of the underworld. With Eurydice now lost to him for a second time, the music of Orpheus' lyre was so sad that it broke the hearer's heart. Alone on the mountainside Orpheus mourned, and day after day the people who lived nearby wept to hear his wailing song. Then one day the sound was heard no more. Some said that the gods, unable to bear the sounds of his lamentation, had struck him with lightning; others that Orpheus had been torn apart by wild beasts, tormented by the pain of his song, or by Maenads, half-crazed women who wandered over the mountains.

However that may be, Orpheus' lyre floated down the River Hebrus and out into the wide sea, playing all the while, and its sweet music echoed across the water. At length the lyre was cast up high on the shores of the island of Lesbos, where it lay neglected until it was overgrown with vines and half-buried under falling leaves. But the winds of the island are known for their melodies, and the nightingales of Lesbos are said to sing more sweetly than those of any other place in the world . . .

INTRODUCTION

At the beginning of the twentieth century an American visitor to the island of Lesbos said that every family on the island had a daughter named Sappho. Today, although you can meet Iphigenias in Greece, Electras and Cassandras, and even Jocastas, you hardly ever meet a Sappho. It is not a name that features in the dictionaries scoured by new parents in any country.

I did once know a girl called Sappho – not in Greece, but in Oxford. It was in the early 1970s and she was an American, a renegade hippie who had run away from her respectable family, worked in a circus and done the drug scene, and who now wanted to settle into domesticity with her undergraduate boyfriend. Her real name was Sue. Another Sappho that I know of was Sappho Durrell, the daughter of Lawrence Durrell (who figures in this book) and herself a writer. Sadly, though she made the ancient Sappho one of her literary models, her personal history all too closely resembled that of her namesake, for she led a difficult and unhappy life and ended by committing suicide in January 1985 at the age of thirty-four.

Other than that, I can think of the Ladies of Llangollen (Lady Eleanor Butler and Sarah Ponsonby), who were celebrated in the early nineteenth century for their romantic friendship and whose dog was called Sappho. Radclyffe Hall had a parrot called Sappho in 1926, but it bit her and ended up being sent to the zoo. More recently Kate Flint, an academic colleague, once had a cat named Sappho. She liked to sleep high up on top of the kitchen cupboards, from where she would take a flying leap on to the floor. I never did find out if this was how she got to be called Sappho, or whether the practice began after she had acquired the name, but I do know that Kate's other cat was called Mrs Pankhurst.

So even in this very small sample of Sapphos, the name conjures up allusions to an activist-feminist, to a Sapphist or a romantic friend, to a writer and a suicide, to a non-conformist free spirit, and to an illustrious woman whose name was venerated by the inhabitants of her native island. In this book you will find other examples of all these kinds of Sapphos, and you will meet many more.

The real Sappho, if not the first Sappho, was a poet. And her name was not 'Sappho' – as we pronounce it – at all. Today, in English, she is all soft sibilants and faded f's, but in fact she is ψάπφ 'Psappho'. In ancient Greek – and, indeed, even in modern Greek – if you hear a native speaker say her name, she comes across spitting and popping hard p's. Ppppsappoppo. We have eased off her name, made her docile and sliding, where she is really difficult, diffuse, many-syllabled, many-minded, vigorous and hard.

Psappho lived on the island of Lesbos, off the coast of what is now Turkey, at the end of the seventh and the beginning of the sixth centuries BC. Beyond these bare facts, we know very little about her poetry, hardly anything about her life, not much more about her society, nothing to speak of about her character and nothing whatsoever about her personal appearance. But this lack of facts has not stopped people – virtually from that day to this – making up stories about her. Quite the contrary. As you will see in reading this anthology, 'Sappho' is not a name, much less a person. It is, rather, a space. A space for filling in the gaps, joining up the dots, making something out of nothing.

This applies as much to Sappho's poetry as to her story. Because Sappho's poetry survives only in fragments, haphazardly quoted or remembered or dug up in garbled versions from rubbish heaps, her work has always been a site of invention for the poets who came after her. The first section of this book, 'The Fragments of Sappho', tells how her literary remains were handed down through history. It gives such versions of the Greek as can be construed from the ancient sources, side by side with later, invented poems that are based on that already-fake Sappho.

When it comes to the life, or rather, the legends, then the connections to a real Sappho become, if anything, still more tenuous. Even in her lifetime Sappho was a name that conjured up a story, and the fabrications that built up around her are set out in the second section, 'The Tenth Muse'. In putting together documents that tell the tales of her later incarnations, I have tried to trace the varied phenomena of Sapphic fashions as they unfolded at particular times and, sometimes, in particular places. For instance, during the Middle Ages, Sappho was a name for 'The Learned Lady', but during the eighteenth century 'Sappho' meant, for some, the kind of woman who was likely to be caught performing a 'Wanton Sapphoic'; and, during the nineteenth century, her reputation in certain circles sank so low that she became a 'Daughter of de Sade'. Sometimes entirely contradictory images of Sappho run simultaneously, as she becomes caught up in particular cultural movements. So in the eighteenth century you will also find her featuring in sections on 'The Sapphic Sublime' and 'Hellenism and Heroes', while in the nineteenth century she was, at two different stages, a literary role-model in 'The Lady with the Lyre' and a politicised feminist heroine in 'The New Woman'.

In all these different times and manifestations there is a fairly consistent cast of characters – both real and imaginary. Like Sappho herself, they appear in different forms, but it is worth introducing these supporting roles.

Aphrodite: The Greek goddess of love, who also appears under her Roman name of Venus, or under the name of *Cypris*, 'the Cyprian', because she is supposed to have been born on Cyprus. She is Sappho's presiding deity – sometimes her ally, sometimes her rival, occasionally her enemy.

Pittacus: The lord or ruler of Lesbos (c. 645–570 BC), who may actually have been in charge during Sappho's lifetime. Sometimes he is a benevolent despot, sometimes a cruel tyrant.

Phaon: Another name for Adonis, one of Aphrodite's lovers, for whose death Sappho wrote some poems of lamentation. One legend says that Phaon was an old ferryman, who rowed Aphrodite across a river and was rewarded with the choice of any gift he desired. When his request for renewed youth was granted, his beauty and vigour became the admiration of all. In many Sappho stories Phaon figures as her beloved, with or without the above prelude. In most of them he is not actually interested in Sappho and scorns her love, which is why she decides to kill herself.

Alcaeus: An ancient Greek lyric poet; also a native of Lesbos and historically Sappho's contemporary. As with Sappho's own poetry, his work survives only in fragments, but there are more substantial remains. He appears in the legends variously as Sappho's friend, her fellow poet, her lover or her rival.

Anacreon: Another ancient Greek lyric poet, whose chief subjects were wine, women and boys, and song. Sappho's poems were often published in editions alongside Anacreon's. He flourished about 532 BC, so at least half a century later than Sappho, although some writers believed that he was her contemporary, so he too occasionally appears as her friend, her fellow poet, her lover or her rival.

Bion: A Greek poet from Smyrna, who wrote pastorals and lived in about 145 BC.

Theocritus: A Greek poet, who flourished in about 282 BC and lived in Syracuse, Sicily.

Archilochus: A Greek poet, writer of elegies, odes and epigrams, most of which are now lost. A native of Paros, he lived in about 685 BC.

Erinna: A Greek poet who wrote hexameter and elegiac poetry and lived in the late fourth century BC. Sometimes she appears as one of Sappho's pupils or companions. Other early women poets occasionally crop up in Sappho's story, although they were not her contemporaries, and include Corinna, Telesilla, Praxilla, Anyte and Nossis.

Atthis: One of Sappho's companions, pupils, girlfriends or novitiates, depending upon which story you are reading. Her name is actually mentioned in what we have of Sappho's Fragments 49, 96 and 131.

Abanthis, Anaktoria, Andromeda, Dica, Gongyla, Gorgo, Gyrinno, Irana, Megara, Mika, Mnasidica: Other companions. Again, all these names are actually mentioned in the Fragments.

Climene, Cydno, Damophyla, Philaenis, Pyrrhine, Theseyle, Telesippa: Yet more companions, along with various other invented names for Sappho's girls. Sometimes one or another of these might appear as a younger rival in love.

Cleis: Sappho's daughter, named in Fragment 132. Cleis is also supposed to have been the name of Sappho's mother.

Charaxus, Larichus, Erigyius: Sappho's brothers. Larichus was said to have poured wine in the civil ceremonies of Lesbos, a duty reserved only for the sons of noble families. Charaxus may have been a wine merchant.

Doricha: Sometimes also called Rhodope. A courtesan with whom Sappho's brother Charaxus was said to have had a liaison of which his sister did not approve. Fragment 5 is said to be about this.

Alcandro, Stesichore: Two of the names (along with many others) for Sappho's supposed father. He tends to appear most often in the fictions of the late eighteenth and early nineteenth centuries.

Cercylas from Andros: Said to be the name of Sappho's husband. However, as it means 'Prick from the Island of Man', it may be the invention of later comic writers.

The main sites of Sappho's story can be mapped out thus. On Lesbos the chief town is Mytilene, but there is also a smaller town on the other side of the island called Eresus, and in some legends – especially once the story of 'the two Sapphos' takes hold – Sappho is supposed to be a native of Eresus. Lydia, a country occupying the centre of the western part of Asia Minor, or Turkey, was the dominant empire in Sappho's time and sometimes figures in her stories. Its capital was Sardis, a city that she mentions in her Fragments. The story of Sappho's exile means that Sicily also appears. Other stories take her to mainland Greece, to Athens and to Mount Olympus, the legendary home of the gods. The other key place is Leucas, or Leucadia, an island in the Ionian sea now known as St Maura, where Sappho is supposed to have thrown herself to her death. The name derives from *leukos*, meaning white, because of the white cliffs of the island. It was also the site of a cult of Apollo, the sun god, which may have included this human sacrifice in its rituals.

As there is an ever-changing cast of characters and a shifting *mise-en-scène* for Sappho's story, so there is a range of props associated with her, and these symbols figure both in her literary and visual representations. Chief among them is the lyre, either four- or seven-stringed and invented, according to legend, by Apollo (the sun god, and the god of music and poetry), and then inherited by Orpheus (son of Apollo, or Oeager, by Calliope, the muse of eloquence and heroic poetry). The ancient *kithara* was a heavy instrument giving a more solemn tone, and was preferred by professional singers and poets, while the *lyra*, fashioned from a tortoiseshell, was lighter. Sometimes Sappho plays another instrument altogether, depending on the fashion of the day; so, a harp or a lute in the Middle Ages, a lyre-guitar in the early nineteenth century. If Sappho is bemoaning her lot, or on the point of ending her life, then the strings of her lyre are untuned, symbolically snapped or the whole instrument may even be broken into fragments. Sometimes her lyre is much more than a musical instrument, also depending on the fashion of the day. It is certainly used suggestively by Algernon Swinburne, by Alphonse Daudet in his novel *Sapho* and by the French painter Barrias.

Second among Sappho's essential kit of props is the laurel wreath, emblem of Apollo and the reward of the victor in both the ancient Greek games and the poetry contest. If the Sappho being presented is upright and in full control, the laurel wreath sits squarely on her head. (Indeed, the moment of her crowning came to represent the height of achievement for a whole generation of women writers who followed the history of Madame de Staël's Sappho-persona in her 1807 novel *Corinne*.) If, on the other hand, Sappho is distraught – with passion, with pain – then her laurel wreath falls unregarded to the ground.

In pictures, poems and stories until the middle of the eighteenth century Sappho generally wears contemporary garments of the period: wimples and a pointed headdress in the Middle Ages, corsets and lawn in the sixteenth century. Then, in the eighteenth century, muslin came in, along with the fashion for Greek simplicity, and thereafter Sappho was almost always associated with tunics and drapery, or the classical *chiton*, until she managed to get into jeans in the late twentieth century. Around the middle of the eighteenth century she also acquired a full set of furniture: tripod lamps, *klismos* chairs, columns, candlesticks, various Pompeian-inspired room sets, and mirrors of burnished bronze or silver. She also began to appear, both in pictures and in certain plays and poems, with one important piece of furniture, in the shape of a bed, or a couch, or a classical-style sofa, and that too stayed with her until the twentieth century. To go with this there was often a pair of cooing doves, to represent lasciviousness. And, for a brief but spectacular period from about 1760 to 1825, she was regularly depicted in the shadow of Vesuvius – the erupting volcano indicating at once Sappho's volatile passions, her literary grandeur and the unknowable chasms of the woman's body.

These variously inventive ways of imagining Sappho indicate how regularly she has been updated and re-interpreted for a contemporary audience. What is it about her work, about her story, that makes Sappho so attractive; that makes her appeal last for 2,000 years and more; and that still speaks to us across that waste of time?

Partly it is the sense of her being there at the beginning of world literature, unknown, strange and yet dimly recognisable, faintly imaginable – a real person whose relics we may yet be able to recover. For many of the poets included here, Tennyson and Baudelaire among them, she was a poetic mother (Baudelaire's poem 'Lesbos' actually begins '*Mère des jeux latins et des voluptés grecques, / Lesbos*') and in returning to her body, to her nurturing body-of-work, they fantasise about their own origin. The fact that that body is mutilated, in pieces – both actually, in terms of the fragmented works, and metaphorically, in terms of her legendary death, broken on the rocks of the sea – makes Sappho all the more seductive. Like the battered torso of the *Venus de Milo*, her injuries repel, and yet the idealised perfection of the imagined whole inspires a nostalgia and a longing that are greater than those directed towards any other object of desire that is present, intact and accessible. Like the enigmatic smile of the *Mona Lisa*, Sappho seems known to us, familiar, capable of being translated into our everyday lives. Yet still she remains utterly remote – if anything, all the more insinuating and full of meaning because she is, and always will be, absent. Just as thousands of tourists came to stare at the blank space on the walls of the Louvre when the *Mona Lisa* was stolen during the early part of the twentieth century, so we still make up stories about the emptiness that is S—o.

Because of this, Sappho functions as an attractive metaphor. Her work is in fragments, just as her body is broken, and since the eighteenth century our culture has entertained a pervading fascination with anything imperfect, destroyed, failed, lost. At the same time what we have of the work, and what others have made up about her life, suggests different qualities, much admired since the time of the Romantics: enthusiasm, passion, commitment. (These same ingredients made the film *Titanic* into a late twentieth-century blockbuster.) As far as we can tell from the Fragments, Sappho was a dedicated poet; a wordsmith who could craft emotion and experience. She seduces still, and is used to seduce still, in fictions both heterosexual and homosexual.

Then there is Sappho's death, or her supposed death. On the one hand, her leap into space represents a sublime moment of will, of self-glorification in a starry sky, and it is no accident that Sappho's leap became her most popular scene in the late eighteenth century, just after the Enlightenment and with the rise of the Romantics. On the other hand, the fall into the abyss suggests human failure – the mind rises up, while the body sinks down – and so Sappho became associated with 'the fallen woman', the sexually suspect carrier of disease and social disruption, during the nineteenth century. Everywhere the many bodies of Sappho express her contradictions. In Tennyson's *The Princess* (1846) her works are 'jewels five-words-long / That on the stretched forefinger of all Time / Sparkle for ever' (II, 355–7). Yet, at the same time, her words are 'burning', her life is hot with lust and love, and – if you are of a censorious frame of mind – her works are worthy of burning, just as she, like a pagan witch, is ripe for condemnation and the punishment of the stake.

The details of Sappho's story make her various and adaptable, depending on the concerns of the historical moment. At particular times the role of the artist was clichéd into the picture of a suffering, solitary life, punished for the aspirations of vision by the pains of loss or failure. Sappho conveniently fits this mould. At other times, for women especially, the conflict between the calls of art and the comforts of love became the particular tension, and here too Sappho fitted. And yet – needing glorious role-models and finding so few – women artists everywhere have invoked the name of Sappho, however problematic it may be. In the eighteenth century there was 'the Swedish Sappho', Hedvig Charlotte Nordenflycht, author of 'Ode to a Hyacinth'; in England Mary Robinson, among many others, was the 'British Sappho'. The 'Russian Sappho' was Sophia Parnock; Anna Karshin was the 'German Sappho'; there was an 'Italian Sappho'; and so on.

Re-incarnated, revived, resuscitated, recalled, remembered, re-invented. One way or another Sappho lives on, in new places, in new mediums, in new ways.

This collection represents a sample of the incarnations of Sappho over the last 2,500 years. There are many more. But in recent times, especially during the past ten years, Sappho has been enjoying a revival. As far as the classical poet is concerned, this revival is partly due to modern scholarship in ancient Greek, as three major new editions appeared in the second half of the twentieth century: Edgar Lobel and Denys Page, *Poetarum Lesbiorum Fragmenta* (1955); Eva-Maria Voigt, *Sappho et Alcaeus: Fragmenta* (1971); and David A. Campbell, *Greek Lyric 1: Sappho and Alcaeus* (for the Loeb Classical Library, 1982). Many new translations, both in prose and verse, have also been published. Then there have been five major critical books on the classical Sappho, by Margaret Williamson (1995), Page DuBois (1995), Lyn Hatherly Wilson (1996), Jane McIntosh Snyder (1997) and edited by Ellen Greene (1996). Any number of scholarly articles on Sappho's Fragments have also appeared. But the biggest growth area of Sappho studies in the last few years has concerned the reception of Sappho's poetry and the cultural transmission of her legends. This anthology, and my forthcoming book on the critical history of Sappho's reception from the Romantic period to the Modern, form a part of this work. It began with a suggestive essay, 'Sapphistries' by Susan Gubar (published in *Signs* in the autumn of 1984) and continued with Joan DeJean's monumental work on the tradition in French (1989). Other important recent books include *Victorian Sappho* by Yopie Prins (1999) and those by Ruth Vanita (1996) and edited by Ellen Greene (1996). All of these books are listed in the Select Bibliography.

At the same time, Sappho maintains her double life. On the one hand, she is a scholar's resource; on the other, she is a popular heroine (or demon). Many people think of her as a poet, but it is probably true to say that today Sappho is equally – or even more? – famous for being a lesbian. That is how her name is used in the titles of two recent collections; Kay Turner's *Dear Sappho: A Legacy of Lesbian Love Letters* (1996) and Emma Donoghue's *What Sappho Would Have Said: Four Centuries of Love Poems Between Women* (1997). Even when she is not named, she is there, for both Gillian Spraggs' anthology *Love Shook My Senses: Lesbian Love Poems* (1998) and Karen McCarthy's *Bittersweet: Contemporary Black Women's Poetry* (1998) take their titles from Sappho (Fragment 47 and Fragment 130 respectively).

Sappho remains, like her own epithet for Aphrodite, 'many-coloured', or 'many minded'. In 1997 the *Independent* headlined an article with 'I can't get no sapphic action' and went on to state: 'Well, now you can. In cinema and living room, lesbians are big on screen this spring', advertising a season of the film fashion for 'lesbian chic'. And yet, at almost the same time, in 1998 the poet Eavan Boland recalled how she had always known Sappho's lines to her daughter Cleis, because she could remember her own mother reciting them to her as a child.

Lesbian, mother, poet, artist, lover, suicide, warning, icon: Sappho.

Who is she? Everyone and no one. Where is she? Everywhere and . . . on Lesbos.

Strangely enough, the name that still clings to her, with one sense, and which is the most entirely remote from the real Sappho of antiquity, is also the name – in a different sense – that brings us closest to her. For Sappho may or may not have been a lesbian. But she certainly was a Lesbian. And there she is still to be found.

When Lady Mary Wortley Montagu sailed among the Greek islands in 1717, she peered into the past and saw Sappho on Lesbos:

> . . . 'tis impossible to imagine anything more agreeable than this journey would have been between two and three thousand years since, when, after drinking a dish of tea with Sappho, I might have gone the same evening to visit the temple of Homer in Chios, and have passed this voyage in taking plans of magnificent temples, delineating the miracles of statuaries, and conversing with the most polite and most gay of human kind. Alas! art is extinct here; the wonders of nature alone remain.

Like Lady Mary, when the American scholar Mary Mills Patrick went to the island in 1910 she saw what Sappho had seen: the abundant wild flowers, the indented coastline with its sandy coves lined with luxuriant green, the olive groves, the dusty white roads, the wide blue sea, the even wider sky. She saw the hollowed-out place where the acropolis once stood; she could make out the circle of the ancient theatre. She bought tiny bronze coins of ancient Mitylene, with a lyre on one side and the head of Sappho on the other. She was shown two columns built into the portico of the Greek church *Therapon* and taken, so it was said, from the entrance to Sappho's school, the House of the Poets. 'Lovers of Greek poetry,' she said, 'should visit Lesbos while the charm of the ancient scenes and customs remains unchanged. The island will always be beautiful, but the old Greek atmosphere which one finds there now will pass away with the onward march of Western civilisation.'

She was right, and she was wrong. When the Greek writer Stratis Myrivilis, a native of Lesbos, wrote his bestselling novel *The Schoolmistress with the Golden Eyes* in 1954, he might have felt bitterly about Patrick's 'onward march of Western civilisation' as he described his hero returning to Lesbos from the horrors of a war that set Greek against Turk and took the cities of the Aegean coast back to the times of barbarian atrocities exchanged between island and mainland. Yet even that state of affairs would have been recognisable to Sappho, just as the flowers and the inlets, the sea and the sky, in Myrivilis' novel would look the same to her eyes.

Now another half-century has passed. The columns are still there, though no coins are to be had in the souvenir shops. Instead, you have to make do with T-shirts, plaster casts of a naked woman bearing the legend 'You have put a torch to my heart' (not a Fragment I recognise), glass pendants and sets of Sappho-with-her-lyre coasters (choice of green or white background). The house rented by Renée Vivien in 1904 can still be seen, and although the 1970s' campsite for lesbians on Lesbos has disappeared, there is still a gay scene in the town of Eressou where, as the *Rough Guide* puts it, Sappho's acolytes can be found 'paying homage' at the 'clothing-optional zone of the beach west of the river mouth', or disporting themselves at the single-sex hotel *Antiopi* or at a bar called *Dhekati Mousa*, 'The Tenth Muse'. A modern mural of 'Sappho and Alcaeus' by the Greek artist Theophilus has appeared on the wall of a former *kafeneion*, now a private house, showing Sappho in gold with a green scarf across her shoulders, listening to Alcaeus playing his golden lyre. The south harbour at Mytilene looks like that on any

Greek island, and the new, yet already shabby, half-finished concrete houses are just the same as they are on Paros or Naxos or Mykonos. But there are hotels called the 'Sappho', and a taverna advertising 'Aphrodite Home Cooking'; and on the quayside stands a larger-than-lifesize statue of Sappho in white Pentelic marble by the Lesbian sculptor Nassos Limnaios. The base is inscribed: 'Come now, delicate Graces and beautiful-haired Muses'. She stands, looking out to sea, her lyre held against her left shoulder, her right hand open and extended and her head erect, as if she is just about to begin a performance.

The quayside statue has only been there since 1965, and the harbour is not the place where you will find Sappho's real presence on Lesbos. But go out from the town, along the white roads and, even after 2,600 years, you will find the flowers and the green valleys, and the winds blowing warm into the island coves, just as they did when Sappho called across the sea to her goddess:

Hither to me from Crete, to this holy temple
here to your grove of appletrees, come, to the altars
smoking with incense, while the cool water
    sifts through

the apple branches; and everywhere
is shaded with roses, while from the shimmering
leaves, an enchanted drowsiness descends
    into the meadow

where horses graze and the spring flowers
blossom, and the winds
blow gently . . .
    . . .

There . . . gracious Cypris
take up the offering, and pour gracefully
into golden cups the nectar that consecrates
    in our festivities . . .

Fragment 2

A NOTE ON THE TEXT

All the Greek texts quoted for Sappho's Fragments 1–168B in the first section of this book are taken, with permission, from Eva-Maria Voigt, *Sappho et Alceaus: Fragmenta* (1971).

The Fragments are numbered according to Voigt's edition. The same numbering is used in Lobel and Page's edition (1955) and in David A. Campbell's Loeb Classical Library edition (1992). The only exception is Fragment 130 where Voigt links two Fragments, – that is those given as Fragment 130 and Fragment 131 in Lobel and Page, and in Campbell – believing them to be parts of the same poem. (Earlier editions, such as Bergk and Wharton, used a different numbering system.)

In the case of Fragment 49 I have included only Wharton's nineteenth century translation, although all the modern editors – Voigt, Lobel and Page, and Campbell – agree that the Fragment continues with

σμίκρα μοι πάις ἔμμεν' ἐφαίνεο κἄχαρις

'You seemed to me a small graceless child . . .'.

The Fragments of Sappho that survive, especially those reconstructed from papyrus texts, are damaged, and the brackets and other editorial marks that appear in the edited Greek texts indicate omissions or tentative readings.

Translations that are not attributed are my own.

The source from which each extract in the later sections of the anthology is taken is noted at the end of the piece, unless it has already been given as the title. Full titles are given in the Complete List of Poems and Extracts, p. 403.

ONE

The Fragments of Sappho

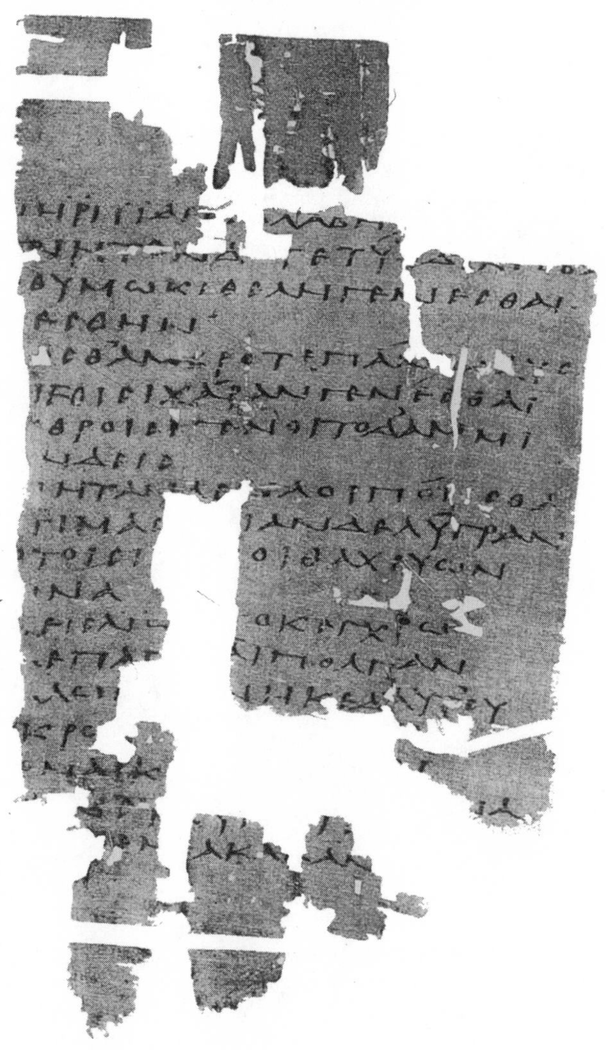

A multilated papyrus dating from the 3rd century A.D. found at Oxyrhynchus (now called Behnasa) in Egypt at the beginning of the 20th century. The text is Sappho's Fragment 5 'To the Nereids' and the ghost of the shape of the Sapphic stanza (three long lines, one short) tantalisingly suggests a frame for all the missing words of the poem. The British Museum.

Sappho's poems, composed 2,600 years ago, are with us still. Her images, her vocabulary, her subjects, her style have influenced the work of poets from her own day until now. But even people who have never read a line of the Classics will recognise Sappho, because the phrases and images that she first used have become so widely popular, so familiar and apparently instinctive that they are used by almost everyone who wishes to speak about the beauty of nature, the pain of love or the evanescence of a changing world. She was in the 1920s' hit parade with:

By the light,
Of the silvery moon,
I want to spoon,
To my honey I'll croon love's tune

(Fragment 34 'the stars and the shining moon . . .'); she is in a jazz song from the 1950s by Carmen McCrae called 'You Took Advantage of Me', which goes:

I'm just an apple on the bough
I knew you'd shake me down

(Fragment 105A 'the sweet apple . . .'); she is in Diana Ross's hit 'Where Did Our Love Go?':

You came into my heart, so tenderly,
With a burning love, that stings like a bee

(Fragments 130 'Love once again . . . limb-loosening . . . bitter sweet . . .' and Fragment 146 'neither honey nor bee . . .'). And she is even in Madonna's controversial single 'Like a Virgin' (Fragment 114, 'where are you, virginity?').

None of these performers would have worried about borrowing from Sappho, or even realised that they were doing so, but from the time of the Roman poets on, Sappho's verse has been imitated, plagiarised, re-invented. In English this process did not begin until the end of the sixteenth century, but once it did, Sappho acquired many new voices. Or, rather, many latterday writers acquired her, ventriloquised her, spoke for her.

In fact, Sappho has no authentic voice in any language, even her own. The Greek given here for each Fragment, taken from the scholarly work of a modern edition, is also a reconstruction, but it reminds us that Sappho and her work should be thought of as something strange, foreign and remote; something that is ultimately unrecoverable, in spite of all the many layers of invention by later writers.

One reason why Sappho must remain so remote is that none of her work was ever written down. She lived at a time when the early civilised world around the Mediterranean was going through a period of transition from an oral tradition to a literate one. Sappho herself would have performed her poems to music, and they would have been either memorised or improvised. But a classical Greek alphabet originated from Miletus not long after her death, and in Egypt and other places it had long been known that papyrus reeds could be made into a material like paper and used for writing on.

There is some argument for suggesting that Sappho's likely knowledge of the new possibilities of literacy contributed to her character as a self-aware poet, recognising in the development consequences for the survival of her work beyond her own lifetime, and even beyond the lifetimes of those who memorised her verses. That poetry could have a long life was something already within her own experience, for she certainly seems to have known the work of her great predecessor Homer, who had lived some 200 years earlier. There are two epigrams from the *Palatine Anthology* that have been attributed to Sappho and, if they are hers, then they do suggest that she was a writer who believed in the power of writing to memorialise and celebrate what is lost, to make it survive through poetry. The first is on the death of Timas, here in a version by J. A. Symonds (1883), and the second on Pelagon the fisherman, here in a version by Michael Field (1889):

> This is the dust of Timas, whom, unwed,
> Persephone locked in her darksome bed:
> For her, the maids who were her fellows shore
> Their curls and to her tomb this tribute bore.

Above a fisher's tomb
Were set his withy-basket and his oar,
The tokens of his doom,
Of how in life his labour had been sore:
A father put them up above his son,
Meniscus over luckless Pelagon.

The most authoritative sources for Sappho's verses are the earliest – that is, papyri fragments, mostly from about the second or third centuries AD – which record her work. But these were written long after Sappho's death, so they are quotations, or memories of memories of her compositions. These papyrus fragments were found at the turn of the last century on rubbish heaps and many of them were badly damaged, some even torn into strips to make bandages for mummies or recycled as useful papyrus (while the poetry written on them was considered pretty useless). The challenge for scholars reconstructing Sappho's work can readily be imagined. In her book *Sappho's Immortal Daughters* (1995), Margaret Williamson gives an amusing account of what it means, by showing what could happen if a scholar had to attempt to recover Shakespeare's speech from *Hamlet*, 'To be or not to be', when all he had was a torn scrap of papyrus with a few random legible words. Add to this the fact that in early writing practice no punctuation was used and, worse still, no gaps between words, and you can see how difficult it was to decipher these early texts.

We do, however, know that Sappho's poems were written down comparatively soon after she died and that there were a great many of them. By the end of the fifth century BC (about 150 years after Sappho died) there was an established trade in manuscript production and a brisk market among rich persons who collected private libraries. Sappho was one author whose works were collected, written down on long papyrus rolls, which were then wrapped around two 'holders' so that you read by feeding the manuscript from one roll to the other. In the early third century BC a library, or museum (House of the Muses), was founded in the Egyptian city of Alexandria, where scholars collected books (or rather papyrus rolls) and developed the systems of comparison and collation that are the staple methods of textual editors even today. At this time Sappho was canonised as one of the great lyric poets and her work ran to Nine Books of verse. One whole book contained her *epithalamia*, songs composed for weddings; another was said to have run to as much as 1,320 lines. Today only just over 200 Fragments survive, most of them only two or three lines long.

So what happened? In the legends, the wholesale destruction of Sappho's oeuvre is attributed to some dramatic event: the earliest stories grew out of the repeated sacking of the library at Alexandria by barbarian hordes. The truth is rather more prosaic and more complicated. As long as manuscripts of Sappho and other Greek lyric poets were treasured, it was worth while for dealers and enthusiasts to go on with the laborious process of making manuscript copies, and undoubtedly there were many copies of Sappho in the wealthiest libraries of the ancient world. In the first century BC there was a great fashion for the Greek lyric poets, which is why the Roman poets Catullus and later Horace knew Sappho and were able to imitate her work. But fashions change, and technologies change too. Gradually it became the custom to cite the language of Athens, Attic, as the true classical Greek, and Sappho's Aeolic dialect was considered provincial. Then, when the book trade improved its materials and switched from papyrus rolls to the more durable parchment codex, it seems that scribes and their employers thought Sappho an arcane taste, not worth the labour of retranscription. Gradually all her Nine Books disappeared.

However, during the years when those manuscripts were copied and recopied, many writers consulted them. And because Sappho was much admired as a stylist, her works were quoted, and those quotations survived from antiquity. From the Middle Ages right up until the end of the nineteenth century Sappho was known only from the snippets quoted by others. Her two most famous fragments, Fragment 1, the so-called 'Ode to Aphrodite', and Fragment 31, 'That man seems to me . . .' were handed down in this way. Fragment 1 was quoted in its entirety in a book entitled *On Literary Composition* by Dionysius of Halicarnassus written in about 30 BC, and Fragment 31 was quoted in part by Longinus in his treatise *On the Sublime*, which was written during the first century AD. (These works by Longinus and Dionysius of Halicarnassus are themselves available today only because they happened to survive another major change in the technology of book production, the invention of the printing press in the sixteenth century, when once again printers made decisions about what they would, and would not, bother to copy from manuscript into type.)

From the Renaissance on, a different kind of development meant that the works of ancient authors were revalued. Once books became a practicable form and comparatively cheap to make and acquire, scholars could begin to collect them and to write yet more books about books. Humanist scholars valued the Greek lyric poets and their status remained high right up to the nineteenth century, when the study of Greek and Latin, 'Greats', was the core of the syllabus at Oxford and Cambridge universities. Sappho's work, in particular, enjoyed a huge revival from the beginning of the eighteenth century, and many new translations and then editions were published, which combed the works of ancient authors for any stray quotation that could be added to the meagre collection of Fragments. In this way the size of her oeuvre increased steadily, if very slowly. Then something happened that radically changed the state of Sappho scholarship.

Towards the end of the nineteenth century farmers in Egypt began to turn up pieces of papyrus as they ploughed new fields. Gradually news of this filtered through to the West, and Germany, France and Britain, in particular, began to send out teams of excavators to see what they might find. In 1895 Bernard Grenfell and Arthur Hunt, two young men from Queen's College, Oxford, set out for Egypt with financial backing from the Egypt Exploration Fund. They settled on a site at a small town about 120 miles south of Cairo, Oxyrhynchus (now called Behnasa). On the outskirts of the town was a group of low mounds. Almost as soon as they began to dig, Grenfell and Hunt realised that it was the huge rubbish dump of a once-thriving town dating from the period of Hellenistic Egypt. The rubbish had been thrown out in about the fifth century AD, but quite a lot of it was much older, often dating from the second to third centuries AD. For months they lived in tents, quarrelled with the cohorts of local workers, piled tiny scraps of torn papyrus into reed baskets, then sifted and deciphered, before packing them up into Huntley and Palmer's biscuit tins and sending them back to Oxford. In the end there were crates and crates of such fragments, and the process of dealing with them goes on to this day. The Egypt Exploration Society began, slowly, to edit and publish the finds. Despite having reached their sixty-sixth volume in the series, the findings are still being published, and the Ashmolean Museum in Oxford still holds crates of fragments in their basement.

Most of the fragments are dross: bills and receipts, IOUs, invitations, inventories, tickets, laundry lists. But one page seemed to record some of the sayings of Jesus. And another tiny scrap, dating from the third century AD, was a copy of a poem by Sappho – a new poem, previously unknown. It is included here as Fragment 5, 'To the Nereids'.

As the work at Oxyrhynchus went on, other Sappho fragments were recovered, including some of the most substantial, such as Fragment 16, 'Some say a host of cavalry . . .', Fragment 44, 'Hector and Andromache . . .', and Fragment 58 '[fleeing?] . . . [was bitten . . . ?] . . . love has got for me the brightness and beauty of the sun'. Altogether the body of Sappho's known work increased considerably. Some of the finds are now in the British Museum, London; others in the Ashmolean and in Berlin. It had been the fantasy of the ages to recover the precious lost Nine Books of Sappho and here, in a shabby, dusty Egyptian town, that overdue dream seemed to be coming true. Excavations continued at Oxyrhynchus into the twentieth century, although irrigation has now destroyed anything that may be left. Other sites in Egypt are still being excavated and some Sappho scholars go on hoping that new finds might turn up one day.

Of the 213 Fragments that are currently known, I have selected thirty, designed to give some indication of the flavour of Sappho's work, her themes and subjects, as well as some sense of the world for which her poetry was created.

We know very little about the actual circumstances in which Sappho's poetry was composed, and many of the wilder guesses are included in the later sections of this anthology. But modern scholarship places Sappho in a privileged and aristocratic world, where she took part in rituals dedicated to the cult of Aphrodite. This does not make her a priestess, but perhaps a leader of young noble women, probably training in the arts and being groomed for an advantageous marriage. This group of young girls (*parthenoi*, virgins, as opposed to *gynaikos*, adult women) figures in many of Sappho's fragments, including Fragment 41, Fragment 57 and Fragment 96.

Fragment 1, the so-called 'Ode to Aphrodite' and the only complete poem of hers to survive from antiquity, would have been written for public performance for this female audience, within the context of the cult of Aphrodite, goddess of love. However, the fact that Sappho names herself in the fifth stanza ('who wrongs you, Sappho?'), combined with the urgent tone of the poem, means that it has often been read like a latterday lyrical effusion, both private and personal. This is also one of the poems that helps to give rise to questions about Sappho's sexuality, because the phrase translated as 'even against her will' in the sixth stanza is feminine in the Greek. As you will see, this does not stop Sappho's earliest translators into English from turning the lover she desires into a man (a 'coy Youth' in John Addison's 1735 version), or even from giving her beloved a name, 'Phaon' (as Francis Fawkes did in 1760).

The next almost-complete poem is Fragment 31, 'That man seems to me . . .' This is probably the most influential of all Sappho's extant verse, partly because it was known relatively early on and partly because it has been translated and interpreted so many times. When Longinus quoted it in the first century AD he cited it as an example of 'love's madness':

> . . . are you not amazed how at one and the same moment she seeks out soul, body, hearing, tongue, sight, complexion as though they had all left her and were external, and how in contradiction she both freezes and burns, is irrational and sane, is afraid and nearly dead, so that we observe in her not one single emotion but a concourse of emotions? All this of course happens to people in love . . .
>
> D. A. Campbell, Loeb translation, 1982

Sappho's catalogue of symptoms, as relayed to us by Longinus, has since become the conventional description of the physical effects of desire, repeated in cultures high and low, from pop songs to Roland Barthes (who quoted Longinus and Sappho in his *A Lover's Discourse: Fragments* of 1977). Certainly Sappho seems to have been an original inventor of the language of sexual desire. Fragment 31 is also important within Western culture because it evokes the psychic geometry of a love triangle, which has since become a commonplace. Sappho looks at, and desires, a girl who is unavailable because she favours a man, who therefore seems, to Sappho, 'equal to the Gods'. Again, this poem contains a crux much discussed by those who argue over Sappho's sexuality. *Chlorotera*, 'I am greener', in stanza four has a feminine ending. (The 'green' adjective has also been a trial to scholars: it might refer to feeling sick or being pale; it may be to do with restored youth, freshness and innocence; or it may be connected to an Homeric image that describes the warrior's fear as 'green'.) So the speaker of the poem is definitely female and, as is clear, her desire is inflamed by the girl, and not the man, in the poem. Translators who are determined to make Sappho into a poet of heterosexual love have gone to great lengths to arrange the poem to suit their view. The simplest method is to make the speaker male, as Catullus did in his imitation of Fragment 31, and as most of the early English translations do. But if a translator had Greek, he (usually he) would have known the sleight of hand he was practising, and it is interesting to note that in 1735 John Addison made it absolutely clear that the speaker was female.

Like the 'Ode to Aphrodite', and perhaps even more so, Fragment 31 has almost always been read as an expression of personal feeling. Recently, however, some critics have put this poem back into Sappho's social context and have suggested that it is an *epithalamium*, a wedding poem, designed to be sung during the celebration of a marriage. In this case the whole work could be read as an elaborate compliment to the bridegroom who has just acquired such a desirable bride. It is certainly clear that many of Sappho's poems were composed for performance at wedding celebrations, and among these would be Fragments 44, 'Hector and Andromache . . . ', and 114 'where are you, virginity?', which Mary Barnard's 1958 translation makes into a whole wedding carol.

Fragments 1 and 31 have been consistently quoted and revised in English since the late sixteenth century, but other poems have gone in and out of fashion. Fragment 2, 'Hither to me from Crete . . .', is an invocation, a prayer for the presence of Aphrodite, but it is the evocation of the natural beauty of Sappho's island world that makes it seductive, and this too was one of Sappho's key themes. Until the twentieth century only a few lines from the middle section of Fragment 2 were known (handed down because they were quoted by the ancient writer Hermogenes in his *Kinds of Style*). Percy Osborn's 1909 translation and Douglas Young's 1943 Scots version are both based on those few lines. Josephine Balmer's 1984 translation, however, is based on the longer four-stanza version, which has become the accepted reading of the poem. Scholars were able to extend this fragment because one of the more unusual finds made at Oxyrhynchus, by the Italian papyrologist Medea Norsa, was an *oistrakon*, a broken piece of terracotta pottery dating from the third century BC, which had this poem inscribed on it, clearly identifiable as Sappho's because of the few lines already known. This piece of terracotta is now kept in a velvet case in the Biblioteca Laurenziana in Florence.

Fragment 16, 'Some say a host of cavalry . . .', and Fragment 44,

'Hector and Andromache . . .', were both papyri found at Oxyrhynchus. These too also seem to be nearly complete, and they are particularly important because they suggest Sappho's knowledge, and rewriting, of Homer's epic poem *The Iliad*.

It has been important to many modern commentators to place Sappho in relation to the works of classical Greece conventionally regarded as 'mainstream' in order to get her away from the categorisation of 'women's poetry' from which she has suffered in the past, and which is inclined to make her work seem flowery and pretty. In fact, it is neither, and some of the more recent translations, especially those by Mary Barnard, David Constantine and Josephine Balmer, attempt to convey the cool and yet impassioned tone, the concrete imagery and the spikiness of style of Sappho's original Greek. Critics have also tried to make Sappho's poems less personal and more political by pointing out, for instance, the realities of Sappho's own time that stood behind poems such as Fragment 16 and Fragment 132, 'I have a golden child . . .' In the late seventh to early sixth centuries BC Lesbos was a vulnerable island, threatened all the time by the immense military capabilities of the province of Lydia (now part of mainland Turkey). So when Sappho speaks of the impressive sight of Lydia's chariots, or prefers her own child to the wealth of Lydia, she is talking about something that would have been all too painfully apparent to her contemporary audiences.

For readers and translators today the comparatively new longer poems, which give an insight into Sappho's time and her literary antecedents, are often the most intriguing. But in the past other Fragments attracted attention. Fragment 55, 'Dead, you shall lie there . . .', has caught the imagination of many translators and has lent itself to numerous different interpretations, from the Countess of Winchilsea's condemnation of 'an insipid beauty' to Richard O'Connell's modern scholar's griping. Fragment 102, 'Truly sweet mother I cannot weave my web . . .', enjoyed a great fashion in the second part of the eighteenth century, perhaps because at the time many women were failing to weave their webs and were taking up the pen instead, citing Sappho as their model. Fragment 104, 'On the Evening Star', on the other hand, has always been a favourite while Fragment 105A and B, 'the sweet apple . . . and the hyacinth . . .', by contrast, did not become really popular with translators until the 1800s, and it is tempting to see in that a connection to the invention of modern notions of sexuality during the nineteenth and early twentieth centuries. I have included one verse, Fragment 168B, 'The moon is set and the Pleiades', which is not now thought to have been composed by Sappho, because it has been so popular across the centuries. The evocation of the night, the delicate suggestiveness of the enveloping dark and the wistful lustfulness of Sappho's 'lying alone' have found their way into many works by English poets, and have been partly responsible for one enduring image of Sappho as a voluptuary.

One of the peculiarities of Sappho translations is that sometimes a writer or a poet will be attracted to just one fragment, while others take on the whole cycle. Until the nineteenth century there was no reliable Greek text to use: John Addison and Francis Fawkes both translated what was then available in their 1735 and 1760 editions of Greek lyric poets. The Greek scholar John Addington Symonds made translations of most of the Fragments then known, for inclusion in H. T. Wharton's important book *Sappho: Memoir, Text, Selected Renderings and a Literal Translation* (1885). With the growth of interest after the Egyptian excavations came the complete-cycle versions of Percy Osborn in 1909, Edward Storer in 1915 and Edwin Marion Cox (an influential early editor of Sappho) in 1925. More recent translators who have attempted all, or almost all, the Fragments include Mary Barnard, Guy Davenport, Richard O'Connell, Diane Rayor, Robert Chandler, Josephine Balmer and Jim Powell.

For convenience, I have called all of the versions that follow 'translations'. So they are, in that they carry Sappho to us across the space of thousands of years, across miles of sea and land, from the world of Lesbos in another culture, another way of thinking. It may be that it is not possible to translate Sappho at all. You can attempt to convey her technical devices, the use of the Sapphic stanza (essentially three long lines, followed by one short) or her distinctive method of *enjambement* (carrying the thought across from one stanza to the next, as in Fragment 1, where the 'whirring wings' of the sparrows that drive Aphrodite's chariot carry her down to earth across stanzas three to four). But sometimes the vocabulary remains intractable or doubtful. Even Sappho's very first word, the beginning of her Fragment 1, 'Ode to Aphrodite', is the subject of dispute. Is it *poikilotron*, 'many-coloured throne', or *poikilophron*, 'many-minded'? As with any translation, the question that faces the writer is whether to naturalise the language and make Sappho into a native –

which is what most early versions do – or make the English strange and let Sappho stay foreign – which is what many more recent versions do.

Added to that is Sappho's special problem: she is in tatters. If the writer who follows 'after Sappho' is brave enough, her empty spaces can become dynamic and her translations suggestive, playing between the Greek fragments of the past and the English of the present, suggesting that other, larger space that will always stretch between us and Sappho, even if we were to hold all those Nine Books in our hands.

In the end, translations date, where original texts do not. And it is new literary texts that many of the writers included here have made. Guy Davenport created a song from Sappho's ravaged Fragment 58, and out of virtually nothing at all Mary Barnard made a memorable poem from Sappho's elusive Fragment 37:

Pain penetrates

Me drop
by drop

Sappho's poetry haunts us still, 2,600 years after her death. Ruth Padel's new poem (see p. 390), written specially for this anthology, uses Sappho's Fragment 96 as a starting point. This Fragment is a poem about love and loss, about the memory of desire and about the poet who sings of all these things. Padel's poem proves that what was true for the ancient writer Dioscorides in the third century BC is still true for us today:

O Sappho, sweetest support of young love
and surely now residing with the Muses . . .
Greetings to you, lady, wherever you are, greetings as to a god:
for your songs are with us still, your immortal daughters.

FRAGMENT I

⊗ Ποι⸥κιλόθρο⸤ν' ἀθανάτ'Αφρόδιτα,
παῖ⸥Δ⸤ίος δολ⸤όπλοκε, λίccομαί cε,
μή μ'⸥' ἄcαιcι ⸤μηδ' ὀνίαιcι δάμνα,
πότν⸥ια, θῦ⸤μον,

ἀλλ⌋ὰ τυίδ' ἔλ⌊θ', αἴ ποτα κἀτέρωτα
τὰ⌋ς ἔμας αὔ⌊δας ἀίοισα πήλοι
ἔκ⌋λυες, πάτρο⌊ς δὲ δόμον λίποισα
χ⌋ρύσιον ἦλθ⌊ες

ἄρ⌋μ' ὐπασδε⌊ ύξαισα· κάλοι δέ σ' ἆγον
ὤ⌋κεες στροῦ⌊θοι περὶ γᾶς μελαίνας
πύ⌋κνα δίν⌊νεντες πτέρ' ἀπ' ὠράνω αἴθε-
ρο⌋ς διὰ μέσσω·

αἶ⌋ψα δ' ἐξίκο⌊ντο· σὺ δ', ὦ μάκαιρα,
μειδιαί⌋σαις' ἀθανάτωι προσώπωι
ἤ⌋ρε' ὄττ⌊ι δηὖτε πέπονθα κὤττι
δη⌋ὖτε κ⌋άλ⌊η⌋μμι

κ⌋ὤττι ⌊μοι μάλιστα θέλω γένεσθαι
μ⌋αινόλαι ⌊θύμωι· τίνα δηὖτε πείθω
..⌋.ςάγην ⌊ἐς σὰν φιλότατα; τίς σ', ὦ
φά⌋πφ', ⌊ἀδίκησι;

κα⌋ὶ γ⌊ὰρ αἰ φεύγει, ταχέως διώξει,
αἰ δὲ δῶρα μὴ δέκετ', ἀλλὰ δώσει,
αἰ δὲ μὴ φίλει, ταχέως φιλήσει
κωὐκ ἐθέλοισα.

ἔλθε μοι καὶ νῦν, χαλέπαν δὲ λῦσον
ἐκ μερίμναν, ὄσσα δέ μοι τέλεσσαι
θῦμος ἰμέρρει, τέλεσον, σὺ δ' αὔτα
σύμμαχος ἔσσο. ⊗

AN HYMN TO VENUS

O *Venus*, Beauty of the Skies,
To whom a thousand Temples rise,
Gayly false in gentle Smiles,
Full of Love-perplexing Wiles;
O Goddess! from my Heart remove
The wasting Cares and Pains of Love.

If ever thou hast kindly heard
A Song in soft Distress preferr'd,
Propitious to my tuneful Vow,

O gentle Goddess! hear me now.
Descend, thou bright, immortal Guest,
In all thy radiant Charms confest.

Thou once didst leave Almighty *Jove*,
And all the Golden Roofs above:
The Carr thy wanton Sparrows drew;
Hov'ring in Air they lightly flew,
As to my Bow'r they wing'd their Way:
I saw their quiv'ring Pinions play.

The Birds dismist (while you remain)
Bore back their empty Carr again:
Then You, with Looks divinely mild,
In ev'ry heav'nly Feature smil'd,
And ask'd, what new Complaints I made,
And why I call'd you to my Aid?

What Phrenzy in my Bosom rag'd,
And by what Cure to be asswaged?
What gentle Youth I would allure,
Whom in my artful Toiles secure?
Who does thy tender Heart subdue,
Tell me, my *Sappho*, tell me Who?

Tho' now he Shuns thy longing Arms,
He soon shall court thy slighted Charms:
Tho' now thy Off'rings he despise,
He soon to Thee shall Sacrifice;
Tho' now he freeze, he soon shall burn,
And be thy Victim in his turn.

Celestial Visitant, once more
Thy needful Presence I implore!
In Pity come and ease my Grief,
Bring my distemper'd Soul Relief;
Favour thy Suppliant's hidden Fires,
And give me All my Heart desires.

Ambrose Philips, 1711

AN HYMN TO VENUS

Many-Scepter'd Queen of Love,
Guile-enamour'd Child of *Jove*,
Ever-honour'd! cease my Smart,
Nor oppress thy Vot'ry's Heart.

But, propitious, Oh descend!
And my tuneful Vows attend.
From thy Father's gold-roof'd Court,
Once they charm'd thy kind Resort.

Thee thy wanton Sparrows drew,
Swift on sable Wings they flew;
As they thro' the raptur'd Air,
Lightly-quiv'ring bore thy Car.

They return'd. You, Goddess, smil'd,
And with Looks divinely mild,
Ask'd, What Griefs my Peace betray'd,
Why I call'd you to my Aid.

Whence my Mind's soft Phrenzy grew?
What coy Youth I would subdue?
Whom engage in artful Toils?
Who my *Sappho*'s Heart beguiles?

Tho' thy Gifts and Thee he slight,
He shall soon with Gifts invite;
Tho' he freeze, he soon shall burn,
Thy fond Victim in his Turn.

Once again, Oh hear my Pray'r!
Loose the Bands of am'rous Care.
Present bless thy Suppliant's Fires,
Grant me all my Heart desires.

John Addison, 1735

HYMN TO APHRODITE

Star-throned incorruptible Aphrodite,
Child of Zeus, wile-weaving, I supplicate thee,
Tame not me with pangs of the heart, dread mistress,
Nay, nor with anguish.
But come thou, if erst in the days departed
Thou didst lend thine ear to my lamentation,
And from far, the house of thy sire deserting,
Camest with golden
Car yoked: thee thy beautiful sparrows hurried
Swift with multitudinous pinions fluttering
Round black earth, adown from the height of heaven
Through middle ether:
Quickly journeyed they; and, O thou, blest Lady,
Smiling with those brows of undying lustre,
Asked me what new grief at my heart lay, wherefore
Now I had called thee,
What I fain would have to assuage the torment
Of my frenzied soul; and whom now, to please thee,
Must persuasion lure to thy love, and who now,
Sappho, hath wronged thee?
Yea, for though she flies, she shall quickly chase thee;
Yea, though gifts she spurns, she shall soon bestow them;
Yea, though now she loves not, she soon shall love thee,
Yea, though she will not!
Come, come now too! Come, and from heavy heart-ache
Free my soul, and all that my longing yearns to
Have done, do thou; be thou for me thyself too
Help in the battle.

John Addington Symonds, 1883

THE ODE TO APHRODITE

Richly-throned goddess, O deathless Aphrodite,
Daughter of Zeus, subtle and sacred one,
Bear not my spirit down with too much suffering,
But rather come to me as sometimes you have come,
When my far prayer has reached your divine presence,

And you have left for me your father's golden house,
Drawn in your chariot shimmering like the dawn;
Your fair fleet sparrows to herald you, whose wings,
Luminous still with the glory of heaven, have flashed
Radiance over earth. Then you have asked me,
How fared my eager heart and all its strong hopes:
'What would you do with love or have love do with you?
Sappho, who treats you cruelly? She who avoids you
Soon with desire shall burn, your gifts requiting
Many times, yours to be whether she will or not.'
Goddess, come once again, free me from longing.
Crown me with victory. O be my own ally.

Edward Storer, 1915

PRAYER TO MY LADY OF PAPHOS

Dapple-throned Aphrodite,
eternal daughter of God,
snare-knitter! Don't, I beg you,

cow my heart with grief! Come,
as once when you heard my far-
off cry and, listening, stepped

from your father's house to your
gold car, to yoke the pair whose
beautiful thick-feathered wings

oaring down mid-air from heaven
carried you to light swiftly
on dark earth; then, blissful one,

smiling your immortal smile
you asked, What ailed me now that
made me call you again? What

was it that my distracted
heart most wanted? 'Whom has
Persuasion to bring round now

'to your love? Who, Sappho, is
unfair to you? For, let her
run, she will soon run after;

'if she won't accept gifts, she
will one day give them; and if
she won't love you – she soon will

'love, although unwillingly . . .'
If ever – come now! Relieve
this intolerable pain!

What my heart most hopes will
happen, make happen; you yourself join forces on my side!

Mary Barnard, 1958

Eternal Aphrodite,
rainbow-crowned,
you cunning, wily child of Zeus,

I beg you

do not break me, Lady,
with the pain of misled love.
But come to me,
if ever in the past
you heard my far-off cries
and heeding, came,
leaving the golden home of Zeus.

In your readied chariot
the beautiful swift sparrows
bore you,
eddying through the mid-air,
their wings a-whirr,
from heaven to the dark earth.

And there they were. And you,
Lady of Joy,
smiling your immortal smile, asked me
what ailed me now,
and why I called again,
and what did my mad heart most crave:

'Whom shall I, Sappho,
lead to be your love?
Who wrongs you now?
For if she flees you, soon she'll chase,
and if she scorns your gifts, why, she will offer hers.
And if she does not love you,
soon she'll love,
even though she does not want.'

Now
come to me again as well
and loose me from this chain of sorrow.
Do for my yearning heart
all it desires,
and be yourself my ally in the chase.

Suzy Q. Groden, 1964

FRAGMENT 2

. .ανοθεν κατιου[c]-
†δευρυμμεκρητε̣cιπ̣[.]ρ̣[ ] |. ναῦον
ἄγνον ὄππ̣[αι] | χάριεν μὲν ἄλcοc
μαλί[αν], | β̣ῶμοι δ' ἔ ⟨ν⟩ι θυμιάμε-
νοι [λι] |β̣ανώτω⟨ι⟩·

ἐν δ' ὔδωρ ψῦχρο⌊ν⌋ | κελάδει δι' ὔcδων
μαλίνων, | βρόδοιcι δὲ παῖc ὀ χῶροc
ἐcκί |αcτ', αἰθυccομένων δὲ φύλλων |
κῶμα †καταιριον·

ἐν δὲ λείμων | ἰ̣π̣π̣όβοτοc τέθαλε
†τω̣τ. . .(.)ριν |νοιc† ἄνθεcιν, αἰ ⟨δ'⟩ ἄηται
μέλλι |χα πν[έο]ιcιν [
[ ]

ἔνθα δὴ cὺ †cυ.αν† | ἔλοιcα Κύπρι
χρυcίαιcιν ἐν κυ|λίκεccιν ἄβρωc
⟨ὀ⟩μ⟨με⟩μεί|χμενον θαλίαιcι | νέκταρ
οἰνοχόειcα

A COOL RETREAT

Boughs with apples laden around me whisper;
Cool the waters trickle among the branches;
And I listen dreamily, till a languor
Stealeth upon me.

Percy Osborn, 1909

'CALLER RAIN FRAE ABUNE'

Caller rain frae abune
reeshles amang the epple-trees:
the leaves are soughan wi the breeze,
and sleep faas drappan doun.

Douglas Young, 1943

Leave Crete and come to me now, to that holy temple,
where the loveliness of your apple grove
waits for you and your altars smoulder
with burning frankincense;

there, far away beyond the apple branches, cold streams
murmur, roses shade every corner
and, when the leaves rustle, you are seized
by a strange drowsiness;

there, a meadow, a pasture for horses, blooms with all
the flowers of Spring, while the breezes blow
so gently . . .

there . . . Cyprian goddess, take and pour
gracefully like wine into golden cups,
a nectar mingled with all the joy
of our festivities

Josephine Balmer, 1984

FRAGMENT 5

⊗ Κύπρι καὶ] Νηρήϊδες, ἀβλάβη[ν μοι
τὸν κασί]γνητον δ[ό]τε τυίδ' ἴκεσθα[ι
κὤσσα Ϝ]ο̣ι̣ θύμω⟨ι⟩ κε θέλη γένεσθαι
πάντα τε|λέσθην,

ὄσσα δὲ πρ]όσθ' ἄμβροτε πάντα λῦσα[ι
καὶ φίλοισ]ι Ϝοῖσι χάραν γένεσθαι
. . . . . . .ἔ]χθροισι, γένοιτο δ' ἄμμι
. . . . . .μ]ηδ' εἶς·

τὰν κασιγ]νήταν δὲ θέλοι πόησθαι
]τίμας, [ὀν]ίαν δὲ λύγραν
]οτοισι π[ά]ροιθ' ἀχεύων
].να

]. εισαϊω[ν] τὸ κέγχρω
]λεπαγ[. .(.)]αι πολίταν
]λλως̣[. . .]νηκε δ' αὖτ' οὐ
]κρω[ ]

]οναικ[ ]εο[ ]. ι
]. . [.]ν· σὺ [δ]ὲ̣ Κύπ̣[ρι]. .
[. . (.)]να
]θεμ[έν]α κάκαν [
]ι. ⊗

'TO THE NEREIDS'

O sovran Nereids, grant me this, I pray,
To bring my brother safe upon his way;
And whatsoe'er his heart hath willed
be all fulfilled!

For that wherein he faulted make amends,
Grant him to be a joy to all his friends,
  To foes a bane, but none be thus
    a harm to us!

And may he to his sister gladly bring
A share in honour; but that bitter sting,
  The *words* he spoke in angry part
    and broke my heart

(Hearing that song of mine that touched him near)
– Yet grant that in the city's welcome here
  He may forget all that, when home
    he *soon* shall come.

C. R. Haines, 1926

O [Cyprian] and Nereids, grant
that my brother come hither unharmed
and that as many things as he wishes in his heart to come
  about
are all brought to pass,

And that he atones for all his former errors,
and is a joy to his [friends],
a [pain] to his enemies; but for us
let there be no misery.

May he wish to do honour to his sister
  . . . painful suffering . . .

. . . millet-seed . . . of the citizens . . .

. . . but you, Cyprian, setting aside . . .

Jane McIntosh Snyder, 1997

FRAGMENT 16

⊗ Ο]ἰ μὲν ἰππήων cτρότον, οἰ δὲ πέcδων,
οἰ δὲ νάων φαῖc' ἐπ[ὶ] γᾶν μέλαι[ν]αν
ἔ]μμεναι κάλλιcτον, ἔγω δὲ κῆν' ὄτ-
τω τιc ἔραται·

πά]γχυ δ' εὔμαρεc cύνετον πόηcαι
π]άντι τ[ο]ῦ̣τ', ἀ γὰρ πόλυ περcκέ̣θο̣ι̣c̣α
κ̣ά̣λ̣λ̣ο̣c̣ [ἀνθ]ρ̣ώπων 'Ελένα [τὸ]ν ἄνδρα
τ̣ὸ̣ν̣ [αρ]ι̣cτον

κ̣αλλ[ίποι]c̣' ἔβα ·'c Τροΐαν πλέοι̣[c̣α
κωὐδ[ὲ πα]ῖδοc οὐδὲ φίλων το[κ]ήων
π̣ά[μπαν] ἐμνάcθ⟨η⟩, ἀλλὰ παράγα̣γ' α̣ὔταν
]cαν

]αμπτον γὰρ [
]. . .κούφωcτ[ ]οη.[.]ν̣
. .]μ̣ε̣ νῦν 'Ανακτορί[αc ὀ]ν̣έ̣μναι-
c' οὐ] παρεοίcαc,

τᾶ]c ⟨κ⟩ε βολλοίμαν ἔρατόν τε βᾶμα
κἀμάρυχμα λάμπρον ἴδην προcώπω
ἢ τὰ Λύδων ἄρματα κἀν ὄπλοιcι
πεcδομ]άχενταc.

].μεν οὐ δύνατον γένεcθαι
].ν ἀνθρωπ[. .(.) π]εδέχην δ' ἄραcθαι
[ ]
[ ]
[ ]
[ ]
[ ]
προc[
—
ὠcδ[
. .].[
.].[.]ω̣λ̣.[
τ' ἐξ ἀδοκή[τω. ⊗

Some say nothing on earth excels in beauty
Fighting men, and call incomparable the lines
Of horse or foot or ships. Let us say rather
Best is what one loves.

This among any who have ever loved
Never wanted proof. Consider Helen: she
Whom in beauty no other woman came near
Left the finest man

In Greece and followed a much worse to Troy
Across the sea and in that city forgot
Father, mother and her baby girl. For where
Cypris led her there

She followed as women will who are all
Malleable under love and easily turned.
My absent Anaktoria do not likewise
Put me from your thoughts.

For one glimpse of your lovely walk, to see
The radiance of your face again I'd give
The chariots of all Lydia and all their
Armoured fighting men.

David Constantine, 1983

ANACTORIA AND HELEN (FRAGMENT 16)

[So]me an army on horseback, some an army on foot
and some say a fleet of ship i[s] the loveliest sight
o[n this] da[r]k earth; but I say it is whatever you desire;

and it is [per]fectly possible to make th[is] clear
to [a]ll; for Helen, the woman who by far surpassed
[all oth]ers in her beauty, l[eft] her husband –
t[he b]est [of all men]

[behind] and sailed [far away] to Troy; she did not spare
a [single] thought for her [ch]ild nor for her dear pa[r]ents
but [the goddess of love] led her astray
[to desire]

. . . for . . .
. . . lightly . . . w[hich
r]emin[d]s me now of Anactori[a]
[although far] away

[who]se [long-]desired footstep, whose radiant, sparkling face
I would rather see [before me] than the chariots
of Lydia or the armour of men
who [f]ight wars [on foot]

. . . impossible to happen
. . . mankind . . . but to pray to [s]hare

(9 lines missing)

unexpecte[dly]

Margaret Williamson, 1995

FRAGMENT 31

⊗ Φαίνεταί μοι κῆνος ἴcoc θέοιcιν
ἔμμεν' ὤνηρ, ὄττιc ἐνάντιόc τοι
ἰcδάνει καὶ πλάcιον ἆδυ φωνεί-
cαc ὐπακούει

καὶ γελαίcαc ἰμέροεν τό μ' ἦ μὰν
καρδίαν ἐν cτήθεcιν ἐπτόαιcεν·
ὠc γὰρ ⟨ἔc⟩ c' ἴδω βρόχε' ὤc με φώνη-
c' οὐδὲν ἔτ' εἴκει,

ἀλλὰ †καμ† μὲν γλῶccα †ἔαγε†, λέπτον
δ' αὔτικα χρῶι πῦρ ὐπαδεδρόμακεν,
ὀππάτεccι δ' οὐδὲν ὄρημμ', ἐπιβρό-
μειcι δ' ἄκουαι,

†έκαδε† μ' ἴδρωc κακχέεται, τρόμοc δὲ
παῖcαν ἄγρει, χλωροτ⌞έρα δὲ π⌟οίαc
ἔμμι, τεθ⌞νάκην δ' ὀ⌟ λίγω 'πιδε⌞ύηc
φα⌟ ίνομ' ἔμ'αὔτ̣[αι.

ἀλλὰ πὰν τόλματον, ἐπεὶ †καὶ πένητα†

'MY MUSE, WHAT AILS THIS ARDOUR?'

My muse, what ails this ardour?
My eys be dym, my lymns shake,
My voice is hoarse, my throte scorcht,
My tong to this roofe cleaves,
My fancy amazde, my thoughtes dull'd,
My head doth ake, my life faints,
My sowle begins to take leave,
So greate a passion all feele,
To think a soare so deadly
I should so rashly ripp up.

Sir Philip Sidney (1554–86)

'HE THAT SITS NEXT TO THEE . . .'

He that sits next to thee now and hears
Thy charming voyce, to me appears
Beauteous as any Deity
That rules the skie.

How did his pleasing glances dart
Sweet languors to my ravish't heart
At the first sight though so prevailed
That my voice fail'd.

I'me speechless, feavrish, fires assail
My fainting flesh, my sight doth fail
Whilst to my restless mind my ears
Still hum new fears.

Cold sweats and tremblings so invade
That like a wither'd flower I fade
So that my life being almost lost,
I seem a Ghost.

Yet since I'me wretched must I dare.

John Hall, 1652

A FRAGMENT OF SAPPHO

Bless'd as the Immortal Gods is he,
The Youth who fondly sits by thee,
And hears and sees thee all the while
Softly speak and sweetly smile.

Twas this depriv'd my Soul of Rest,
And rais'd such Tumults in my Breast;
For while I gaz'd, in Transport toss'd,
My Breath was gone, my Voice was lost:

My Bosom glow'd; the subtle Flame
Ran quick through all my vital Frame;
O'er my dim Eyes a Darkness hung;
My Ears with hollow Murmurs rung:

In dewy Damps my Limbs were chill'd;
My Blood with gentle Horrours thrill'd;
My feeble Pulse forgot to play;
I fainted, sunk, and dy'd away.

Ambrose Philips, 1711

AN ODE

On a YOUNG MAID whom she lov'd.

Happy as a God is he,
That fond Youth, who plac'd by thee,
Hears and sees thee sweetly gay,
Talk and smile his Soul away.

That it was alarm'd my Breast,
And depriv'd my Heart of Rest.
For in speechless Raptures tost,
Whilst I gaz'd, my Voice was lost.

The soft Fire with flowing Rein,
Glided swift thro' ev'ry Vein;

Darkness o'er my Eyelids hung;
In my Ears faint Murmurs rung.

Chilling Damps my Limbs bedew'd;
Gentle Tremors thrill'd my Blood;
Life from my pale Cheeks retir'd;
Breathless, I almost expir'd.

John Addison, 1735

Thy fatal shafts unerring move,
I bow before thine altar, Love.
I feel thy soft resistless flame
Glide swift through all my vital frame.

For while I gaze my bosom glows,
My blood in tides impetuous flows,
Hope, fear, and joy alternate roll,
And floods of transports whelm my soul.

My faltering tongue attempts in vain
In soothing murmurs to complain;
Thy tongue some secret magic ties,
Thy murmurs sink in broken sighs.

Condemned to nurse eternal care,
And ever drop the silent tear,
Unheard I mourn, unknown I sigh,
Unfriended live, unpitied die.

Tobias Smollett, 1741

ODE II

Happy the youth, who free from care
Is seated by the lovely Fair!
Not Gods his ecstacy can reach,
Who hears the music of thy speech;
Who views entranc'd the dimpled grace,
The smiling sweetness of thy face.

Thy smiles, thy voice with subtil art
Have rais'd the fever of my heart;
I saw Thee, and unknown to rest,
At once my senses were oppress'd;
I saw Thee, and with envy toss'd,
My voice, my very breath, was lost.

My veins a throbbing ardour prove
The transport of a jealous Love;
Ev'n in the day's meridian light
A sickly languor clouds my sight;
A hollow murmur wounds my ear,
I nothing but confusion hear.

With current cold and vital streams
Trill, slowly trill along my limbs;
Pale as the flow'ret's faded grace
An icy chillness spreads my face;
In life's last agony I lie,
– Doom'd, in a moment doom'd to die.

E. Burnaby Greene, 1768

'PEER OF GODS HE SEEMETH . . .'

Peer of gods he seemeth to me, the blissful
Man who sits and gazes at thee before him,
Close beside thee sits, and in silence hears thee
    Silverly speaking,
Laughing love's low laughter. Oh this, this only
Stirs the troubled heart in my breast to tremble!
For should I but see thee a little moment,
    Straight is my voice hushed;
Yea, my tongue is broken, and through and through me
'Neath the flesh impalpable fire runs tingling;
Nothing see mine eyes, and a noise of roaring
    Waves in my ears sounds;
Sweat runs down in rivers, a tremor seizes

All my limbs, and paler than grass in autumn,
Caught by pains of menacing death, I falter,
Lost in the love trance.

John Addington Symonds, 1883

Peer of the gods is that man, who
face to face, sits listening
to your sweet speech and lovely
laughter.

It is this that rouses a tumult
in my breast. At mere sight of you
my voice falters, my tongue
is broken.

Straightway, a delicate fire runs in
my limbs; my eyes
are blinded and my ears
thunder

Sweat pours out: a trembling hunts
me down. I grow paler
than dry grass and lack little
of dying.

William Carlos Williams, 1958

[The man or hero loves Anaktoria, later Sappho; in the end, he withdraws or dies.]

I set that man above the gods and heroes –
all day, he sits before you face to face,
like a cardplayer. Your elbow brushes his elbow –
if you should speak, he hears.

The touched heart madly stirs,
your laughter is water hurrying over pebbles –
every gesture is a proclamation,
every sound is speech . . .

Refining fire purifies my flesh!
I hear you: a hollowness in my ears
thunders and stuns me. I cannot speak.
I cannot see.

I shiver. A dead whiteness spreads over
my body, trickling pinpricks of sweat.
I am greener than the greenest green grass –
I die!

Robert Lowell, 1962

FRAGMENT 34

ἄστερες μὲν ἀμφὶ κάλαν σελάνναν
ἂψ ἀπυκρύπτοισι φάεννον εἶδος
ὄπποτα πλήθοισα μάλιστα λάμπῃ
γᾶν. . . .

* * *

ἀργυρία

THE FULL MOON

Stars above their faces in awe are hiding,
While the Moon, with beauty the world adorning,
At the full, with silvery beams delightful,
Shines from Olympus.

Percy Osborn, 1909

Stars around the luminous moon – how soon they
hide away their glitter of diamond light, when

she floats over, and at the full, refulgent,
glamours the landscape . . .

John Frederick Nims, 1990

FRAGMENT 44

Κυπρο̣.[–2 2–]ας̣·
κᾶρυξ ἦλθε̣ θε̣[–10–]ελε̣[. . .].θεις
Ἴδαος ταδεκα. . .φ[. .].ις τάχυς ἄγγελος
⟨« ⟩
τάς τ' ἄλλας Ἀσίας .[.]δε.αν κλέος ἄφθιτον·
Ἕκτωρ καὶ συνέταιρ̣[ο]ι ἄγοι̣ς' ἐλικώπιδα
Θήβας ἐξ ἰέρας Πλακίας τ' ἀπ̣' [ἀϊ]ν⟨ν⟩άω
ἄβραν Ἀνδρομάχαν ἐνὶ ναῦσιν ἐπ' ἄλμυρον
πόντον· πόλλα δ' [ἐλί]γματα χρύσια κἄμματα
πορφύρ[α] καταΰτ[με]να, ποί̣κ̣ι̣λ' ἀθύρματα,
ἀργύρα̣ τ̣' ἀνά̣ρ⸤ι⸥θμα ⸤ποτή⸥ρ⸤ια⸥ κἀλέφαις».
ὢς εἶπ'· ὀτραλέως δ' ἀνόρουσε πάτ[η]ρ̣ φίλος·
φάμα δ' ἦλθε κατὰ πτ̣όλιν εὐρύχο̣ρ̣ο̣ν φίλοις.
αὔτικ' Ἰλίαδαι σατίναι[ς] ὐπ' ἐυτρόχοις
ἆγον αἰμιόνοις, ἐ̣π̣[έ]βαινε δὲ παῖς ὄχλος
γυναίκων τ' ἄμα παρθενίκα[ν] τ. .[. .].σφύρων,
χῶρις δ' αὖ Περάμοιο θυγ[α]τρες[
ἴππ[οις] δ' ἄνδρες ὔπαγον ὐπ' ἄρ̣[ματα
π[ ]ες ἠίθ̣εοι, μεγάλω[ς]τι δ̣[
δ[ ]. ἀνίοχοι φ[. . . . .].[
π̣[']ξα. ο[
⟨ desunt aliquot versus ⟩
ἴ]κελοι θέοι[ς
] ἄγνον ἀολ[λε
⸤ὄ̣ρματα̣ι̣⸥[ ]νον ἐς Ἴλιο[ν
⸤αὖλος δ' ἀδυ[μ]έλης̣⸥[ ]τ' ὀνεμίγνυ[το
⸤καὶ ψ[ό]φο[ς κ]ροτάλ⸥[ων]ως δ' ἄρα πάρ[θενοι
⸤ἄειδον μέλος ἄγν̣⸥[ον, ἴκα]νε δ' ἐς α̣ἴ̣θ̣[ερα
⸤ἄχω θεσπεσία̣ γελ̣⸥[
⸤πάνται δ' ἦς κὰτ ὄδο⸥[ις
⸤κράτηρες | φίαλαί τ' ὀ⸥[. . .]υεδε [. .]. . εακ[.].[
⸤μύρρα κα|ὶ κασία λίβ⸥ανός τ' ὀνεμείχνυτο

⌊γύναικες δ' ἐλέλυσδο⌋ν ὄσαι προγενέστερα[ι
⌊πάντες δ' ἄνδρες ἐπ⌋ήρατον ἴαχον ὄρθιον
⌊πάον' ὀνκαλέοντες⌋ Ἐκάβολον εὐλύραν
⌊ὔμνην δ' Ἔκτορα κ'Α⌋νδρομάχαν
θεο⟨ε⟩ικέλο[ις. ⊗

the herald came . . .
Idaios . . . swift messenger

'. . . and the rest of Asia . . . unceasing fame:
Hektor and his friends bring a sparkling-eyed girl
from holy Thebes and everflowing Plakia –
delicate Andromache – in ships on the brine
sea; many gold bracelets, fragrant
purple robes, iridescent trinkets,
countless silver cups, and ivory.'
So he spoke. Hektor's dear father leapt up;
the report reached friends through the wide city.
At once Trojan men harnessed mules
to the smooth-running carriages, a whole throng
of women and slender-ankled maidens stepped in;
apart from them, Priam's daughters . . .
and the unwed men yoked horses
to the chariots . . . , far and wide . . .
. . . charioteers . . .

. . . like gods
. . . sacred gathering
hastened . . . to Troy,
the sweet melody of reed-pipe and [kithara] mingled,
sound of castanets, the maidens
sang a holy song, a silvery divine echo
reached the sky, [laughter] . . .
and everywhere through the streets . . .
mixing-bowls and drinking-bowls . . .
myrrh, cassia, and frankincense together.
The elder women all cried out 'Eleleu,'
and all the men shouted high and clear
invoking Paion, the archer skilled in lyre,
and they praised Hektor and Andromache, godlike.

Diane Rayor, 1991

FRAGMENT 47

῎Εροc δ' ἐτίναξέ ⟨μοι⟩
φρένας, ὠc ἄνεμος κὰτ ὄρος δρύcιν   έμπέτων

like a cyclone
shattering oak
love smote
my heart

Richard O'Connell, 1975

Love
shakes my heart like the wind rushing down on
the mountain oaks.

M. L. West, 1993

FRAGMENT 49

⊗ Ἠράμαν μὲν ἔγω cέθεν, Ἄτθι, πάλαι ποτά

I loved thee once, Atthis, long ago.

T. H. Wharton, 1885

FRAGMENT 55

κατθάνοιcα δὲ κείcηι οὐδέ ποτα   μναμοcύνα cέθεν
ἔccετ' οὐδὲ †ποκ'† ὔcτερον· οὐ γὰρ   πεδέχηιc βρόδων
τῶν ἐκ Πιερίαc, ἀλλ' ἀφάνηc κἀν   'Αίδα δόμωι
φοιτάcηιc πεδ' ἀμαύρων νεκύων ἐκπεποταμένα.

MELINDA ON AN INSIPID BEAUTY

You, when your body life shall leave,
Must drop entire into the grave;
Unheeded, unregarded lie,
And all of you together die:
Must hide that fleeting charm, that face in dust,
Or to some painted cloth the slighted image trust;
Whilst my fam'd works shall thro' all times surprise,
My polish'd thoughts, my bright ideas rise,
And to new men be known, still talking to their eyes.

Anne Finch, Countess of Winchilsea (1661–1720)

Whene'er the Fates resume thy breath,
  No bright reversion shalt thou gain;
Unnotic'd shalt thou sink in death,
  Nor ev'n thy memory remain:
For thy rude hand ne'er pluck'd the lovely rose,
Which on the mountain of Pieria blows.

To Pluto's mansions shalt thou go,
  The stern, inexorable king,
Among th' ignoble shades below
  A vain, ignoble thing;
While honour'd Sappho's muse-embellish'd name
Shall flourish in eternity of fame.

Francis Fawkes, 1760

SAPPHO'S CURSING

Woman dead, lie there;
No record of thee
Shall there ever be,
Since thou dost not share
Roses in Pieria grown.
In the deathful cave,
With the feeble troop

Of the folk that droop,
Lurk and flit and crave,
Woman severed and far-flown.

William Cory, 1891

SAPPHIC FRAGMENT

'Thou shalt be – Nothing.' – OMAR KHAYYÁM
'Tombless, with no remembrance.' – W. SHAKESPEARE

Dead shalt thou lie; and nought
Be told of thee or thought,
For thou hast plucked not of the Muses' tree:
And even in Hades' halls
Amidst thy fellow-thralls
No friendly shade thy shade shall company!

Thomas Hardy (1901)

UNKNOWN TO FAME

Thee no worship awaits, nameless among shades in Avernus' hall;
Ne'er may glory be thine, ne'er to the world mem'ry thy name recall.
Thee no roses adorn; roses a bard blest by the Muse may gain;
Thine, to be but a wraith viewless amid shadowy shapes inane.

Percy Osborn, 1909

'DEID SALL YE LIGG . . .'

Deid sall ye ligg, and ne'er a memorie
sall onie hain, or ae regret for ye,
sin that ye haena roses o Pierie.

In Hades' howff a gangrel ghaist ye'll flee,
amang derk ghaists stravaigan sichtlesslie.

Douglas Young, 1943

Undistinguished you'll lie
[even with your Ph.D.]
in Hell.
For you gave nothing to poetry
but a superior smile.

Richard O'Connell, 1975

FRAGMENT 58

].[
].δα[
]
].α
]ῢγοιcα̣[ ]

].[. .]. .[ ]ι̣δάχθην
]χυ θ[ʹ]ο̣ι̣[.]αλλ[. . . . . .]ύταν
].χθο.[.]ατί.[. . . . .]εισα
]μένα ταν[. . . . ώ]νυμόν cε̣
]νι θῆται cτ[ύ]μα[τι] προ̣κοψιν

]πων κάλα δῶρα παῖδες
]φιλάοιδον λιγύραν χελύνναν
πά]ντα χρόα γῆρας ἤδη
λεῦκαί τ' ἐγένο]ντο τρίχες ἐκ μελαίναν

]α̣ι̣, γόνα δ' [ο]ὐ φέροιcι
]ηcθ' ἴcα νεβρίοιcιν
ἀ]λ̣λὰ τί κεν ποείην;
] οὐ δύνατον γένεcθαι
] βροδόπαχυν Αὔων

ἔc]χατα γᾶc φέροιcα[
]ο̣ν ὔμωc ἔμαρψε[
]άταν ἄκοιτιν
]ι̣μέναν νομίcδει
]αιc ὀπάcδοι

˪ἔγω δὲ φίλημμ' ἀβροσύναν,˩
] τοῦτο καί μοι
τὸ λά˪μπρον ἔρως ἀελίω καὶ τὸ
κά˩λον λέ˪λ˩ογχε.⊗

] called you
] filled your mouth with plenty
] girls, fine gifts
] lovesong, the keen-toned harp
] an old woman's flesh
] hair that used to be black
] knees will not hold
] stand like dappled fawns
] but what could I do?
] no longer able to begin again
] rosy-armed Dawn
] bearing to the ends of the earth
] nevertheless seized
] the cherished wife
] withering is common to all
] may that girl come and be my lover
I have loved all graceful things . . . and this
Eros has given me, beauty and the light of the sun.

Guy Davenport, 1995

FRAGMENT 94

τεθνάκην δ' ἀδόλωϲ θέλω·
ἅ με ψιϲδομένα κατελίμπανεν
πόλλα καὶ τόδ' ἔειπ[ε̣] [μοι·
ὤιμ' ὠϲ δεῖνα πεπ[όνθ]αμεν,
Ψάπφ', ἦ μάν ϲ' ἀέκοιϲ' ἀπυλιμπάνω.

τὰν δ' ἔγω τάδ' ἀμειβόμαν·
χαίροιϲ' ἔρχεο κἄμεθεν
μέμναιϲ', οἶϲθα γὰρ ὤϲ ⟨ϲ⟩ε πεδήπομεν·

αἰ δὲ μή, ἀλλά ϲ' ἔγω θὲλω
ὄμναιϲαΐ [. . .(.)].[. .(.)].ε̣αι
ὀ̣ϲ̣[– 10 –] καὶ κάλ' ἐπάϲχομεν·

πọ[λλοις γὰρ στεφάν]οις ἴων
καὶ βρ[όδων . . .]κίων τ' ὔμοι
κα. .[– 7 –] πὰρ ἔμοι π⟨ε⟩ρεθήκα⟨ο⟩

καὶ πọ̀λλαις ὐπα⌋θύμιδας
πλέκ⌊ταις ἀμφ' ἀ⌋πάλαι δέραι
ἀνθέων ἐ̣[– 6 –] πεποημέναις.

καὶ π. . . . .[ ]. μύρωι
βρενθείωι̣ .[ ]ρ̣υ[. .]ν
ἐξαλ⟨ε⟩ίψαο κα̣[ὶ ⌊βασ]ι̣ληίωι

καὶ στρώμν[αν ἐ]πὶ μολθάκαν
ἀπάλαν παρ[ ]ο̣ν̣ων
ἐξίης πόθο̣[ν].νίδων

κωὔτε τις[οὔ]τ̣ε̣ τι
ἶρον οὐδ' ὐ[ ]
ἔπλετ' ὄππ̣[οθεν ἄμ]μες ἀπέσκομεν,

οὐκ ἄλσος .[ ].ρος
]ψοφος
] . . . οιδιαι

TO ATTHIS

Atthis has not come back to me: truly I long to die.
Many tears she wept at our parting, saying:
'Sappho, how sad is our fate. I leave you unwillingly.'
To her I answered: 'Go on your way happily and
Do not forget me, for you know how I love you.
But if you should forget, then I will remind you
How fair and good were the things we shared together,
How by my side you wove many garlands of violets and
Sweet-smelling roses, and made of all kinds of flowers
Delicate necklaces, how many a flask of the finest myrrh
Such as a king might use you poured on your body,
How then reclining you sipped the sweet drinks of your
choice.'

Edward Storer, 1915

FRAGMENT 96

] cαρδ.[. .]
πόλ]λακι τυίδε̣ [.]ων ἔχοιcα

ὠcπ.[. . .].ώομεν, .[. . .]. .χ[. .]
cε †θεαcικελαν ἀρι-
γνωτα†, cᾶι δὲ μάλιcτ' ἔχαιρε μόλπαι̣·

νῦν δὲ Λύδαιcιν ἐμπρέπεται γυναί-
κεccιν ὤc ποτ' ἀελίω
]δύντοc ἀ βροδοδάκτυλοc ⟨cελάννα⟩

πάντα περ⟨ρ⟩έχοιc' ἄcτρα· φάοc δ' ἐπί-
cχει θάλαccαν ἐπ' ἀλμύραν
ἴcωc καὶ πολυανθέμοιc ἀρούραιc·

ἀ δ' ⟨ἐ⟩έρcα κάλα κέχυται, τεθά-
λαιcι δὲ βρόδα κἄπαλ' ἄν-
θρυcκα καὶ μελίλωτοc ἀνθεμώδηc·

πόλλα δὲ ζαφοίταιc' ἀγάναc ἐπι-
μνάcθειc' Ἄτθιδοc ἰμέρωι
λέπταν ποι φρένα κ[.]ρ . . . βόρηται·

κῆθι δ' ἔλθην ἀμμ.[. .]. .ιcα τό̣ δ' οὐ
νωντα[. .]υcτο̣νυμ̣[. .(.)] πόλυc
γαρύει̣ [. .(.)]αλο̣γ[. . . . .(.)]τ̣ο̣ μέccον·

ε]ὔ̣μαρ[εc μ]ὲ̣ν οὐ.α.μι θέαιcι μόρφαν ἐπή[ρατ]ον ἐξίcω
cθ̣αί cυ[. .]ρ̣ο̣c ἔχη⟨ι⟩cθα[. . .]. νίδηον

[ ]το̣[. . .(.)]ρατι-
μαλ[ ].εροc
καὶ δ[.]μ̣[ ]οc 'Αφροδίτα

καμ̣[ ] νέκταρ ἔχευ' ἀπὺ
χρυcίαc [ ]ν̣αν
. . .(.)]απουρ̣[ ] χέρcι Πείθω
[ ]θ[. .]η̣cενη
[ ]ακιc
[ ]. . . . . .αι

[ ]εc τὸ Γεραίcτιον
[ ]ν̣ φίλαι
[ ]υ̣cτον οὐδενο[
[ ]ερον ἴξο[μ

TO ATTHIS

Atthis, far from me and dear Mnasidika,
Dwells in Sardis;
Many times she was near us
So that we lived life well
Like the far-famed goddess
Whom above all things music delighted.

And now she is first among the Lydian women
As the mighty sun, the rose-fingered moon,
Beside the great stars.

And the light fades from the bitter sea
And in like manner from the rich-blossoming earth;
And the dew is shed upon the flowers,
Rose and soft meadow-sweet
And many-coloured melilote.
Many things told are remembered of sterile Atthis.

I yearn to behold thy delicate soul
To satiate my desire . . .

Richard Aldington, 1914

THON TIME WE AA WONNED

Thon time we aa wonned thegither,
she was shair o ye then, and worshippt ye neist;
she loed your singan abune aa ither.

Braw amang Lydian leddies nou
she gaes, like the rose-fingert mune
wi aa the starns about her brou,

eftir the sun's doungangan. The leam
streiks out on the monie-fleurit hauchs
and kelters owre the saut sea's stream.

Doun draps the dauch in a bonnie shouer,
roses blaw rowthie, and saft chervil,
and the hinnie-sawrit clover-fleur.

Stravaigan aften her lane she'll gae,
thinkan lang til her gentie Atthis,
forfant in spreit, and her hert wae.

Douglas Young, 1943

FRAGMENT 102

⊗ Γλύκηα μᾶτερ, οὔ τοι δύναμαι κρέκην τὸν ἴcτον
πόθωι δάμειcα παῖδος βραδίναν δι' 'Αφροδίταν

'YOUNG WANTON *CUPID*'S DARTS AND BOW'

Young wanton *Cupid*'s Darts and Bow
Have forc'd thy Spindle from thee now;
Thy wool, and all *Minerva*'s Toils
Are charming *Heber*'s Beauty's Spoils;
He lives thy Mind's continual Theme,
And you can think on nought but him.

Thomas Creech (1659–1700)

Come, gentle mother, cease your sharp reproof,
My hands no more can ply the curious woof,
While on my mind the flames of Cupid prey,
And lovely Phaon steals my soul away.

Francis Fawkes, 1760

A PASTORAL SONG

My mother bids me bind my hair
  With bands of rosy hue,
Tie up my sleeves with ribbons rare,
  And lace my bodice blue.

'For why,' she cries, 'sit still and weep,
  While others dance and play?'
Alas! I scarce can go or creep,
  While Lubin is away.

'Tis sad to think the days are gone,
  When those we love were near;
I sit upon this mossy stone,
  And sigh, when none can hear,

And while I spin my flaxen thread,
  And sing my simple lay,
The village seems asleep, or dead,
  Now Lubin is away.

Anne Hunter, 1794

SONG

As o'er her loom the Lesbian Maid
    In love-sick languor hung her head,
Unknowing where her fingers stray'd,
    She weeping turn'd away, and said
'Oh, my sweet Mother – 'tis in vain –
    I cannot weave, as once I wove –
So wilder'd is my heart and brain
    With thinking of that youth I love!'

Again the web she tried to trace,
    But tears fell o'er each tangled thread;
While, looking in her mother's face,
    Who watchful o'er her lean'd, she said
'Oh, my sweet Mother – 'tis in vain –

I cannot weave, as once I wove –
So wilder'd is my heart and brain
With thinking of that youth I love!'

Thomas Moore (1779–1852)

'MOTHER, I CAN NOT MIND MY WHEEL'

Mother, I can not mind my wheel;
My fingers ache, my lips are dry:
Oh! if you felt the pain I feel!
But Oh, who ever felt as I?
No longer could I doubt him true . . .
All other men may use deceit;
He always said my eyes were blue,
And often swore my lips were sweet.

Walter Savage Landor (1775–1864)

Sweet mother, I the web
Can weave no more;
Keen yearning for my love
Subdues me sore,
And tender Aphrodite
Thrills my heart's core.

Moreton John Walhouse, 1877

'MINNIE, I CANNA CAA MY WHEEL'

Minnie, I canna caa my wheel,
or spin the oo or twyne the tweel.
It's luve o a laddie whammles me.
Ech, the wanchancie glamarie.

Douglas Young, 1943

Sweetest mother, I cannot work the loom –
Slender Aphrodite fills me with longing for a boy.

Robert Chandler, 1998

FRAGMENT 104

A

Ἕcπερε πάντα φέρηιc ὄcα φαίνολιc ἐcκέδαc’ Αὔωc,
φέρηιc ὄιν, φέρηιc αἶγα, φέρηιc ἄπυ μάτερι παῖδα

B

ἀcτέρων πάντων ὀ κάλλιcτοc

Oh Hesperus! thou bringest all good things –
Home to the weary, to the hungry cheer,
To the young bird the parent's brooding wings,
The welcome stall to the o'erlabour'd steer;
Whate'er of peace about our hearthstone clings,
Whate'er our household gods protect of dear,
Are gather'd round us by thy look of rest;
Thou bring'st the child, too, to the mother's breast.

George Gordon, Lord Byron, 1821

The ancient poetess singeth, that Hesperus all things bringeth,
Smoothing the wearied mind: bring me my love, Rosalind.
Thou comest morning or even; she cometh not morning or evening.
False-eyed Hesper, unkind, where is my sweet Rosalind?

Alfred, Lord Tennyson, 1830

Most beautiful of all the stars
O Hesperus, bringing everything
the bright dawn scattered:

you bring the sheep, you bring the goat,
you bring the child back to her mother.

Jim Powell, 1993

FRAGMENT 105

A

οἶον τὸ γλυκύμαλον ἐρεύθεται ἄκρωι ἐπ' ὔσδωι,
ἄκρον ἐπ' ἀκροτάτωι, λελάθοντο δὲ μαλοδρόπηες·
οὐ μὰν ἐκλελάθοντ', ἀλλ' οὐκ ἐδύναντ' ἐπίκεσθαι

B

οἴαν τὰν ὐάκινθον ἐν ὤρεσι ποίμενες ἄνδρες
πόσσι καταστείβοισι, χάμαι δὲ τε πόρφυρον ἄνθος . . .

ONE GIRL

(A combination from Sappho)

Like the sweet apple which reddens upon the topmost bough,
A-top on the top-most twig, – which the pluckers forgot,
somehow, –
Forgot it not, nay, but got it not, for none could get it till now.

Like the wild hyacinth flower which on the hills is found,
Which the passing feet of the shepherds for ever tear and wound,
Until the purple blossom is trodden into the ground.

Dante Gabriel Rossetti, 1870

LIKE THE SWEET APPLE

Like the sweet apple that reddens
At end of the bough –
Far end of the bough –
Left by the gatherer's swaying,
Forgotten, so thou.

Nay, not forgotten, ungotten,
Ungathered (till now).

Henry Vere de Stacpoole (1863–1951)

As the apple ripening on the bough, the furthermost
Bough of all the tree, is never noticed by the gatherers,
Or, being out of reach, is never plucked at all.

Edward Storer, 1915

FRAGMENT 114

(νύμφη). παρθενία, παρθενία, ποῖ με λίποισ' ἀ⟨π⟩οίχηι;
(παρθενία). †οὐκέτι ἥξω πρὸς σέ, οὐκέτι ἥξω†

Maidenhood, maidenhood, whither art thou gone from me?
Never, O, never again, shall I return to thee.

Edwin Marion Cox, 1925

BRIDESMAIDS' CAROL II

First Voice Virginity O
my virginity!

Where will you
go when I lose
you?

Second Voice I'm off to
a place I shall
never come back
from
Dear Bride!
I shall never
come back to you

Never!

Mary Barnard, 1958

CHILDREN'S SONG

Childhood, childhood where have you gone?
Will you come back to us?
Will you come back?
Ever come back?

Never come back again.
Never come back.
Never.

Peter Whigham, 1984

FRAGMENT 130

⊗Ἔρος δηὖτέ μ' ὁ λυσιμέλης δόνει,
γλυκύπικρον ἀμάχανον ὄρπετον

Lo, Love once more, the limb-dissolving King,
The bitter-sweet impracticable thing,
Wild-beast-like rends me with fierce quivering.

John Addington Symonds, 1883

Percussion, salt and honey,
A quivering in the thighs;
He shakes me all over again,
Eros who cannot be thrown,
Who stalks on all fours
Like a beast.

Eros makes me shiver again
Strengthless in the knees,
Eros gall and honey,
Snake-sly, invincible.

Guy Davenport, 1965

FRAGMENT 131

῎Ατθι, cοὶ δ' ἔμεθεν μὲν ἀπήχθετο
φροντίcδην, ἐπὶ δ' Ἀνδρομέδαν πότη⟨ι⟩

TO ATTHIS

Hateful my face is to thee,
Hateful to thee beyond speaking,
Atthis, who fliest from me
Like a white bird Andromeda seeking.

Henry Vere de Stacpoole (1863–1951)

FRAGMENT 132

⊗ Ἔcτι μοι κάλα πάιc χρυcίοιcιν ἀνθέμοιcιν
ἐμφέρη⟨ν⟩ ἔχοιcα μόρφαν Κλέιc ⟨ ⟩ ἀγαπάτα,
ἀντὶ τᾶc ἔγωὐδὲ Λυδίαν παῖcαν οὐδ' ἐράνναν . . .

I have a child, a lovely one,
In beauty like the golden sun,
Or like sweet flowers of earliest bloom;
And Claïs is her name, for whom
I Lydia's treasures, were they mine,
Would glad resign.

John Herman Merivale, 1833

Sleep, darling

I have a small
daughter called
Cleis, who is

like a golden
flower
        I wouldn't

take all Croesus'
kingdom with love
thrown in, for her

Mary Barnard, 1958

FRAGMENT 137

θέλω τί τ' εἴπην, ἀλλά με κωλύει
αἴδως . . .
. . . .

αἰ δ' ἦχες ἔςλων ἴμερον ἢ κάλων
καὶ μή τί τ' εἴπην γλῶςς' ἐκύκα κάκον,
αἴδως †κέν cε οὐκ† ἦχεν ὄππα-
τ' ἀλλ' ἔλεγες †περὶ τῶ δικαίω†

THE LOVES OF SAPPHO AND ALCAEUS

Alcaeus I fain would speak, I fain would tell,
But shame and fear my utterance quell.
Sappho If aught of good, if aught of fair
Thy tongue were labouring to declare,
Nor shame should dash thy glance, nor fear
Forbid thy suit to reach my ear.

Anon. (D. K. Sandford?), 1832

FRAGMENT 146

μήτε μοι μέλι μήτε μέλιccα

It is clear now:

Neither honey nor
the honey bee is
to be mine again

Mary Barnard, 1958

[From our love]
I want neither
the sweetness of honey
nor the sting of the bees

Josephine Balmer, 1984

FRAGMENT 150

οὐ γὰρ θέμις ἐν μοιcοπόλων ⟨δόμωι⟩
θρῆνον ἔμμεν' ⟨. . . . . . .⟩ οὔ κ' ἄμμι πρέποι τάδε

Must I remind you, Cleis,

That sounds of grief
are unbecoming in
a poet's household?

and that they are not
suitable in ours?

Mary Barnard, 1958

FRAGMENT 168B

⊗ Δέδυκε μὲν ἀ cελάννα
καὶ Πληΐαδεc· μέcαι δὲ
νύκτεc, παρὰ δ' ἔρχετ' ὤρα,
ἔγω δὲ μόνα κατεύδω.

The *Pleiads* now no more are seen,
Nor shines the silver Moon serene,
In dark and dismal Clouds o'ercast;
The love appointed Hour is past:
Midnight usurps her sable Throne,
And yet, alas! I lie alone.

Francis Fawkes, 1760

The moon, with silver-gleaming eye
Smiling a paly light,
Has pass'd, long pass'd the noon of night:
The *Pleiades* no more
Cheer with their glimm'ring lamps the sky.
Ah! long with envious wing has flown
The Love appointed hour,
While I, perfidious man, with amorous moan,
Sink on my couch abandon'd, and alone.

E. Burnaby Greene, 1768

The weeping Pleiads wester,
And the moon is under seas;
From bourn to bourn of midnight
Far sighs the rainy breeze:

It sighs from a lost country
To a land I have not known;
The weeping Pleiads wester,
And I lie down alone.

The rainy Pleiads wester,
Orion plunges prone,
The stroke of midnight ceases,
And I lie down alone.

The rainy Pleiads wester
And seek beyond the sea
The head that I shall dream of,
And 'twill not dream of me.

A. E. Housman (1936)

MOONSET

from the Greek of Sappho

δέδυκε μὲν ἁ σελάννα
καὶ πληΐαδες, μέσαι δέ
νύκτες, παρὰ δ' ἔρχετ' ὥρα,
ἔγω δὲ λονα κατεύδω.

The meen's awa, the Sisters set,
The mid hour o' the nicht has gane,
But, O, my Laddie comesna yet,
An' dowff I lie my leeve alane.

William Christie, 1971

TWO

The Tenth Muse

The earliest extant portrait of Sappho, in a drawing based on the original vase painting which dates from the late 6th century B.C., about eighty years after Sappho's death. The vase is in the Czartoryski collection, 142333 in the National Musuem, Warsaw. The drawing is from G. Perrot and C. Chipiez, *Histoire de l'art dans l'antiquité* (Paris, 1914), vol. 10.

Sappho's reputation as a poet spread abroad even in her own lifetime. One anecdote comes down to us about Solon of Athens, a near-contemporary of hers who lived c. 640/635–561/560 BC. One evening at dinner his nephew sang a song of Sappho's over the wine, and Solon was so taken with this that he asked the boy to teach it to him. When a friend asked him why he was so eager, Solon replied, 'So that I may learn it and then die.'

Many references to Sappho and her works can be gleaned from the surviving writings of other ancient authors. The most important of these are collected in the *Testimonia* printed in the Loeb Classical Library edition of Sappho, *Greek Lyric I, Sappho and Alcaeus*, edited by David A. Campbell (1982). These passing allusions make clear how important Sappho was in antiquity, but they are not the only evidence. She was also celebrated in art, in coins and in plays.

The earliest picture that we have is a figure on a Greek vase dating from about the end of the sixth century BC, so quite soon after her death. This vase, now in the Czartoryski Collection, in the National Museum in Warsaw, shows Sappho standing, lyre in hand. On another, later *hydria* or water vase, now in the National Museum in Athens, her name actually appears, and here she is depicted seated, reading from a papyrus roll, while her pupils stand around, one of them holding a lyre. In yet another, in the Staatliche Antikensammlungen und Glyptothek, Munich, she is shown in dialogue with her fellow countryman and poet, Alcaeus. From the first century AD to about the third, Sappho's portrait appeared on many of the coins issued at Mytilene. And we know from a reference in one of Cicero's speeches that she was sufficiently famous to have had a statue erected to her at Syracuse by the noted sculptor Silanion (*Test.* 24) – a statue that may have borne the inscription 'My name is Sappho, and I surpassed women in poetry as greatly as Homer surpassed men' (*Test.* 57).

In the theatre, in a comedy by Antiphanes dating from about the fourth century BC, the poet apparently set riddles for the other characters. Only a tiny fragment of this comedy survives, but it includes one of Sappho's riddles:

Sappho: There's a feminine creature that keeps
its babes in its bosom always,
And dumb though those babes may be

loud is the cry that they raise
Reaching to any they choose
whether by field or by flood –
Absent he hears it, and present
he's deaf though his hearing be good.

Sappho's father tries the answer 'the state', but he is wrong. The answer is *epistole* ('letter'), which is feminine in Greek:

Sappho: The feminine creature's an epistle, then,
And the babes it carries, offspring of the pen;
Though dumb, they speak far off to whom they choose,
And, near the reader, you'll not hear his news.

It is an interesting scenario. The literary tradition had only recently taken over from the oral, and yet here is Sappho – a woman and a poet – vaunting the powers of the feminine *epistole*, but in the process also making a claim for the significance of her own voice, which will be heard far and wide, across a whole world, so long as readers, silently, attend to her.

In the last centuries BC, while Alexandria was the great centre of learning in the ancient world and Sappho's own works were still valued, she was paid many flowery compliments as the 'tenth Muse', as shown in the epigram attributed to Plato (c. 427–348 BC): 'Some say that there are nine Muses . . . but how careless, look again, . . . Sappho of Lesbos is the tenth'; or as the 'mortal Muse', which was the name given to her by Antipater of Sidon (fl. c. 100 BC). This was also the time when Sappho came to be associated with the Hellenistic women writers, Erinna, Moero, Anyte and Nossis. They are all listed in a 'garland' of lyric poets by the Greek writer Meleager, who put together an anthology of epigrams in around 100 BC and described Sappho's work as 'little, but all roses'. But it was only Nossis, who lived in Locri in southern Italy around the third century BC, who specifically mentioned Sappho in one of her epigrams:

If, stranger, you sail to Mytilene of the lovely dances
to find inspiration in the flower of Sappho's graces
tell them there that Locri has borne one dear to the Muses and to her;
and know that my name is Nossis, and then go.

Greek Anthology 7.718

At around the same time the legend of Sappho's leap from the Leucadian rock began to appear. The Greek comic playwright Menander (c. 342–292 BC) produced a drama called *The Lady from Leukas*, of which a few fragments and disjointed lines survive, including this:

> *Chorus*: Where Sappho first, so runs the story,
> In wild love chase of Phaon proud
> Leapt from a far-seen promontory,
> O hearkening now to the vow we vowed
> Grant praise, great King,
> Of thy Shrine shall ring
> Upon the cliff Leucadian.

In all, there seem to have been at least five ancient comedies called *Sappho*, by Diphilus, Ephippus, Ameipsias, Amphis and Antiphanes, all probably based on the stories that now began to circulate about her. There was also one play called *Phaon*, by Plato Comicus, and at least three others (as well as Menander's) apparently called *The Leucadian* or *The Lady from Leukas*. What there is of these plays still in existence is collected in *The Fragments of Attic Comedy*, edited by John Maxwell Edmonds. Though Menander made Sappho the first to take the Leucadian leap, he was employing poetic licence, for the legends actually tell of many others who had tried the leap, which was supposed to be a kill-or-cure remedy for hopeless passion. That too, was an invention, based on folk memories of a primitive ritual sacrifice to Apollo, in which some guilty and unlucky person was thrown off the cliff in order to propitiate the god. Strabo, writing in the early years AD, repeated the story of Sappho's leap in his *Geography* (*Test.* 23), and from that time on it became inextricably bound up with Sappho's name.

As for Phaon and his rather sudden significance in Sappho's story, that was probably the result of a literary mix-up. 'Phaon' is another name for Adonis, the beloved of the goddess Aphrodite, who was wounded by a wild boar in the chase. Sappho wrote poems naming Adonis and lamenting his demise in the name of Aphrodite, and later interpreters seem to have assumed that she was speaking in her own persona and confessing a personal passion. Little changes in the literary world: the same assumptions are regularly made today about writers, especially women writers.

About the time of these early comic plays Sappho began to acquire a new character and, eventually, a bad name. She was still being praised by literary commentators: Posidippus, for instance, writing in about the first half of the third century BC, composed an epigram (here translated by J.W. Mackail) that clearly drew on his knowledge of some of her Fragments:

> Doricha, long ago thy bones are dust, and the ribbon of thy hair and the raiment scented with unguents, wherein once wrapping lovely Charaxus round thou didst cling to him, carousing into dawn; but the white leaves of the dear ode of Sappho remain yet and shall remain speaking thine adorable name, which Naucratis shall keep here so long as a sea-going ship shall come to the lagoons of the Nile.

For centuries Lesbos had been known as a place of sensual delights and the women of the island, especially, were noted for their skills in the arts of love. In many ways this popular stereotyping was probably a perverted recognition of the real situation, when Sappho took part in the cult of Aphrodite and composed *epithalamia* for the girls of the island. From there it was but a short step to make her into a sensualist, and thence into the quintessential poet of love.

This is exactly what she was for the Roman poet Catullus (84–54 BC). He composed a sequence of famous poems addressed to 'Lesbia' – and the name is significant with regard to Sappho – a married woman with whom he carries on a sophisticated dalliance. 'Let us live, my Lesbia', he says in one poem, 'and let us love / and we will value at nothing the censorious talk of old men . . . Give me a thousand kisses, and then a hundred / and then another thousand and a second hundred . . .' Catullus' poem LI, '*Ille mi par esse deo videtur*', is one of the most famous of this series, and yet it is not his at all, but an imitation of Sappho's Fragment 31. That the practice of lyric poetry – Sappho's sensual poetry, as Catullus has reconfigured it – is something set apart from the male world of business and state is made quite clear in the new conclusion that Catullus gives to the Fragment (see stanza four). Sappho was gradually becoming fit only for the boudoir.

The Roman poet Horace (68–5 BC) also admired Sappho: 'How narrowly I missed . . . seeing . . . Sappho complaining to her Aeolian lyre about the girls of her city', he wrote (*Carmina* 2. 13. 21–3). But he it was who called Sappho *mascula* ('masculine') in an aside in which he compares her use of metre with that of another Greek lyric poet (*Epistolae* 1. 19. 28). The term stuck, and was repeated by at least one other later writer, who worried away at what it might mean: '"Masculine Sappho", either because she is famous for her poetry, in which men more often excel, or because she is maligned as having been a tribad' (*Test.* 17). Add to that a misunderstanding of a passage from Seneca (c. 4 BC–AD 65), where he was actually making a joke about futile and foolish lines of scholarly enquiry – 'the birthplace of Homer, . . . the real mother of Aeneas, whether Anacreon was addicted more to lust or to liquor, whether Sappho was a prostitute, and other matters that you should forget if you ever knew them . . .' (*Letters to Lucilius* 88.37, *Test.* 22) – and you can see how Sappho's name was being declined.

One of the most influential contributions to the Sappho myth was that of Ovid (43 BC–AD 18) in his 'Sappho to Phaon', number XV of his *Letters of the Heroines*. The jokey tone of the letter is clear from the start. Ovid plays with the idea that Phaon will not recognise Sappho's handwriting because, of course, it *is not* hers. It is Ovid's, and he has, in effect, forged her signature, by usurping her name and her voice. Ovid's authorship has sometimes been disputed, but this idea of Sappho – a sententious elderly bluestocking, once enamoured of her girls, but converted to heterosexual love by the manly beauty of the younger Phaon – was thoroughly integrated into the legend. (Only an extract from Ovid is given in this section, because the most famous version of 'Sappho to Phaon' is Alexander Pope's English translation dating from 1707, later included in full.)

For the Roman writers then Sappho was, at best, a poet of love; worse, a nymphomaniac; and, worst of all, a lover of women. She is implied in the scandalous *Dialogues of the Courtesans* 5 by Lucian (c. 120–90 AD), where Leana confides to Clonarium about her strange experiences with a rich Lesbian called Megilla, who is in love with her 'just like a man'. But Maximus of Tyre (c. AD 161–80) explains this phenomenon in Sappho's history in terms of a Greek custom, a 'Socratic art of love':

> What Alcibiades and Charmides were to him, Gyrinna and Atthis and Anactoria were to her; what the rival craftsmen Prodicus and Gorgias and Thrasymachus and Protagoras were to Socrates, Gorgo and Andromeda were to Sappho.
>
> (*Test.* 20)

Philostratus (d. AD 244) saw Sappho's relationship to her girls as part of her poetic legacy, as her practice was carried on by Damophyla and others of her associates (*Test.* 21). Thus by about the third century AD Sappho, the woman, had a dubious reputation, while Sappho, the poet, owned a glorious name. The complimentary judgments of Dionysius of Halicarnasuss (fl. c. 25 BC) on the elegance of Sappho's Fragment 1 (*Test.* 42), and of Longinus (first century AD) on the conviction of Sappho's Fragment 31, were still recorded and remembered, and other writers cited her as an eminent stylist.

Little wonder, then, that this was the time when the theory of the two Sapphos began to appear. Aelian (fl. c. AD 200) wrote in his *Historical Miscellanies*, 'I understand that there was in Lesbos another Sappho, a courtesan, not a poetess' (*Test.* 4). And by the time the *Suda* (an encyclopaedia dating from the tenth century AD) was compiled 'Sappho' received two entries. One for the lyric poetess: 'She had three brothers ... she was married to a very wealthy man ... and she had a daughter by him, called Cleis. She had three companions and friends, Atthis, Telesippa and Megara, and she got a bad name for her impure friendship with them ... She wrote nine books of lyric poems, and she invented the plectrum ...' (*Test.* 2). And one for the 'other Sappho': 'A Lesbian from Mytilene, a lyre-player. This Sappho leapt from the cliff of Leucates and drowned herself for love of Phaon the Mytilenaean. Some have said that she too composed lyric poetry' (*Test.* 3). But then the *Suda*, compiled so late in the day, can be no means be taken seriously. It gives no fewer than eight possible names for Sappho's father. And it tells us that her husband was called 'Cercylas' and that he traded from 'Andros' – which in Greek would be like saying that he was called 'Prick' and came from 'the island of Man'. Already the absurdities and calumnies of the comic playwrights appear in Sappho's stories as fact.

Two last speculative details come down to us from antiquity. The first is that Sappho was 'small and dark, like the nightingale'. 'In appearance she seems to have been contemptible and quite ugly, being dark in complexion and of very small stature,' says a biography dating from the late second or early third century AD found on an Oxyrhynchus papyrus (*Test.* 1). We do not need to take this very seriously, but the other detail may have been based on fact: that is the evidence of an inscription on a marble from the island of Paros, which mentions Sappho sailing into exile from Mytilene to Sicily (*Test.* 5). This adds another element that would recur in the later legends of Sappho.

A red figure *hydria* (water jar) dating from the mid to late 5th century B.C.. Sappho reads from a papyrus scroll, one of her companions holds a tortoiseshell lyre and another holds a garland. National Museum, Athens, NM 1260.

LI

Ille mi par esse deo videtur,
ille, si fas est, superare divos,
qui sedens adversus identidem te
spectat et audit

dulce ridentem, misero quod omnis
eripit sensus mihi; nam simul te,
Lesbia, aspexi, nihil est super mi
[vocis in ore]

lingua sed torpet, tenuis sub artus
flamma demanat, sonitu suopte
tintinant aures, gemina teguntur
lumina nocte.

otium, Catulle, tibi molestumst:
otio exultas nimiumque gestis.
otium et reges prius et beatas
perdidit urbes.

That man, to me, seems like a god,
if anything, he seems to surpass the gods,
who, sitting opposite you, over and over again
looks, and listens

to your sweet laughter, – that is what made me
miserable, all
my senses snatched away; for as soon as you
Lesbia, come in my sight, nothing is left me
[no voice in my mouth]

instead my tongue is leaden, certain, yet subtle
down my limbs
a flame runs through me, a sound of humming
rings in my ears, double darkness wraps me round
my eyes are night

idleness, Catullus, is bad for you:
in indulgence you exult and in foolish play.
Idleness, that has ruined kings before now,
lost cities.

Gaius Valerius Catullus (c. 84–54 BC)

SAPPHO PHAONI

Ecquid, ut adspecta est studiosae littera dextrae,
Protinus est oculis cognita nostra tuis –
an, nisi legisses auctoris nomina Sapphus,
hoc breve nescires unde movetur opus?
Forsitan et quare mea sint alterna requiras
carmina, cum lyricis sim magis apta modis.
flendus amor meus est – elegiae flebile carmen;
non facit ad lacrimas barbitos ulla meas.
Uror, ut indomitis ignem exercentibus Euris
fertilis accensis messibus ardet ager.
arva, Phaon, celebras diversa Typhoidos Aetnae;

me calor Aetnaeo non minor igne tenet.
nec mihi, dispositis quae iungam carmina nervis,
proveniunt; vacuae carmina mentis opus!
nec me Pyrrhiades Methymniadesve puellae,
nec me Lesbiadum cetera turba iuvant.
vilis Anactorie, vilis mihi candida Cydro;
non oculis grata est Atthis, ut ante, meis,
atque aliae centum, quas hic sine crimine amavi;
inprobe, multarum quod fuit, unus habes.
Est in te facies, sunt apti lusibus anni –
o facies oculis insidiosa meis!
sume fidem et pharetram – fies manifestus Apollo;
accedant capiti cornua – Bacchus eris!
et Phoebus Daphnen, et Cnosida Bacchus amavit,
nec norat lyricos illa vel illa modos;
at mihi Pegasides blandissima carmina dictant;
iam canitur toto nomen in orbe meum.
nee plus Alcaeus, consors patriaeque lyraeque,
laudis habet, quamvis grandius ille sonet.
si mihi difficilis formam natura negavit,
ingenio formae damna repende meo.
sim brevis, at nomen, quod terras inpleat omnes,
est mihi; mensuram nominis ipsa fero.

SAPPHO TO PHAON

So, when you inspected this elegant letter composed by my right hand
Did your eye know at once that this was mine?
Or, if you hadn't read my signature, Sappho,
Would you not have known whence this brief word came?
Perhaps you will ask why I resort to couplets
When I am better suited to the lyric mode?
Well, I must weep for my love – and elegy is the weeping style . . .
I cannot make my lyre adjust to my tears.
I burn, – as fierce flames fanned by winds,
Scorch the fertile plains with their ardour.
The fields where Phaon lives are far away by Typhoean Aetna
But my heat is like Aetna's and no less a fire consumes me.

Nor am I capable of arranging a well-ordered poem;
  an empty head is the thing for poetry!
Neither the girls of Pyrrha or Methymna
  Nor the Lesbian maids, nor all the rest arouse me.
Vile is Anactoria, vile to me now is blonde Cydro,
  Atthis delights not my eyes as she once did,
Nor any of the other hundred that I loved without crime.
  Unworthy One! what the many once had, is now yours
  alone.
Beauty is in you, your youth is apt for delight and makes
  A beauty which fascinates my eyes!
Take up the lyre and shine – then you are Apollo;
  Grow horns on your head – behold, you are Bacchus!
And Phoebus Apollo loved Daphne, and Bacchus, Ariadne of
  Knossis,
  Yet neither the one nor the other knew the lyric mode.
While, for me, the Muses, daughters of Pegasus, dictate
  delightful verses,
  So that my name is praised throughout the world.
Not even Alcaeus, who shares my country and career,
  Has more praise, though he does sing more grandly.
If, to me, nature was unkind and denied me beauty
  I am recompensed with genius.
If I am short, an illustrious name, known throughout the world
  Is mine; take the measure of me from my fame.

Ovid (43 BC–AD 18)

THREE

The Learned Lady

Surrounded by books and musical instruments, an educated Sappho in medieval head-dress plays the lute, while the amorous couple just glimpsed through the doorway many hint at the erotic connotations of her work that shadowed her illustrious reputation. A woodcut illustration to an edition of Boccaccio's *De Claris Mulieribus* made at Ulm, Germany in 1473. Hind, *History of Woodcut* II.

Just before the beginning of the Dark Ages, about the ninth century AD, Sappho's poetry disappeared. That much is fact. But this sudden absence has given rise to one of her most enduring legends: that Sappho, the pagan poet of love, Sappho the tribade, Sappho the outspoken woman, had her works destroyed, publicly burned, by the fanatical hands of the early Christians.

It is a beguiling image: Byzantine emperors clothed in the wealth of looted nations and fervent with the ardour of a new-found faith, directing cartloads of ancient papyrus rolls towards the pyre; or the gnarled and jewelled hands of Popes caressing, for the last time, those precious relics that recorded the heated words of Sappho, before consigning them to the flames.

Burning Sappho: 'subtle fire' in her limbs in her own Fragment 31. Burning Sappho: the sentence that condemns the heretic who speaks of carnal love. Burning Sappho: reaching out beyond her own time and space to light up the world with desire. It seems such a fitting explanation for the disappearance of her poetry that the story is told and retold by later commentators. It is true that in his *Speeches to the Greeks* in about AD 180 the ascetic Tatian, one of the early fathers of the Church, did describe Sappho as a *gynaikon pornikon erotomanes*, 'a sensual love-mad woman', and that he also called her *hetaira*, 'a courtesan', but the public burning of her books is, so far as we can tell, only a story.

The tale first seems to have been written down in the early years of the Renaissance. Cardan, a humanist writing in about 1550, said that Gregory Nazianzen instigated the public destruction of her works in AD 380. Then Joseph Scaliger, another humanist scholar and expert classical philologist writing at the end of the sixteenth century, declared that the writings of Sappho and other lyric poets were burned both at Rome and at Constantinople in 1073, on the instructions of Pope Gregory VII (Hildebrand). Finally, Petrus Alcyonius wrote in a book published in 1707 that, as a boy, he had heard another earlier scholar, Demetrios Chalkondylas, say that under the Byzantine emperors the ecclesiastical authorities burned the works of the Greek lyric writers because they contained 'the passions, obscenities and follies of lovers'.

The latest copies to survive of Sappho's poems, directly transmitted from antiquity and, almost certainly copied themselves from some lost papyri, are parchment codex pages dating from the sixth and seventh centuries AD. A sixth-century parchment now in Berlin is the source, for instance, of Sappho's Fragment 94, 'Frankly I wish I were dead . . .'. But by about the end of this century Paul the Silentiary wrote an epigram that suggests that her works were not only considered voluptuous, but also entirely inaccessible:

> Soft Sappho's kisses, soft embraces of her snowy limbs, soft every part of her, but her soul is of unyielding adamant. For her love stops at her lips; the rest belongs to her virginity. And who could endure this? Perhaps one who has borne it will endure the thirst of Tantalus easily.

In the ninth century there may have been copies of Sappho's poetry in the great libraries of Constantinople, which succeeded Alexandria as a centre of learning. But repeated sackings and burnings of the city, including that by the Crusaders in 1204, destroyed everything collected there. This, too, adds fuel to the story of Sappho's burning.

If Sappho's works did not survive the Dark Ages intact, her reputation fared rather better. The early medieval humanists and scholars were more interested in Latin than in Greek, so copies of the Latin poets were made in many monasteries for sale to private libraries. The works of Ovid, in particular, were widely studied and he became a textbook for medieval students of the Classics. The *Heroides* (*Letters of the Heroines*), which includes Letter XV, 'Sappho to Phaon', was not regarded as the most important of his works, but it none the less warranted enough attention to result in several manuscript copies, some of which still exist. The earliest, the *Codex Parisinus 8242* and the *Codex Etonensis*, date from the eleventh century, but neither includes Letter XV – one reason why scholars have sometimes disputed its authorship. The best authority for Letter XV is the *Codex Francofurtanus*, dating from the thirteenth century, and, from about that time on, the fictional Sappho, as created by Ovid, began to travel the medieval scholarly world.

Ovid was the source used by the Italian writer Giovanni Boccaccio (1313–75) when he compiled his *De Claris Mulieribus* (*Of Famous Women*). This deals exclusively with women of antiquity, who were not necessarily admirable, but rather notorious. Sappho, however, benefits from Boccaccio's intense admiration for poetry and poets, and gets off rather lightly. She is praised for her abilities in the arts, which are difficult 'even for well-educated men', and she is given a noble lineage as befits Boccaccio's concept of her elevated calling. All the same, though he does not go into the full details of her amours, Boccaccio does moralise on the failure of her poetry to soften her lover's heart.

When Christine de Pisan (c. 1363–1431) came to write her *Le Livre de la Cité des Dames* (*The Book of the City of Ladies*) in the early fifteenth century she took Boccaccio as her source. She quotes him extensively, but expands on his praises for Sappho and, significantly, makes no mention whatsoever of love, or a lover, or of any failure of her talent. Christine's Sappho is an intellectual woman, matched with seventeen other 'ladies of learning and skill', including Minerva, Circe and Medea. It is clear, too, that Christine herself identifies with her list of learned ladies. Guided by the Three Virtues – Reason, Rectitude and Justice – Christine is introduced first to 'Ladies of political and military accomplishment'. Then Christine asks Reason 'whether God has ever wished to ennoble the mind of woman with the loftiness of the sciences?' She goes on: 'I wish very much to know this because men maintain that the mind of women can learn only a little.' Reason replies with a proto-feminist argument that rings down the centuries: 'Women know less . . . because they are not involved with many things, but stay at home', and because 'the public does not require them to get involved in the affairs which men are commissioned to execute'.

All the same, Christine says, that does not mean that women's minds are less capable than men's, and she recites her catalogue of eighteen examples, with Sappho as the third. Unlike Boccaccio, Christine's exemplars are not all derived from antiquity. She takes it upon herself (I. 14. 4) to instruct Reason in the achievements of her own contemporaries, and mentions one Anastasia: '. . . so learned and skilled in painting manuscript borders and miniature backgrounds that one cannot find an artisan in all the city of Paris who can surpass her . . . And I know this from experience, for she has executed several things for me which stand out among the ornamental borders of the great masters.'

Whether or not Anastasia ever portrayed Sappho herself, several images of Sappho as learned lady decorated the pages of medieval manuscripts. She is shown wearing unlikely medieval headdresses, surrounded by books and musical instruments, often playing a harp or a lute, in illustrations to Boccaccio and de Pisan. In one woodcut that was made in Venice in 1501 to illustrate an early printed edition of Ovid's *Heroides* she is shown as a priestess, a laurel wreath on her head, as she pours out a libation over a sacred flame. Behind her one woman writes a letter, another plays a viol, while others stand in groups conversing decorously with men.

Christine de Pisan's *Book of the City of Ladies*, like her earlier work *Epistres du débat sur le Roman de la Rose* (*Letters on the Debate on the Romance of the Rose*), was partly inspired by her desire to exonerate women from the stereotypes about their fickleness, guile and sensuality propagated by certain clerics in the Middle Ages. Ludovico Ariosto's brief mention of Sappho in his *Orlando Furioso* (1516) serves a similar purpose. Thinking about her achievements in learning leads him to observe that 'In our own day I can clearly see such virtues evident among fair ladies . . .'

By the sixteenth century the intellectual woman was ready to claim her place and Sappho kept her good name. In Italy Raphael included her – the only mortal woman – in his painting of Parnassus on the walls of the Stanza della Segnatura in the Vatican (1511–12). And in England Thomas More (c. 1477–1535), whose own daughters were highly educated, was one of the many Renaissance classical scholars who helped to restore a widespread interest in Greek and in the literature of the ancient world. He composed a Greek and Latin version of the epigram by Plato about the tenth Muse, and seems to have had no interest in the more salacious aspects of her story.

While the new breed of scholar-humanists attempted to explain the destruction of the classical literary heritage by attributing it to the bigotry of the early Church, the new printing press meant that manuscript sources were ferreted out of monasteries all over Europe. Sappho's name began to crop up in widely disseminated printed commentaries on Ovid and Catullus. Her actual poems appeared too: Fragment 1 in a very early printed edition of Dionysius of Halicarnassus produced in Venice by Aldus Manutius in 1508, and Fragment 31 in the first printed edition of Longinus' *On the Sublime* made in 1554. In the meantime Robert Estienne, the king's printer in France, printed a new copy of Dionysius of Halicarnassus in 1547, and his son Robert eventually included both Fragments 1 and 31, as well as nearly forty other Fragments, under the name of Sappho in his early printed edition of the Greek lyric poets produced in 1566. A body of work was once more beginning to accrue to Sappho's name, and the story of these early efforts by French scholars and printers is told in Joan DeJean's *Fictions of Sappho: 1546–1937* (1989).

In France at this time the poet Louise Labé (c. 1520–66), like

Christine de Pisan before her, began to see in Sappho, the original woman poet, a desirable model and a promise. In a poem from 1555 she praises Apollo 'who gave me the lyre whose verses / so often sang of the Lesbian loves'. Sappho's status during the Renaissance was apparently so relatively secure that it was possible for the playwright John Lyly (c. 1554–1606) – described in one edition of his works as 'Wittie, Comicall, *Facetiously-Quicke and* unparalleld' – to put on a play before Queen Elizabeth I in which an allegorical Sappho (who would, of course, have been played by a boy) figured as a lady who was rich, learned, of noble birth and presiding over her own court at Syracuse.

In *Sappho and Phao* (1584) the character of the poetess is a dramatic portrait of the queen, certainly intended as a compliment, showing the learned princess commanding poetry and language in a witty exchange of puns and double meanings. Modern scholars assign a date of 1582 to the performance of this play, because the Duke d'Alençon was then in England to woo the queen. He is Phao, hastily departing from Syracuse at the end of the play (just as Alençon went back to France), while the virgin Sappho triumphs over erotic passion, taking Cupid as her own son and dismissing Venus, so that Sappho herself will be the new 'queen of love'. 'I will direct these arrows with better aim,' she says, 'and conquer mine own affections with greater modesty.' Sappho will henceforth 'rule the fancies of men', as the queen devotes herself to her people and her state.

Given Lyly's celebration of Sappho's honour, it is all the more surprising to encounter John Donne's homosexual poet in his 'Sappho to Philaenis', whose inventive linguistic skills are at once devious and seductive. Some of Donne's modern editors have been troubled by this poem and have questioned its attribution, on no firmer ground than their own anxiety. But just as Sappho in Lyly's play would have been a cross-dressed boy, so here Donne's own literary transvestism is an experiment in dealing with questions about poetry: 'Where is that holy fire, which verse is said / To have? Is that enchanting force decayed?' The quibbling about where poetry comes from, whose voice it speaks with, gives the poem an enduring resonance.

Donne (1572–1631) certainly seems to have known Sappho's poetry, and the fact that Sir Philip Sidney (1554–86) had already produced a version of her Fragment 31 in his *Old Arcadia* suggests that that particular poem, at least, was well known to educated Elizabethans. This is the poem to which Donne seems to be referring in line sixteen, when his Sappho says 'when gods to thee I do compare' (echoing 'That man is equal to the Gods . . .'). But then Sappho becomes a reflection of Donne; one poet speaking as another poet, just as his Sappho making love to another girl sees only her own mirror-image. By the end Donne touches his own self though he masquerades in Sappho's dress: 'Likeness begets such strange self flattery, / That touching myself, all seems done to thee'. And indeed *Donne* to thee – which is exactly what it is.

Philaenis is a generic name for a bucolic nymph, or indeed shepherdess, in the pastorals of the sixteenth century. But Donne's choice of name may also have been suggested by a possible knowledge of the Roman poet Martial, who addresses one of his more virulently rude epigrams (7. 67) to Philaenis. (She in turn may have been named after the supposed author of a Greek erotic handbook dating from the third century BC.) Martial's Philaenis is a tribade and prides herself on her manliness: she has eleven girls and several boys a day, she mud-wrestles, drinks hard and vomits like a hero. Donne's Sappho, at the beginning of the seventeenth century, may have been as witty as the queen, as learned as Christine de Pisan's or Boccaccio's heroines, but she ushers in a new lascivious Sappho who is ready to cavort with both female and male alike.

SAPPHO, POETESS OF LESBOS

The poetess Sappho was a girl from the city of Mytilene in the island of Lesbos. No other fact has reached us about her origin. But if we examine her work, we will see part of what time has destroyed restored to her; that is, the fact that she was born of honourable and noble parents, for no vile soul could have desired to write poetry, nor could a plebeian one have written it as she did. Although it is not known when she flourished, she nevertheless had so fine a talent that in the flower of youth and beauty she was not satisfied solely with writing in prose, but, spurred by the greater fervour of her soul and mind, with diligent study she ascended the steep slopes of Parnassus and on that high summit with happy daring joined the Muses, who did not nod in disapproval. Wandering through the laurel grove, she arrived at the cave of Apollo, bathed in the waters of Castalia, and took up Phoebus' plectrum. As the sacred nymphs danced, this girl did not hesitate to strike the strings of the cithara and bring forth melody.

All these things seem very difficult even for well-educated men. Why say more? Through her eagerness she reached such heights that her verses, which according to ancient testimony were very famous, are still brilliant in our own day. A bronze statue was erected and consecrated to her name, and she was included among the famous poets. Certainly neither the crown of kings, the papal tiara, nor the conqueror's laurel is more splendid than her glory. But, if the story is true, she was as unhappy in love as she was happy in her art. For she fell in love with a young man and was the prey of this intolerable pestilence either because of his charm and beauty or for other reasons. He refused to accede to her desires, and, lamenting his obstinate harshness, Sappho wrote mournful verses. I should have thought that they were elegiacs, since they are appropriate to such subjects, had I not read that she scorned the verse forms used by her predecessors and wrote a new kind of verse in a metre different from others. This kind of verse is still named Sapphic after her. Are the Muses to be blamed? They were able to move the stones of Ogygia when Amphion played, but they were unwilling to soften the young man's heart in spite of Sappho's songs.

Giovanni Boccaccio (1313–75), *Of Famous Women*,
trans. Guido A. Guarino, 1964

HERE SHE SPEAKS OF SAPPHO, THAT MOST SUBTLE WOMAN, POET AND PHILOSOPHER

'The wise Sappho, who was from the city of Mytilene, was no less learned than Proba. This Sappho had a beautiful body and face and was agreeable and pleasant in appearance, conduct and speech. But the charm of her profound understanding surpassed all the other charms with which she was endowed, for she was expert and learned in several arts and sciences, and she was not only well-educated in the works and writings composed by others but also discovered many new things herself and wrote many books and poems. Concerning her, Boccaccio has offered these fair words couched in the sweetness of poetic language: "Sappho, possessed of sharp wit and burning desire for constant study in the midst of bestial and ignorant men, frequented the heights of Mount Parnassus, that is, of perfect study. Thanks to her fortunate boldness and daring, she kept company with the Muses, that is, the arts and sciences, without being turned away. She entered the forest of laurel trees filled with many boughs, greenery and different coloured flowers, soft fragrances and various aromatic spices, where Grammar, Logic, noble Rhetoric, Geometry and Arithmetic live and take their leisure. She went on her way until she came to the deep grotto of Apollo, god of learning, and found the brook and conduit of the fountain of Castalia, and took up the plectrum and quill of the harp and played sweet melodies, with the nymphs all the while leading the dance, that is, following the rules of harmony and musical accord." From what Boccaccio says about her, it should be inferred that the profundity of both her understanding and of her learned books can only be known and understood by men of great perception and learning, according to the testimony of the ancients. Her writings and poems have survived to this day, most remarkably constructed and composed, and they serve as illumination and models of consummate poetic craft and composition to those who have come afterward. She invented different genres of lyric and poetry, short narratives, tearful laments

Sappho playing a harp, in a garden with her attendant ladies. From a Dutch illuminated manuscript of Christine de Pisan's *The Book of the City of Ladies* (1475). The British Museum, Add. 20698 fol.73.

and strange lamentations about love and other emotions, and these were so well made and so well ordered that they were named "Sapphic" after her. Horace recounts, concerning her poems, that when Plato, the great philosopher who was Aristotle's teacher, died, a book of Sappho's poems was found under his pillow.

'In brief this lady was so outstanding in learning that in the city where she resided a statue of bronze in her image was dedicated in her name and erected in a prominent place so that she would be honoured by all and be remembered for ever. This lady was placed and counted among the greatest and most famous poets, and, according to Boccaccio, the honours of the diadems and crowns of kings and the mitres of bishops are not any greater, nor are the crowns of laurel and victor's palm.'

Christine de Pisan, *The Book of the City of Ladies*, 1405,
trans. Earle Jeffrey Richards, 1983

IN FEATS OF ARMS

In feats of arms, as in the cultivation of the Muses, the women of old achieved distinction, and their splendid, glorious deeds irradiated the whole earth. Harpalice and Camilla achieved fame for their practised skill in battle; Sappho and Corinna shine, on account of their learning, with a radiance that night will never darken. Women have proved their excellence in every art in which they have striven; in their chosen fields their renown is clearly apparent to anyone who studies the history of books. If the world has long remained unaware of their achievements, this sad state of affairs is only transitory – perhaps Envy concealed the honours due to them, or perhaps the ignorance of historians. In our own day I can clearly see such virtues evident among fair ladies that ink and paper is needed with which to record it all for posterity; this way, too, the calumnies of evil tongues may be drowned in perpetual shame.

Ludovico Ariosto, *Orlando Furioso*, Canto 20, 1516,
trans. Guido Waldman, 1974, 1983

Musas esse novem referunt, sed prorsus aberrant.
Lesbica iam Sappho Pieris est decima.

Εννέα τας Μούσας φασίν τινες· ως ολιγώρως
Ηνίδε και Σαπφώ Λεσβόθεν η δεκάτη.

There are said to be nine Muses, but this is clearly a mistake.
For Lesbian Sappho of Pieris is the Tenth.

Thomas More (c. 1477–1535), *Complete Works*, Vol. 3

SAPPHO AND PHAO

[*The bed-curtains are drawn back and* SAPPHO *is discovered in bed, with* ISMENA *in attendance. Phao and Mileta approach.*]

Ismena [*To Sappho*] Phao is come.
Sappho Who? Phao? Phao – let him come near. But who sent for him?
Mileta You, madam.
Sappho I am loath to take any medicines, yet must I rather than pine in these maladies. Phao, you may make me sleep, if you will.

[*Exeunt* MILETA *and* ISMENA.]

Phao If I can I must, if you will.
Sappho What herbs have you brought, Phao?
Phao Such as will make you sleep, madam, though they cannot make me slumber.
Sappho Why, how can you cure me when you cannot remedy yourself?
Phao Yes, madam, the causes are contrary. For it is only a dryness in your brains that keepeth you from rest. But –
Sappho But what?
Phao Nothing, but mine is not so.
Sappho Nay, then I despair of help if our disease be not all one.
Phao I would our diseases were all one.
Sappho It goes hard with the patient when the physician is desperate.
Phao Yet Medea made the everwaking dragon to snort when she, poor soul, could not wink.

In Raphael's painting of *Parnassus* (1511–1512) in the Camera della Segnatura in the Vatican at Rome Sappho is the only mortal woman included (as opposed to Muses and allegorical figures). She wears the laurel wreath, her name is on a scroll in her hand, and a 16th century version of a lute is propped up beside her. Vatican Museums and Galleries, Italy/Bridgeman Art Library.

Sappho Medea was in love, and nothing could cause her rest but Jason.

Phao Indeed, I know no herb to make lovers sleep but hearts-ease, which, because it groweth so high, I cannot reach, for –

Sappho For whom?

Phao For such as love.

Sappho It groweth very low, and I can never stoop to it, that –

Phao That what?

Sappho That I may gather it. But why do you sigh so, Phao?

Phao It is mine use, madam.

Sappho It will do you harm, and me too, for I never hear one sigh but I must sigh also.

Phao It were best then that your ladyship give me leave to be gone, for I can but sigh.

Sappho Nay, stay; for, now I begin to sigh, I shall not leave though you be gone. But what do you think best for your sighing to take it away?

Phao Yew, madam.

Sappho Me?

Phao No, madam, yew of the tree.

Sappho Then will I love yew the better. And indeed I think it would make me sleep too; therefore, all other simples set aside, I will simply use only yew.

Phao Do, madam, for I think nothing in the world so good as yew.

John Lyly, *Sappho and Phao*, Act III, 1584, ed. David Bevington

SAPPHO TO PHILAENIS

Where is that holy fire, which verse is said
  To have? is that enchanting force decayed?
Verse, that draws Nature's works, from Nature's law,
  Thee, her best work, to her work cannot draw.
Have my tears quenched my old poetic fire;
  Why quenched they not as well, that of desire?
Thoughts, my mind's creatures, often are with thee,
  But I, their maker, want their liberty.
Only thine image, in my heart, doth sit,
  But that is wax, and fires environ it.

My fires have driven, thine have drawn it hence;
  And I am robbed of picture, heart, and sense.
Dwells with me still mine irksome memory,
  Which, both to keep, and lose, grieves equally.
That tells me how fair thou art; thou art so fair,
  As, gods, when gods to thee I do compare,
Are graced thereby; and to make blind men see,
  What things gods are, I say they are like to thee.
For, if we justly call each silly man
  A little world, what shall we call thee then?
Thou art not soft, and clear, and straight, and fair,
  As down, as stars, cedars, and lilies are,
But thy right hand, and cheek, and eye, only
  Are like thy other hand, and cheek, and eye.
Such was my Phao awhile, but shall be never,
  As thou wast, art, and, oh, mayst thou be ever.
Here lovers swear in their idolatry,
  That I am such; but grief discolours me.
And yet I grieve the less, lest grief remove
  My beauty, and make me unworthy of thy love.
Plays some soft boy with thee, oh there wants yet
  A mutual feeling which should sweeten it.
His chin, a thorny hairy unevenness
  Doth threaten, and some daily change possess.
Thy body is a natural paradise,
  In whose self, unmanured, all pleasure lies,
Nor needs perfection; why shouldst thou then
  Admit the tillage of a harsh rough man?
Men leave behind them that which their sin shows,
  And are as thieves traced, which rob when it snows.
But of our dalliance no more signs there are,
  Than fishes leave in streams, or birds in air.
And between us all sweetness may be had;
  All, all that Nature yields, or Art can add.
My two lips, eyes, thighs, differ from thy two,
  But so, as thine from one another do;
And, oh, no more; the likeness being such,
  Why should they not alike in all parts touch?
Hand to strange hand, lip to lip none denies;
  Why should they breast to breast, or thighs to thighs?
Likeness begets such strange self flattery,

That touching myself, all seems done to thee.
Myself I embrace, and mine own hands I kiss,
And amorously thank myself for this.
Me, in my glass, I call thee; but alas,
When I would kiss, tears dim mine eyes, and glass.
O cure this loving madness, and restore
Me to me; thee, my half, my all, my more.
So may thy cheeks' red outwear scarlet dye,
And their white, whiteness of the galaxy,
So may thy mighty, amazing beauty move
Envy in all women, and in all men, love
And so be change, and sickness, far from thee.
As thou by coming near, keep'st them from me.

John Donne (1572–1631)

FOUR

Nymphs and Satyrs

As a court lady in ringlets and rouge, Sappho with bared breasts figures in a crude illustration to a ballad sheet, but she is still framed with a laurel wreath. 'The Loves of Damon and Sappho' (c. 1680), from *Ancient Songs and Ballads collected by the Earl of Oxford* (London, 1773), Vol. II. The British Library.

During the seventeenth century France was the centre of Sappho scholarship. The pioneering work of Henri Estienne, in publishing Sappho's Fragments under her own name, was followed by two important works by the classical scholar Tanneguy Le Fèvre: a Greek-Latin edition of Anacreon and Sappho (1660), and a summary of the lives of the Greek poets, *Abrégé des vies des poètes grecs*, written for the twelve-year-old Comte de Limoges and published in 1664. The first French translation of Fragment 31 by Rémy Belleau had appeared in 1556, but the first French translation of a *collection* of Sappho's poems did not appear until 1670. It was by Du Four de la Crespelière, who included her in his translation *Les Odes amoureuses, charmantes, et bachiques des poètes grecs Anacreon, Sappho, et Theocrite*. Four years later Nicolas Boileau translated Longinus' *On the Sublime* into French, and his version of Sappho's Fragment 31 became immensely popular. Finally came Anne Le Fèvre Dacier's French translation of 1681, and Baron de Longepierre's of 1684. Consecutive French editions of Sappho prefaced the Fragments with a 'life of Sappho', and this became the convention in almost all later translations.

These biographies were generally based on little more than the author's personal prejudices, but seventeeth-century French scholars were in a better position to own such prejudices than their contemporaries in Britain. In 1652 John Hall published the first English translation of Longinus – and therefore an early English version of Fragment 31 – but still it was the legends, and not the poetry, of Sappho that dominated. During the 1630s there was a celebrated French singer at the court of Charles I and Queen Henrietta Maria, called Madame Coniack, whom the poet Thomas Randolph cast as a version of Sappho when he addressed a poem (or possibly two poems) to her under the name of 'Lesbia'. The first, which begins 'I chanc'd sweet Lesbia's voice to heare . . .', bore the title 'Upon a very deformed Gentlewoman, but of a voice incomparably sweet' (or, in another copy, 'Upon the French Woman with the hard face that singes in Masques at Court').

The legends that Randolph was using were those concerning Sappho's alleged ugliness, as well as her poetic skill. Other Sapphic legends were not of a kind to appeal during the years of the seventeenth century when the Puritans were in power. But with the Restoration all sorts of lusty Greeks came back into fashion, among them Sappho, who appears as a reluctant maid ('A Virgin I will dye / Diana I will obey') succumbing to the blandishments of an eager admirer in an anonymous ballad published in about 1680. The ballad sheet for *The Loves of Damon and Sappho, or, The Shepherd Crown'd with Good Success* was printed up complete with four little woodcuts showing 'Sappho' in ringlets and court dress with her breasts exposed, and the shepherd Damon sporting an elaborate curly wig.

Rather closer to the genuine antique was Alexander Radcliffe's version of Ovid's Letter XV, in his *Ovid's Travestie* of 1681. Here 'Saff' – as she is known to her lover – is a ballad singer, starving in the time-honoured writer's garret, with a caged linnet that refuses to sing rather than a tuneless lyre, and with a particular grudge against Phaon, 'her Companion and Partner in the Chorus', because he has run off with her ring and her 'Petticoat with Gimp'. Radcliffe's updating of Ovid is done with panache: Apollo and Bacchus in the original become 'The Mayor (God bless him)' and the 'worthy Sheriffs', while Sappho's girls, the maids of Pyrrha and Methymna, become 'Sue Smith' and 'Doll Price' who '. . . offers very fair, / She'l Sing along with me for Quarter-share . . .'

William Bosworth's posthumously published long poem *The Chast and Lost Lovers, Lively shadowed in the persons of Arcadius and Sepha* (1651) offers another seventeenth-century Sappho. Little is known about Bosworth (c. 1607–c. 1650) other than that he was supposed to have written his work when he was only nineteen. It is a comparatively rare book (not surprisingly, given that it was published during the reign of Cromwell), and the type is so poor that odd words occasionally appear, such as Sappho's 'lyribliring tunes', which may be a misprint for 'lyrioliring', or 'lyre-obliging'.

Bosworth does not seem to have known much about the original of his story. His Sappho, living in a tower on Lesbos with a 'grove / Bedeck'd with pearls, and strew'd about with love', is straight out of an old-fashioned chivralric romance, and the tale about Phaon's exile, which has brought him from his kingdom of Illyris to Lesbos, may be a garbled half-memory of the story of Sappho's exile in Sicily. It is tempting, on the one hand, to view Phaon's tale of civil insurrection in the light of events in contemporary Britain ('what fruits seditions bring / May well be guesst, for every one was King'), but if Bosworth did write the poem when he was nineteen, that cannot be the case. In this version Phaon is not unfaithful or heartless, but dies of political despair, while Sappho's death, first stabbing herself with his sword and then throwing herself into the river, gives her the ennobled status of honour satisfied.

One of the most interesting aspects of Bosworth's poem is his portrayal of Sappho as a poet whose voice first attracts Phaon's attention. Unlike the conventional situation between nymphs and their swains, it is she who makes the first move, and Phaon reproaches her: 'Immodest girl . . . why art so rude / To woo? / when virtuous women should be woo'd, / And scarce obtain'd by wooing . . .'

This was a period that produced many women poets, both at home and abroad, and while not all of them were as 'immodest' in their verses as Bosworth's Sappho, her name, from this time on, becomes a synonym for the woman writer. In France Madeleine de Scudéry was popularly called 'the French Sapho' because she rewrote Ovid's story in her *Lettres Amoureuses de divers auteurs de ce temps* (1641) and, even more explicitly, in her *Les Femmes illustrés ou Les Harangues héroïques* (1642). Here de Scudery develops a fiction for Sappho that focuses on her writing, without much reference to her life, or to her amorous history. But ten years later, in the last volume of her famous novel *Artamène ou le Grand Cyrus* (1649–53), de Scudery returned to Sappho to give her a scrupulous biography painstakingly gleaned from ancient sources.

The 'English Sappho' at this time was Katherine Phillips (1631–64), whose close attachments to her female friends (especially as expressed in her poems to 'Rosania' and 'Lucasia'), and cult of intense romantic relationships, meant that she acquired the name for more than just her literary reputation.

Aphra Behn (1640–89) was more outspoken and, quite possibly, more experienced. 'To the Fair Clarinda, Who Made Love to Me, Imagin'd More than Woman' – one of several poems that speak frankly about sex – is particularly intriguing for its device of imagining Clarinda as a man in order to explain desire ('And let me call thee, Lovely Charming Youth. / This last will justify my soft complaint'), but then returning her to her female incarnation, in order to escape one kind of unchaste behaviour, even while she cheerfully risks another.

The cross-dressing implied, if not carried out, in Behn's poem is reminiscent of the strategies used by other women writers. For instance, in the play *The Convent of Pleasure* (1668) by Margaret Cavendish, Duchess of Newcastle (c. 1624–74), Lady Happy decides to 'incloister [her]self from the World' with a group of like-minded women who have forsworn the company of men because they 'make the Female Sex their slaves'. Into Lady Happy's well-ordered 'convent' arrives 'a great Foreign Princess . . . a Princely brave Woman truly, of a Masculine Presence'. The princess seeks, and receives, Lady Happy's permission to wear men's clothes:

> I observing in your several Recreations, some of your ladies do accoustre Themselves in Masculine-Habits, and act Lovers-parts; I desire you will give me leave to be sometimes so accoustred and act the part of your loving Servant.

In the end it turns out that the princess is indeed a man, but not before Lady Happy has been wooed – and won – by the princess as a woman.

Lady Happy's story has, if you see it that way, a happy ending. The writings of women like the Duchess of Newcastle and Aphra Behn suggest that the seventeenth century perceived gender as something not innate, but 'performed', as modern theory would put it. Behn characterises Clarinda as both woman and man – Cloris and Alexis at once. She concludes that she will make 'Aphrodite' (Clarinda's female self) into her friend, and Hermes (Clarinda's male self) into her lover. It is a cryptogram that spells 'Hermaphrodite' – according to myth, the son of Aphrodite and Hermes, who loved, and became of one body with, the nymph Salmacis. And as with Clarinda, so with Sappho in the fictions that now began to proliferate around her.

William Walsh's *A Dialogue Concerning Women* (1691) is hardly a '*Defence of the Sex*' as its subtitle claims. When his character Misogynes, 'Woman-hater', gets on to the subject of 'Women of Understanding', Sappho does not fare well. Women, he says, are certainly as capable as men in some things. In 'the business of Lust', for example, Sappho was as 'witty' as any man, but what was the result? 'Not content with our Sex, she begins Amours with her own, and teaches us a new sort of Sin, that was follow'd not only in Lucian's time, but is practis'd frequently in Turkey at this day.'

Walsh's allusion to Lucian's *Dialogues of the Courtesans*, and to the popular idea of the goings-on in Turkish harems, indicates that some in the seventeenth century were well aware of tribades and their ways. Nicholas Rowe's 'Song', from Giles Jacob's *Treatise of*

Hermaphrodites (1718), thoroughly enjoys its own picture of the mutual entertainment devised by Sappho and Philenis.

Sappho's stock, then, had fallen pretty low. Pierre Bayle's entry for her in his influential *Dictionnaire historique et critique* (1697), translated into English in 1710, gets straight past the poetry and on to the prurience: 'Sappho always passed for a Famous Tribas'. Bayle (1647–1706) does excuse her on the grounds that 'the Women of the Ile of Lesbos . . . were very subject to this Passion', and he exonerates her from the charge being 'the Inventor of it'. He also points out that she was punished for her preference ('If her Design was to pass by and neglect the other half of Mankind, she was frustrated in her Expectation'), but he is still determined to insist upon Sappho's sexual orientation.

It is sometimes said that Sappho does not become a lesbian Lesbian until the nineteenth century. The truth is that there is almost always some *frisson* of suggestion throughout her history, and sometimes it predominates. In his *Abrégé des vies des poètes grecs* (1664) Sappho's early French biographer Tanneguy Le Fèvre was clear about Fragment 31; it is 'an ode of sixteen lines addressed to a girl with whom she was in love'. And though he leaves out 'the word' that would describe what Sappho was – he was writing for a twelve-year-old, after all – he goes on confidently: 'I mean, Monsieur, that Sappho was of a very amorous complexion, and that not being satisfied with that which other women find in the company of men who are not disagreeable to them, she wanted to have mistresses.'

It was a woman who first made a serious effort to rescue Sappho from her libidinous selves. Le Fèvre's daughter Anne, later Dacier, was a classical scholar like her father, and when she published her erudite translation of Sappho in 1681, she gave the poet a heterosexual story about a husband who died while she was young, a string of eager suitors and a torrid affair with Phaon. 'I believe,' said Le Fèvre Dacier, '. . . that envy inspired those who wrote the calumnies with which they attempted to blacken her.' Pierre Bayle's emphasis in his *Dictionary* is an answer to this. In a footnote he says:

> I cannot blame the charity of Mrs Le Fèvre who has endeavoured for the Honour of *Sappho* to render the fact uncertain; but I think her too reasonable to be vexed at us for believing our own Eyes. The Ode which *Longinus* has mention'd, is not in the Style of a Friend writing to a Friend: It favours of Love all over, and not of Friendship: Otherwise, *Longinus*, who was so good a Judge,

> would not have brought it as a Model of the Art with which great Masters represent things: He would not, I say, have given us as an Example of that Art, the manner wherewith the Symptoms of an Amorous Fury are collected in that Ode . . . and *Plutarch* would not have cited this same Ode to prove that Love is a Divine Fury . . . To conclude, I leave it to a new Father *Sanchez* to decide, whether a Married Woman, who had complied with the Passion of *Sappho*, would have Committed Adultery and made her Husband a Cuckold? I do not know whether this question has escaped the inexhaustible Curiosity of the Casuists about Matrimonial Causes.

Bayle completes his argument by citing Baron Longepierre, Sappho's last French translator in the seventeenth century, who said that, after the death of her husband, Sappho 'renounced Marriage, but not the pleasure of loving'. So passionate was her nature that she 'wholly gave her selfe to it, and loved all manner of ways, far beyond the bounds which Modesty naturally prescribes for her Sex . . . Many beautiful Women are put in the Number of her Mistresses.'

The struggle here, between women who would like to bear the name of a latterday Sappho and men bent on reproving her – and, by implication, them – was to become even more intense in the eighteenth century.

THE LOVES OF DAMON AND SAPPHO, OR, THE SHEPHERD CROWN'D WITH GOOD SUCCESS

You Lovers all that would successful be;
Be not too bashful, but in Love be free:
Time but your passion and you'l never fail,
There is a time when you'l be sure prevail.
Maids will deny, its true, but soon will yield,
If once you charge, they soon will lose the Field:
Though they deny, it is but for a fashion,
For when they do, they have the greatest passion.

A pleasant New Play-house Song, To the Tune of, *Hail to the Myrtle Shades*

Come turn thy Rosie face,
leave blushing at me my Dear,
Let's kindly now imbrace,
whilst Cupid does banish all fear:
The Neighbouring Swains are gone
to water their flocks you see:
And now we are all alone,
in pleasure let us be free.

I fancy now to be
like Adam in Paradice;
Then let me taste the Tree
of pleasures, and be not nice:
For Beauty fades away,
Old Age will waste it quite:
And time for none will stay,
then let's pursue Delight.

Under this Spreading shade,
all near to this Chystal Spring,
Our vows they shall be pay'd,
while the Birds do pleasantly sing:
A yielding in your Eyes,
my Sappho I do behold:
Then let us act our joys,
before that our passion's cold.

The blooming Spices smell,
and Summer is in her Pride,
Come let us sport a while,
and Sappho shall be my Bride:
With Flowers I'le crown thy brow
thou shalt be Queen of the Field:
Where all plenty does grow,
Oh then my fair Sappho yield.

See Earth Embroyder'd smiles,
and all things do gay appear:
While time our love beguiles,
come blush no more my dear:
Let's search for joys unknown,

and each of us trade in bliss:
Fair Nymph we are alone,
in you shall no more resist.

Alas, my Damon, fie,
do not a poor Nymph betray:
A Virgin I will dye,
Diana I will obey:
Then think, kind Swain, no more
to flatter yourself with Love:
God Cupid I'le ne'r adore
nor rank him with powers above.

O say not so my joy,
for Beauty's ne'r made in vain:
Not use is to destroy
what the powers above ordain:
Hark how the birds invite,
and Love with their Song do charm
Alluring to delight,
while thus we hold arm in arm.

No more sweet Damon spare,
my blushes that do arise:
O fie kind Shepherd forbear,
and do not a Maid surprize.
I am too young for Love,
and must not as yet be won:
Oh help ye Powers above
or I shall be quite undone.

In vain fair Nymph you strive,
for passion will have its way:
And he that did love contrive,
in these shades you must obey.
Alas, I resistance loose,
and now can resist no more:
What coy I did refuse,
Love's pleasures do over-pow'r.

Witness this pleasant Grove,
I to denyal was bent:

Had not you forced my love,
but now I shall ne'r repent:
No, never my Dear, for we
our mutual joys will encrease:
So happy we will be,
and live in an endless peace.

FINIS

c. 1680, from *Ancient Songs & Ballads*,
collected by the Earl of Oxford, 1773

SAPPHO TO PHAON

THE ARGUMENT

Sapho was a Lady very Eminent for Singing of Ballads, and upon an extraordinary Pinch, could make One well enough for her Purpose: She held a League with one *Phaon*, who was her Companion and Partner in the *Chorus*; but Phaon deserted his Consort for the Preferment of a Rubber in the *ba'nnio*. *Sapho* took this so to heart, that she threatens to break her Neck out of a Garret Window; which, if effected, might prove her utter Destruction. Authors have not agreed concerning the execution of her Design. But however she Writes him this loving and terrifying Epistle.

When these my doggrel Rhimes you chance to see,
You hardly will believe they came from me,
Till you discover *Sapho*'s Name at bottom,
You'l not imagine who it is that wrote 'em:
I, that have often Sung – *Young* Phaon *strove*,
Now Sing this doleful Tune – *Farewel my Love*;
I must not Sing new Jiggs – the more's the Pity,
But must take up with some old Mournful Ditty.
You in the *Bannio* have a Place, I hear;
I in my Garret Sweat as much, with Fear;
You can rub out a Living well enough,
My Rent's unpaid, poor *Sapho* must rub off;
My Voice is crack't, and now I only houl,
And cannot hit a Treble for my Soul:
My Ballads lye neglected on a Shelf,
I cannot bear the Burthen by my self;

Doll Price the Hawker offers very fair,
She'l Sing along with me for Quarter-share;
Sue Smith, the very same will undertake,
Their Voice is like the winding of a Jack.
Hang 'em, I long to bear a Part with you,
I love to Sing, and look upon you too;

Besides, you know when Songs grow out of fashion,
That I can make a Ballad on occasion.
I am not very Beautiful, – God knows;
Yet you should value one that can Compose;
Despise me not, though I'm a little Dowdy,
I can do that – same – like a bigger Body:
Perhaps you'l say, I've but a tawny Skin;
What then? you know my Metal's good within.
What if my Shoulder's higher than my Head?
I've heard you say, I'm Shape enough a-Bed:
The Mayor (God bless him) or the worthy Sheriffs
Do very often meet with homely Wives.
Our Master too; that little scrubbed Draper,
Has he not got a Lady that's a Strapper?
If you will have a Beauty, or have none,
Phaon must lye – *Phaon* must lye alone:
I can remember, 'fore my Voice was broke,
How much in praise of me you often spoke,
And when I shook a Trill, you shook your Ears,
And swore I Sung like, what d'ee call 'em – Spheres;
You kiss'd me hard, and call'd me Charming witch,
I can't do't now, if you wou'd kiss my Breech.
Then you not only lik'd my airy Voice,
But in my Fleshly part you did Rejoice;
And when you clasp'd me in your brawny clutches,
You swore I mov'd my Body like a Dutchess;
You clap'd my Buttocks, o're and o're agen,
I can't believe that I was crooked then.
Beware of him, you Sisters of the quill,
That sing at *Smithfield-Bars*, or *Saffron-Hill*,
Who, for an honest Living, tear your Throat;
If *Phaon* drinks w'ye, you're not worth a groat:
And Ladies know, 'twill be a very hard thing
To sink from him the smallest Copper-farthing;

Avoid him all – for he has us'd me so,
Wou'd make your hearts ake, if you did but know.
My Hair's about my Ears, as I'm a Sinner,
He has not left me worth a Hood or Pinner.
Phaon by me unworthily has dealt,
Has got my Ring, – though 'twas but Copper gilt;
Yet that which vexes me, – Th' ungrateful Pimp
Has stole away my Petticoat with Gimp;
Has all my Things, but had he left me any
I can't go out alone, to get a Penny.
Phaon, I should have had less cause to grieve,
If like a Man of Sense, you'd taken leave:
That you'd be gone, had I been ne'r so certain,
We might have drank a Pot or two at parting;
Or fry'd some Bacon with an Egg; or if
Into some Steaks, we'd cut a pound of Beif,
And laugh'd awhile, that had been somthing like;
But to steal off, was but a sneaking Trick.
My Landlady can tell, how I was troubled,
When I perceiv'd my self so plainly bubbled:
I ran like mad out at the Alley-Gate
To overtake you, but it was too late:
When I consider'd I had lost my Coat,
If I had had a Knife, I'd cut my Throat;
Yet notwithstanding all the ills you did,
I Dream of you as soon as I'm in Bed;
You tickle me, and cry, Do'st like it *Saff*?
Oh wondrous well! and then methinks I laugh.
Sometimes we mingle Legs, and Arms, and Thighs,
Something between the sheets, methinks does rise:
But when I wake, and find my Dream's in vain,
I turn to sleep, only to Dream again.
When I am up, I walk about my Garret
And talk I know not what – just like a Parrot:
I move about the Room from Bed to Chair,
And have no Satisfaction any where.
The last time I remember you lay here,
We both were dry ith' Night, and went for Beer:
Into the Cellar by good luck we got,
What we did there, I'm sure you ha'n't forgot:

There stands, you know, an antiquated Tub,
'Gainst which, since that, I often stand, and rub;
Only to see't, as much delight I take
As if the Vessel now were full of Sack;
But more to add unto my Discontent,
There's been no Drink ith' Cellar since you went.
There's nothing but affords me Misery,
My Linnet in the Cage, I fear will dye:
The Bird is just like me in every thing;
Like me it pines, like me it cannot Sing.
Now *Phaon*, Pray take notice what I say,
If you don't bring the things you took away;
You know, my Garret is four Stories high;
From thence I'll leap, and in the Streets I'll die:
May be you will refuse to come – Do – do,
Y'had best let *Sapho* break her Neck for you.
Your afflicted Consort, Sapho.

Alexander Radcliffe, *Ovid's travestie: a burlesque upon Ovid's 'Epistles'*, 1681

THE CHAST AND LOST LOVERS

Lively shadowed in the persons
of *Arcadius* and *Sepha*, and illustrated
with the severall stories of
Haenion and *Antigone*, *Eramio* and *Amissa*,
Phaon and *Sappho*, *Delithason* and *Verista*:
Being a description of severall Lovers
smiling with delight, and with hopes fresh
as their youth, and fair as their beauties
in the beginning of their Affections,
and covered with Blood
and Horror in their conclusion.

To this is added the Contestation betwixt
Bacchus and *Diana*, and certain Sonnets of the
Author to AURORA.

Digested into three Poems, by Will. Bosworth, Gent.

A prominent laurel wreath, and a tiny lyre. *Sappho* by Carlo Dolci in a portrait in a collection at the Corsini Palace, Florence. Engraving by Robert Strange (1764), published in London in 1787.

Then, 'cause one way did lead to both their towers,
He took her magic hand, and with whole showers
Of tears first washt them, then with a faint kiss
Dried them, and walking homeward told her this.

THE STORY OF PHAON AND SAPPHO

'In Lesbos famous for the comic lays,
That us'd to spring from her o'erflowing praise,
Twice famous Sappho dwelt, the fairest maid
Mitelin had, of whom it once was said
Amongst the Gods a sudden question was,
If Sappho or Thalia did surpass
In lyribliring tunes: it long remain'd,
Till Mnemosyne the mother was constrain'd
To say they both from her begetting sprang,
And each of th' other's warbling Lyra sang.
There was a town in Lesbos, now defac'd,
Antissa nam'd, by Neptune's arms embrac'd;
There Sappho had a tower, in it a grove
Bedeck'd with pearls, and strew'd about with love;
Leucothean branches overspread the same,
And from the shadows perfect odours came.
To dress it most there was a purple bed,
All wrought in works, with azure mantles spread;
The tables did unspotted carpets hold
Of Tyrian dyes, the edges fring'd with gold.
Along this grove there stealing ran a spring,
Where Sappho tun'd her Muse, for she could sing
In golden verse, and teach the best a vein
Beyond the music of their sweetest strain.
Here while she sang, a ruddy youth appear'd,
Drawn by the sweetness of the voice he heard;
"Sing on," said he, "fair lady, let not me,
Too bold, give period to your melody.
Nor blame me for my over-bold attempt,
(Although I yield of modesty exempt
In doing this) and yet not over-bold,
For whoso hears the voice, and doth behold
The lips from whence it comes, would be as sad

As I, and trust me, lady, if I had
But skill to tempt you and so sweet a touch,
Assure you, you yourself would do as much."
She answers not, for why the little God
Had touch'd her heart before, and made a rod
For one contempt was past; she view'd him hard,
Whose serious looks made Phaon half afear'd
She was displeas'd; about to go she cries,
"Stay, gentle knight, and take with thee the prize,
To thee alone assur'd." The boy look'd pale,
But straight a ruddy blush did make a veil
T' obscure the same; while thus he panting stood,
A thousand times he wisht him in the wood
From whence he came, and speaking not a word,
Let fall his hat, his javelin, and his sword.
She being young, and glad of an occasion,
Stoopt down to take them up; he with persuasion
Of an half showing love, detains her hand
From it, and with his fingers made the band
To chain them fast, (now Love had laid his scene
And draw'd the tragic plot, whereon must lean
The ground of all his acts) . . .
. . . For (lady) so it past between the lovers,
That after little pause Sappho discovers
Those kindled flames which never can expire,
But his contempt adds fuel to her fire.
"Immodest girl," he said, "why art so rude
To woo? when virtuous women should be woo'd,
And scarce obtain'd by wooing." "O forbear,"
Sweet Sappho cried, "if I do not prepare
A just excuse by none to be denied,
Never let me –" so sat her down and cried.
He, mov'd for pity more to see her tears,
Than toucht with any loyal love he bears,
Sat down by her, while she despairing, laid
Her eyes on his, her hands on his, and said, . . .
. . . "Now for the fault whereof I am accus'd,
O blame me not, for 'tis no fault I us'd;
For if affection spurs a man to love,
'Tis that affection needs must make him move
His suit to us, and we, when we affect,

And see the like from them, seem to neglect
Their scornèd suit, but so our frowns appear,
Mixt with a faint desire, and careful fear
It should displease them, that we may unite
A careless love with an entire delight.
Again, when men do see a curious stone,
The only hopes of their foundation,
How often do they slight with scornful eye,
Neglect, disgrace, dispraise and spurn it by,
The more to move and stir up an excess
Of disrespect, and make the value less.
Even so we handle men, who still endure
A thousand deaths, to train us to their lure;
And were we sure they could not us forsake,
We'd dally more, even more delight to make.
Even so as men are caught, even so are we,
When we affect those that our service flee;
What kind salutes, embraces and constraints
Ought we to use? lest our untun'd complaints
Unpitied die, and we with sorrow's scope,
As free from pleasure die, as free from hope.
Thou art a stranger, Phaon, to this place,
But I have known thy name, and know thy race;
Eumenion stories do thy honour tell,
Istria, Eumenion, knew thy parents well,
Whose fathers' head upheld the weighty crown
Of Illyris, which none could trample down;
Though many envied, free from harm he laid
His bones to rest, with whom the crown decay'd.
Now Fate, to show a model of her power,
On thy Illyricum began to lower;
Thy household gods, acquainted with the cries
Of thy decaying subjects, cast their eyes
This way and that; 'twas yours, O Gods, to bid
Denial to sedition that was hid
In Catalinian breasts, and to surcease
The period of your domestic ease.
In this uproar (what fruits seditions bring
May well be guesst, for every one was King)
The better sort prepar'd for thee and thine

A waftage over the belov'd Rhyne,
To Lesbos this; thou hadst not long been here,
But private envy did thy walls uprear,
And did beguile to all posterity
Thee of thy glory, and the crown of thee . . .
. . . Here wast thou brought, here hast thou daily stay'd,
And (while thy better subjects sought thee) play'd,
Beguiling time away; perhaps you'd know
What mov'd the powers to permit thee so
Untimely ruin: know they did anoint
Thee King of famous Lesbos, and appoint
This means alone to make their power approv'd,
And bring thee here of me to be belov'd."
To this faint speech he intermission made
With heavy sighs, and then, "Fair lady" said,
"The Heav'ns have robb'd me of succeeding bliss,
And hid me from those means to grant you this
I most desire; behold, my love, I die,
My trou[b]led soul methinks doth seem to fly
Through silent caves and fields; two pleasant gates
Ope wide to take me in, wherein there waits
A crown of gold, neither by arm or hand
Supported, but of its free power doth stand,
Now sits upon my head: these things I see,
And yet I live; can this a vision be?"
About to stir, "O stir me not," he cries,
"My feet stick fast; Sappho, farewell," and dies.
While yet he speaks, my parents' wayward fate
Must be accompanied with the date
Of my despisèd life, a fearful rind
Of citron trembling red doth creeping bind
His not half-closèd speech; his curlèd hair,
Which gallants of his time did use to wear
Of an indifferent length, now upward heaves
Towards the skies their gold refulgent leaves.
Sappho at this exclaims, laments, invokes
No power nor God, but seeks by hasty strokes,
As a fit sacrifice unto her friend,
From her belovèd breast her soul to send.
Awhile she silent stood, belike to think,

Which was the safest way for her to drink
Of the same cup her Phaon did; at last
(As evil thoughts will quickly to one haste)
She saw the spring that ran along the grove,
"'Tis you, fair streams, must send me to my Love.
Behold, dear Love, with what impatient heat
My soul aspires to mount to that blest seat,
Where thou blest sit'st; stretch out thy sacred hand,
And with safe conduct draw me to that land,
That we may taste the joys the valley yields;
And hand in hand may walk th' Elysian fields."
This said, she turns her face unto the tree,
And kissing it, said, "If thou still canst see,
Behold how irksome I enjoy that breath,
Which still detains my meeting thee in death":
With that she saw his sword, which she did take,
And having kiss'd it for the owner's sake,
Salutes her breast with many weeping wounds,
Then casts herself into the spring, and drownds.'

William Bosworth, 1651

TO THE FAIR CLARINDA, WHO MADE LOVE TO ME, IMAGIN'D MORE THAN WOMAN

Fair lovely Maid, or if that Title be
Too weak, too Feminine for Nobler thee,
Permit a Name that more Approaches Truth:
And let me call thee, Lovely Charming Youth.
This last will justify my soft complaint,
While that may serve to lessen my constraint;
And without Blushes I the Youth pursue,
When so much beauteous Woman is in view.
Against thy Charms we struggle but in vain
With thy deluding Form thou giv'st us pain,
While the bright Nymph betrays us to the Swain.

In pity to our Sex sure thou wert sent,
That we might Love, and yet be Innocent:

For sure no Crime with thee we can commit;
Or if we shou'd – thy Form excuses it.
For who, that gathers fairest Flowers believes
A Snake lies hid beneath the Fragrant Leaves.

Thou beauteous Wonder of a different kind,
Soft *Cloris* with the dear *Alexis* join'd;
When e'r the Manly part of thee, wou'd plead
Thou tempts us with the Image of the Maid,
While we the noblest Passions do extend
The Love to *Hermes*, *Aphrodite* the Friend.

Aphra Behn, 1688

A DIALOGUE CONCERNING WOMEN

A conversation takes place in the park between Misogynes and Philogynes, a hater and a lover of women respectively. Misogynes gets rather more to say, and here he tackles the question of women and learning . . .

But there are doubtless, you will say, Women of Understanding: Pray where are they? Is it your Prudent Woman, your good Houswife, who is plaguing all the World with her Management, and instructing everybody how to feed Geese and Capons? Or is it your Politician, who is always full of Business, who carries a Secretary of State's Office in her Head, and is making her deep Observations upon every days News? Or is it your Learned Woman, who runs mad for the love of hard words, who talks a mixt Jargon, or *Lingua Franca*, and has spent a great deal of time to make her capable of talking Nonsense in four or five several Languages? What think you, Sir, do you not wish for your Visitant again, as the more tolerable folly of the two? Do not you think Learning and Politicks become a Woman as ill as riding astride? And had not the Duke of *Brittaine* reason, who thought a Woman knowing enough, when she cou'd distinguish between her Husband's Shirt and his Breeches?

Do not you, in answer to these, fetch me a *Sappho* out of *Greece*; a *Cornelia*, the Mother of the *Gracchi*, out of *Rome*; an *Anna Maria Schurman* out of *Holland*; and think that in shewing me three

Learned Women in three thousand years, you have gain'd your point; and from some few particular Instances, prov'd a general Conclusion: If I shou'd bring you half a dozen Magpies that cou'd talk, and as many Horses that cou'd dance, you wou'd not, I suppose, for all that, chuse out the one to converse with, or the other to walk a Corant.

But wou'd you see 'em to their best advantage? Would you have their Wit, Courage, and Conduct display'd? Take 'em upon the business of Lust; That can make *Sappho* witty, *Aloisia* Eloquent, a Country-wife Politick; That can humble *Messalina*'s Pride to walk the Streets; can make tender *Hippia* endure the Incommodities of a Sea-Voyage, can support the Queen of *Sheba* in a Journey to *Solomon*, and make *Thalestris* search out *Alexander* the Great: In this particular, I must confess, we ought to submit to 'em, and with shame allow 'em the preference. I cannot reflect upon the Stories of *Semiramis*'s lying with all the handsomest men in her Army, and putting 'em to Death afterwards; of her offering her Son the last Favour; of *Messalina* the Empresses prostituting her self in the publick Stews; and of Queen *Joan* of *Naples* providing a Bath under her Window, where she might see all the lustiest young men naked, and take her choice out of 'em, without such an admiration as their Heroick Actions deserve. *Sappho*, as she was one of the wittiest Women that ever the World bred, so she thought with Reason it wou'd be expected she shou'd make some additions to a Science in which all Womankind had been so successful: What does she do then? Not content with our Sex, she begins Amours with her own, and teaches us a new sort of Sin, that was follow'd not only in *Lucian*'s time, but is practis'd frequently in *Turkey* at this day. You cannot but be sensible, Sir, that there is no necessity of going so far for Instances of their Lewdness, and were it civil to quote the Lampoons, or write the Amours of our own Time, we might be furnish'd with Examples enow nearer home.

Here, Madam, I cou'd not forbear telling my Friend, that his Disputant grew Scurrilous. He told me, considering him as a Woman-hater, he thought 'twas no more than his Character requir'd; and that if I compar'd his Discourse with what others had said against 'em, I shou'd think him a very well-bred Man.

William Walsh, *A Dialogue Concerning Women, Being a Defence of the Sex. Written to Eugenia*, 1691

Sappho was one of the most renowned Women of all Antiquity for her Verses and her Amours. She was a Native of *Mitylene* in the Isle of *Lesbos*, and lived in the time of *Alceus* her Country-Man, and in the time of *Stesichorus*, that is to say, in the 42 Olympiad, six hundred and ten Years before JESUS CHRIST. She Composed a great Number of Odes, Epigrams, Elegies, Epithalamiums, etc. All her Verses run upon Love, and had such Natural and moving Charms that 'tis no wonder if she was called the tenth Muse. *Strabo* looks on her as a Wonder, and says that never any Woman could come near her in Poetry. There remains nothing of so many Poems she made but some small Fragments which the Ancient Scholiasts have cited, and a Hymn to *Venus*, and an Ode to one of her Mistresses; for you must know that her Amorous Passion extended even to the Persons of her own Sex, and this is that for which she was most cried down. *Suidas* has preserved the Names of 3 of her Mistresses, who spoiled her Reputation and defamed themselves by a strange singularity which was imputed to their Commerce. He has also preserved the Names of 3 of her Female Scholars whom she did, without doubt, initiate in her Mysteries. Since *Lucian* does not observe that the Women of the Isle of *Lesbos*, who he says were very Subject to this Passion, Learned it of *Sappho*, 'tis better to imagine that she found it already Established in her Country than to make her the Inventer of it. Be it as it will, *Sappho* always passed for a Famous *Tribas*, and some think that it was for this Reason, that some Sirnamed her *Mascula Sappho*. If her Design was to pass by and neglect the other half of Mankind, she was frustrated of her Expectation; for she fell desperately in Love with *Phaon*, and did in vain all that she could to make him love her: But he despised her and Forced her by his Coldness to throw her self from a high Rock to extinguish her devouring Flame. O! what a Cruelty! She had been long before the Widow of one of the Richest Men of the Isle of *Andros*, called *Cercala*, by whom she had a Daughter called *Cleis*. And so the Mother of *Sappho* was called. I do not know her Father's Name; for there are eight assigned to her by Authors. She had 3 Brothers, one of which called *Charaxus* dealt in Wine from *Lesbos* in *Egypt*, and fell in love there with a Famous Curtesan, by some, called *Rhodope*, but *Sappho* calls her *Doricha*. She was very Angry with her Brother about this Engagement. It's said that the *Mitylenians* did her the Honour after her Death, to stamp their Money with her Image. Some Authors make mention of another *Sappho*.

Mr *Moreri* found one in *Martial*, only thro' an extreme Inadvertency. We read in *Aristotle* the Proof *Sappho* made use of to shew that Death is an Evil. The Gods, said she, have Judged it so, for otherwise they would die. There was in the *Prytaneum* of *Syracusa*, a most beautiful Statue of *Sappho*: See what *Cicero* says of it, when he reproaches *Verres* with Stealing it. It was the work of *Silanion*, and probably the same that *Tatian* speaks of reproaching the *Gentiles* with the Honour they paid to dishonest Women.

Pierre Bayle, *An Historical and Critical Dictionary*, English translation 1710

SONG

While *Sappho*, with harmonious airs,
Her dear *Philenis* charms,
With equal joy the nymph appears,
Dissolving in her arms.

Thus to themselves alone they are,
What all Mankind can give;
Alternately the happy pair
All grant, and all receive.

Like the twin-stars, so fam'd for friends,
Who set by turns, and rise;
When one to *Thetis*' lap descends,
His brother mounts the skies.

With happier fate, and kinder care,
These nymphs by turns do reign,
While still the falling, does prepare
The rising, to sustain

The joys of either sex in love,
In each of them we read,
Successive each, to each does prove,
Fierce youth and yielding maid.

Nicholas Rowe (1674–1718)

FIVE

Wanton Sapphoics

H. Gravelot Inv. J. Aliamet Sculp.

Ton Vaiſseau ſur les Mers s'enfuit au gré des Vents,
Le ſoufle de la mort glace auſsitôt mes ſens.

Ton Vaisseau sur les Mers s'enfuit au gré des Vents
Le soufle de la mort glace aussitôt mes sens.

Sappho, the abandoned woman, in Hubert François Gravelot's frontispiece to Blin de Sainmore's translation of Ovid *Lettre de Sapho a Phaon* (1766). The British Library.

Among the many Classics-inspired works of the young Alexander Pope (1688–1744) was a verse translation of Ovid's 'Sappho to Phaon'. This version of 1707 became immensely popular and Pope's Ovidian picture of a Sappho dishevelled and miserable, unable any longer to compose and fantasising hopelessly in her dreams, became one of the most persistent images of Sappho in English. Pope himself, though largely self-taught, had enough Latin and Greek (he later went on to translate Homer's *Iliad* and *Odyssey*) to know that this was not the whole truth. He was also, at various times, friendly with two of Sappho's champions in the early eighteenth century: Ambrose Phillips (1674–1749), who translated Sappho's Fragments 1 and 31 in 1711; and Joseph Addison (1672–1719) who, in 1711, founded *The Spectator* with Richard Steele (1672–1729) and published there two important early articles on the life and works of Sappho. Yet Pope, perhaps more than anyone else, was responsible for a marked decline in Sappho's reputation, and his libels were not confined to the historical personage of the classical poetess, but extended to include his contemporaries among women writers.

Lady Mary (Pierrepont) Wortley Montagu (1689–1762) was the daughter of the Duke of Kingston. Though entirely self-educated – she said that she 'stole the Latin language' in her father's library at Thoresby – she aspired to be a writer. In that library she found Anne Dacier's translation of Sappho, and the works of Madeleine de Scudéry. In order to escape from a forced marriage, she eloped and settled in London from 1714, where she cultivated the wits of the day – among them Pope and Addison. Lady Mary was celebrated for her beauty and her wit, and when she travelled with her husband's embassy to Turkey in 1716–18 she wrote a volume of travel *Letters*, which circulated in manuscript and added to her fame. Pope was one of the recipients, and his admiration was extravagant; he was, he said, as 'pleased with some Fragments of hers, as I am with Sappho's'. He insisted on moving to Twickenham to be near her, and arranged for her to be painted in Turkish costume by the eminent portaitist Godfrey Kneller.

But then something happened. Quite what, as well as quite when, is still a mystery. Isobel Grundy suggests in her biography *Lady Mary Wortley Montagu: Comet of the Enlightenment* (1999) that it may have been connected with political differences, as well as Pope's growing friendship with Jonathan Swift (whom Lady Mary despised). The results of the rift were spectacular, for Pope began to publish accusations against Lady Mary, all under the name of 'Sappho'. He began with personal hygiene:

> As *Sappho*'s diamonds with her dirty smock;
> Or *Sappho* at her toilet's greasy task,
> With *Sappho* fragrant at an evening mask . . .
>
> *Moral essays*, Epistle II, 24

and went on to her state of health:

> Slander or Poyson, dread from Delia's Rage,
> Hard Words or Hanging, if your Judge be *Page*
> From furious *Sappho* scarce a milder Fate,
> P—x'd by her Love, or libell'd by her Hate . . .
>
> *Imitations of Horace*, Satires II, I, 81–4

and then on to her morals and her appearance:

> *To Ld. Hervey & Lady Mary Wortley*
>
> When I but call a flagrant Whore unsound,
> Or have a Pimp or Flaterer in the Wind,
> Sapho enrag'd crys out your back is round,
> Adonis screams – Ah! Foe to all Mankind!
>
> Thanks, dirty Pair! you teach me what to say,
> When you attack my Morals, Sense, or Truth,
> I answer thus – poor Sapho you grow grey,
> And sweet Adonis – you have lost a Tooth.

Pope's repeated attacks on Lady Mary – that she was dirty, promiscuous, syphilitic and vain – became a sideshow in literary London. Even her good actions were used against her. She had, for instance, been an early champion of innoculation against smallpox, using a method she had seen in Turkey. So her friends really had been 'poxed' by her love, but not in the way Pope implied. Everyone knew who was meant, but, though Lady Mary did her best to reply in kind, the soubriquet of 'Sappho' created a problem. It was obvious – went the argument from Pope's camp – that no one but a 'lewd and infamous Creature' could be meant by 'Sappho', so why did Lady Mary insist on identifying herself with the name?

In spite of these troubles, Lady Mary never did renege on the name – or the work – of Sappho. When she fell in love with Francesco Algarotti she wrote a poem of desire modelled on Fragment 31, and at one point she had among her papers a translation of Fragment 1. Others went on calling her 'Sappho', renowned for '*Verse* and *Satire* keen' according to one writer; and she was hailed in a French poem by Antonio Conti as 'Montaigu Sapho nouvelle'.

Pope called other women 'Sappho' as well, and for him it was almost always a term of abuse for women writers. In a complimentary poem addressed to Anne Finch, Lady Winchilsea (1661–1720) – who published under the name of 'Ardelia' and wrote at least one version of Sappho's own Fragment 55 – Pope wrote:

> In vain you boast Poetick Dames of yore,
> And cite those Sapphoes wee admire no more;
> Fate doom'd the fall of ev'ry female Wit,
> But doom'd it then when first Ardelia writ.

Sappho remained the measure for women poets throughout the century, although the mud still stuck to the antique original. In 1743 Katherine Phillips was still being named as 'the English Sappho' in late editions of her work, as here in 'The Crooked Sixpence'. In 1765 Lord Lyttleton compared Elizabeth Carter favourably to Sappho: 'Greece shall no more / Of Lesbian Sappho boast, whose wanton Muse, / Like a false Syren, while she charm'd, seduc'd / To guilt and ruin . . .' ('On Reading Mrs Carter's Poems in Manuscript', 1765). And Anna Aikin complimented Elizabeth Rowe in similar terms: 'Such were the notes our chaster Sappho sung / And every Muse dropped honey on her tongue. / Blest shade! How pure a breath of praise was thine, / Whose spotless life was faultless as thy line' ('Verses on Mrs Rowe', 1773).

It was not surprising that these writers were circumspect. The libels that had gathered around the name of Sappho were not restricted to Pope's invective. In the anonymous *Lesbia: A Tale* (1756) she appeared as a teenage sexpot, and the story of her seduction – and its inevitable results – ends with a moral:

> When Frailty once subdues the Will,
> Then Woman will be Woman still.

But there was worse. In 1736 a certain William King set out to revenge himself upon Lady Frances Brudenell, Duchess of Newburgh. In *The Toast* he satirised her as 'Myra', the leader of a group of ladies, including her friend Lady Allen, who appears as 'Ali' or 'Lady Al-n' and is portrayed as 'Myra's' lover and familiar:

> . . . in-crawl'd her own *Imp*
> In a scaly small Body, contors'd like a Shrimp.
> In a Rapture she stroak'd it, and gave it the Teat,
> By the Suction to raise sympathetical Heat.
> Then by *Hecate* she swore, *she was sated with Men*;
> Sung a wanton *Sapphoic*, and stroak'd it agen . . .

The libels on all the ladies lampooned here include accusations of tribadism, backed up with mock-learned notes from classical sources where the grossest circumstances (including explanations about the activities of Sappho) are given in Latin. The author does, however, note in English and with some satisfaction that 'there seems to have been a peculiar Act of Justice in the Punishment of *Sappho*, who killed herself at last for the Love of a Man'.

What particularly bothers King, and many others of his kind, is Lady Frances' allegiances with her own sex. In the concluding 'Ode to Myra' he spells it out:

> What if *Sappho* was so naught [naughty]?
> I'll deny, that thou has taught
> How to pair the Female Doves,
> How to practise *Lesbian* Loves:
> But when little AL is spread
> In her Grove, or on thy Bed,
> I will swear, 'tis Nature's Call,
> 'Tis exalted Friendship all.

Practical systems of support, romantic friendships and dreams of a female community ran through the lives and writings of educated women from the end of the seventeenth century. I have mentioned the Duchess of Newcastle's *The Convent of Pleasure* (1668), but a more influential text was Mary Astell's *A Serious Proposal to the Ladies* (1694). Written 'By a Lover of her Sex', Astell (1666–1731) suggested the establishment of supportive communities for unmarried women, financed by dowries. She was also a friend of Lady Mary Wortley Montagu, writing a preface for her *Embassy Letters*.

From these few suggestive facts it was easy to come to greater conclusions, and titillating hints about women who like women began to appear in many different places.

In 1749 a popular volume was published under the title *Satan's Harvest Home.* The subtitle explains all: *Or, the Present State of Whorecraft, Adultery, Fornication, Procuring, Pimping, Sodomy, and the Game at Flatts (Illustrated by an Authentick and Entertaining Story), And other* SATANIC WORKS *daily propagated in this good Protestant Kingdom.* The anonymous author quotes word for word the passage about Sappho that appeared in William Walsh's *A Dialogue Concerning Women* (1691), except that he adds that her 'new sort of sin' is practised 'frequently in *Turkey*, as well as at *Twickenham* at this Day'.

Twickenham, of course, was where Lady Mary Wortley Montagu lived. Two years later she appeared, disguised as the character of 'Lady Bell', in a novel by John Cleland, *Memoirs of a Coxcomb* (1751). Here Cleland compares 'Lady Bell' to Sappho, not for her poetry, but for her capacity for – and ingenuity in – sexual pleasure.

Twickenham was again said to be the scene for 'the game of flatts' when Anne Conway Damer (1749–1828) inherited Horace Walpole's house at Strawberry Hill. She was an aristocrat and an artist and, after her marriage ended with her husband's suicide, an independent woman. The rumours about her affairs were rife, and those women who were supposed to have been her 'mistresses' were many. The anonymous pamphlet *A Sapphick Epistle, from Jack Cavendish, to the Honourable and most beautiful Mrs D—R* (c. 1782?) is apparently addressed to her, but gives us another eighteenth-century Sappho: 'She was the first Tommy the world has upon record; but to do her justice, though there hath been many more Tommies since, yet we never had but one Sappho.'

'Jack Cavendish's' pamphlet muddles up classical sources with popular prejudice, and feminist politics with romantic friendship and lesbian sex. The serious side of his accusations, as far as independent women of the period were concerned, is clear from his placing the whole argument within a philosophical frame when he refers (sceptically) to 'chaste platonick love and law, / As taught in France by Jacques Rousseau', or when he sends up separatist agitators: 'Ye Sapphic saints, how ye must scorn / The dames with vulgar notions born, / Who prostitute to man'. Just at the time when new freedoms were being proposed, Sappho was being put in her place, made into a warning to all women who consorted with women or interested themselves in the politics of gender.

From the late eighteenth century one standard way to condemn a strong woman was to whisper about what she did with other women. Scandalous pamphlets (with pornographic illustrations) accused Marie Antoinette; Napoleon told stories about what went on in a marble bath between Nelson's mistress Emma, Lady Hamilton and Queen Marie Caroline of Naples; and, in fiction, you knew where you were with the Marquise de Merteuil, because she was at it too. Bawdy publications treated of tribades and their ways, as discussed in Emma Donoghue's *Passions Between Women: British Lesbian Culture 1668–1801* (1993). Of those who took Sappho's name in vain, there is a rare little book entitled *The Sappho-An. An Heroic poem of three cantos, in the Ovidian stile, describing the pleasures which the fair sex enjoy with each other . . . found among the papers of a lady of quality . . .* (1740) that was clearly read – by men – and may have been on display in public places, because the University of Kansas has a copy that is annotated with an address in Covent Garden, 'Tom's Coffee House, April 10, 1749'.

One of the most popular of these curious publications was *La Nouvelle Sapho, ou Histoire de la Secte Anandryne* (1789), also called *Histoire d'une Jeune Fille* and *Anandria, La Jolie T—* (tribade?). It was published anonymously by Mathieu François Pidanzat de Mairobert (though the Sappho sections may have been written by Mayeur de Saint-Paul), who was a friend of the Paris police chief and a member of a Salon that specialised in salacious gossip. It purported to reveal the secrets of a private club called 'La Loge de Lesbos', in which the actress Judith Raucourt was said to be a leading light.

In the extract included here a young novitiate describes the ceremonial temple of the Sect, before going on with the story of her initiation. A bust of Sappho presides over the scene, along with a bust of Mademoiselle d'Éon (1728–1810), who was in fact not a woman, but a man, and whose story was one of the most celebrated of the eighteenth century. (At the peak of a highly successful career as a soldier-diplomat and spy, d'Éon liked to put it about that he was really a woman. On his return from England to France in 1777 the king decreed that it was unfitting for him – or rather, as everyone had been convinced, her – to masquerade as a man, and so d'Éon was required thereafter to assume feminine dress and, what most distressed him, was forbidden to wear the king's uniform.) Reprinted many times at the end of the eighteenth century, *La Nouvelle Sapho* was also available in England, and was included in a pornographic work of ten volumes published in London as *L'Espion Anglais*, 'The English Spy'.

La Nouvelle Sapho is pretty explicit. I have chosen a tame extract. At the end of the eighteenth century, on the eve of the French Revolution, society was changing. Mary Wollstonecraft was writing *Vindication of the Rights of Woman*, Madame de Staël would soon be standing up to Napoleon. And yet Sappho – that model for the woman writer, that illustrious name for the noble woman – had become a dirty word.

SAPPHO TO PHAON

A TRANSLATION OF OVID'S HEROIC EPISTLE, XV

Say, lovely youth that dost my heart command,
Can Phaon's eyes forget his Sappho's hand?
Must then her name the wretched writer prove,
To thy remembrance lost as to thy love?
  Ask not the cause that I new numbers choose,
The lute neglected and the lyric Muse:
Love taught my tears in sadder notes to flow,
And tuned my heart to elegies of woe.
  I burn, I burn, as when through ripened corn
By driving winds the spreading flames are borne.
Phaon to Aetna's scorching fields retires,
While I consume with more than Aetna's fires.
No more my soul a charm in music finds;
Music has charms alone for peaceful minds:
Soft scenes of solitude no more can please;
Love enters there, and I'm my own disease.
No more the Lesbian dames my passion move,
Once the dear objects of my guilty love:
All other loves are lost in only thine,
Ah, youth ungrateful to a flame like mine!
Whom would not all those blooming charms surprise,
Those heavenly looks and dear deluding eyes?
The harp and bow would you like Phoebus bear,
A brighter Phoebus Phaon might appear:

Would you with ivy wreathe your flowing hair,
Not Bacchus' self with Phaon could compare:
Yet Phoebus loved, and Bacchus felt the flame;
One Daphne warmed and one the Cretan dame;
Nymphs that in verse no more could rival me
Than e'en those gods contend in charms with thee.
The Muses teach me all their softest lays,
And the wide world resounds with Sappho's praise.
Though great Alcaeus more sublimely sings,
And strikes with bolder rage the sounding strings,
No less renown attends the moving lyre
Which Venus tunes and all her Loves inspire.
To me what Nature has in charms denied
Is well by wit's more lasting flames supplied.
Though short my stature, yet my name extends
To heaven itself and earth's remotest ends:
Brown as I am, an Aethiopian dame
Inspired young Perseus with a generous flame:
Turtles and doves of different hue unite,
And glossy jet is paired with shining white.
If to no charms thou wilt thy heart resign
But such as merit, such as equal thine,
By none, alas, by none thou canst be moved;
Phaon alone by Phaon must be loved.
Yet once thy Sappho could thy cares employ;
Once in her arms you centred all your joy:
No time the dear remembrance can remove,
For oh how vast a memory has love!
My music then you could for ever hear,
And all my words were music to your ear:
You stopt with kisses my enchanting tongue,
And found my kisses sweeter than my song.
In all I pleased, but most in what was best;
And the last joy was dearer than the rest:
Then with each word, each glance, each motion fired,
You still enjoyed, and yet you still desired,
Till all dissolving in the trance we lay,
And in tumultuous raptures died away.
  The fair Sicilians now thy soul inflame:
Why was I born, ye gods, a Lesbian dame?
But ah, beware Sicilian nymphs, nor boast

That wandering heart which I so lately lost;
Nor be with all those tempting words abused:
Those tempting words were all to Sappho used.
And you that rule Sicilia's happy plains,
Have pity, Venus, on your poet's pains.
  Shall fortune still in one sad tenor run
And still increase the woes so soon begun?
Inured to sorrow from my tender years,
My parent's ashes drank my early tears:
My brother next, neglecting wealth and fame,
Ignobly burned in a destructive flame:
An infant daughter late my griefs increased,
And all a mother's cares distract my breast.
Alas, what more could Fate itself impose,
But thee, the last and greatest of my woes?
No more my robes in waving purple flow,
Nor on my hand the sparkling diamonds glow;
No more my locks in ringlets curled diffuse
The costly sweetness of Arabian dews;
Nor braids of gold the varied tresses bind
That fly disordered with the wanton wind.
For whom should Sappho use such arts as these?
He's gone whom only she desired to please!
Cupid's light darts my tender bosom move;
Still is there cause for Sappho still to love;
So from my birth the Sisters fixed my doom,
And gave to Venus all my life to come:
Or, while my Muse in melting notes complains,
My yielding heart keeps measure to my strains.
By charms like thine, which all my soul have won,
Who might not – ah, who would not be undone?
For those, Aurora Cephalus might scorn,
And with fresh blushes paint the conscious morn:
For those, might Cynthia lengthen Phaon's sleep,
And bid Endymion nightly tend his sheep:
Venus for those had rapt thee to the skies,
But Mars on thee might look with Venus' eyes.
O scarce a youth, yet scarce a tender boy!
O useful time for lovers to employ!
Pride of thy age, and glory of thy race,
Come to these arms and melt in this embrace!

The vows you never will return, receive;
And take at least the love you will not give.
See, while I write, my words are lost in tears:
The less my sense, the more my love appears.
  Sure 'twas not much to bid one kind adieu:
At least, to feign was never hard to you.
'Farewell, my Lesbian love,' you might have said;
Or coldly thus, 'Farewell, O Lesbian maid.'
No tear did you, no parting kiss receive,
Nor knew I then how much I was to grieve.
No lover's gift your Sappho could confer;
And wrongs and woes were all you left with her.
No charge I gave you, and no charge could give
But this – 'Be mindful of our loves, and live.'
Now by the Nine, those powers adored by me,
And Love, the god that ever waits on thee; –
When first I heard (from whom I hardly knew)
That you were fled and all my joys with you,
Like some sad statue, speechless, pale I stood;
Grief chilled my breast and stopt my freezing blood;
No sigh to rise, no tear had power to flow,
Fixed in a stupid lethargy of woe.
But when its way the impetuous passion found,
I rend my tresses and my breasts I wound;
I rave, then weep; I curse, and then complain;
Now swell to rage, now melt in tears again.
Not fiercer pangs distract the mournful dame
Whose first-born infant feeds the funeral flame.
My scornful brother with a smile appears,
Insults my woes, and triumphs in my tears;
His hated image ever haunts my eyes; –
'And why this grief? thy daughter lives,' he cries.
Stung with my love and furious with despair,
All torn my garments and my bosom bare,
My woes, thy crimes, I to the world proclaim;
Such inconsistent things are love and shame.
'Tis thou art all my care and my delight,
My daily longing and my dream by night, –
O night, more pleasing than the brightest day,
When fancy gives what absence takes away,
And, dressed in all its visionary charms,

Restores my fair deserter to my arms!
Then round your neck in wanton wreath I twine;
Then you, methinks, as fondly circle mine:
A thousand tender words I hear and speak;
A thousand melting kisses give and take:
Then fiercer joys; I blush to mention these,
Yet, while I blush, confess how much they please.
But when with day the sweet delusions fly,
And all things wake to life and joy, but I;
As if once more forsaken, I complain,
And close my eyes to dream of you again:
Then frantic rise; and, like some fury, rove
Through lonely plains, and through the silent grove,
As if the silent grove and lonely plains,
That knew my pleasures, could relieve my pains.
I view the grotto, once the scene of love,
The rocks around, the hanging roofs above,
That charmed me more, with native moss o'er-grown,
Than Phrygian marble or the Parian stone:
I find the shades that veiled our joys before;
But, Phaon gone, those shades delight no more.
Here the pressed herbs with bending tops betray
Where oft entwined in amorous folds we lay;
I kiss that earth which once was pressed by you,
And all with tears the withering herbs bedew.
For thee the fading trees appear to mourn,
And birds defer their songs till thy return:
Night shades the groves, and all in silence lie, –
All but the mournful Philomel and I:
With mournful Philomel I join my strain;
Of Tereus she, of Phaon I complain,
A spring there is whose silver waters show,
Clear as a glass, the shining sands below:
A flowery lotos spreads its arms above,
Shades all the banks and seems itself a grove;
Eternal greens the mossy margin grace,
Watched by the sylvan genius of the place:
Here as I lay, and swelled with tears the flood,
Before my sight a watery virgin stood:
She stood and cried, – 'O you that love in vain,
Fly hence and seek the fair Leucadian main:

There stands a rock from whose impending steep
Apollo's fane surveys the rolling deep;
There injured lovers, leaping from above,
Their flames extinguish and forget to love.
Deucalion once with hopeless fury burned;
In vain he loved, relentless Pyrrha scorned.
But when from hence he plunged into the main
Deucalion scorned, and Pyrrha loved in vain.
Haste, Sappho, haste, from high Leucadia throw
Thy wretched weight, nor dread the deeps below.'
  She spoke, and vanished with the voice: I rise,
And silent tears fall trickling from my eyes.
I go, ye nymphs, those rocks and seas to prove:
How much I fear, but ah, how much I love!
I go, ye nymphs, where furious love inspires;
Let female fears submit to female fires:
To rocks and seas I fly from Phaon's hate,
And hope from seas and rocks a milder fate.
Ye gentle gales, beneath my body blow,
And softly lay me on the waves below.
And thou, kind Love, my sinking limbs sustain,
Spread thy soft wings and waft me o'er the main,
Nor let a lover's death the guiltless flood profane.
On Phoebus' shrine my harp I'll then bestow,
And this inscription shall be placed below:
'Here she who sung, to him that did inspire,
Sappho to Phoebus consecrates her lyre:
What suits with Sappho, Phoebus, suits with thee;
The gift, the giver, and the god agree.'
  But why, alas, relentless youth, ah, why
To distant seas must tender Sappho fly?
Thy charms than those may far more powerful be,
And Phoebus' self is less a god to me.
Ah, canst thou doom me to the rocks and sea,
O far more faithless and more hard than they?
Ah, canst thou rather see this tender breast
Dashed on these rocks that to thy bosom pressed?
This breast, which once, in vain! you liked so well;
Where the Loves played, and where the Muses dwell.
Alas, the Muses now no more inspire;
Untuned my lute, and silent is my lyre;

My languid numbers have forgot to flow,
And fancy sinks beneath the weight of woe.
  Ye Lesbian virgins and ye Lesbian dames,
Themes of my verse and objects of my flames,
No more your groves with my glad songs shall ring;
No more these hands shall touch the trembling string:
My Phaon's fled, and I those arts resign:
(Wretch that I am, to call that Phaon mine!)
Return, fair youth, return, and bring along
Joy to my soul and vigour to my song.
Absent from thee, the poet's flame expires;
But ah, how fiercely burn the lover's fires!
Gods, can no prayers, no sighs, no numbers move
One savage heart, or teach it how to love?
The winds my prayers, my sighs, my numbers bear;
The flying winds have lost them all in air.
Or when, alas, shall more auspicious gales
To these fond eyes restore thy welcome sails?
If you return, ah, why these long delays?
Poor Sappho dies while careless Phaon stays.
O launch the bark, nor fear the watery plain:
Venus for thee shall smooth her native main.
O launch thy bark, secure of prosperous gales:
Cupid for thee shall spread the swelling sails.
If you will fly – (yet ah, what cause can be,
Too cruel youth, that you should fly from me?)
If not from Phaon I must hope for ease,
Ah, let me seek it from the raging seas;
To raging seas unpitied I'll remove:
And either cease to live or cease to love.

Alexander Pope, 1707

CROOKED SIX-PENCE, WITH A LEARNED PREFACE

It is but reasonable, that the Purchaser should know what he is to expect from this Edition of *The Crooked Six-pence*; and that the rather, because there is publickly Sold by the Booksellers of *London* and *Westminster*, a little blank Poem, called the *Splendid Shilling*,

'Sappho listening to the insinuation of Love:
Of Cupid's dang'rous wiles fond Maid beware,
Nor fall incautious in his fatal snare'.
In an obscure re-working of 'mother and child' images G.B. Cipriani's popular prints of Sappho portray her without any of her professional attributes, but with pertly exposed breasts, as she listens to the 'insinuations' of Cupid. Drawn by I. Mannin, engraved and published by G.B. Cipriani, (Dublin, c. 1783).

falsely attributed to the admired Author of those ungingling Poems *Cyder* and *Blenheim* . . .

. . . As to the Author's Surname, I grant with Alacrity it was *Phillips*. But does it therefore follow that it must be *John Phillips*? Have we not had many in this Nation of the Name of *Phillips*, successful in their addresses to the Muses? Does there not even now exist a Poet of that Name, deservedly celebrated for Pastorals truly Natural, and who in the Namby-Pamby kind may justly be stiled λεπτεπιλεωτότεζος *Sed quid opus est verbis*? Many Words will not fill a Sack. It was not the real Name of our *English Sappho*, the incomparable *Orinda, Katharine Phillips*? *Ea est, ipsa est*; that, that is she, the very individual *Phillips* that originally composed this our *Crooked Six-pence*. If the *Grecian* Poetess should be put in Competition with our *English Sappho*, may we not justly say

Castior hæc, & non doctior fuit? MARTIAL

The Title Page, Christian Name, and Sex of the Author, being thus by Conjecture more than probable recovered, it necessarily follows, that the Verses of the Poem itself were given differently from what they now appear in the vulgar Editions.

Mrs *Katharine Phillips* flourished in the Decline of the last Century, in the *Augustan* Reign of *Charles I.* much about the Time that *Milton*'s *Paradise Lost* first appeared in the World, *viz.* in the Year *1667*.

Anon., 1743

THE TOAST

This is a libellous satire on 'Myra' (Lady Frances Brudenell, Duchess of Newburgh) written by William King, an Oxford don who, during a stay in Dublin, had taken Lady Frances to court over a debt of several thousand pounds, and lost. In Book II a group of fashionable gentlemen sets out to toast the ladies, beginning with 'the household of Jove' and moving on to those they despise, including Myra and her familiar, an imp called Ali . . .

They began (as 'twas meet) with the Houshold of *Jove*;
With the Goddesses all, and Court Ladies above.
But they hail'd the great Queen, who gives Charms to the rest,
Still Herself of all Beings and Fairest confest.
Then to *Thetis* they fill'd, and the Nymphs of her Train,
Who inchant with their Voices, and smooth the rough Main;
Merry *Nereids*, by *Venus* well fashion'd to please:
For the Goddess remembers she sprung from the Seas.
Next are toasted the *Naiads*, who murmuring glide,
Or in Rivers roll rapid, where Urn Gods reside.
Then the tall *Hamadryads*, who sport in the Groves:
Nor the Eyes of the Sun can discover their Loves.
Then the little bright *Donnas*, who flit thro' the Air:
Not a *Silph* was forgot, who was deem'd to be fair . . .
  They rejected the *Jilt*, and *Coquet*, and the *Prude*;
And the Nymphs, who took Money, or who were too lewd:
Pretty *Cloe* had sold herself twice to the *Jews*,
And *Corinna* had often been seen in the Stews.
  They excepted more justly all Nations of *Picts*,
Who supply by Machin'ry their various Defects.

Not a Counterfeit Belle cou'd their prying escape,
Who had made a new Face, or had mended her Shape.
One was censur'd for combing her Eye-brows with Lead,
And another for spreading a Grain of *French* Red.
Little *Ali*, whom erst I invok'd for my Goddess,
Now alas! was untoasted for wearing steel Bodice.
  Yet the Dames, who pollute their own Sex, they lik'd worse,
And the *Tribads* were all set aside with a Curse:
Nor a *Sappho*, says *Phœbus*, shall please with her Songs;
Nor *Homassa*, cries *Vol*, would I touch with my Tongs.
  By Exceptions so nice, such severe Regulation,
Scarce suffic'd the whole Globe for one Night's Compotation.

William King, *The Toast. An Heroick poem in four books, written originally in Latin by Frederick Scheffer: now done into English, and illustrated with Notes and Observations by Peregrine O'Donald*, 1736

LESBIA: A TALE

Lesbia the fair, the gay, the young,
The Joy, the *Burden* of my Song,
Was at fifteen what Men adore,
And envious Women blacken o'er.
Not *Alexander*'s Mistress, which
Inspir'd such tuneful Parts of Speech,
Should, half so soon, with all her Art,
Enchant a Soul, or steal an Heart,
Reclaim a philosophic Look,
Or wean a Scholar from his Book,
As inexperienc'd *Lesbia* seen,
At artless innocent fifteen.
  'Twas at a Moon-light Morning Hour,
When Fairies take their fansied Tour,
And Poets, restless Night and Day,
Snore out a Poem or a Play,
That tir'd with Pillow, Sleep, and Ease,
She gather'd Scraps of Thought like these:
'My good Mamma has now confest,
'The *Parsley-Bed* was all a Jest,
'Contriv'd by Nurses sage to gull

'Children that never went to *School.*
'*Eroto*'s rev'rend Youth declares,
''Tis plain as A, B, C, or Pray'rs,
'That I am now a Woman grown,
'And such are never blest *alone.*
'He says, through universal Nature
'There's a Propensity in Creature,
'Which fans the Fire of youthful Blood,
'To thaw the Ice of Solitude.
'Hence every Bird and every Beast
'Chuse a Companion from the rest,
'Whose soothing social Chear is tasted,
'When Pastures fail, or Fruits are blasted.
'All but the Phœnix, hapless Bird,
'That erst *Arabia*'s Sons admir'd,
'Which having many a tedious Year,
'Sought for a Mate both far and near;
'Resolves the lonesome World to shun,
'And with her Wings collects the Sun;
'In whose hot Beams, her Nest of Spice,
'And she herself flame in a trice.
  'Great Lengths indeed he oft will go,
'And, quotes a Text to prove it so.
'He says 'tis only Lovers know,
'Or taste of happiness below,
'That they who foster Nature's Fire
'Find all Things jump to their Desire;
'While ev'ry Virgin in the Nation
'Is in a State of *Reprobation*'
Thus ended *Lesbia*'s Meditation.

Anon., 1756

A SAPPHICK EPISTLE, FROM JACK CAVENDISH, TO THE HONOURABLE MRS D—R

Was there a Maid of Lesbos* Isle,
That ever did refuse to smile,
When Sappho deign'd to woo?
And yet she left their rosy cheeks,
And all their little modest freaks,
For Phaon – most untrue.

Ah! hapless woman, to confide
In man, and sigh to be the bride;
A vessel full of care:
Would you the wiser Sappho learn,
You might your happiness discern,
And shun a sharp despair.

When Sappho, the fair Lesbian belle,
Had gain'd the knack to read and spell;
She woo'd the Graces all:
No wench of Mytelene's Town,
Or black, or fair, or olive brown,
Refus'd her amorous call.

By Penny-post she sent her odes,
To matrons, widows, whores and bawds,
And won them to her will:
For who, Ah tell me cou'd refuse,
The pow'r of such a pleading muse,
The language of her quill?

* Lesbos, an Isle of the Ægean Sea, famous for the birth of Miss Sappho, who was the first young classic maid that bestowed her affections on her own sex: She wrote better poesy than either Mrs Montague, Mrs Grenville, Miss Carter, or Miss Aikin, but yet her verses failed when she came to address the cold Phaon. So when an old maid, and unfit for man's love, she pursued the young girls of Mytelene, and seduced many. She was the first Tommy the world has upon record; but to do her justice, though there hath been many Tommies since, yet we never had but one Sappho.

No more the Lesbian dames my passion move,
Once the dear objects of my guilty love.

Mr Pope, and Mr Publius Naso Ovid, the first a waspish English Poet, the latter the most accomplished Roman Gentleman in the reign of Augustus, have given evidence to this heterogeneous passion of Sappho.

Thus happy Sappho past her time,
In making love, and making rhime,
        To all the Lesbian maids:
Who were more constant and more kind,
More pure in soul, more firm of mind,
        Than all the Lesbian blades.

Thrice sensible, discerning dame,
That first pursued the hallow'd flame,
        Of chastity and joy:
That left the brutal clasp of man,
Jove's trite, dull, delegated plan,
        And e'en his Gany-boy.

When this pure scheme the dame pursued.
There was no sin in being lewd,
        It brought no mean disgrace:
'Twas chaste platonick love and law,
As taught in France by Jacques Rousseau,
        That wonder of his race.

His Eloisa was a wife,
A pattern of domestic life,
        Most pious sage and true:
And Mr Wolmar was a man,
Made on the old, tame, stale, cold plan,
        And cuckolded by St Preue.

But now my muse hath ta'en a dance,
And led me off, full frisk to France,
        Which was not my intention;
To Lesbos Isle I meant to stick,
To praise, and visit every nick,
        By help of some invention.

Ah tell me Lady (for you can)
What little joy there is in Man,
        The rough, unweildy bear:
Ah Sappho! I adore thy name,
That did the vulgar Wretch disclaim,
        For the more lovely Fair.

O! think how Phaon us'd the dame,
Curse on his impious heart and name,
        Curse on his cold disdain:
A cruelty, like his, would prove
To me a perfect cure for love,
        Of ev'ry vig'rous swain.

But thank my stars, I have no cause,
To rail at man, or human laws,
        To me they're kind and true:
But I detest the jealous race,
I'd rather see Almeria's face.
        Or gaze on pretty C—.

Oh wou'd the sex pursue my plan,
And turn upon the monster man,
        What would they not escape:
A thousand woes, a thousand pains,
Swellings, distortions, cramps and strains,
        The ruin of each shape.

Tell me, for you are vers'd in love,
Did you from man sweet transports prove,
        To counterpoise the pain?
Can one so slender and so mild,
Support the torments of a child,
        Nor reprobate the chain.

The marriage chain, Oh hell on earth!
The iron shackle of all mirth,
        Life's purgatory here:
For woman had been gay, if free,
Nor curs'd to raise up pedigree,
        To peasant and to peer.

Dear Lady, such is woman's state,
With Charlotte, or with Russia's Kate,
        Or Moll, or Peg, or Nan:
All sigh, and soon as fledg'd, to have
Some mere, male creature for a slave,
        To prime their little pan.

Small's then the touch-hole, not being old,
The colour lead, or carrot gold,
Or brown, or white or black:
But think, what a fair maid must bear,
When some rough marksman to a hair,
Shoots at the little crack . . .

. . . Ah! were the gentle sex like you,
Joy wou'd be rational and true,
And women might have fame:
You are a pattern of a wife,
That could resign a husband's life,
To raise a Sapphick name.

Ah! Mytelene's beauteous maid,
Could I possess thee in the shade,
And sober D— by:
You ne'er should wish for puerile joy,
Nor whimper for the scornful boy,
Like Mrs Chicken.

Curse on my stars, that I was born,
In such an age of lust and scorn.
Oh, Sappho, had'st thou been
Alive in these rude, filthy days,
Thy verses had been all in praise
Of me and beauty's queen.

Oh! had it been my wretched fate,
That Phaon had made me his hate,
What then had been my case?
Like D— I had scorn'd the youth,
Kiss'd every female's lovely mouth,
And follow'd ev'ry face . . .

Anon. (addressed to Anne Damer), c. 1782?

The hour of my initiation into the mysteries of the sect of the Anandrynes was fixed for the following day, and I was to be admitted with full honours. This extraordinary ceremony was too overwhelming for me to forget any of the minutest details, and without doubt it is the most curious episode of my history.

At the centre of the temple is an oval salon decorated with the kind of allegorical figures that one usually sees in such places, raised up in all their pride, while nothing lights up the scene except a skylight that forms a belt of light and extends out over the statues that I speak of. At the time of their assemblies they give precedence to a small statue of *Vesta*, about the size of an ordinary woman, that descends majestically, with her feet poised on a globe, into the middle of the assembly so that she can preside over it. At a certain distance one can discern the chain of iron that holds her, so that she rests suspended in

Pag. 26.
Approchez, mon enfant, venez vous asseoir à côté de moi.

The innocent heroine meets the president of the Anandrynes. This anonymous semi-pornographic novel was published in London and Paris though 'Lesbos' was sometimes given as the place of publication, and its story line lampooned goings on among a notorious lesbian set in Paris. It was often reprinted at the end of the eighteenth century and of the nineteenth century. *La Nouvelle Sapho ou Histoire de la Secte Andandryne* (Paris, 1789). The British Library.

Pag. 38.
Belle présidente et vous cheres
compagnes, voici une postulante.

The initiation of the postulant. Note the oval shaped room, the altar, the billing doves and the presiding statue. *La Nouvelle Sapho ou Histoire de la Secte Andandryne* (Paris, 1789). The British Library.

mid air. Unless you are accustomed to this miracle, it is a terrifying sight.

A corridor circles around the sanctuary of the goddess, and this is the place where two tribades parade during the assembly, meticulously guarding all the gates and approaches. The only entry is through the middle, where there is a gate with a double door. On the opposite side of this, you see a black marble slab inscribed, in letters of gold, with the verses that I will soon recite to you: At each of the extremities of the oval is a space for a little altar where there is a flame, lit and tended by none but the guardians. On the altar to the right as you enter is the bust of Sapho, as the oldest and the best known of the Tribades. The place on the altar to the left was vacant until recently, but it has now been graced with the bust of Mademoiselle d'Eon, that illustrious modern woman, most worthy of figuring in the sect Anandryne. But, as yet, she has achieved little, and we wait to see if she'll come out of the same mould as the voluptuous Mademoiselle Houdon.

All around and into the distance were placed, on the many shelves cladding the walls, the busts of the beautiful Greek girls whom Sapho celebrated as her companions. At the base you could read the names of *Thelesyle*, *Amythone*, *Cydno*, *Megara*, *Pyrrine*, *Andromeda*, *Cyrine*, *&c.* In the middle was a bed raised up in the form of a basket lit by two lamps either side. Here reposed the president and her pupil. All around the salon, seated on Ottoman sofas, piled with cushions, were women, with limbs intertwined, or gazing into each other's eyes. Each couple was composed of a mother and a novice, or in the mystic terms, of an 'incubus' and a 'succubus'. The walls were covered with sculpture of superior workmanship, where the chisel had traced in a hundred places, with unique precision, and in the most naturalistic manner, the various private parts of woman, those parts that are described in the chart of 'wedded love' in the *natural history* of Monsieur de Buffon.

This is an exact description of the sanctuary, and I do believe that I have left nothing out. Hear now the manner of my initiation.

Anon., 1789

SIX

The Sapphic Sublime

Sappho in the midst of Sublime '*sturm und drang*' as she prepares to throw herself from the cliff in William Beechey's ink and wash sketch from the 1790's. Department of Prints and Drawings, British Museum.

Sappho led a double life in the eighteenth century. Popularly her name was a term of abuse, but among scholars she acquired a newly furnished reputation. In Germany, Johann Christian Wolf produced a Latin edition of her Fragments (1773) and other translations and editions also appeared, especially towards the end of the century. Poinsinet de Sivry (1758), J. J. Moutonnet-Clairfons (1773), E. Billardon de Sauvigny (1777, Amsterdam) and J. B. Grainville (1796) translated her into French. In England, Joseph Addison wrote his *Spectator* articles, and John Addison (1735), Francis Fawkes (1760), Edward Burnaby Greene (1768) and Edward Du Bois (1799) wrote English translations, while several Latin editions also appeared. There were translations into Italian by G. M. Pagnini (1793 and 1794) and into Spanish by Don Ignacio de Luzan (1776).

While all this scholarly work brought more substantial Sapphos before the public, it was the invention – or, rather, the rediscovery – of the notion of 'the sublime' in art that made Sappho into a popular icon. John Hall had published an English translation of Longinus' first-century treatise *Peri Hypsous* (*On the Sublime*) in 1652, but the real beginning of the eighteenth-century's obsession with the sublime dates from 1674, when Nicolas Boileau's popular French translation was published. In England, the immediate results were a Latin edition by John Hudson (1710) and an English translation by William Smith (1739). Sappho's most famous poem, Fragment 31, 'That man seems to me . . .', was quoted by Longinus as an example of 'the sublime' and, for nearly 150 years as definitions of the sublime governed arguments and trends in aesthetics, Sappho became part of that picture.

Joseph Addison (1672–1719) had already written his two influential articles on Sappho for *The Spectator* in 1711, when he contributed to the dissemination of the idea of the sublime with a series of *Spectator* articles on 'The Pleasures of the Imagination' (21 June to 3 July 1712). Another important early theorist was John Baillie, who published *An Essay on the Sublime* in 1747. But it was Edmund Burke's vastly influential book *A Philosophical Enquiry into the Origin of Our Ideas of the Sublime and Beautiful* (1757, revised and expanded edition 1759) that set out the principles that were now to dominate.

Although it was a book about aesthetics, Burke's *Philosophical Enquiry* also drew on concepts of gender difference that were just beginning to harden into the categories of a constructed 'masculine' and 'feminine'. These concepts would underpin the 'separate spheres' of the male and female worlds in the nineteenth century, and still colour commonplace perceptions of appropriate gender behaviour today. According to Burke, 'those virtues which cause admiration' (fortitude, justice, wisdom) went into the manly category of 'the sublime', while those that inspire love (easiness of temper, compassion, kindness and liberality) went into the 'softer' category of 'the beautiful'. Mark Akenside's 'Ode XIII. On Lyric Poetry' sets up the same opposition. Alcaeus, Sappho's fellow poet and countryman (and the 'Lesbian patriot' referred to in the first stanza included here), is portrayed in terms of 'the sublime', as his verses pour out 'shame and vengeance' on the 'perfidious' lords of his native island. By contrast Sappho, in the second stanza, expresses 'the beautiful' in 'melting airs' that mimic the sentiments of her own Fragment 1, 'The Ode to Aphrodite'.

George Dyer's 'Ode XXVI. The Resolve, Supposed to be Written by Sappho' also exploits a contrast between 'the sublime' and 'the beautiful'. But his Sappho ends by bemoaning her addiction to 'tenderer loves', and she characterises herself as 'Beauty's weak captive'. She regrets this failing, because it compromises her commitment to 'the love of praise', and to her high calling as a poet, which is construed in terms of 'the sublime':

> . . . I will listen to wild ocean's roar,
> Or, like some out-cast solitary shade,
> Will cling upon the howlings of the wind,
> Till I grow deaf with listening, cold and blind.

For although Sappho is a woman, and although her poetry is lyric (that is, feeling) rather than epic (that is, heroic), Longinus' definitions – as reworked by the theorists of the eighteenth century – plus the fictions of Sappho's legends made her into an examplar of the 'masculine' category of the sublime, rather than the 'feminine' category of the beautiful. For instance, in early eighteenth-century writings on the sublime there was considerable emphasis on a move to challenge the authority of tradition and formulaic rhetoric, in favour of the authenticity of individual experience and personal expression. Fragment 31, with its emphasis on the physical experience of desire and the intimate relation of private feeling, obviously fits in with this move. As the century wore on, and theories of the sublime opened out into the promotion of a Romantic sensibility and the moral value of the poet's role, Sappho was easily remade into a model Romantic poet. Her work (even such little as was available to the eighteenth century) ranged over many topics, and was free-thinking and broad in tone, even while it retained the character of personal conviction. It was this that linked her writing with tenets of the sublime, as described, for instance, by Joseph Addison in 1712:

> The mind of man naturally hates everything that looks like a restraint upon it ... On the contrary, a spacious horizon is an image of liberty, where the eye has room to range abroad, to expiate at large on the immensity of its views, and to lose itself amidst the variety of objects that offer themselves to its observation.

Above all, the cirumstances of Sappho's legend made her into an icon of the sublime. One moment in particular was repeated and reworked: the scene of Sappho's leap. Quite suddenly, this was the image that began to appear in engravings, paintings, statues, poems and plays. Numberless Sapphos leaped from innumerable cliffs, and if there was one thing that everyone knew about her, it was not her poetry or her story, but the means of her end.

Robert Southey's 'Sappho: A Monodrama' (1793) positions her on one of those cliffs, puts a Gothic curse into her mouth ('Oh haunt his midnight dreams, black Nemesis!') and nerves her to an extravagance of reaction as she prepares to destroy herself ('Tremendous height! / Scarce to the brink will these rebellious limbs / Support me'). The natural terror of the cliff height itself makes the scene of Sappho's suicide sublime. In describing great, or sublime, scenery – as opposed to the beautiful, which is distinguished by luxuriance – Addison singled out just such settings. The sublime lies, he said, in:

> the prospects of an open champaign country, a vast uncultivated desert, of huge heaps of mountains, high rocks and precipices, or a wide expanse of waters, where we are not struck with the novelty or beauty of the sight, but with that rude kind of magnificence which appears in many of these stupendous works of nature.

And then there is the effect of Sappho's emotions, rendered artistically, on the mind of the audience. When Addison wrote that 'The two leading passions, which the more serious parts of poetry stir up in us, are terror and pity', he was anticipating Edmund Burke's famous definition of the character of the sublime in art:

> The passions which belong to self-preservation, turn on pain and danger . . . they are delightful when we have an idea of pain and danger, without being actually in such circumstances . . . Whatever excites this delight, I call *sublime* . . .

Sappho's leap fitted Burke's category and, as the Romantics indulged a taste for the horrific or grand, for the terrifying or the extreme, so the scene of Sappho's suicide gave that *frisson* of delicious excitement to the viewer, without any threat of real danger. As Addison put it:

> When we look on hideous objects, we are not a little pleased to think that we are in no danger of them. We consider them at the same time, as dreadful and harmless; so that the more frightful appearance they make, the greater is the pleasure we receive from the sense of our own safety.

Recent theorists have pointed out that this was no cheap fairground thrill, but a serious exercise. As far as Burke (1729–97) was concerned, the best antidotes to the kinds of debilitation, fear and self-doubt that were besetting eighteenth-century Europe at a time of widespread civil and military agitation, were the practices of contemplating large and awe-inspiring scenes, and testing out one's own reactions to such artificially produced prospects. 'The best remedy,' he wrote, 'for all these evils is exercise or *labour*; and labour is a surmounting of *difficulties*, an exertion of the contracting power of the muscles; and as such resembles pain, which consists in tension or contraction, in every thing but degree.'

When Mary Robinson (1758–1800) published her sonnet sequence *Sappho and Phaon* in 1796 she was setting herself and her readers just such an exercise. 'As poetry,' she said in her Preface, 'has the power to raise, so has it also the magic to refine.' In her address 'To the Reader' she explains her choice of subject:

> The story of the LESBIAN MUSE . . . presented to my imagination such a lively example of the human mind, enlightened by the most exquisite talents, yet yielding to the destructive controul of ungovernable passions, that I felt an irresistible impulse to attempt the delineation of their progress; mingling with the glowing picture

of her soul, such moral reflections, as may serve to exite that pity, which, while it proves the susceptibility of the heart, arms it against the danger of indulging a too luxuriant fancy.

In the forty-four sonnets of her sequence Robinson sets the 'feminine' susceptibility to love against the 'masculine' enlightenment that should govern the ambitions of the intellectual woman. Her retelling of the tale in Burkean terms is offered in the hope that it will create a 'sympathy in the mind of the susceptible reader'.

And she clearly does mean the intellectual *woman* reader. Mary Robinson was – had been – an actress and the mistress of the Prince of Wales, later George IV. But she was also a friend of Mary Wollstonecraft (1759–97). More than that, Robinson followed the example of her friend in producing (under the pseudonym of Anne Frances Randall) a pamphlet, first published in 1799 as *Thoughts on the Condition of Women* and reprinted later that same year under the title *Letter to the Women of England on the Injustice of Mental Subordination.* It begins, 'Custom, from the earliest periods of antiquity, has endeavoured to place the female mind in the subordinate ranks of intellectual sociability', and goes on to cite eminent females to support her case for woman's elevation – among them Anne Dacier, Lady Mary Wortley Montagu and, of course, Sappho herself, whom she calls 'this celebrated woman'. Robinson ends, 'Should this Letter be the means of influencing the minds of those to whom it is addressed, so far as to benefit the rising generation, my end and aim will be accomplished.'

When Edmund Burke composed his *Philosophical Enquiry* he was not just writing about aesthetics. The emphasis on the authenticity of personal experience, and the strenuous effort that he recommended in any approach to the sublime, were two aspects of his work that linked it, first, to the democratic ideals that were new in the eighteenth century and, second, to the work ethic that would dominate and would lead eventually to the making of the English middle class. Most critical writing on Burke concentrates on the effects and results that this had for men. But it had far-reaching effects for women, too. As Mary Wollstonecraft (his opponent, but also his disciple, in some ways) had seen, women were the single largest disenfranchised class. And so, when Mary Robinson chose to write about Sappho in terms of the sublime, she was making a case for the rights of all capable, intelligent and ambitious women.

Some people got the message. When Robert Southey's 'Sappho: A

Monodrama' was first published in 1793 it was in a volume that began with a poem to Mary Wollstonecraft, whom he greatly admired. Samuel Taylor Coleridge (1772–1834), another friend of Robinson's, indicated his high opinion of her work by writing a poem addressed to her when she lay, ill and impoverished, in her cottage at Windsor. In 'A Stranger Minstrel: Written [to Mrs Robinson] a Few Weeks Before her Death' (1800) Coleridge envisaged himself on the heights of Mount Skiddaw in the Lake District, wishing that Mary Robinson was with him to appreciate the magnificence and terror of the scene. He imagines that the mountain, 'ancient Skiddaw, stern and proud', speaks to him about her, and tells him how her poetry has reached even this mountainous wildnerness:

'Nay, but thou dost not know her might,
The pinions of her soul how strong!
But many a stranger in my height
Hath sung to me her magic song,
Sending forth his ecstasy
In her divinest melody,
And hence I know her soul is free,
She is where'er she wills to be,
Unfetter'd by mortality'.

In his poem 'Alcaeus to Sappho' (1800), Coleridge pays Mrs Robinson a similar compliment. As 'Alcaeus', he sets up 'the beautiful' in the person of a girl who loves him, but writes that, while others may think this the most exquisite sight in the world, he knows that 'Sappho's' sublime intellectual powers make hers 'The fairest face on earth'.

In spite of Coleridge's understanding, the late eighteenth century was a difficult period of transition for women writers, for women thinkers, for women, for Sappho. Elizabeth Moody's comic poem 'Sappho Burns Her Books and Cultivates the Culinary Arts' (1798) wittily transposes elements of Sappho's many past legends into that troubled present, sets cleverness against cookery, high art against *haute cuisine* and shows how *Peri Hypsous*, 'On the Sublime' could so easily descend to *Peri Bathous*, 'On the Bathetic'.

SAPPHO, inspired by Love, compoſes an Ode to VENUS.

An engraving by the Facius brothers of one of Angelika Kauffmann's many Sappho paintings. The writing is the beginning of Fragment 1, the Ode to Aphrodite', the lyre and laurel wreath are conventional attributes, while the erupting volcano introduces a new association. Published by John Boydell, (London, 1778). Department of Prints and Drawings, British Museum.

ODE XIII. ON LYRIC POETRY

Broke from the fetters of his native land,
  Devoting shame and vengeance to her lords,
With louder impulse and a threatening hand
  The Lesbian patriot smites the sounding chords:
    Ye wretches, ye perfidious train,
    Ye cursed of gods and free-born men,
      Ye murderers of the laws,
    Though now ye glory in your lust,
  Though now ye tread the feeble neck in dust,
Yet Time and righteous Jove will judge your dreadful cause.

But lo, to Sappho's melting airs
  Descends the radiant queen of Love:
She smiles, and asks what fonder cares
  Her suppliant's plaintive measures move:
Why is my faithful maid distressed?
Who, Sappho, wounds thy tender breast?
  Say, flies he? – Soon he shall pursue:
Shuns he thy gifts? – He soon shall give:
Slights he thy sorrows? – He shall grieve,
  And soon to all thy wishes bow.

Mark Akenside (1721–70)

ODE XXVI. THE RESOLVE

SUPPOSED TO BE WRITTEN BY SAPPHO

Yes, I have loved: yet often have I said,
Love in this breast shall never revel more;
But I will listen to wild ocean's roar,
Or, like some out-cast solitary shade,
Will cling upon the howlings of the wind,
Till I grow deaf with listening, cold and blind.
But, ah! enchantress, cease that tender lay,
Nor tune that lyre to notes thus softly slow;
Those eyes, oh take those melting eyes away!
Nor let those lips with honey'd sweets o'erflow,
Nor let meek Pity pale that lovely cheek,
Nor weep, as wretches their long sufferings speak:
With forms so fair endued, oh! Venus, why
Are Lesbian maids, or with such weakness I?
Do Lesbian damsels touch the melting lyre?
My lyre is mute; and I in silence gaze;
As tho' the muse did not this breast inspire,
I lose, in tenderer loves, the love of praise.
Oh! Sappho, how art thou imprisoned round,
Beauty's weak captive, fast-enchained with sound!
Frail, frail resolve! vain promise of a day!
I see, I hear, I feel, and melt away.

George Dyer (1755–1841)

The earlier of Theodore Chasseriau's two paintings of Sappho throwing herself from the rock of Leucata. The hurrying sky reflects her internal drama at the moment immediately before the fall. Exhibited at the Paris Salon, 1849. The Louvre, Paris.

SAPPHO: A MONODRAMA

Scene: the promontory of Leucadia

This is the spot: – 'tis here Tradition says
That hopeless Love from this high towering rock
Leaps headlong to Oblivion or to Death.
Oh 'tis a giddy height! my dizzy head
Swims at the Precipice – 'tis death to fall!

Lie still, thou coward heart! this is no time
To shake with thy strong throbs the frame convuls'd;
To die, – to be at rest – oh pleasant thought!
Perchance to leap and live; the soul all still,
And the wild tempest of the passions husht
In one deep calm; the heart, no more diseas'd
By the quick ague fits of hope and fear,
Quietly cold;
Presiding Powers look down!
In vain to you I pour'd my earnest prayers,
In vain I sung your praises: chiefly thou
VENUS! ungrateful Goddess, whom my lyre
Hymn'd with such full devotion! Lesbian groves,
Witness how often at the languid hour
Of Summer twilight, to the melting song
Ye gave your choral echoes! Grecian maids
Who hear with downcast look and flushing cheek
That lay of love, bear witness! and ye youths,
Who hang enraptur'd on the empassion'd strain,
Gazing with eloquent eye, even till the heart
Sinks in the deep delirium! and ye too
Shall witness, unborn Ages! to that song
Of warmest zeal; ah witness ye, how hard
Her fate who hymn'd the votive hymn in vain!
Ungrateful Goddess! I have hung my lute
In yonder holy pile: my hand no more
Shall wake the melodies that fail'd to move
The heart of Phaon – yet when Rumour tells
How from Leucadia Sappho hurl'd her down
A self-devoted victim – he may melt
Too late in pity, obstinate to love.

Oh haunt his midnight dreams, black NEMESIS!
Whom, self-conceiving in the inmost depths
Of CHAOS, blackest NIGHT long-labouring bore,
When the stern DESTINIES, her elder brood,
And shapeless DEATH, from that more monstrous birth
Leapt shuddering! haunt his slumbers, Nemesis!
Scorch with the fires of Phlegethon his heart,
Till helpless, hopeless, heaven-abandon'd wretch
He too shall seek beneath the unfathom'd deep
To hide him from thy fury.

How the sea
Far distant glitters as the sun-beams smile
And gayly wanton o'er its heaving breast!
Phæbus shines forth, nor wears one cloud to mourn
His votary's sorrows! God of Day shine on –
By Men despis'd, forsaken by the Gods
I supplicate no more.

How many a day,
O pleasant Lesbos! in thy secret streams
Delighted have I plung'd, from the hot sun
Screen'd by the o'er-arching grove's delightful shade,
And pillowed on the waters: now the waves
Shall chill me to repose

Tremendous height!
Scarce to the brink will these rebellious limbs
Support me. Hark! how the rude deep below
Roars round the rugged base, as if it called
Its long-reluctant victim! I will come.
One leap, and all is over! The deep rest
Of Death, or tranquil Apathy's dead calm
Welcome alike to me. Away vain fears!
Phaon is cold, and why should Sappho live?
Phaon is cold, or with some fairer one –
Thought worse than death!

She throws herself from the precipice.

Robert Southey, 1793

SONNET IV

Why, when I gaze on Phaon's beauteous eyes,
  Why does each thought in wild disorder stray?
  Why does each fainting faculty decay,
And my chill'd breast in throbbing tumults rise?
Mute, on the ground my Lyre neglected lies,
  The Muse forgot, and lost the melting lay;
  My down-cast looks, my faultering lips betray,
That stung by hopeless passion, – Sappho dies!
  Now, on a bank of Cypress let me rest;
Come, tuneful maids, ye pupils of my care,
  Come, with your dulcet numbers soothe my breast;
And, as the soft vibrations float on air,
  Let pity waft my spirit to the blest,
To mock and barb'rous triumphs of despair!

Mary Robinson, *Sappho and Phaon,* 1796

Sappho as priestess; pen and ink sketch by Giuseppe Bossi (c.1780), who also engraved a head for the frontispiece to Alessandro Verri's novel *Le Avventure di Saffo* (Rome, 1780). Department of Prints and Drawings, British Museum.

SONNET VII

Come, Reason, come! each nerve rebellious bind,
  Lull the fierce tempest of my fev'rish soul;
  Come, with the magic of thy meek controul,
And check the wayward wand'rings of my mind:
Estrang'd from thee, no solace can I find,
  O'er my rapt brain, where pensive visions stole,
  Now passion reigns and stormy tumults roll –
So the smooth Sea obeys the furious wind!
  In vain Philosophy unfolds his store,
O'erwhelm'd is ev'ry source of pure delight;
  Dim is the golden page of wisdom's lore;
All nature fades before my sick'ning sight:
  For what bright scene can fancy's eye explore,
'Midst dreary labyrinths of mental night?

Mary Robinson, *Sappho and Phaon,* 1796

SONNET XXXVI

Lead me, Sicilian Maids, to haunted bow'rs,
  While yon pale moon displays her faintest beams
  O'er blasted woodlands, and enchanted streams,
Whose banks infect the breeze with pois'nous flow'rs.
Ah! lead me, where the barren mountain tow'rs,
  Where no sounds echo, but the night-owl's screams,
  Where some lone spirit of the desart gleams,
And lurid horrors wing the fateful hours!
  Now goaded frenzy grasps my shrinking brain,
Her touch absorbs the crystal fount of woe!
  My blood rolls burning through each gasping vein;
Away, lost Lyre! unless thou can'st bestow
  A charm, to lull that agonizing pain,
Which those who never lov'd, can never know!

Mary Robinson, *Sappho and Phaon,* 1796

ALCAEUS TO SAPPHO

How sweet, when crimson colours dart
Across a breast of snow,
To see that you are in the heart
That beats and throbs below.
All Heaven is in a maiden's blush,
In which the soul doth speak,
That it was you who sent the flush
Into the maiden's cheek.

Large steadfast eyes! eyes gently rolled
In shades of changing blue,
How sweet are they, if they behold
No dearer sight than you.

And, can a lip more richly glow,
Or be more fair than this?
The world will surely answer, No!
I, Sappho, answer, Yes!

Then grant one smile, tho' it should mean
A thing of doubtful birth;
That I may say these eyes have seen
The fairest face on earth!

Samuel Taylor Coleridge, 1800

SAPPHO BURNS HER BOOKS AND CULTIVATES THE CULINARY ARTS

[On Miss R.P.'s Saying she would find Love only if she did so]

Companions of my favourite hours,
By winter's fire, in summer's bowers,
That wont to chase my bosom's care,
And plant your pleasing visions there!
Guarini, Dante, honoured names,
Ah, doomed to feel devouring flames!
Alas, my Petrarch's gentle loves!

My Tasso's rich enchanted groves!
My Ariosto's fairy dreams,
And all my loved Italian themes!
I saw you on the pile expire,
Weeping I saw the invading fire;
There fixed remained my aching sight,
Till the last ray of parting light
The last pale flame consumed away,
And all dissolved your relics lay.

  Goddess of Culinary Art,
Now take possession of my heart!
Teach me more winning arts to try,
To salt the ham, to mix the pie;
To make the paste both light and thin,
To smooth it with a rolling-pin;
With taper skewer to print it round,
Lest ruder touch the surface wound.
Then teach thy votary how to make
That fair rotundo – a plum-cake;
To shake the compound sweets together,
To bake it light as any feather,
That, when complete, its form may show
A rising hillock topped with snow;
And how to make the cheesecake, say,
To beat the eggs and turn the whey;
To strain my jelly fair and clear,
That here no *misty fog* appear;
But plain to view each form may rise
That in its glassy bosom lies.

  Now fancy soars to future times,
When all extinct are Sappho's rhymes;
When none but cooks applaud her name,
And naught but recipes her fame.
When sweetest numbers she'll despise,
When Pope shall sing beneath *minced-pies*,
And Eloise in her *tin* shall mourn
Disastrous fate and love forlorn;
Achilles too, that godlike man,
Shall bluster in the *patty-pan*;

And many a once-loved Grecian chief
Shall guard from flames the roasting beef.

Then, when this transformation's made,
And Sappho's vestments speak her trade;
When girt in towels she is seen,
With cuffs to keep the elbows clean:
Then, Sorceress, she'll call on thee!
Accomplish then thy fair decree!
If, like your sisters of the heath,
Whose mystic sound betrayed Macbeth,
Fallacious charms your arts dispense,
To cheat her with ambiguous sense;
Severest torments may you prove! –
Severest – disappointed love.

Elizabeth Moody (née Greenly), 1798

SEVEN

Hellenism and Heroes

Enrico Tresham inv. e inc.
Venere salva Faone
Mi trasse dall' onda in alto fuori, subitamente per l' aere volando.
Libro III. Cap. VI.

Inspired by Alessandro Verri's 1780 novel, the Irish artist Henry Tresham produced a set of twelve evocative aquatints illustrating the story and celebrating the beauty of the male body, *Le Avventure di Saffo* (Rome, 1784). Tresham was part of the set surrounding the Swiss artist Henry Fuseli in Rome and the friend of two other artists who made Sappho-derived images, the sculptor Antonio Canova and the Scottish painter Hugh Douglas Hamilton. Department of Prints and Drawings, British Museum.

In the Museo Nazionale in Naples two rooms on the first floor are dedicated to showing the finds from the so-called Villa dei Papiri at Herculaneum. There are bronzes and mosaics, portions of frescos and marble statues; there are pieces of furniture and other decorative items. But what most people miss are the things that gave the villa its name.

Just inside the first door is a small, atmospherically controlled glass case. In it are the remains of a couple of papyrus rolls. They look like nothing at all. If the warder happens to draw the attention of passing tourists to the case, they stare at it, uncomprehending. Unless you know about the two spindles that wind on the roll, it is impossible to understand that this is an ancient book. Unless you realise that these charred and blackened ribbons once displayed the writings of antiquity, it is impossible to imagine how these precious relics stirred the imagination of the eighteenth century.

The 'father of Classicism' was Johann Joachim Winckelmann (1717–68) whose monumental works, *Thoughts on Greek Works of Painting and Sculpture* (1755) and *History of the Art of Antiquity* (1764) promoted an ideal of Greek art – noble in its simplicity, pure in its proportions, grand and yet retaining a distinctive spiritual quality. This ideal was to influence not only succeeding German writers such as Goethe and Schiller, but also many later English writers and thinkers on the aesthetic, especially Walter Pater. Although he was an authority on both Greek and Roman antiquities, Winckelmann's fame was based on the work he pursued in Rome where, from 1755, he worked in the library of Cardinal Alessandro Albani cataloguing the Florentine Stosch collection of engraved sealstones and working on his history. To Rome came others, attracted by the immediacy of the classical past to be found there. Some of these foreigners settled there for a time; others passed through on the Grand Tour, visiting Rome, Naples, Venice and, to a lesser extent, Florence.

In the eighteenth century Italy was the new Greece. The real Greece was ruled by the Ottoman Empire, and visiting Northerners could see few traces of her ancient glory. Lady Mary Wortley Montagu had lamented in 1717 that 'art is extinct here; the wonders of nature alone remain'. But in Italy caches of Greek art did remain: in the marble sculptures in the Vatican, both Greek originals and

Roman copies; in the rare and expensive ancient cameos brought from Constantinople and offered for sale in Venice; in the collections of Greek red-figured *hydria* and vases brought here long ago by waves of migration from ancient Greece, avidly sought by connoisseurs such as Sir William Hamilton (1730–1803), British envoy to the court at Naples. Above all, the remnants of ancient Greek civilisation were to be found in the many archaeological sites across the country that pandered to a new branch of scholarship and quickly created a new fashion. Fortresses and towns, tombs and temples were excavated by enterprising Italians, and by foreigners too, and the market in antiquities flourished. Itinerant artists like the Irishman Henry Tresham (1751–1814) would subsidise their travels by dealing in artefacts. Even Sir William was not above financing his collection by selling on hoards of bronze items, candelabra, mirrors and lamps to fellow enthusiasts at home, and, as each new site opened, scholars and speculators raced each other to the scene.

No site generated as much interest – or rivalry, or rapaciousness – as the excavations at Herculaneum and Pompeii. Local people living around the Gulf of Naples had long known that there were treasures to be extracted from the volcanic deposits along the seashore, left there after the famous eruption of Vesuvius in AD 79. But the first official public notice of the sites came in 1711 when Emmanuel-Maurice de Lorraine, later the Duc d'Elbeuf, a general in the Austrian army serving in Naples, decided to build himself a seaside villa at Portici. One story goes that his workers, busy sinking a well, came across coloured marbles far below ground and realised that here was the site of an ancient city. The more cynical version says that d'Elbeuf wanted to decorate his beach-house with antique marble and deliberately purchased a property where the local landowner had, years before, made some finds in digging her well at nearby Resina.

In investigating his plot, d'Elbeuf had workmen build narrow tunnels around the shaft, and soon the men were crawling up from below bringing decorative marbles and portrait heads, as well as life-size statues, from a building that they believed to be a temple (it was actually the Theatre at Herculaneum). Then d'Elbeuf was recalled to Austria, and eventually the property was acquired by Charles of Bourbon in 1746. He too had decided, in 1738, to build himself a villa on a nearby plot. The task of construction went to an engineer, Rocque Joachin Alcubierre, who soon realised the possibilities for excavation (and spent much energy in claiming for himself the glory of having been the discoverer of Herculaneum). Alcubierre employed another engineer, Karl Weber, to undertake much of the work, and at this early stage it was due to Weber's painstaking records and drawings that classical historians began to learn about the buried city. The history of Weber's role in the excavations is told in Christopher Charles Parslow's *Rediscovering Antiquity: Karl Weber and the Excavation of Herculaneum, Pompeii, and Stabiae* (1998).

One of Weber's most important finds was the Villa dei Papiri. His forced labourers came across a circular pavilion, buried some thirty yards below the surface, in 1750. Over the next eleven years this huge villa gave up its treasures; marbles, bronzes, mosaics and the papyrus scrolls. The first hoard, discovered in October 1752, was reported by Camillo Paderni in an open letter to the Royal Society of London:

> [One room] appears to have been a library, adorned with presses, inlaid with different sorts of wood, disposed in rows; at the top of which were cornices, as in our own times. I was buried in this spot for more than twelve days, to carry off the volumes found there; many of which were so perished, that it was impossible to remove them.

Undoubtedly a great deal more was lost than was saved. When the workmen first found the papyrus scrolls they had no idea what they were. They trampled over them, sliced into them with their spades, tossed them back into the tunnels they were back-filling. When someone did notice their cylindrical shape and their curious winding-spindles, it was assumed, to begin with, that these were rolls of burned cloth, or nets, used for hunting or fishing. At last, according to the ironical account of Padre Antonio Piaggio, a priest brought from Rome in 1753 to decipher the findings, Paderni spotted the characters on the rolls, rushed to the palace and, cutting one open with a knife, tried to impress upon the king and queen the immense value of this 'hidden treasure'.

If the monarchs did not immediately recognise the importance of the charred and broken fragments paraded before them, the world did. The treasure did not include any Sappho, but because her Nine Books were among the great losses of antiquity it was not long before fantasies began to build around the anticipation of new discoveries. This was helped by two factors. The first was the current movement towards demands for women's rights, and the development of the notion of the intellectual woman, who often looked to antiquity for role-models. The second – and the two are not unconnected – was the discovery of 'Sappho's portrait'.

In 1758 a bust of 'Sappho' was recovered from the great peristyle of the Villa dei Papiri. In April 1756 a statue – sometimes called 'Sappho', sometimes called 'Berenice' – had been found, again in the Villa dei Papiri. There was also a mosaic of a woman, dark-haired and serious, called 'Sappho'; and, most evocative of all, a painted portrait tondo of a bust of 'Sappho' discovered in 1759 (along with a companion tondo of a man) in a room in the Cuomo property on the Royal Road in Pompeii (all are now in the Museo Nazionale in Naples).

None of these can be real portraits. Nor can we even be sure that they were ever meant to represent Sappho, but it is telling that this was the attribution given to them at this time. The fresco, in particular, keeps Sappho's name, and the identification seems as inevitable and natural today to the curators of exhibitions at the Museo Nazionale and to the postcard-sellers in the Louvre as it did then to the excavators of Pompeii. It shows a young woman, curly-haired and wearing a distinctive netted headdress, holding a writing tablet in one hand and a stylus in the other, which she places thoughtfully to her lips, as if in search of inspiration.

The finds at Pompeii, along with the current fashion for all things Hellenic, gave impetus to several new Sappho fictions and influenced two in particular. Étienne Lantier's *Voyages d'Antenor en Grèce et en Asie* (1797) was translated into English two years later with the full title of *The Travels of Antenor in Greece and Asia: from a Greek Manuscript found at Herculaneum: including Some Account of Egypt.* The story begins with an unnamed narrator travelling to Naples, attempting to visit the smoky tunnels of the excavations (as many Grand Tourists actually did), then witnessing the work in progress on the papyri finds:

> They consisted of cylindric rolls, nearly in the form of rolled tobacco. The first folds were so difficult to open, that it was necessary to make use of a machine to draw out, by means of screws, this black and shattered parchment upon linen or unctuous paper. As soon as the decypherer had discovered a word, he wrote it down; guessing at those which were illegible by the sense and connection of the sentence: and though these writings

had no points or commas, the learning and intelligence of the persons employed supplied all these defects.

The chief of the scholars at work here hopes to discover the lost glories of ancient literature, and is not interested in a 'very voluminous roll in Greek' noticed by the narrator. The narrator persuades the scholar to allow him to take it away to Paris for translation, and so discovers that this is the autobiography of one Antenor, who was supposed to have been born, in ancient times, to a virgin priestess at Ephesus, and to have lived to the age of 108, when he composed his memoirs. In the course of Antenor's travels he happens to arrive at Leucadia on the very day when Sappho is due to take the leap (which is where the extract in this section begins). But before Sappho attempts it, she confides another manuscript to Antenor, and it is this that he is supposed to be reading from when he tells the story of her life.

The romance of found-manuscripts also influenced Vincenzo Imperiale's *La Faoniade: Inni et Odi di Saffo* (1784). This was supposed to be a translation from the Greek of a hitherto unknown work by Sappho, recently discovered on papyri found in a stone box by the 'famous Russian scholar Ossur' while he was visiting the Cape of Leucadia. It purports to be 'the only complete work we have of Saffo' and consists of an epic love poem about Sappho's love for Phaon. The work was translated – and the hoax continued – by J. B. Grainville in his *Hymnes de Sapho, nouvellement découvertes et traduite pour la première fois en français* (1796).

Lantier, Imperiale and Grainville were all capitalising on an antiquarian fad that affected every fashionable household in Europe. It was responsible for 'Pompeii'-style decoration in many drawing rooms, for cameo and print collections in many libraries, for lyre-guitars and tripod lamps; and even for the hair bound up in scarves and shawls, for the muslin shifts and bare feet, displayed in many famous pictures of celebrated beauties, like Emma Hamilton in her picture '*en Sibylle*' by Élisabeth Vigée Lebrun (c. 1790–1), or Madame Récamier in her portrait by David (1800), or even the Empress Joséphine in the park at Malmaison in her portrait by Prud'hon (c. 1806). And there were books to go along with the décor and the furniture, the clothes and the hairstyle.

One of the earliest of these was Alessandro Verri's novel *Le Avventure di Saffo*, published in Italy in 1780, reprinted many times and translated into English by John Nott (without acknowledgement of Verri) in 1803. In this typically eighteenth-century tale of reason overthrown by sensibility, Saffo is an impressionable teenager, overly influenced by a diet of too many novels. After Phaon's miraculous transformation, he competes in the games at Mytilene, and the moment Saffo spies his oiled and well-muscled body she is inspired to compose her first poem. After many trials, she attempts to follow Phaon to Sicily. But he is delayed by a shipwreck, and she is taken in by Eutychius, a wise and enlightened scholar who tries – vainly in the end – to encourage the cultivation of Saffo's intellect, as opposed to her passions, and to promote her talent for composition. The novel seems to have become a souvenir for the Grand Tourist, for a copy in the Bodleian library, Oxford, printed at Rome in 1803, bears the signature 'Georgiana Craven. 1803'. The Irish artist Henry Tresham, part of the circle gathered around the Swiss artist Henry Fuseli in Rome, and also a friend of the Italian sculptor Antonio Canova, was inspired by Verri's novel to produce a set of eighteen aquatints illustrating scenes from *Le Avventure di Saffo* (1784). These beautiful prints, too, were among the trinkets collected by northern visitors to Rome.

The most important and influential of all the antiquarian novels of the eighteenth century, however, was the Abbé Barthélemy's *Voyage du jeune Anacharsis en Grèce*. First published in 1788, it was reprinted regularly well into the nineteenth century. It was translated into English in 1794 and many times thereafter, and into Italian in 1801. This strange book retained its immense popularity throughout the long period of revolution, in spite of the fact that Jean-Jacques Barthélemy (1716–95) was an ardent royalist and that his book was originally published 'Avec approbation, et Privilège du Roi'. Its full title in English is *Travels of Anacharsis the Younger in Greece during the Middle of the Fourth Century before the Christian Era*, and each of its many volumes (four in the first edition, but expanded to nine by 1791) is copiously annotated with references to classical literary sources. In Volume II, Chapter 3 (in the 1817 English translation) Anacharsis visits Lesbos and hears the story of Sappho – the extract included in this section.

Anacharsis the Younger eventually spawned a whole industry, for it was followed up by abridged versions, as well as scholarly *Maps, Plans, Views and engravings of the relevant antique Coins*. As late as 1846 C. P. Landon published a *Numismatique du Voyage du Jeune Anacharsis*. Lantier's *Voyages d'Antenor* (1797) was both an attempt to capitalise on Barthélemy's success and a sly take-off of the

Abbé's weighty erudition. In the end, the antiquarian fashion gained a less elevated reputation, and in 1801 a highly popular volume by J.-B. Chaussard appeared in Paris, entitled *Fêtes et Courtisanes de la Grèce: Supplément aux Voyages d'Anacharsis et d'Antenor*, in which a long section appears under 'S' for Sappho.

The erotically stressed poetess portrayed in *Fêtes et Courtisanes* would eventually take over in the nineteenth century, but in the 1790s Sappho, or Saffo, or Sapho was still an inspiration. Mary Robinson's sonnet sequence *Sappho and Phaon* (1796, see 'The Sapphic Sublime') was largely informed by her reading of Barthélemy, and in all three of these antiquarian fictions (Verri, Barthélemy and Lantier) Sappho figures as an intellectual. In Verri she can argue aesthetics and politics with Eutychius; in Barthélemy she is praised for her 'force of genius', though the rumours of her 'infamous manners' are deplored; in Lantier she is a leading light in cultured Athens and undertakes to teach Phaon astronomy and geography, as well as tutoring him so efficiently in music and poetry that, after he has left her, he gains a great reputation as a scholar and artist-performer.

This is where a new strand starts to take over. For gradually over the last years of the eighteenth century it became no longer Sappho's story, but Phaon's, or at least some other man's, whether lover, sophist or scholar.

In Verri's novel the sight of Phaon's naked body shakes Sappho into poetry; a scene brilliantly realised in Plate 1 of Henry Tresham's series of aquatints, '*Saffo si accende per Faone*' ('Sappho is enflamed by Phaon'). In Lantier, too, she first falls when she sees him working out at the gymnasium in Athens. Then, in both Verri and Lantier, there is an older, wiser man who tries to put Sappho on the right path of reason. Even the fact that Sappho only comes to the reader through the agency of a man – whether the voyagers Anacharsis or Antenor, or Lantier's unnamed papyrus-rescuing narrator – suggests how far these Sappho-stories had started to give a precedence to masculine investment and supremacy. In this period of revolution masculine values ruled, except when they were espoused by women. Thus power was transferred from Sappho to Phaon, or some other man.

Vincenzo Imperiale's *Inni et Odi di Saffo* (1784) was part of this trend, pretending, as it did, that these newly discovered verses were a hymn of praise to Phaon's many virtues. Philip Freneau's poem 'The Monument of Phaon' (1770) is in the same vein, as he becomes the sole subject of her verses, and even the discovery of Phaon's tomb is relayed to her by another, male, traveller Ismenius. Freneau (1752–1832) was an American poet – indeed, he was called by some the 'father of American poets' – whose works were popular during the years of the American War of Independence: '. . . the productions of his pen animated his countrymen in the darkest days of '76 and the effusions of his muse cheered the desponding soldier as he fought the battles of freedom'.

The hero-worship that began to characterise the 'Napoleonic' fictions of Sappho is even more explicit in the pictures that multiply at this time. For instance, in a comparatively little-known painting by Jacques-Louis David of 1809 (now in the Hermitage Museum, St Petersburg), Sappho is seated and has been playing her lyre up until the moment when Phaon arrives – upright and centred in the frame – so that Cupid takes the instrument from her hand: the bed in the background clearly beckons. And in a suite of sixteen engravings by Anne-Louis Girodet Trioson, designed to illustrate his own translation of the Fragments of Sappho (1827), the heroic naked male body is frequently displayed centre-page. Sometimes it is that of Phaon, sometimes Sappho's husband, and even, in one plate, '*un poète*' – possibly Alcaeus, but more likely Anacreon, who, although exceedingly well endowed, lies unheroically abed while he is harangued by Sappho on the glories of art and the duties owed to one's native land.

Girodet and David, with many other painters who took up the Sappho theme (such as Antoine-Jean Gros, Louis Ducis and François Gérard), were very much part of the Napoleonic camp, as his court painters and his (official and unofficial) propagandists. And there was one particular woman whom Napoleon and his crew especially wanted to degrade: the woman who, most of all, deliberately made herself into the new image of Sappho.

Germaine Necker, Baronne de Staël (1766–1817), published her famous novel *Corinne, or Italy* in 1807. It was not the first, nor would it be the last, time that she invoked the memory of Sappho, for she had written verses on the classical poet in her youth, and she went on to write a play *Sapho, drame en cinq actes*, which was published posthumously in 1821. But it was *Corinne* that made a new story for a modern Sappho. The novel was enormously popular and went through many reprintings. When it was translated into English by Isabel Hill in 1833, the English *improvisatrice* L.E.L. (Letitia Elizabeth Landon) provided metrical versions for Corinne's verses.

That 1833 translation was illustrated with an engraving of a painting by François Gérard. It showed Madame de Staël herself as Corinne, experiencing her last scene of triumph, just as her talents are about to fail. Corinne is seated at Cape Miseno on the Gulf of Naples, with Vesuvius rising in the background. She looks up to the skies as she finishes a recitation, and the native populace and foreign tourists crowd round in admiration. But the lyre has fallen from her hand and, centre-stage, is a man (her lover Lord Nelvil), who will soon desert her and bring about her demise.

In the end, Corinne does die. But not before she has tutored Lord Nelvil's little daughter, and passed on her own skills and ambition. And not before the most glorious moment in her history: when she is crowned at the Capitol in Rome in recognition of her achievements as a poet and *improvisatrice*. This scene would inspire countless women in the nineteenth century – many forgotten, others well known – including the poet Elizabeth Barrett Browning and novelist George Eliot.

A portrait tondo of a young woman dating from about the 1st century A.D., and found at Pompeii in the 1760's. It was called – then and now – *Portrait of Sappho*, though it was discovered with a companion tondo of a man. This was one of at least three images unearthed in the excavations and assigned the name of Sappho; there is no reason to assume that the attribution is correct, but this picture evokes such a convincing image of the contemplative writing woman that it makes the connection to the ancient poet seem natural and inevitable. Museo Nazionale 9084, Naples.

Eutychius remained some little time with her; and it seemed as if the silence of night, and the calm of solitude, invited their souls to disclose themselves with greater confidence than in the busy day. After a short pause, then, the girl, turning to him, said: 'I have often been considering within myself during the last hours, which you seem to have passed with your usual cheerfulness, whence it could happen that you live in this retirement; it must be from some cause which I cannot divine, that you prefer it to the city, where you might live in greater splendour. Nor have I yet dared to ask you what country you are of; so that I may say I know much, and yet little, of you; for I greatly admire your humanity and your virtue: I also prize your understanding: at the same time I am ignorant of your history, and of your birth-place, which, producing such natives, must assuredly be the happiest of climes.' 'You perceive, however,' replied Eutychius, 'that it is not so to me, since I do not dwell in it.' 'Certainly,' answered Sappho, 'the country of men such as yourself can only be the universe.' 'Think not,' added Eutychius, 'that being disgusted with Syracuse, which, since you wish to know it, is my country, has determined me to live in this solitude, unless it were for a concurrence of unpleasing events: two enemies, most cruel to a feeling and liberal mind, in my youthful days waged unkind war against me; so that, overcome with worldly cares which I for a long time foolishly bore, alleviating also my mind by time and change of place, I have resolved to finish the short career of human life, now approaching towards its goal, in this spot; forgetting the past, and trusting to heaven for the present as well as the future.' 'O, you are indeed happy!' exclaimed Sappho: 'why cannot I partake of your tranquillity? But who were these enemies you spoke of?' Eutychius answered, 'Love and tyranny; for you must know,' and as he spoke he seated himself facing to her, who listened with extreme attention, 'that I have seen in my time my country free, and then subject to the sway of a tyrant, whose race at present holds it in slavery. I, with the better part of my fellow-citizens, endeavoured, during these revolutions, to transmit to our posterity that same form of republic which our ancestors established with their blood. But, as will be the case when antient virtue decays, and all discipline grows corrupt, it became by degrees more pleasing to be a slave in the midst of vice, than to be free with prudence. The bravery of a few was therefore ineffectual to counteract the supineness of the many. In history we often find that the best of citizens have attempted to cure the ills of their diseased country, in the same way as surgeons cure some injuries, by amputation. I then, with all due reverence for the fame of those who undertook so glorious a task, withdrew myself from the unwelcome fight of such disgraceful struggles, not through a low love of life, but from the moderate principles of wise, and, as I think, of true philosophy. For, when liberty is oppressed in such a manner that there are no means of making it revive but by a conspiracy, it is manifest from experience that scarce any other effects are produced, than the sacrifice of every remnant of good, the triumph of wickedness, and the establishment of tyranny. The multitude will not second any daring project, and renounces that gift which becomes valueless, namely liberty: the rich prize their own wealth beyond their country, nor will they endanger it by a hazardous revolution: the great become the necessary instruments of despotic government, and monarchical splendour delights them more than republican equality; so that all parties would concur in rendering remedies slow to operate on the mortal evil; and he who thinks otherwise will find, from consequences, that these lofty ideas produce only an ostentatious disturbance. But we should not withhold this consideration, that the good are every where few in number; and that, even among the partisans of liberty, there are those who have no other wish than to tempt a better fortune amid the violence of a revolution: therefore, weighing my debt to my country, and my country's debt to me as being her son, I saw that this mother, aged, infirm, and reduced to vile servitude, understood not kindness, and could not be grateful. I therefore left her, but with agonizing reluctance; and I chose, instead of my own country, this starry sky, this sea, this air, which are common to all, under the just and unvaried rule of the deity, who inhabits a temple so worthy of himself.' Whilst he uttered these words, he drew near the door, pointing to the heavens, and added: 'Look, my girl, if any one, who contemplates that boundless space, spangled over with unnumbered fires, in the midst of which not only Syracuse but our whole earth is only as an atom of dirt, can complain that he wants either an altar for his country's sacrifices, or a fane wherein to worship the gods, or an opportunity for the exercise of virtue. If fortune than gave to me a confined country, I chose myself this, which is, as you see, a most spacious dwelling.' 'Truly so!' replied Sappho: 'it corresponds with your ideas.' 'O my charming guest!' interrupted Eutychius, 'my ideas were perhaps greater than Syracuse; but they become humble and subdued in the presence of the universe, for the understanding has not capacity to comprehend so vast a scope; and after we have strained it to extend over such an expanse, we find that fatigue and wonder is all the result.

Alessandro Verri, *The Adventures of Saffo*, 1780, trans. John Nott, 1803

TRAVELS OF ANACHARSIS THE YOUNGER IN GREECE

Alcæus and Sappho, who are both entitled to a place in the first class of lyric poets, flourished at Mytilene. Alcæus was born with a restless and turbulent disposition, and seemed at first inclined to adopt the profession of arms, which he preferred to every other pursuit. His house was filled with swords, helmets, shields, and cuirasses; but on his first essay in the field he shamefully fled, and the Athenians, after their victory, branded him with disgrace, by suspending his arms in the temple of Minerva at Sigæum. He made great pretensions to the love of liberty, but was suspected of harbouring a secret wish for its destruction. With his brothers, he first joined Pittacus, to expel Melanchrus, tyrant of Mytilene, and then took part with the malecontents to subvert the government of Pittacus. The violence and indecency of the abuse which he lavished on that prince evinced nothing but his jealousy. Banished from Mytilene, he some time after returned at the head of the exiles, and fell into the hands of his rival, who took the noblest revenge by pardoning him.

Poetry, love, and wine, consoled him for his disgrace. His early writings were filled with invectives against tyranny; he now sang the gods, and above all the deities who preside over pleasures; he sang his loves, his warlike labours, his travels, and the miseries of banishment. His genius required to be stimulated by intemperance; and it was in a kind of intoxication that he composed those works that have acquired him the admiration of posterity. His style, uniformly adapted to his subject, has no other defects but what arise from the language spoken at Lesbos. He unites harmony with vigour, and richness with precision and perspicuity. He soars almost to the height of Homer, when he describes battles, or would make a tyrant tremble.

Alcæus had conceived a passion for Sappho, and he one day wrote to her: 'I wish to explain myself, but shame restrains me.' – 'Your countenance would not blush,' answered she, 'were not your heart culpable.'

Sappho was accustomed to say, 'I am actuated by the love of pleasures and of virtue. Without virtue nothing is so dangerous as riches, and happiness consists in the union of both.' She used likewise to say: 'This person is distinguished by his figure, that by his virtues; the one appears beautiful at a first view, the other not less so at a second.'

I was one day repeating these and many similar expressions to a citizen of Mytilene, and added: 'The figure of Sappho is seen upon your coins, and you profess the highest veneration for her memory. How is it possible to reconcile the sentiments she has left us in her writings and the honours you publicly decree her with the infamous manners with which she is privately reproached.' He answered me, 'We are not sufficiently acquainted with particulars to form a competent judgment of her life.' Strictly speaking, no conclusion can be drawn in her favour from the love she professes for virtue, nor from the honours we pay to her talents. When I read some of her works, I dare not acquit her; but she had merit and enemies, and I dare not condemn her.

After the death of her husband, she devoted her leisure hours to letters, and undertook to inspire the Lesbian women with a taste for

Emma, Lady Hamilton as Terpsichore, Polyhymnia and Calliope, the three Muses of choral dance and song, of sublime hymn, and epic poetry, by Hugh Douglas Hamilton (c.1789–1790). The multiplying of Emma's image refers to the famous 'Attitudes', her speciality from 1786 as Sir William Hamilton's mistress in Naples. The Hamilton Collection, Lennoxlove, East Lothian, Scotland.

literature. Many of them received instructions from her, and foreign women increased the number of her disciples. She loved them to excess, because it was impossible for her to love otherwise, and she expressed her tenderness with all the violence of passion. Your surprise at this will cease, when you become better acquainted with the extreme sensibility of the Greeks and discover that amongst them the most innocent connections often borrow the impassioned language of love. Read the dialogues of Plato, you will there see in what terms Socrates speaks of the beauty of his pupils. Yet no person knew better than Plato how pure the intentions of his master were. Nor was there less purity perhaps in those of Sappho. But a certain facility in her manners, and warmth in her expressions, were but too well calculated to expose her to the hatred of some women of distinction, humbled by her superiority, and of some of her disciples who happened not to be the objects of her preference. To this hatred, which broke forth into violence, she replied by truths and irony, which completely exasperated her enemies. She then complained of their persecutions, and this was a new crime. Compelled at length to fly, she repaired to Sicily in search of an asylum, where, I am told, it is intended to erect a statue to her. If the rumours you speak of are, as I believe them to be, without foundation, we may learn from her example, that great indiscretions are sufficient to tarnish the reputation of every person exposed to the eye of the public and posterity.

'The sensibility of Sappho was extreme.' – 'She was then exceedingly unhappy,' said I. 'Undoubtedly she was,' replied he. 'She loved Phaon, who forsook her. After various attempts to bring him back, despairing of happiness either with him or without him, she took the leap of Leucata, and perished in the waves. 'Death has not effaced the stain imprinted on her character; and perhaps,' added he, concluding his discourse, 'it will never be obliterated; for envy, which fastens on illustrious names, does indeed expire, but bequeaths her aspersions to that calumny, which never dies.'

Sappho has composed hymns, odes, elegies, and a number of other pieces, principally in a kind of metre of which she was herself the inventress. All of these abound in happy and brilliant expressions with which she has enriched the language.

Several of the Grecian women have cultivated poetry with success, but none have hitherto attained to the excellence of Sappho, and among the other poets there are few indeed who have surpassed her. What an attention does she display in the selection of her words and subjects! She has painted all the most pleasing objects in nature. She has painted them in the most harmonising colours; and so skilful is she in their distribution, as always to produce the happiest combination of light and shade. Her taste is transcendent even in the mechanism of her style, in which, by an address which gives not the least idea of labour, we meet with no dissonant clashings, no violent shocks between the elements of language; and the most delicate ear would scarcely discover in a whole poem a few sounds which it had been better to suppress. So perfect is the ravishing harmony of her style, that, in the greatest part of her productions, her verses flow with more grace and softness than those of Anacreon and Simonides.

But with what force of genius does she hurry us along when she describes the charms, the transports and intoxication of love! What scenery! what warmth of colouring! Agitated like the Pythia by the inspiring god, she throws on the paper her words that burn. Her sentiments fall like a cloud of arrows, or a fiery shower about to consume every thing. She animates and personifies all the symptoms of this passion, to excite the most powerful emotions in our souls.

At Mytilene was it that I traced this feeble sketch of the talents of Sappho, guided by the judgment of several persons of information and abilities; it was in the silence of meditation, in one of those beautiful nights so common in Greece, on hearing, under my windows, a melting voice, accompanied by the lyre, sing an ode, in which that illustrious Lesbian abandons herself, without reserve, to the impression made by beauty on her too susceptible heart. Methought I saw her languid, trembling, and as if thunderstruck; deprived of her understanding and her senses; alternately blushing and turning pale; yielding to the diversified and tumultuous emotions of her passion, or rather of all the jarring passions of her soul.

Abbé Barthélemy, *Travels of Anacharsis the Younger in Greece during the Middle of the Fourth Century before the Christian Era*, 1788, English translation 1817

THE MONUMENT OF PHAON

Phaon, the admirer of Sappho, both of the isle of Lesbos, privately forsook this first object of his affections, and set out to visit foreign countries. Sappho, after having long mourned his absence (which is the subject of one of Ovid's finest epistles), is here supposed to fall into the company of Ismenius a traveller, who informs her that he saw the tomb of a certain Phaon in Sicily, erected to his memory by a lady of the island, and gives her the inscriptions, hinting to her that, in all probability, it belonged to the same person she bemoans. She thereupon, in a fit of rage and despair, throws herself from the famous Leucadian rock, and perishes in the gulph below.

Sappho

No more I sing by yonder shaded stream,
  Where once intranc'd I fondly pass'd the day,
Supremely blest, when Phaon was my theme,
  But wretched now, when Phaon is away!

Of all the youths that grac'd our Lesbian isle
  He, only he, my heart propitious found,
So soft his language, and so sweet his smile,
  Heaven was my own when Phaon clasp'd me round!

But soon, too soon, the faithless lover fled
  To wander on some distant barbarous shore –
Who knows if Phaon is alive or dead,
  Or wretched Sappho shall behold him more.

Anne-Louis Girodet Trioson translated the fragments of Sappho and Anacreon, with black and white engravings in the flat 'antique vase' style made popular in England by John Flaxman. Girodet's illustrations include authentic ancient detail of household goods copied from items recently excavated. Anne-Louis Girodet Trioson et M. Coupin, *Recueil de Compositions dessinées par Girodet* (Paris, 1827), Department of Prints and Drawings, British Museum.

Ismenius

As late in fair Sicilia's groves I stray'd,
  Charm'd with the beauties of the vernal scene
I sate me down amid the yew tree's shade,
  Flowers blooming round, with herbage fresh and green.

Not distant far a monument arose
  Among the trees and form'd of Parian stone,
And, as if there some stranger did repose,
  It stood neglected, and it stood alone.

Along its sides dependent ivy crept,
  The cypress bough, Plutonian green, was near,
A sculptur'd Venus on the summit wept,
  A pensive Cupid dropt the parting tear.

Strains deep engrav'd on every side I read,
  How Phaon died upon that foreign shore –
Sappho, I think your Phaon must be dead,
  Then hear the strains that do his fate deplore: . . .

Sappho

. . .
Ah, faithless Phaon, thus from me to rove,
And bless my rival in a foreign grove!
Could Sicily more charming forests show
Than those that in thy native Lesbos grow –
Did fairer fruits adorn the bending tree
Than those that Lesbos did present to thee!
Or didst thou find through all the changing fair
One beauty that with Sappho could compare!
So soft, so sweet, so charming and so kind,
A face so fair, such beauties of the mind –
Not Musidora can be rank'd with me
Who sings so well thy funeral song for thee! –
I'll go! – and from the high Leucadian steep
Take my last farewell in the lover's leap,
I charge thee, Phaon, by this deed of woe
To meet me in the Elysian shades below,
No rival beauty shall pretend a share,
Sappho alone shall walk with Phaon there.

She spoke, and downward from the mountain's height
Plung'd in the plashy wave to everlasting night.

Philip Freneau, 1770

SAPPHO TAKES THE LEUCADIAN LEAP

On the fatal day when Sappho was to take the leap, we hired a boat, and kept paddling about the base of the promontory. The sea was covered with small vessels ranged in a semicircle, and leaving a space in the middle to receive the self-devoted victim, while eight excellent swimmers were ready to rescue her from the inexorable waves. The summit of the rock was also crowded with spectators, whom the great celebrity of the heroine of the day had drawn from all parts to witness this horrid scene. She went to the temple of Apollo, to render the god propitious to her; and the priests having immolated a heifer, declared the auspices in her favour.

Sappho came forth from the temple without her veil or her accustomed ornaments of flowers, and with dishevelled hair advanced between two priests to the edge of the rock. She cast her eyes around on the spectators, and surveyed the height of the leap with a firm and tranquil countenance, while every one was intent upon all her motions, waiting, in mournful silence, the event of this dreadful experiment. Thrice did she advance to the edge of the promontory, and thrice, with involuntary terror, drew back from the fatal abyss. At length the priests having exhorted and encouraged her, she returned again to the edge of the precipice. With sympathetic horror we beheld her raising her hands and eyes to heaven, and advancing with rapid step to the edge of the rock, whence she threw herself into the dreadful abyss. In mid air she rolled over, and falling into the gulf below, instantly disappeared. The clamours and terrors of the spectators now found vent, and the swimmers plunged into the sea in search of her. They soon found her, and brought her to the shore, where they extended her on the beach, cold and inanimate as marble. An immense crowd presently collected around her, crying out, 'She is dead! she is dead!' but I laid my hand upon her heart, and felt that some warmth still remained, nor had it entirely ceased to move. 'No, no,' cried I; 'she lives! Help, help, and we shall save her!' The attendants now chafed her, and gave her cordials, till at length she began to breathe and opened her eyes, which she fixed upon me,

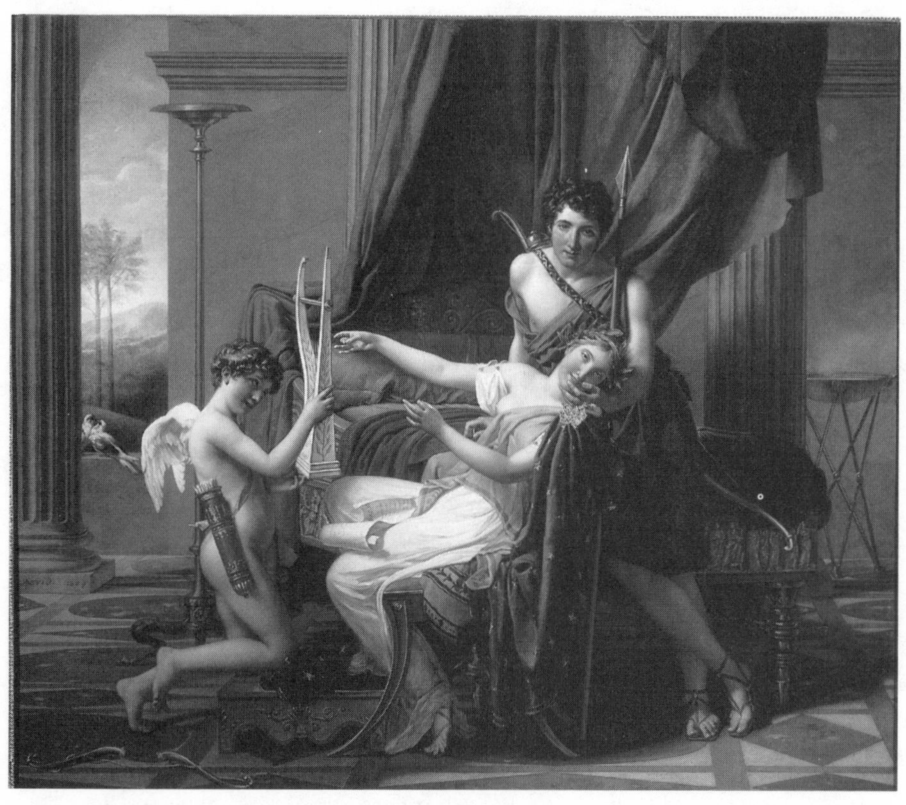

Sappho and Phaon by Jacques-Louis David (1809). David was only one of many eminent French painters who acted as (official and unofficial) propagandists for Napoleon and who also happened to paint pictures of Sappho. This was not entirely coincidental, for David's picture, like those by painters such as Gros, Gerard, Ducis, and Vafflard show Sappho – representative type of the intellectual woman loathed by Bonaparte – in various debilitated positions. Here she is displaced from centre stage by the manly Phaon, and disabled by his erotic attentions. Hermitage Museum, St Petersburg, Russia/Bridgeman Art Library.

and strove to raise herself to speak to me. 'To thee, whosoe'er thou art,' said she, 'I entrust the care of my funereal rites! I die a victim to love and ingratitude! Should you ever see the perfidious Phaon, tell him the fate of a wretch whose love he has repaid with death.' – 'No, no,' said I; 'live, and again become the ornament and the glory of the world!' – 'Glory!' exclaimed she: ''tis but a splendid chimera! for, alas! I only leave mortals upon the earth.' With these words she expired. – We all burst into tears, and Phanor and myself having given instructions to the priests to perform the obsequies of the unfortunate Sappho, and promised to attend the ceremony ourselves, hastened from a scene of woe too afflicting for us to contemplate.

We now walked for some time along the beach, lost in thoughtful and melancholy silence; for I wished to give Phanor time to reflect on this lamentable catastrophe. At length, after a considerable interval, I exclaimed, 'What a wretched fate, for one who possessed such brilliant talents, so cultivated a mind, and so tender a heart!' – 'Yes,' replied he, 'it is a wretched fate indeed!' – 'What do you think,' said I, 'of this Leucadian leap, and its method of curing hopeless love?' – 'I think it an infallible remedy,' answered Phanor. – 'And have you still,' rejoined I, 'any inclination to try the experiment?' – 'It is on that,' said he, 'I was reflecting. I confess my desire is somewhat cooled.' – 'It is sufficient,' said I, 'to cool any one's enthusiasm. You must surely agree that it is an act of folly?' – 'Indeed,' replied he, 'it has some appearance of it.' – 'Suppose, then,' said I, 'we set off to-morrow?' – 'I have no objection,' he replied; 'for I begin to be somewhat reconciled to life.' Soon after we met the two unfortunate lovers of Sicyon, who were to leap next after Phanor, when my friend told them he would give up his turn to whichever of them was the most anxious to try the experiment. Philoxenes immediately thanked him, but confessed he thought the remedy rather too desperate; that he had rather live an injured husband than be a lifeless corpse; and therefore left to his companion, who was much younger than himself, the glory of the exploit. But the latter immediately replied that he would not avail himself of his kindness, and that the beautiful Agarista might consecrate her virginity to the infernal Hecate, or Prosperine, or whomsoever she pleased; but that he would not take the leap even for the sake of Helen herself. Thus did the fatal end of Sappho save three insensate lovers from almost certain perdition, while the priests of the temple on the rock no doubt attributed their cure to the miraculous influence of the holy island.

I told the two travellers, that Sappho had entrusted me with the history of her loves, and that if they pleased I would read it to them. We therefore took a seat on the sea shore, reclining on a heap of moss and sea-weed, when I opened the manuscript and read as follows.

THE OBSEQUIES OF SAPPHO

We were now interrupted by a message that the funereal procession of Sappho was about to commence; upon which we immediately set off to join it, and Phanor went to apprise the priests of Apollo that he had abandoned his intention of taking the Leucadian leap. To this they replied by urging the obligation of his oath: but he answered, that although it was true he had taken the oath, he had since sworn by the manes of Sappho not to fulfil it.

The corpse had already been washed and anointed with perfumed essences, and clothed in a rich and splendid garment. It lay at the door of the temple, near a vessel of lustral water, with which all those who had touched the body purified themselves. Her head was covered with a veil, and we adorned it with a chaplet of laurel interwoven with flowers. A priest then placed a cake of flour and honey in her hand, to appease the dog Cerberus, and under her tongue a piece of money, to give Charon for her passage over the Styx.

Thus exposed, the body lay there the remainder of the day and the whole of the night, attended by several women, who sent forth the most vehement groans and lamentations, while some of them cut off locks of their hair, and threw it on the coffin, which was of cypress.

The procession took place, according to the laws of Athens, before sun-rise. It was led by men playing on the flute, who were followed by others clothed in black, and casting their eyes upon the earth. Next to these came the funereal car, and the whole was closed by a number of women. In this order we ascended a little hill destined for the tomb, where the funeral pile was raised. Upon this was placed the body, turned towards the west, and the pile was set fire to with torches. While the flame was rising, we poured libations around it, and threw into the fire flowers, honey, bread, meat, and some of Sappho's clothes, calling thrice upon her name. As soon as the body was consumed, the ashes were gathered in an urn, and buried in the earth. Near it was erected a funereal marble, on which was represented a lyre as a symbol of poetry, and under it the following epitaph:

> Here Sappho lies, from weeping Græcia torn:
> Ye Muses, Graces, Loves, for ever mourn!

We planted some elms round the grave, and again called thrice upon the deceased, accompanying this last adieu with the bitterest tears. Those who had attended the procession were invited to the funeral feast, where we eulogised the genius and talents of Sappho. When we parted, we embraced each other tenderly, and took our last farewell as if we should never meet again.

After thus performing these sad offices to the dead, we resumed the perusal of her manuscript beneath the shade of an impending rock, where we enjoyed the cool of the sea-breeze and the silence of retirement.

Étienne Lantier, *The Travels of Antenor in Greece and Asia: from a Greek manuscript found at Herculaneum*, 1797, English translation 1799

CORINNE AT THE CAPITOL

Oswald awoke in Rome. The dazzling sun of Italy met his first gaze, and his soul was penetrated with sensations of love and gratitude for that heaven, which seemed to smile on him in these glorious beams. He heard the bells of numerous churches ringing, discharges of cannon from various distances, as if announcing some high solemnity. He enquired the cause, and was informed that the most celebrated female in Italy was about that morning to be crowned at the Capitol, – Corinne, the poet and improvisatrice, one of the loveliest women of Rome. He asked some questions respecting this ceremony, hallowed by the names of Petrarch and of Tasso: every reply he received warmly excited his curiosity.

There can be nothing more hostile to the habits and opinions of an Englishman than any great publicity given to the career of a woman. But the enthusiasm with which all imaginative talents inspire the Italians, infects, at least for the time, even strangers, who forget prejudice itself among people so lively in the expression of their sentiments.

The common populace of Rome discuss their statues, pictures, monuments, and antiquities, with much taste; and literary merit, carried to a certain height, becomes with them a national interest.

On going forth into the public resorts, Oswald found that the streets through which Corinne was to pass had been adorned for her reception. The herd, who generally throng but the path of fortune or of power, were almost in a tumult of eagerness to look on one whose soul was her only distinction. In the present state of the Italians, the glory of the fine arts is all their fate allows them; and they appreciate genius of that order with a vivacity which might raise up a host of great men, if applause could suffice to produce them – if a hardy life, strong interest, and an independent station were not the food required to nourish thought.

Oswald walked the streets of Rome, awaiting the arrival of Corinne: he heard her named every instant; every one related some new trait, proving that she united all the talents most captivating to the fancy. One asserted that her voice was the most touching in Italy; another, that, in tragic acting, she had no peer; a third, that she danced like a nymph, and drew with equal grace and invention: all said that no one had ever written or extemporised verses so sweet; and that, in daily conversation, she displayed alternately an ease and an eloquence which fascinated all who heard her. They disputed as to which part of Italy had given her birth; some earnestly contending that she must be a Roman, or she could not speak the language with such purity. Her family name was unknown. Her first work, which had appeared five years since, bore but that of Corinne. No one could tell where she had lived, nor what she had been, before that period; and she was now nearly six and twenty. Such mystery and publicity, united in the fate of a female of whom every one spoke, yet whose real name no one knew, appeared to Nevil as among the wonders of the land he came to see. He would have judged such a woman very severely in England; but he applied not *her* social etiquettes to Italy; and the crowning of Corinne awoke in his breast the same sensation which he would have felt on reading an adventure of Ariosto's.

A burst of exquisite melody preceded the approach of the triumphal procession. How thrilling is each event that is heralded by music! A great number of Roman nobles, and not a few foreigners, came first. 'Behold her retinue of admirers!' said one. 'Yes,' replied another; 'she receives a whole world's homage, but accords her preference to none. She is rich, independent; it is even believed, from her noble air, that she is a lady of high birth, who wishes to remain unknown.' – 'A divinity veiled in clouds,' concluded a third. Oswald looked on the man who spoke thus: every thing betokened him a person of the humblest class; but the natives of the South converse as naturally in poetic phrases as if they imbibed them with the air, or were inspired by the sun.

At last four spotless steeds appeared in the midst of the crowd, drawing an antiquely shaped car, beside which walked a maiden band in snowy vestments. Wherever Corinne passed, perfumes were thrown upon the air; the windows, decked with flowers and scarlet hangings, were peopled by gazers, who shouted, 'Long live Corinne! Glory to beauty and to genius!'

This emotion was general; but, to partake it, one must lay aside English reserve and French raillery; Nelvil could not yield to the spirit of the scene, till he beheld Corinne.

Attired like Domenichino's Sibyl, an Indian shawl was twined among her lustrous black curls, a blue drapery fell over her robe of virgin white, and her whole costume was picturesque, without sufficiently varying from modern usage to appear tainted by affectation. Her attitude was noble and modest: it might, indeed, be perceived that she was content to be admired; yet a timid air blended with her joy, and seemed to ask pardon for her triumph. The expression of her features, her eyes, her smile, created a solicitude in her favour, and made Lord Nelvil her friend even before any more ardent sentiment subdued him. Her arms were transcendently beautiful; her figure tall, and, as we frequently see among the Grecian statues, rather robust – energetically characteristic of youth and happiness. There was something inspired in her air; yet the very manner in which she bowed her thanks for the applause she received, betrayed a natural disposition sweetly contrasting the pomp of her extraordinary situation. She gave you at the same instant the idea of a priestess of Apollo advancing towards his temple, and of a woman born to fulfil the usual duties of life with perfect simplicity; in truth, her every gesture elicited not more wondering conjecture, than it conciliated sympathy and affection. The nearer she approached the Capitol, so fruitful in classic associations, the more these admiring tributes increased: the raptures of the Romans, the clearness of their sky, and, above all, Corinne herself, took electric effect on Oswald. He had often, in his own land, seen statesmen drawn in triumph by the people; but this was the first time that he had ever witnessed the tender of such honours to a woman, illustrious only in mind. Her car of victory cost no fellow mortal's tear; nor terror nor regret could check his admiration for those fairest gifts of nature – creative fancy, sensibility, and reason. These new ideas so intensely occupied him, that he noticed none of the long-famed spots over which Corinne proceeded. At the foot of the steps leading to the Capitol the car stopped, and all her friends rushed to offer their hands: she took that of Prince Castel Forte, the nobleman most esteemed in Rome for his talents and character. Every one approved her choice. She ascended to the Capitol, whose imposing majesty seemed graciously to welcome the light footsteps of woman. The instruments sounded with fresh vigour, the cannon shook the air, and the all-conquering Sibyl entered the palace prepared for her reception.

In the centre of the hall stood the senator who was to crown Corinne, surrounded by his brothers in office; on one side, all the cardinals and most distinguished ladies of Rome; on the other, the members of the Academy; while the opposite extremity was filled by some portion of the multitude who had followed Corinne. The chair destined for her was placed a step lower than that of the senator. Ere seating herself in presence of that august assembly, she complied with the custom of bending one knee to the earth: the gentle dignity of this action filled Oswald's eyes with tears, to his own surprise; but, in the midst of all this success, it seemed as if the looks of Corinne implored the protection of a friend, with which no woman, however superior, can dispense; and he thought how delicious it were to be the stay of her, whose sensitiveness alone could render such a prop necessary. As soon as Corinne was seated, the Roman poets recited the odes and sonnets composed for this occasion: all praised her to the highest; but in styles that described her no more than they would have done any other woman of genius. The same mythological images and allusions must have been addressed to such beings from the days of Sappho to our own. Already Nelvil disliked this kind of incense for her: he fancied that he could that moment have drawn a truer, a more finished portrait; such, indeed, as could have belonged to no one but Corinne.

Germaine de Staël, *Corinne, or Italy*, 1807, trans. Isabel Hill, 1833

EIGHT

The Lady with the Lyre

Germaine de Staël *en Corinne* by Elisabeth Vigée Le Brun (1806–7). It was the artist's idea to portray the novelist as her own fictional character drawn from her famous work of 1807, and she also supplied the mountain setting and the so-called Temple of the Sibyl at Tivoli for the background. De Staël may not have liked the picture much, for she later had it copied in a watered down version in contemporary dress where her arms are covered, her mouth closed, and her face shown in an altogether prettier and softer light. Musée d'Art et d'Histoire, Geneva.

In 1808 Élisabeth Vigée Lebrun painted a portrait of Madame de Staël as Corinne (now in the Musée des Beaux Arts, Geneva). It was not the writer's idea that she should be portrayed in the character of her own fictional heroine, but the artist's. Nearly twenty years earlier Vigée Lebrun had executed what she considered her masterpiece, a famous picture of Emma Hamilton '*en Sibylle*', and for this one of Corinne she mimicked her own conception. Corinne – or Madame de Staël – is captured in a moment of poetic rapture. Her lips are slightly parted, her eyes are raised upward, she strikes the lyre in her hand. Behind her rises a steep slope, crowned with the small round temple known as the Temple of the Sibyl at Tivoli. She wears a simple tunic and a peplum bordered with a Greek motif. But if you had not read *Corinne*, if you did not recognise Madame de Staël, it would be hard to know that this was what the picture represented. Given all the attributes, it would look like an imaginary picture of Sappho.

In tracing the ebb and flow of classical fashions, the shifting currents of alternate praise and blame in the fictions of Sappho, it is clear that specific tensions at particular times gave rise to contradictory, but often related, cultural trends. Different interested parties jostle one another, competing for possession of Sappho's image. At the same time as Sappho was condemned in pornographic literature, and belittled in heroic and Napoleonic fictions, she was being applauded and admired in women's circles. It is very striking, for instance, to note how many women artists at this period produced pictures of Sappho, and it became a fashion for society ladies to have themselves portrayed holding a lyre or other musical instrument, or to be shown singing or performing poetry.

There was more to this than the pleasure of a pretty pose. Angelika Kauffman, for instance, painted at least two pictures of Sappho, and engraved at least two others. She also painted a chimneypiece for a London drawing room with a picture of Sappho that was said to be a self-portrait. In around 1781 her painter husband Antonio Zucchi produced a work sometimes entitled *Music and Poetry*, sometimes *Sappho and Homer*, for which again Kauffman was said to be the model. Kauffman's reference to her own aspirations is clear, but sometimes the code is not so easy to read. Around 1802 the English artist Richard Westall painted a *Portrait of the Artist's Wife as Sappho* (now in the Walker Art Gallery, Liverpool). As we know nothing about her, it is hard to say what claims he, or his wife, were pressing.

Over and over again in these pictures a facet of artistic activity is emphasised. Whether actually shown playing a musical instrument (as in Vigée Lebrun's *Madame de Staël en Corinne*), or writing a poem (as in Kauffman's two Sappho engravings), or simply in the moment of intense contemplation that might precede literary composition, these women are always shown *doing* that something. This was an age when women as performers came into their own. On the professional stage there were famous female actors to be seen (Mary Robinson among them); in the opera house the demise of the castrati meant that the diva had arrived; in Italy you could witness the impromptu effusions of an *improvisatrice* like Corilla Olimpica (whose career was partly reflected in that of de Staël's Corinne); in Sir William Hamilton's palace at Naples his wife, Emma, performed her famous 'Attitudes' for his guests; and in countless humbler homes charades, monodramas and amateur theatricals occupied the women as much as – perhaps even more than – the men. As 'the first' woman poet, as the original woman composer and performer of her own work, Sappho was an attractive subject.

Just as many early operas were based on the story of Orpheus, because his role as poet-singer makes it so peculiarly suited to the form, so Sappho too was used, early on, as an operatic subject. Most of these early operas (and ballets and plays) came out of France, and one of the earliest was Venard de Jonchère's *Sapho, opéra en trois actes*, produced at the Théâtre Lyrique at Barbou in 1772. Others included Emphis and Cournol's *Sapho* (1818), and Sappho as a suitable subject for opera lived on with Giovanni Pacini's *Saffo* (1840) and Charles Gounod's *Sapho* (1851). There were also minor pieces by Bree (in Dutch), by Schwartzendorf and Kanne (in German), by Reicha (in Bohemian) and Lissenko (in Russian).

I have come across only the one ballet, Charles-Louis Didelot's *Sappho and Phaon*, as performed at the Haymarket Theatre in London in 1797 with music by Joseph Mazzinghi. Obviously there is not much scope for performing poetry here, but the fact that it was advertised as a '*Grand Ballet Érotique*' suggests that the emphasis was still very much on the performing (woman's) body. That same year saw the production of William Mason's play *Sappho* (1797), which suggests similar interests, especially in the cross-dressing scene. Mason's transvestite Sappho may owe something to an earlier fiction, Claude de Sacy's novel *Les Amours de Sapho et de Phaon*

(1775), in which, because Phaon is a wild man living in the woods who has 'sworn eternal hatred to the sex', Sappho has to resort to dressing as a man in order to secure the confidence of her macho hero. Yet whether or not Sappho actually gets to wear the trousers, the fact is that in taking on an active performing and desiring role she is still, in many of these texts, usurping male privilege.

Numerous French plays (none of them included here) took Sappho as their theme, among them that created by the Princesse de Salm-Dyck, Constance Pipelet (or Citoyenne Pipelet). Her *Sapho, tragédie mêlée de chants* with music by Martini, was staged in 1794 during the revolution and, just after the end of the Terror, at the Théâtre des Amis de le Patrie. Other French dramas included Madame de Staël's (unperformed) *Sapho* (1816), Hippolyte de La Morvonnais's *Sapho, drame lyrique en deux actes* (1824), Philoxene Boyer's *Sapho, drame en un acte* (1850), Arsène Houssaye's *Sapho, drame antique en trois actes* (1850, written for the great tragic actress, Rachel), Paul Juillerat's *La Reine de Lesbos, drame antique* (1854) and Armand Silvestre's *Sapho* (1881). Little wonder that Houssaye, when he was director of the Opéra Comique in Paris, had cause to complain of 'that everlasting Sappho'.

In Germany there were at least two Sappho plays (not included here), suggesting the growing German interest that would eventually dominate Sappho scholarship in the nineteenth century. One of these was by the eminent dramatist Franz Grillparzer (1791–1872), whose *Sappho* (1818) was performed many times, widely translated and is still highly regarded.

Grillparzer had first come to the idea of Sappho when he happened one night to meet a friend walking through the Prater, the great park in the centre of Vienna. The friend told him that the opera was looking for a libretto, and suggested that Grillparzer undertake it, with Sappho as the subject. He took himself next day to the Imperial Library to search out Sappho's Fragments, then wrote his tragedy instead. But the concept of performing, impersonating and ventriloquising Sappho was one that underpinned not only portraits, plays and operas of the period, but poems as well. The Sapphic premise in these poems varies greatly, depending upon the knowledge and expertise of the latterday poet. Percy Bysshe Shelley's 'To Constantia, singing' (1822) casts Constantia in Sappho's performing role, and the speaker in the role of her audience. But he is still the poet, writing the poem that makes her into a pretty picture, and in evoking his own reaction to Constantia's singing, Shelley quotes a version of Sappho's Fragment 31:

> My brain is wild, my breath comes quick/ . . .
> I am dissolved in these consuming ecstasies.

Tennyson's 'Fatima' (1832) is a cross-dressing poem, in that it speaks from the woman's point of view. It may owe something to Shelley, but it is clearly linked to Fragment 31, for when it was first published in 1832 it bore no title, only an epigraph in Greek: the first line of Sappho's poem. Tennyson (1809–92) had Greek and knew his Sappho very well, from his early schooldays when his father taught him, and on throughout his life when he kept up with developments in Greek scholarship and actually purchased many of the important new editions of Sappho coming out of France and Germany. Fragment 31, in particular, was an important source for him, and he quoted Sappho many times in his early writings, as well as allowing her tone and style to permeate much of his mature work.

The women poets, on the other hand, for the most part did not have Greek. So for them it was the *legends* that counted, and a whole chorus of women poets singing 'Sappho's Last Song', on her behalf, grew up in the nineteenth century, beginning with the works of Felicia Hemans (1793–1835) and L.E.L. (Letitia Elizabeth Landon, 1802–38) and continuing in writers such as Christina Rossetti (1830–94) and Caroline Norton (1808–77). The oft-repeated theme of this song is art-versus-love, or the suffering of the woman who may be admired in public, but is neglected in private. L.E.L. and Christina Rossetti both wrote at least two poems on the subject of Sappho. Her possibilities are never exhausted, and often artists return to her again and again.

Elizabeth Barrett Browning (1806–61) is one of the few women poets of the nineteenth century who did read Greek, and yet she – to some extent deliberately – tried to keep clear of Sappho, apart from one translation of a supposed Sappho Fragment, 'The Song of the Rose', that she found in the *Greek Anthology*, and a brief mention in 'A Vision of Poets' (1844), which takes up the theme of the price paid by the woman-artist:

> And Sappho, with that gloriole
> Of ebon hair on calméd brows.

O poet-woman! none forgoes
The leap, attaining the repose!

The various 'Modern Sapphos' collected in this anthology suggest some of the major currents in the thought and art of the nineteenth century: Charles Kingsley's pagan heroine is restless with ambition and lack of faith; Matthew Arnold's Victorian parallel to the (heterosexualised) speaker in Sappho's Fragment 31 is a practical woman who waits and hopes, prepared to settle for the less-than-perfect love of a man who will turn to her when his present passion has faded into 'fatigue, discontent, and dejection'. Christina Rossetti's Sappho is a Pre-Raphaelite shade sighing for rest and making a ghostly presence out of linguistic absences; while Hans Schmidt's little 'Sapphische Ode' – famously set to music by Johannes Brahms – is Sapphic only in metre and theme (in its reference to the attributed 'Song of the Rose'), but otherwise is essentially Victorian in its yearning expression of the dualities of love found and love lost, love's pleasure and love's pain.

It is easy to assume that all these ladies with lyres are parlour Sapphos: domesticated, pretty, scaled down. But Sappho's impersonations were, even here, more than a matter of raiding the dressing-up box. In the 1840s in particular Sappho was cast in the role of a revolutionary, albeit one who is doomed to failure. Giovanni Pacini's opera *Saffo* opens with the poetess using her oratory to challenge the authoritarian rule of the priests of Apollo, rousing the people to rebel against the cruel law that condemns victims to sacrifice themselves in the ritual leap of Leucadia. Later on she actually overturns the altar of Apollo, and although she eventually regrets and is punished for her blasphemy, the spectacle of a daring Sappho, defying gods and men, is the image that remains.

Gounod's opera also has a revolutionary background. Phaon and the poet Alcaeus are part of a conspiracy to murder Pittacus, the tyrant of Lesbos. Sappho, being a woman, is not an active party to the plot, but when blackmailed by the unscrupulous courtesan Glycera, she shows herself to be a valiant accomplice, in that she prefers death – and her lover's mistaken condemnation – to betrayal and the failure of the cause. When the opera was first performed in 1851 the producers were not permitted to sell the libretto in the theatre, and the censor demanded that some of Alcaeus' lines were cut where the music carried an echo of the 'Marseillaise'.

'The cause' in Caroline Norton's mind was the tyranny of man –

domestic, rather than public. In 'The Picture of Sappho' Norton conjures up not one, but many Sapphos. They multiply in the imagined pictures that were indeed created by many different artists from the middle of the eighteenth century on:

> Thou! whose impassion'd face
> The Painter loves to trace,
> Theme of the Sculptor's art and Poet's story . . .

They multiply too in the various emotions of dismay, mourning, anxiety and despair that are rehearsed in the succeeding stanzas of the poem. For Norton each of these images of Sappho was much more than a stylised set of Attitudes. Like Christine de Pisan, like Lady Mary Wortley Montagu, like Mary Robinson, Norton was a woman who saw in Sappho's story some ancient reflection of her own present trials. She had – perforce – made herself into a champion of women's rights because of her own miserable experiences in a marriage where her unscrupulous husband had left her physically abused, destitute (taking even the money she herself had earned) and without the guardianship of her own children. 'A married woman in England,' she wrote with some justification, 'has no *legal existence*; her being is absorbed in that of her husband.' It was a predicament that she fought with vehemence, and that made her a byword in English society. Long after her own personal troubles were at an end, the name of Caroline Norton was likely to be pronounced either with pity or with scorn.

At the end of Norton's poem, Sappho's individual experiences are wiped out in the light of the generality of her sex; 'Thou wert a WOMAN, and wert left despairing!' Sappho, no matter how glorious, is condemned by the law of man that undervalues and despises her. One despairing fact remains for ancient Sappho and for all her succeeding nineteenth-century 'Sapphos' alike: that their words will be lost, unheard, and their identity denied. Norton's poem, says Yopie Prins in *Victorian Sappho* (1999), is a postscript added to Sappho's authentic signature, endlessly repeating the many inscriptions of Sappho's name reflected in the many mirrors of history: P.S., P.s., Psappho.

SAPPHO AND PHAON: A GRAND EROTIC BALLET, IN FOUR ACTS

COMPOSED BY M. DIDELOT
And performed for the First Time. April 6, 1797, at the
KING'S THEATRE, HAYMARKET

The Music by MR MAZZINGHI
The Scenery by MR GREENWOOD
The Dresses by MR SEITINI

DRAMATIS PERSONAE

SAPPHO, *a celebrated Artist of Mitylenis*	*Mad. Rose*
DAMOPHILE, *Sappho's favourite Pupil*	*Mad. Hilligsberg*
VENUS	*Mlle. Parisot*
ADONIS	*Miss Menage*
CUPID	*Master Menage*
ZEPHYRUS	*Signor Gentilli*
VULCAN	*M. Fialon*
PHAON, a young Waterman	*M. Didelot*
ALCEUS, a celebrated Poet	*Mr Simpson*
NEMESIS	*Mr Simpson*
FIRE	*Signor Gentilli*
HYPOCRISY	*M. Fialon*

Iron, Poison, Crime, Death, Despair, Remorse, Attendants of Nemesis, Graces, Sappho's Pupils, Tritons and Nymphs, Cupids, Shepherds and Shepherdesses.

The Scene is in Mitylenis and the Neighbourhood, on the Sea Shore.

ADVERTISEMENT

Loaded with the favours of the Public, emboldened by the flattering manner in which my productions were received last year, and several *Pas de Deux* and *Pas de Trois* this season, I venture a great Work, and presume to take a loftier flight.

The subject of Sappho, which never was brought upon the stage as a Ballet (that I know of) appears pleasing to me, indeed the more so, as it gives me an opportunity of bringing forwards in an equally shining manner three favourites of the public, Rose, Hilligsberg, and Parisot; and that, although an author may wish it, he but seldom finds great subjects with that advantage.

The celebrated Sappho left nothing to her posterity but a few pieces of poetry carefully collected. These enable us to judge of her taste, of her genius, and lead us to regret that she left no more.

We only learn that she loved Phaon, that he was ungrateful; left her for one of her pupils; returned to her more through pride than love, and abandoned her once more – that she followed him even to Sicily, and that, unable to gain his heart, she threw herself into the deep from the rock of Leucate. We learn also, that she was beloved and most cruelly treated by three famous men of that time, who could never obtain any return.

Sappho, in one of her charming pieces of poetry, says that Venus came oftentimes to her palace – in another, she relates that Venus gave beauty to Phaon, who took her in his boat, when under a mortal form she hid herself from the God's looks.

It is upon that basis that I have framed this Ballet – I have chosen the *Erotic* style as the fittest to Sappho's character and a Ballet – the different Episodes of Venus and Adonis, Phaon's Education, the Cause of his Inconstancy, the Temple of Revenge, Damophile and Sappho's ugliness, and the *Dénouement*, are entirely the children of my fancy; but have of themselves a moral allegorical sense, which shows that virtue and ingratitude meet with their reward.

As to the Scene of the *Palace of Vengeance*, I have perhaps ventured in it strokes somewhat too bold, but what is a picture without shades? – could Apelles himself have painted with only carmine, blue and white? – besides, what instruments of vengeance could I have presented to Sappho's choice, but iron, fire, poison, crime, and hypocrisy? and is it possible to bring them on the stage without strongly representing their characteristicks?

Woe to the artist, who does but unleave roses, without daring to gather any for fear of the thorns! – In fine, since it is given to great masters only always to keep within true limits, I chuse rather to overpass my aim, than not to be able to obtain it; and if I have gone too far, I can soon correct my mistake.

One will easily see that I have for a moment deprived Sappho of her beauty, only to render her more interesting, to show the goodness of her heart, and to accelerate the *dénouement*. I hope I shall be forgiven not carrying her to Leucate, on account of the impossibility: I have changed Leucate into a common rock, and the religious intention of Sappho into a despair very natural to a sensible heart, whose love is rejected – Besides, the religious action of leaping from Leucate did not follow the march of the work, such as I have composed it; and would only have thrown a damp upon the *dénouement*.

. . . .

ACT IV

SCENE I

The Scene represents a picturesque and verdant Spot. – An elevated Rock commands the Sea.

Damophile loads Phaon with the most endearing caresses. They express in a *pas de deux* their different sensations; they play with Cupid, who attempts to escape, but he is soon retaken, and tied to a tree: they afterwards free him, but with the greatest precautions – Soon, more cunning than they have been prudent, he cuts his ties, and flies away; then he cedes to their wishes, and flying to their arms, teaches them that Love cannot be mastered.

Night surprises them; and a drapery, curiously grouped by zephyrs and suspended to *cariatides* of the finest marble, covers a couch, towards which Damophile and Phaon are conducted by Cypris's son. – Phebe reflecting her pallid face on the scarcely agitated waves, spreads a silver light over the landscape. The stars scintillate; every thing invites to repose. Love, placing himself between the lovers, orders the zephyrs to flutter round them – when they fall into a calm and profound sleep.

SCENE II

Meanwhile the earth shakes – the fearful zephyrs fly away, and let fall the drapery they supported – the three hellish monsters, Crime, Remorse and Despair, come out of an abyss – A thick smoke proceeds, and flames surround them by intervals – the two last hold a looking-glass in their terrible hands.

They surround the bed, so lately the asylum of Zephyrs, Pleasure, and Happiness: With their horrid paws they open the curtains – Remorse presses and agitates by turns Damophile and Phaon, who seem in their dreams to feel the most cruel pangs – Crime, seizing Damophile as most culpable, changes her beautiful features into frightful forms, and wakes her – Remorse hastens to show her the looking-glass, in which she sees herself; she knows not in her fright what causes her the most horror, the monsters who surround her, or herself. – Phaon, also awakens, and is seized by Despair – At the first noise, Cupid has taken his flight, and remains suspended in the air.

SCENE III

In the same moment, Venus and Sappho enter – 'Sappho, thou art already revenged: how thy presence adds to Damophile's torment!' – Phaon is petrified; and the Furies fly towards the Goddess, applauding themselves for what they have done. The trembling Damophile approaches her mistress, and begs in vain her forgiveness – Venus forbids Sappho granting it. Cupid, surprised at all this, flies to his mother, from whom he receives a severe reprimand – 'But, what signifies all this?' says Cupid to Venus – 'let Phaon adore Sappho, I order it' – 'I will obey' – and satisfied, Venus gives him a kiss.

The three inexorable daughters of Hell wish Phaon to share Damophile's fate. Sappho has hardly time enough to throw herself before him, to screen him from their fury, and she receives at the same moment the horrid features, which, by Venus's secret orders, disappear from Damophile's charming countenance. The looking-glass intended for Phaon is presented to Sappho, who perceives at once her own ugliness, and her rival's beauty. The wretched woman throws herself at Venus's feet, and begs to have her former beauty restored. – Venus, feigning not to be able to relieve her, seems to say: – 'thou would'st spare Phaon, Fate's decrees must be fulfilled – Adieu, I can no more protect thee' – and she disappears, after ordering the cruel Deities to re-enter the abysses from whence they came, and after speaking to her son.

SCENE IV

'Ah! seems to say the tender and unhappy Sappho, ah! they all betray me.' – 'Oh! Sappho, cast a look of pity on your Phaon; it is your heart, 'tis your noble soul I adore . . . I was unfaithful . . . forgive, and I shall be the happiest of men. Sappho, do but forgive, and I renounce every thing for you, . . . Damophile, inconstancy, I renounce all.' – 'Cruel; I adored, I still adore you; but' – 'Ah! Sappho, sweet friend, so basely betrayed, see me at your feet, imploring forgiveness.' – Sappho's tender soul cannot resist their entreaties, their remorse – 'ungrateful, so dearly beloved, I forgive you both . . . but what! . . . (*fraught with despair*) my lyre is broken, my beauty is lost, and . . . I cannot live to happiness, I must die' – She seems to take a firm resolution, and addressing Damophile and Phaon: – 'go, love one another, be happy together . . . Phaon give me thy hand; Damophile, thine; . . . embrace the wretched Sappho' – Her sobs stifle her; her tears flow abundantly – She attempts to unite their hands; but her heart revolts at the thought of that cruel sacrifice – She flies, and it is in vain that Phaon and Damophile try to prevent her; they lose sight of her among the windings of the trees. – She ascends the rock, reaches the summit that commands the sea, at the moment that Phaon and Damophile appear on the opposite side – bids them an eternal adieu, and throws herself headlong into the deep – Phaon follows her; and Damophile is going to share their fate.

SCENE V

But what a prodigy! – Sappho suspended in the air, supported by clouds, surrounded by Cupids and Zephyrs, appears in the midst of Venus's court, and at the Goddess's feet. Love presents her lyre crowned with roses and myrtles – Phaon is at her feet, supported by the nymphs of the deep; and Damophile, suspended in the air by Zephyrs, opens her arms towards them.

The rocks, trees, and forest, disappear; and a marble palace appears in their place. The *coup-d'oeil* is bounded by a piece of water, in which Nymphs and Cupids are at play; some riding upon swans, some walking on the clouds that suspend Venus: whilst Sappho's pupils fill the inside of the temple.

Sappho has already recovered her first form; her lover is forgiven; and Damophile owns her faults in her friend's arms. The clouds descend gradually, open and show the remainder of the palace, which prolongs itself in immense gardens, well watered. The pleasant green, the cascades, the architecture, the little Cupids, who play fancifully upon the surface of the water, betwixt the trees and the columns, form a picturesque prospect that embellishes the spectacle of Phaon's union to Sappho.

A car drawn by two white steeds, appears from the bosom of the earth. – Sappho, Phaon and Damophile enter it; and, followed by the celestial court, they set off for Mitylenis.

FINIS

Music by Joseph Mazzinghi (1765–1844),
ballet by Charles-Louis Didelot (1767–1837)

After Venus makes her miraculous gift of perfect beauty to Phaon, the famous poet Sappho falls in love with him. He too is enraptured, but rather with her poetry and her fame than with her, and no sooner do they plight their troth than he takes ship for Sicily and there woos a shepherdess, Doris, much to the dismay of her aged father, Agenor, who sees Phaon for the philanderer he is. When Sappho arrives in Sicily in pursuit of Phaon, she disguises herself as a shepherd in order to gain the confidence of the local shepherds and get an introduction to Doris . . .

SCENE VI

Changes to the bower of Doris

DORIS

Ye solitary shades, once more receive
Your love-lorn visitant! Let my poor limbs
Fall on your fragrance! O that they might soon
Sink into sleep eternal! that Agenor
Might find his daughter here depriv'd of breath,
And wipe from her pale brow the dews of death!

Ye powers! this load of life remove,
Who gave the boon to be enjoy'd;
Behold that boon a burthen prove;
Behold your gen'rous aim destroy'd!
Change then to death your gift divine;
The gift that gladly I resign.
[*She reclines on the turf in a pensive attitude.*]

SCENE VII

LYCIDAS, SAPPHO, DORIS

Lyc. Heard ye that pensive strain? it was the voice
Of Doris. See, reclin'd upon yon bed
Of fragrant violets, she sits and weeps!
Hasten, I pray thee, and with some soft air
Chase from her breast the cloud of black despair.
[*Lycidas retires behind the bower, while Sappho sits down at her feet, plays a pastoral symphony on her reed, and then sings.*]
Sap. The youth, that gazes on thy charms,

Rivals in bliss the Gods on high,
Whose ear thy pleasing converse warms,
Thy lovely smile his eye.
But trembling awe my bosom heaves,
When plac'd those heav'nly charms among;
The sight my voice of power bereaves,
And chains my torpid tongue.
Thro' ev'ry thrilling fibre flies
The subtle flame; in dimness drear
My eyes are veil'd; a murm'ring noise
Glides tinkling thro' my ear;
Death's chilly dew my limbs o'erspreads,
Shiv'ring, convuls'd, I panting lie;
And pale, as is the flower that fades,
I droop, I faint, I die!

Dor. Who art thou, bright-ey'd spirit? for those strains
Bespeak thee more than human. Tell me, which
Of the tun'd spheres thou guid'st, and why hast left
The chiming orb to sooth my mortal ear
With thy celestial warblings?

SCENE VIII

PHAON

What do I see? a rival at her feet!
He clasps her hands, devours it with his kisses.
Rouse thee, rash swain, and stand prepar'd to meet
An injur'd lover's fury!

[*Lycidas rushes from behind the bower.*]

Lyc. Stand there first,
And meet the fury of that injured lover,
Who first has right of vengeance!

Pha. Him I've caught
In am'rous dalliance; he shall first be punish'd,
Thee I can scorn at leisure.

[*He runs at Sappho, strikes her on the breast, she falls.*]

Dor. Stay thee, Phaon,
Ah me! the shepherd swoons. Good Lycidas,
Prevent a deadlier blow.

[*Lycidas seizes the crook of Sappho, and stands before the bower to guard it, while Doris kneels and supports her.*]

Lyc. Base murderer, pause!

In me behold a man whose firmer arm
Is brac'd to meet thy prowess, vile assassin,
I dare thee to the combat!
Pha. No, poor shepherd,
Thy heart enough is wounded! Hie thee hence:
My wrath shall not assist the scorn of Doris,
Curst with the pang of unsuccessful love,
Go bear away thy woes, and quit the grove.
Where the willows skirt the brook,
  Go, and weave a garland green,
Leave thou there thy scrip and crook,
  Vent in tears thy jealous spleen:
Heave thou there thy last sad sigh,
Drop into the stream, and die.

Sap. Die, didst thou say? I hop'd I had been dead;
But death, like Phaon, has deceiv'd poor Sappho.
Dor. and Lyc. Sappho!
Pha. Just Heav'ns! it is, it is my Sappho,
And I have wounded her perhaps to death!
Sap. Would to that Heav'n thou hadst! but thou may'st still
Achieve the deed; behold this bruised breast!
O! with thy dagger give a kinder blow,
And I shall be at peace.
Pha. O torture! torture!
Where shall I turn? how hide me from myself?

SCENE IX

AGENOR

Whence springs this tumult? need I ask the cause,
When that licentious wretch appears before me?
But who the wounded swain?
Dor. Hear, sire, and wonder.
'Tis Lesbian Sappho; she whose tuneful fame –
Sap. Ah! spare the praise, or turn that praise to pity.
Yes; pity her, whom fate ordain'd to prove
The sharpest pangs of agonising love.

Sappho. O! if thy aged heart can feel,
Ev'n from that venerable eye
My woes might bid the tears to steal,

And not debase its dignity. [*To Agenor*]

Ag. See, at thy call they freely flow!

Ag.Do.Lyc. We all partake in Sappho's woe!

Pha. Shall I, that sorrow's impious cause,
Not add my true repentant tear?

Ag.Sap. / *Do.Lyc.* Traitor, avaunt! the vengeance fear
That on thy head thy falsehood draws!

Ag. Fly from his presence, hapless fair!
Fly to my hospitable gate:

Dor. There let this breast thy friendship share;

Lyc. There let my zeal on both await.

Pha. Shall I be banish'd from the grove,
Deny'd my folly to atone?

Ag.Sa. / *Ph.Do.* / *Lyc.* Such is the righteous doom of Jove:
So justice thunders from his throne!

[*Exeunt – Phaon on the opposite side.*]

William Mason, 1797

TO CONSTANTIA, SINGING

Thus to be lost and thus to sink and die,
  Perchance were death indeed! – Constantia, turn!
In thy dark eyes a power like light doth lie,
  Even though the sounds which were thy voice, which burn
Between thy lips, are laid to sleep;
  Within thy breath, and on thy hair, like odour it is yet,
And from thy touch like fire doth leap.
  Even while I write, my burning cheeks are wet,
  Alas, that the torn heart can bleed, but not forget!

A breathless awe, like the swift change
  Unseen, but felt in youthful slumbers,
Wild, sweet, but uncommunicably strange,
  Thou breathest now in fast ascending numbers.
The cope of heaven seems rent and cloven
  By the enchantment of thy strain,
And on my shoulders wings are woven,

To follow its sublime career,
Beyond the mighty moons that wane
Upon the verge of nature's utmost sphere,
Till the world's shadowy walls are past and disappear.

Her voice is hovering o'er my soul – it lingers
O'ershadowing it with soft and lulling wings,
The blood and life within those snowy fingers
Teach witchcraft to the instrumental strings.
My brain is wild, my breath comes quick –
The blood is listening in my frame,
And thronging shadows, fast and thick,
Fall on my overflowing eyes;
My heart is quivering like a flame;
As morning dew, that in the sunbeam dies,
I am dissolved in these consuming ecstasies.

I have no life, Constantia, now, but thee,
Whilst, like the world-surrounding air, thy song
Flows on, and fills all things with melody.
Now is thy voice a tempest swift and strong,
On which, like one in trance upborne,
Secure o'er rocks and waves I sweep,
Rejoicing like a cloud of morn.
Now 'tis the breath of summer night,
Which when the starry waters sleep,
Round western isles, with incense-blossoms bright,
Lingering, suspends my soul in its voluptuous flight.

Percy Bysshe Shelley, 1822

THE LAST SONG OF SAPPHO

Suggested by a beautiful sketch, the design of the younger Westmacott. It represents Sappho sitting on a rock above the sea, with her lyre cast at her feet. There is a desolate grace about the whole figure, which seems penetrated with the feeling of utter abandonment.

Sound on, thou dark unslumbering sea!
My dirge is in thy moan;
My spirit finds response in thee,
To its own ceaseless cry – 'Alone, alone!'

Yet send me back one other word,
Ye tones that never cease!
Oh! let your secret caves be stirr'd,
And say, dark waters! will ye give me peace?

Away! my weary soul hath sought
In vain one echoing sigh,
One answer to consuming thought
In human hearts – and will the wave reply?

Sound on, thou dark unslumbering sea!
Sound in thy scorn and pride!
I ask not, alien world, from thee,
What my own kindred earth hath still denied.

And yet I loved that earth so well,
With all its lovely things!
– Was it for this the death-wind fell
On my rich lyre, and quench'd its living strings?

– Let them lie silent at my feet!
Since broken even as they,
The heart whose music made them sweet,
Hath pour'd on desert-sands its wealth away,

Yet glory's light hath touch'd my name,
The laurel-wreath is mine –
– With a lone heart, a weary frame –
O restless deep! I come to make them thine!

Give to that crown, that burning crown,
Place in thy darkest hold!
Bury my anguish, my renown,
With hidden wrecks, lost gems, and wasted gold.

Thou sea-bird on the billow's crest,
Thou hast thy love, thy home;
They wait thee in the quiet nest,
And I, th' unsought, unwatch'd-for – I too come!

I, with this winged nature fraught,
These visions wildly free,
This boundless love, this fiery thought –
– Alone I come – oh! give me peace, dark sea!

Felicia Hemans (1793–1835)

SAPPHO'S SONG

Farewell, my lute! – and would that I
  Had never waked thy burning chords!
Poison has been upon thy sigh,
  And fever has breathed in thy words.

Yet wherefore, wherefore should I blame
  Thy power, thy spell, my gentlest lute?
I should have been the wretch I am,
  Had every chord of thine been mute.

It was my evil star above,
  Not my sweet lute, that wrought me wrong;
It was not song that taught me love,
  But it was love that taught me song.

If song be past, and hope undone,
  And pulse, and head, and heart, are flame;
It is thy work, thou faithless one!
  But, no! – I will not name thy name!

Sun-god! lute, wreath are vowed to thee!
  Long be their light upon my grave –
My glorious grave – you deep blue sea
  I shall sleep calm beneath its wave!

L.E.L. (Letitia Elizabeth Landon), 1824

Ode in a Grecian Urn. In a garden setting with antique columns in the background, a woman wearing Greek robes and an *à la Sapho* headdress plays the *kithara* as the frontispiece to the 1832 edition of the popular illustrated album of poetry and prose *The Keepsake* (London, 1831).

FATIMA

O Love, Love, Love! O withering might!
O sun, that from thy noonday height
Shudderest when I strain my sight,
Throbbing through all thy heat and light,
  Lo, falling from my constant mind,
  Lo, parched and withered, deaf and blind,
  I whirl like leaves in roaring wind.

Last night I wasted hateful hours
Below the city's eastern towers:
I thirsted for the brooks, the showers:
I rolled among the tender flowers:
  I crushed them on my breast, my mouth;
  I looked athwart the burning drouth
  Of that long desert to the south.

Last night, when some one spoke his name,
From my swift blood that went and came
A thousand little shafts of flame
Were shivered in my narrow frame.
  O Love, O fire! once he drew
  With one long kiss my whole soul through
  My lips, as sunlight drinketh dew.

Before he mounts the hill, I know
He cometh quickly: from below
Sweet gales, as from deep gardens, blow
Before him, striking on my brow.
  In my dry brain my spirit soon,
  Down-deepening from swoon to swoon,
  Faints like a dazzled morning moon.

The wind sounds like a silver wire,
And from beyond the noon a fire
Is poured upon the hills, and nigher
The skies stoop down in their desire;
  And, isled in sudden seas of light,
  My heart, pierced through with fierce delight,
  Bursts into blossom in his sight.

My whole soul waiting silently,
All naked in a sultry sky,
Droops blinded with his shining eye:
I *will* possess him or will die.
  I will grow round him in his place,
  Grow, live, die looking on his face,
  Die, dying clasped in his embrace.

Alfred, Lord Tennyson, 1832

SONG OF THE ROSE

ATTRIBUTED TO SAPPHO

(From Achilles Tatius)

If Zeus chose us a King of the flowers in his mirth,
  He would call to the rose and would royally crown it,
For the rose, ho, the rose! is the grace of the earth,
  Is the light of the plants that are growing upon it.
For the rose, ho, the rose! is the eye of the flowers,
  Is the blush of the meadows that feel themselves fair –
Is the lightning of beauty, that strikes through the bowers
  On pale lovers who sit in the glow unaware.
Ho, the rose breathes of love! ho, the rose lifts the cup
  To the red lips of Cypris invoked for a guest!
Ho, the rose, having curled its sweet eaves for the world,
  Takes delight in the motion its petals keep up,
As they laugh to the Wind as it laughs from the west.

Elizabeth Barrett Browning, 1850

SAPPHIC ODE

Roses I plucked at night from the dark hedgerow;
they breathed a sweeter scent than ever by day.
But the twigs stirred and plentifully showered
dew that made me wet.

I was never so thrilled as by the scent of the kisses
that I plucked at night from the shrub of your lips;
and you too, stirred in spirit like the roses,
were bedewed with tears.

Hans Schmidt, 'Sapphische Ode', 1880s,
set to music by Johannes Brahms, op. 94 no. 4, 1884

A MODERN SAPPHO

They are gone – all is still! Foolish heart, dost thou quiver?
  Nothing stirs on the lawn but the quick lilac-shade.
Far up shines the house, and beneath flows the river –
  Here lean, my head, on this cold balustrade!

Ere he come – ere the boat by the shining-branch'd border
  Of dark elms shoot round, dropping down the proud stream,
Let me pause, let me strive, in myself make some order,
  Ere their boat-music sound, ere their broider'd flags gleam.

Last night we stood earnestly talking together;
  She enter'd – that moment his eyes turn'd from me!
Fasten'd on her dark hair, and her wreath of white heather –
  As yesterday was, so to-morrow will be.

Their love, let me know, must grow strong and yet stronger,
  Their passion burn more, ere it ceases to burn.
They must love – while they must! but the hearts that love
    longer
  Are rare – ah! most loves but flow once, and return.

I shall suffer – but they will outlive their affection;
  I shall weep – but their love will be cooling; and he,
As he drifts to fatigue, discontent, and dejection,
  Will be brought, thou poor heart, how much nearer to thee!

For cold is his eye to mere beauty, who, breaking
  The strong band which passion around him hath furl'd,
Disenchanted by habit, and newly awaking,
  Looks languidly round on a gloom-buried world.

Through that gloom he will see but a shadow appearing,
  Perceive but a voice as I come to his side –
But deeper their voice grows, and nobler their bearing,
  Whose youth in the fires of anguish hath died.

So, to wait! – But what notes down the wind, hark! are
    driving?
  'Tis he! 'tis their flag, shooting round by the trees!
– Let my turn, if it *will* come, be swift in arriving!
  Ah! hope cannot long lighten torments like these.

Hast thou yet dealt him, O life, thy full measure?
  World, have thy children yet bow'd at his knee?
Hast thou with myrtle-leaf crown'd him, O pleasure?
  – Crown, crown him quickly, and leave him for me!

Matthew Arnold, 1849

SAPPHO

She lay among the myrtles on the cliff;
Above her glared the noon; beneath, the sea.
Upon the white horizon Atho's peak
Weltered in burning haze; all airs were dead;
The cicale slept among the tamarisk's hair;
The birds sat dumb and drooping. Far below
The lazy sea-weed glistened in the sun;
The lazy sea-fowl dried their steaming wings;
The lazy swell crept whispering up the ledge,
And sank again. Great Pan was laid to rest;
And Mother Earth watched by him as he slept,
And hushed her myriad children for a while.
She lay among the myrtles on the cliff;
And sighed for sleep, for sleep that would not hear,
But left her tossing still; for night and day
A mighty hunger yearned within her heart,
Till all her veins ran fever; and her cheek,
Her long thin hands, and ivory-channelled feet,
Were wasted with the wasting of her soul.

Then peevishly she flung her on her face,
And hid her eyeballs from the blinding glare,
And fingered at the grass, and tried to cool
Her crisp hot lips against the crisp hot sward:
And then she raised her head, and upward cast
Wild looks from homeless eyes, whose liquid light
Gleamed out between deep folds of blue-black hair,
As gleam twin lakes between the purple peaks
Of deep Parnassus, at the mournful moon.
Beside her lay her lyre. She snatched the shell,
And waked wild music from its silver strings;
Then tossed it sadly by. – 'Ah, hush!' she cries;
'Dead offspring of the tortoise and the mine!
Why mock my discords with thine harmonies?
Although a thrice-Olympian lot be thine,
Only to echo back in every tone
The moods of nobler natures than thine own.'

Charles Kingsley, 1847

SAPPHO

I sigh at day-dawn, and I sigh
When the dull day is passing by.
I sigh at evening, and again
I sigh when night brings sleep to men.
Oh! it were better far to die
Than thus for ever mourn and sigh,
And in death's dreamless sleep to be
Unconscious that none weep for me;
Eased from my weight of heaviness,
Forgetful of forgetfulness,
Resting from pain and care and sorrow
Thro' the long night that knows no morrow;
Living unloved, to die unknown,
Unwept, untended and alone.

Christina Rossetti, 1846

WHAT SAPPHO WOULD HAVE SAID HAD HER LEAP CURED INSTEAD OF KILLING HER

Love, Love, that having found a heart
   And left it, leav'st it desolate; –
   Love, Love, that art more strong than Hate,
More lasting and more full of art; –
O blessèd Love, return, return,
Brighten the flame that needs must burn.

Among the stately lilies pale,
   Among the roses flushing red,
   I seek a flower meet for my head,
A wreath wherewith to bind my veil:
I seek in vain; a shadow-pain
Lies on my heart; and all in vain.

The rose hath too much life in it;
   The lily is too much at rest.
   Surely a blighted rose were best,
Or cankered lily flower more fit;
Or purple violet, withering
While yet the year is in its spring.

I walk down by the river side
   Where the low willows touch the stream;
   Beneath the ripple and sun-gleam
The slippery cold fishes glide,
Where flags and reeds and rushes lave
Their roots in the unsullied wave.

Methinks this is a drowsy place:
   Disturb me not; I fain would sleep:
   The very winds and waters keep
Their voices under; and the race
Of Time seems to stand still, for here
Is night or twilight all the year.

A very holy hushedness
   Broods here for ever: like a dove
   That, having built its nest above

A quiet place, feels the excess
Of calm sufficient, and would fain
Not wake, but drowse on without pain.

And slumbering on its mossy nest
  Haply hath dreams of pleasant Spring;
  And in its vision prunes its wing
And takes swift flight, yet is at rest.
Yea, is at rest: and still the calm
Is wrapped around it like a charm.

I would have quiet too in truth,
  And here will sojourn for a while.
  Lo; I have wandered many a mile,
Till I am foot-sore in my youth.
I will lie down; and quite forget
The doubts and fears that haunt me yet.

My pillow underneath my head
  Shall be green grass; thick fragrant leaves
  My canopy; the spider weaves
Meet curtains for my narrow bed;
And the dew can but cool my brow
That is so dry and burning now.

Ah, would that it could reach my heart,
  And fill the void that is so dry
  And aches and aches; – but what am I
To shrink from my self-purchased part?
It is in vain; is all in vain;
I must go forth and bear my pain.

Must bear my pain, till Love shall turn
  To me in pity and come back.
  His footsteps left a smouldering track
When he went forth, that still doth burn.
Oh come again, thou pain divine,
Fill me and make me wholly thine.

Christina Rossetti, 1848

SAPPHO: A NEW GRAND SERIOUS OPERA

PERFORMED AT THE
THEATRE ROYAL, DRURY LANE
ON SATURDAY, APRIL 1, 1843

DRAMATIS PERSONAE

Alcander	*MR H. PHILLIPS*
Phaon	*MR ALLEN*
Lysimachus	*MR STRETTON*
Hippias	*MR J. REEVES*
Dirce	*MRS SERLE*
Sappho	*MISS CLARA NOVELLO*
Climene	*MRS ALFRED SHAW*

Greek Youths, Priests of Apollo, Guards, Augurs, Grecian Maidens, etc.

ACT I

THE OLYMPIC CROWN

SCENE – *The Exterior of the Circus*

[*At the rising of the curtain tumultuous applause is heard, with prolonged clapping of hands.*]

Voices from the Circus (Chorus)

Ah, voice of heaven! Thee should it waken,
Soul of the slain! mourn we thy doom.

[*A moment of silence, to which succeeds an increasing murmur, which rises to a tumult with appalling shouts.*]

Hence from the Circus! Sorrow and evil
Are in thy presence. Go, murd'rer! Leave us! Go!

[*Alcander rushes from the Circus in the greatest disorder, the marks of extreme anger on his countenance. Hippias enters on the opposite side.*]

Hip. What tumult?

[*Alcander, his lips convulsed with passion, is unable to reply.*]

What fearful raging clamour! It resounds,
Wild as the roaring of the rous'd Egean,
When storms arise.

Alc. If anger do not choak my utt'rance; hear me!
Thou knowest that Olympia ne'er could boast

Games of the splendour that it now beholdeth.
Thither Greece hath called her people! her leaders,
Her monarchs, her sacred priesthood, all now are here.
The laurel, crown of the bard, now is contested.
Strains full of mourning, Sappho attuned:
Antigonus, fam'd in fearful story,
She sang. How to forget the faithless Temisto;
He sought Leucadia, its fatal leap had braved,
And found his tomb in the engulphing sea.
'Perish then,' cried she, 'this rite unholy!'
And, on its ministers,
Called she the anger, the vengeance of Greece.
Lo! at her bidding rise the enraged people
And me, the priest of the Leucadian Phœbus.
Can I speak it? – words fail me!
Me they spurn forth with shame.

[*Trembling he covers his face with both hands, and sinks upon a stone seat.*]

Hip. I freeze with horror.

Alc. (*rising and looking threateningly towards the Circus.*) Tremble! haughty Sappho.
Heaven's and its ministers' hate shall pursue thee.
Yet, pure as she appeared, Hippias,
Ah, with no hatred first I beheld her!

[*His bearing loses all trace of anger, his tone is calm but feeling.*]

Ah! her accents, so sweetly flowing,
Seem'd to speak to me well-known greeting:
Thro' my slumbers had I seen her
As a vision often fleeting,
By such transport was I moved
As rejoining are beloved.
Ah! no language can declare
Thoughts my soul can hardly bear.
Direful omens full of sorrow,
Chill me with fear, with wild alarm.

Chorus, from the Circus

Hail to thee! first in glory!
Hail! Honour waits upon thee!
Sister of Muses call we thee,
Name that thy song hath won thee.

Thou hast the slain recalled!
Thou hast avenged a king!

Music by Giovanni Pacini, libretto by Giuseppe Cammarano, 1840

SAPPHO

Sappho: O ma lyre immortelle,
Qui, dans les tristes jours,
A tous mes maux fidele
Les consolais toujours . . .

. . . O my lyre immortal,
Even on the saddest days
Of all my pain, faithful,
And consoling always!
Vain now your voice so calm
Thou to suffering e'er alert
You cannot give the balm,
Which will soothe o'er my hurt:
The wound is in my heart!
Only death can cure this smart!

Farewell, lights of the world,
Descend under the sea;
When the waves above me swirl,
Sweet rest shall come to me.

The day about to dawn,
Phaon, will shine for you;
Your thoughts for me are few
As you greet this waking morn . . .
Open wide, bitter gulf, open now to me
I shall sleep forever in the boundless sea!

(*She climbs to the top of the rock.*)

Open wide, bitter gulf, open now to me
I shall sleep forever in the boundless sea!

(*She throws herself into the water below.*)

END OF THE OPERA

Music by Charles Gounod, libretto by Émile Augier, 1851

SAPPHO

An etching by Queen Victoria, February 1841, in an image which gives Sappho none of her conventional attributes (except the clifftop) yet where her profile closely resembles that of the young queen herself. Victoria's interest may have been inspired by reading about Giovanni Pacini's new opera *Saffo* which was premiered in Naples in November 1840, though it was not performed in London until April 1843. Christian Brinton, 'Queen Victoria as Etcher', in *The Critic* (June, 1900)

THE PICTURE OF SAPPHO

Thou! whose impassion'd face
The Painter loves to trace,
Theme of the Sculptor's art and Poet's story –
How many a wand'ring thought
Thy loveliness hath brought,
Warming the heart with its imagined glory!

Yet, was it History's truth,
That tale of wasted youth,
Of endless grief, and Love forsaken pining?
What wert thou, thou whose woe
The old traditions show
With Fame's cold light around thee vainly shining?

Didst thou indeed sit there
In languid lone despair –
Thy harp neglected by thee idly lying –
Thy soft and earnest gaze
Watching the lingering rays
In the far west, where summer-day was dying –

While with low rustling wings,
Among the quivering strings
The murmuring breeze faint melody was making,
As though it wooed thy hand
To strike with new command,
Or mourn'd with thee because thy heart was breaking?

Didst thou, as day by day
Roll'd heavily away,
And left thee anxious, nerveless, and dejected,
Wandering thro' bowers beloved –
Roving where *he* had roved –
Yearn for his presence, as for one expected?

Didst thou, with fond wild eyes
Fix'd on the starry skies,
Wait feverishly for each new day to waken –
Trusting some glorious morn

Might witness his return,
Unwilling to believe thyself forsaken?

And when conviction came,
Chilling that heart of flame,
Didst thou, O saddest of earth's grieving daughters!
From the Leucadian steep
Dash, with a desperate leap,
And hide thyself within the whelming waters?

Yea, in their hollow breast
Thy heart at length found rest!
The ever-moving waves above thee closing –
The winds, whose ruffling sigh
Swept the blue waters by,
Disturb'd thee not! – thou wert in peace reposing!

Such is the tale they tell!
Vain was thy beauty's spell –
Vain all the praise thy song could still inspire –
Though many a happy band
Rung with less skilful hand
The borrowed love-notes of thy echoing lyre.

FAME, to thy breaking heart
No comfort could impart,
In vain thy brow the laurel wreath was wearing;
One grief and one alone
Could bow thy bright head down –
Thou wert a WOMAN, and wert left despairing!

Caroline Norton (1808–77)

NINE

Daughter of de Sade

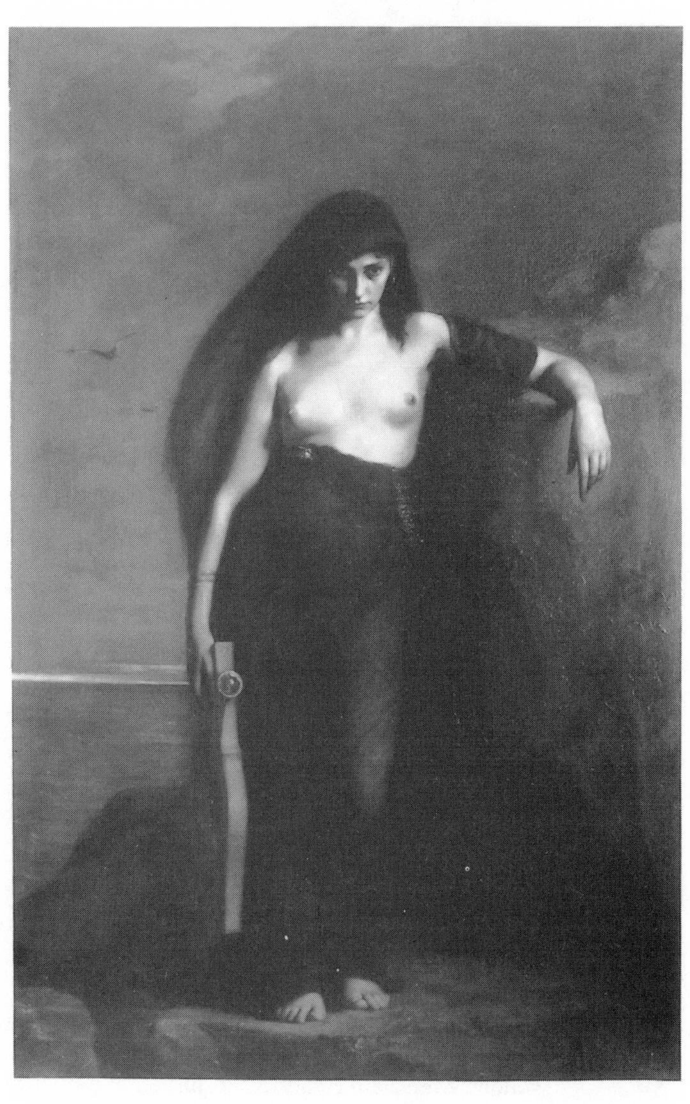

Sappho by Charles-Auguste Mengin, (1877). Sultry and sullen, Sappho may be dressed in mourning, but her see-through weeds suggest that she is a black widow. Manchester City Art Gallery.

If Sappho began the nineteenth century as the lady with the lyre, by the 1850s she was more lyre than lady. After the many editions that marked the epitome of French Sappho scholarship in the previous century, the main centre of academic endeavour in the Classics now moved to Germany. France was still very much involved, and editions like Jean-François Boissonade's of 1825 were widely bought and read. In Britain, too, a continuing interest in classical scholarship meant that new translations appeared, taken to a wider public by lengthy articles in the popular learned journals. In April 1832 *The Edinburgh Review*, for instance, carried an article entitled 'Greek Authoresses' by D. K. Sandford, which reviewed some new translations and turned into a discussion about women and poetry. 'Sappho,' he wrote, 'was known chiefly for her love, her leap, her looks, and her lyrics.' In that order.

The Germans took their Greeks rather more seriously. From the 1770s to about the 1850s more than twenty new editions and translations of Sappho were published, often along with other Greek lyric poets. Of these the most important were those by Heinrich Friedrich Magnus Volger (1810), Christian Friedrich Neue (1827) and Theodor Bergk (1854 and 1882). Bergk, in particular, became the standard edition in any language. When Henry Thornton Wharton produced his influential English edition of Sappho in 1885 he used Bergk's Greek as his source, and this work was only superseded by the scholarly editions of the twentieth century. Another significant German production was F. G. Schneidewin's *Delectus Poesis Graecorum Elegiacae, Iambicae, Melicae. – Sapphonis Mitylenaeae*, published in Göttingen in 1838. This added a few new Fragments to Sappho's oeuvre, and was one of the scholarly works known to readers abroad, including the English poet, Alfred, Lord Tennyson.

Even as all this learned industry was being expended on Sappho's behalf, her name and reputation were still suspect. So suspect that in 1816 Friedrich Gottlieb Welcker published a treatise entitled *Sappho von einem herrschenden Vorurtheil befreyt* ('Sappho freed from a reigning prejudice'). The prejudice in question, though barely named in the work, was that of her sexuality. In a bizarre, convoluted argument Welcker suggests that Sappho was neither homosexual nor heterosexual, but chaste. His 'evidence' for this is the fact that

Sappho's poems were admired in antiquity and, he says, 'no educated Greek would have thought these were beautiful love poems if something monstrous and disgusting had been going on in them'. The feminine, he argues, with a theoretical angle that predates the assumptions of the Victorians, was an idealised and pure concept for the ancient Greeks, and Sappho exemplified this role in her lyrical spirituality. She could not therefore have been subject to base and sensual passion. Nor – and this is where Welcker takes up an unlikely position as an early champion of 'Greek love' – would she have been capable of the profound and ennobling passion that characterised the relation between man and boy, between teacher and pupil, in ancient Greece.

Welcker's defence of Sappho was long-lived and influential, though it existed side by side with contradictory readings and theories. On his journeys from England, Byron could joke that he would attempt Sappho's leap and hope to survive to return home. In 1819 in *Don Juan* he celebrated 'The isles of Greece! the isles of Greece! / Where burning Sappho loved and sung', but in Canto XLII he added the poet to a list of forbidden classical authors:

> Ovid's a rake, as half his verses show him,
> Anacreon's morals are a still worse sample,
> Catullus scarcely had a decent poem,
> I don't think Sappho's Ode a good example,
> Although Longinus tells us there is no hymn
> Where the sublime soars forth on wings more ample.

In France, Jean-François Boissonade read the Greek of Sappho's Fragment 1 and knew what it said: 'I didn't want to write *if he flees*; I didn't dare write *if she flees*. I decided to use *one*, which reproduces the ambiguity of the Greek.' And at about the same time Allier de Hauteroche's *Notice sur la courtisane Sapho, née à Eresos, dans l'île de Lesbos* (1822) returned to the ancient idea of there having been 'two Sapphos' – one a respectable poet and teacher, the other a notorious courtesan. This was one method of cleaning up the Sapphic act, while keeping in view the salacious fictions that had come to surround the name of Sappho and that were to dominate in the latter part of the nineteenth century. Colonel William Mure, the author of *A Critical History of the Language and Literature of Ancient Greece* (1850), was one who argued that Sappho was not only an expert in 'the Ideal Love of the Greeks', but also the high priestess of a decadent sensuality typical of Lesbos in its decline.

Paris, however, was the scene for a new proscribing of Sappho's name. From about the 1830s to the 1850s lesbians were all the rage, whether in fictions like Théophile Gautier's *Mademoiselle de Maupin* (1835) and Honoré de Balzac's *La Fille aux Yeux d'Or* (1835) and *Seraphitus-Seraphita* (1854) or in the real-life salons, where writers and independent women like George Sand were not above suspicion. Sappho's converts were many, present and past. In a volume entitled *Mémoires de Christine Reine de Suède* (1830), Queen Christina of Sweden was made to confess her early passion for '*la belle Ebba Sparre*', one of her ladies-in-waiting. It was, she said, all the fault of her education:

> Alas! it was my youthful aptitude that set me on the way. The burning tenderness of Sappho for the young Lesbians, that strange and unusual desire, I felt more than anything else in reading the little of her poetry that remains to us. Yes, and everything that the poetess said that touched, that transported in the love of the Lesbians, I felt with the same vehemence for my divine Ebba.

Sappho had become a sexual exotic, and just as she had presided over the salons of the sophisticated 'Anandrynes', or had authorised the bloodthirsty pleasures of the tribades who called themselves 'followers of Sappho' in de Sade's *L'histoire de Juliette, ou les Prospérités du vice* (1797), so she fell again, into the hands of the decadents.

In 1845 Charles Baudelaire (1821–67) announced the forthcoming publication of a new volume of poems to be titled *Les Lesbiennes*. In fact the work did not appear until 1857 and, when it did, it was actually called *Les Fleurs du Mal*. But there still remained in the collection three specifically lesbian poems, 'Femmes Damnées', 'Lesbos' and 'Femmes Damnées: Delphine et Hippolyte', of which the two last were among the six '*pièces condamnées*' that Baudelaire was directed to excise, as a result of the obscenity trial that made *Les Fleurs du Mal* one of the most notorious texts of the nineteenth century. Baudelaire's Lesbos is a strange female world, remote from any morality or judgment, where the 'victims' of an '*exces des baisers*' are also acolytes, dedicated with a holy passion to the exploration of '*des voluptués grécques*'. As in so many of de Sade's strung-out scenes, there is some confusion here as to who is doing what to whom. Sappho's body blends into the secret places of her island; she is the queen of these 'vestals' and yet she is the sacrifice who dies on the day of her 'blasphemy' – unspecified, but bodily, and suggestively sexual.

Baudelaire's most ardent English disciple was Algernon Charles Swinburne (1837–1909), who rewrote Sappho, both from the Greek and filtered through the French of Baudelaire, in several of his poems. In 'Anactoria' (1866), Sappho goes on at length, inexhaustibly delineating the tortures she will both inflict and suffer. 'The Sappho of Anactoria,' said the critic Douglas Bush in 1937, 'is not merely the descendant of Libitina and Priapus, she is the daughter of de Sade.'

The ancestral connections are also made by the poets. Both Baudelaire and Swinburne saw themselves to some extent as Sappho's heirs: Baudelaire made himself into the inheriting poet who looks out 'with his piercing eye', scrutinising the sea for Sappho's broken body, which his own work will restore; Swinburne, especially in one poem, 'On the Cliffs', made Sappho into his muse and 'sister'. And Sappho's function, as far as Swinburne is concerned, is to deal out punishment. In her *Victorian Sappho* (1999), Yopie Prins sets out a witty reading that links Swinburne's addiction to flagellation, with his academic passion for Greek metre and his bodily taste for the exhilaration of a vigorous swim in the beating waves of the sea. Writing to his friend George Powell in 1868, Swinburne looks forward to a beach holiday, 'to satiate my craving (ultra Sapphic and plusquam Sadic) lust after the sea'. For both Baudelaire and Swinburne, Sappho was the mother, '*la mère*', and in the sea, '*la mer*'.

And she was a stern mistress. In her guise as a dominatrix she also appears in George Moore's slight verse drama 'Sappho'. Here the princess Megara is in love with Hylas, a handsome young man who desires Sappho. Sappho wants to have her wicked way with Megara, so when the princess asks the poetess to grant her the favour of allowing her to pretend to be Sappho and get one night of love with the deceived Hylas, Sappho agrees. There are two conditions: first, Megara will thereafter submit to Sappho; second, Megara will kill Hylas in the morning. At the climax, outside in the dawn, Sappho sings an English translation of Baudelaire's 'Femmes Damnées' neatly done up into Sapphic stanzas.

Sadeian Sappho survived in the works of many other writers of the 'Decadence', including Paul Verlaine's *Parallèlement* (1889) and

Arthur Symons' *Lesbia and Other Poems*. She has also had many twentieth-century interpreters, some of them highly unlikely; Aldous Huxley and Philip Larkin are among those who translated one or the other of Baudelaire's 'lesbian' poems. In this strand of Sapphic invention the Fragment that receives a great deal of attention is Fragment 105A and B, 'the sweet apple' and 'the hyacinth'. The reaching after the unattainable, the trampling into the dirt, is repeated by poets as diverse as Dante Gabriel Rossetti (whose version of Fragment 105 appears in 'The Fragments of Sappho'), Emily Dickinson, Arthur Symons and Olive Custance in 'Love's Firstfruits' (included in 'Return to Mytilene').

The ideal out of reach; the real soiled – this was the underlying theme in a number of Sappho works from the mid-nineteenth century, including three with a linked genealogy that begins with a statue, goes on to a novel and ends with an opera.

In the late 1840s and early 1850s the French sculptor James Pradier produced two Sappho statues: one small, standing Sappho cast in silver; the other large, seated and in marble. Both were highly sexualised in their characteristics, and both were freely available in copies for sale. This, combined with rumours that the model was either the tragic actress Rachel or the writer Louise Colet (best known as the mistress of Gustave Flaubert) meant that these Sapphos were no better than they should be. Drawing on this tale of two Sapphos, the novelist Alphonse Daudet (1840–97) published *Sappho: Parisian Manners: A Realistic Tale* in 1884. His heroine is a prostitute who has been the model for a famous statue of Sappho created by one of her lovers, and the inspiration for a poem 'The Book of Love', composed by another. She is helpfully named 'Fanny Legrand', but is universally known as 'Sapho'. Her new lover, a young provincial called Jean Gaussin, has no idea how Fanny acquired her nickname. Then one day, after he has been living with Fanny for a year, he meets Fanny's old lover, the sculptor Caoudal, and Caoudal explains. 'Sappho' has done it all:

> Such arms, shoulders still a trifle thin – but that suited the ardent Sappho. And as a woman, a mistress! What rapture to be drawn from that fleshly form, what sparks from that flint; a key-board where never a note was wanting. The whole gamut! As La Gournerie used to say.

La Gournerie, the fictional poet, here stands in for the real-life

Alphonse de Lamartine (1790–1869), who had written 'L'Élégie antique' (1816) in imitation of Sappho's Fragment 31. Lamartine's declaration on the nature of passion became a catchphrase in Paris, repeated by many of the Decadents including Swinburne and Gabriele d'Annunzio: '*L'amour, c'est la lyre à sept cordes, et j'ai joué de toutes*' ('Love is a lyre with seven strings, and I have played them all').

Daudet's novel is set firmly in the contemporary Parisian '*monde*'. When Gaussin comprehends Fanny's shop-soiled status, he remembers the gossip columns about 'Sappho, Cora, Caro, Phryne', a list of pseudonyms that hints at the rumours about courtesans and the lesbian fashion of the 1840s and 1850s. And yet Daudet is also aware of older Sapphic fictions. When, at the end of the novel, Gaussin arranges to meet Fanny at Marseilles to set off for a new life abroad, he stays at the Hôtel du Jeune Anacharsis.

Daudet's novel was made into an opera, *Sapho*, with a libretto by Henry Cain and Arthur Bernède and music by Jules Massenet. It was premièred in November 1897 with Emma Calve in the title-role, and a convention grew up for Fanny to be played in alternate scenes as seductress and fishwife. In a bizarre footnote to this Sapphic history, Oscar Wilde, newly released from prison, saw the opera in 1897 in the company of Lord Alfred Douglas and at the invitation of Pierre Louys.

Fanny Legrand was by no means the only Sappho on stage in the nineteenth century. Francis Cowley Burnand (1836–1917) was a Cambridge classicist who specialised in burlesque dramas based on the myths of the ancient world. Thus he gave to the English stage such gems as *Dido: The Celebrated Widow* (1860), *Ixion: or, the Man at the Wheel* (1863) and *Helen: or, Taken from the Greek* (1866). His *Sappho; or, Look Before You Leap!* (1870) plays cleverly with the facts and fancies of Sappho, and reveals just how much knowledge of the legends Burnand expected from his audiences at the popular London theatres. His Sappho is another one of these older, knowing women, but she is also a transvestite: 'Sappho should be played by a gentleman, and be got up to represent a very prim middle-aged lady.' And yet not so very prim either, for, according to the play's prospectus, she 'had conceived a burning passion for Phaon, and loved him fondly, devotedly, with all the gushing ecstasy of a young girl of fifty'. Then, with the discovery of his infidelity:

A March hare was nothing to Sappho in her rabid state; and

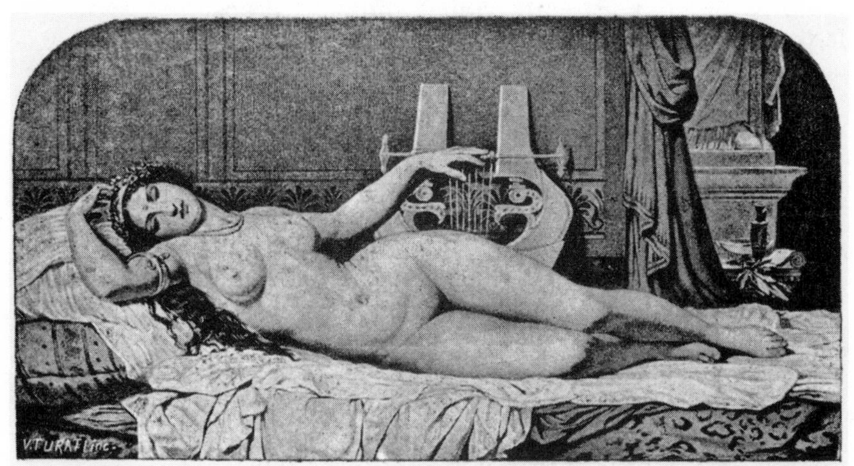
Sapho di M. BARRIAS
(da una fotografia).

'Love is a lyre with seven strings and I have played them all'; *Sapho d'Ereze* (1847) by Felix Joseph Barrias. The present whereabouts of the original are now, sadly, unknown but this photograph was published in A. Cipollini's *Saffo* (Milan, 1890).

finally, with the idea of casting herself for an entirely new part, she took the necessary steps up the Leucadian rock, for taking a sensation header into the sea. Considering her value as a poetess and musician, everybody thought that such an action was literally throwing herself away.

The Sadeian Sappho of Swinburne and Baudelaire had dwindled from *femme fatale* into pantomine dame, but, even at her most suggestive, she had never been subject to so much *double entendre*.

LESBOS

Mother of latin games and lecherous greek loves,
Lesbos, where kisses now languid, now keen,
Burning like the sun, or cooling like melon,
Ornament the night and the shining days;
Mother of latin games and lewd greek love,

Lesbos, where kisses cascade down
Thrust without fear into your fathomless deeps,
And run by turns sobbing and laughing,
Stormy and secret, seething and profound;
Lesbos, where kisses rain eternally down!

Lesbos, where Phrynes are drawn each to the other,
Where no sigh goes without its answering echo,
Where the stars admire you equally with Paphos,
And Venus with good reason is jealous of Sapho!
Lesbos, where Phrynes seduce each and the other,

Lesbos, land of warm and langorous nights,
Where before the mirror's sterile desire!
Girls with hollowed eyes and yearning flesh,
Caress the ripe fruits of their youth;
Lesbos, land of warmth and languor in the nights,

Let old Plato frown with austere eye;
You exact your pardon with an extravagance of kisses,
Queen of the secret empires, adored and noble land,
Whose refinements are ever inexhaustible,
So, let old Plato's austere eye frown on.

You extract forgiveness through eternal martyrdom,
Inflicted without remorse on ambitious hearts,
Who are drawn far from us by that radiant smile
Glimpsed vaguely on the edge of other skies!
You claim forgiveness with eternal martyrdom!

Which of the gods will dare, Lesbos, to be your judge
And condemn your pale face in travail,
If the golden balances cannot weigh the flood
Of tears that have poured into the sea in torrents?
Which of the gods dares, Lesbos, to be your judge?

What do the laws of the just and the unjest want with us?
Virgins with simple hearts, the honour of the archipelago,
Your religion like any other is august,
And love laughs at Hell and Heaven!
What do they want of us the laws of the just and the unjust?

For Lesbos from all the earth has chosen me
To sing the secrets of your virgins in flowers,
And in infancy I was admitted to the dark mystery
Of the wild laughter mingled with sobering tears;
For Lesbos has chosen me from all the earth.

And since then I watch at the summit of Leucate,
Like a sentinel with eye piercing and sure,
That lies on the watch night and day for brig or tartane or
frigate,
The moment their forms shimmer far away on the blue;
And since then I watch over the summit of Leucate

To know if the sea will be indulgent and kind,
And among the cries that the rock retains
One evening will bring back to Lesbos, who will forgive,
The adored cadaver of Sapho, which left us.
To know if the sea was goodhearted and kind!

The body of the male Sapho, lover and poet
More beautiful than Venus in her gloomy pallor!
– The eye of blue is vanquished by the dark eye that marked
The dark circle traced by sadnesses
On the body of the male Sapho, lover and poet!

– Fairer than Venus standing over the world
And pouring out the treasures of her serene view
And the radiance of her blonde youth
On the old Ocean enchanted with his daughter;
More beautiful than Venus exalting over all the world!

– Sapho, who dies on the day of her blasphemy,
When she insulted the rite and cult she'd devised,
And made her beautiful body supreme fodder
For a brute whose pride punished the impiety
Of her who, died on the day of her blasphemy.

And ever since that time Lesbos laments,
And, spite of the honours rendered by the universe,
She is high every night with the cry of torment

That pushes toward Heaven from the deserted shore!
And ever since that day Lesbos laments!

Charles Baudelaire (1857)

'"HEAVEN" – IS WHAT I CANNOT REACH!'

'Heaven' – is what I cannot reach!
The Apple on the Tree –
Provided it do hopeless – hang –
That – 'Heaven' is – to Me!

The Colour, on the Cruising Cloud –
The interdicted Land –
Behind the Hill – the House behind –
There – Paradise – is found!

Her teasing Purples – Afternoons –
The credulous – decoy –
Enamoured – of the Conjuror –
That spurned us – Yesterday!

Emily Dickinson, c. 1861, published 1896

ANACTORIA

τίνος αὖ πὺ πειθοῖ
μὰψ σαγηνεύσας φιλότατα
Sappho

My life is bitter with thy love; thine eyes
Blind me, thy tresses burn me, thy sharp sighs
Divide my flesh and spirit with soft sound,
And my blood strengthens, and my veins abound.
I pray thee sigh not, speak not, draw not breath;
Let life burn down, and dream it is not death.
I would the sea had hidden us, the fire
(Wilt thou fear that, and fear not my desire?)
Severed the bones that bleach, the flesh that cleaves,
And let our sifted ashes drop like leaves.
I feel thy blood against my blood: my pain

Famed pornographer and Sadeian Sappho; Felicien Rops's suggestive frontispiece to Stephane Mallarmé's *Les Poesies* (Paris, 1891).

Pains thee, and lips bruise lips, and vein stings vein.
Let fruit be crushed on fruit, let flower on flower,
Breast kindle breast, and either burn one hour.
Why wilt thou follow lesser loves? are thine
Too weak to bear these hands and lips of mine?
I charge thee for my life's sake, O too sweet
To crush love with thy cruel faultless feet,
I charge thee keep thy lips from hers or his,
Sweetest, till theirs be sweeter than my kiss:
Lest I too lure, a swallow for a dove,
Erotion or Erinna to my love.
I would my love could kill thee; I am satiated
With seeing thee live, and fain would have thee dead.
I would earth had thy body as fruit to eat,
And no mouth but some serpent's found thee sweet.
I would find grievous ways to have thee slain,
Intense device, and superflux of pain;
Vex thee with amorous agonies, and shake
Life at thy lips, and leave it there to ache;
Strain out thy soul with pangs too soft to kill,
Intolerable interludes, and infinite ill;
Relapse and reluctation of the breath,
Dumb tunes and shuddering semitones of death.
I am weary of all thy words and soft strange ways,
Of all love's fiery nights and all his days,
And all the broken kisses salt as brine
That shuddering lips make moist with waterish wine,
And eyes the bluer for all those hidden hours
That pleasure fills with tears and feeds from flowers,
Fierce at the heart with fire that half comes through,
But all the flowerlike white stained round with blue;
The fervent underlid, and that above
Lifted with laughter or abashed with love;
Thine amorous girdle, full of thee and fair.
And leavings of the lilies in thine hair. . . .

Algernon Charles Swinburne, from 'Anactoria', 1866

When *La Nouvelle Sapho* was reprinted for the voracious Victorian pornographic market Felicien Rops provided suitably salacious illustrations. Frontispiece to *Anandria, ou Confessions de Mademoiselle Sapho, avec la clef* (Lesbos, 1778–1866 [Paris, 1866?]), The British Library.

SAPPHO

SCENE II

The sleeping chamber of Sappho, a marble-walled room divided by an immense richly embroidered curtain hanging by large rings from an iron rod, with bread-fruit ornaments at each end; against the curtain a low couch raised upon lion's claws, upon which Megara sits half reclining, gazing upon Hylas, who lies by her side in a profound slumber. Close by her hand at the head of the couch is a small tripod on cloven feet, upon it an inlaid casket with a jewelled dagger. The floor is of multicoloured marble; on the left, nearly in the middle of the room, placed on a table of a precious wood, is a female figure holding in her extended arms a mirror of polished metal. On the right is a statue of Sappho.

MEGARA

Hath heaven aught more fair to show than this?
Sweet breast, sweet limbs, sweet hands, sweet hair.
Are they not end enough for all desire,
Though it be set with wings that darken sun

And starry throng? O Earth! most fruitful mother!
O perfect mother! Mother ever bountiful
Of gifts! What sweeter than thy lakes and streams?
What goodlier than thy sun-unfolded fields
Of sky, thy corn fields and thy sea fields hoar,
And vineyards waxing from the green to red
Fruit in their sun appointed time? What form
Diviner than these supple moulded limbs,
These passion-parted lips, so good to kiss,
This tender throat half hidden in the hair,
And these full arms entwined around me yet?
What is there holier than thy nakedness,
Implacable relentless Venus, born
Of sea-foam and the bitterer foam of blood?
Thy shrine is built upon the world's great want,
Thy worshipper is man, and thy hands fill
The measure of his pleasure and his pain,
For thou art one with life and life is one
With thee.

SAPPHO *(heard singing outside)*

'Have not high Gods longing with loathing given,
And our sleepings woven around with dreamings
And the whole world crowned with a crown of sorrow
Filling it full with . . .

MEGARA (*interrupting*)

The moon looks not upon the daytime yet,
But sits as a yellow-faced Egyptian queen
Filled with the languors of a southern love
Amid the purple starrèd draperies
That fold her throne. Then why doth Sappho come?
What need the imminent hour of messenger?

SAPPHO (*continuing*)

'Thorns of passion, weakness, and fervid willing,
Hope, the green shoot grafting of weary grieving,
Love, the sense-smit shuddering of the spirit,
Weeping and laughter . . .

MEGARA

The stars grow pale as aspen leaves, the night
Dies fast, and round her trailing garments cling
My dreams like children round a dying mother.
(*looking at him*)
God making thee just dreamt of woman, sweet,
Thou shouldst e'er lie head laid across my knees,
And dream adown the shifting agonies
Of Love's steep seasons, seeing the green flower catch
On red and pleasure wane to weariness,
In dreaming passing interludes of love
And weariness to pleasure wax again
In molten mood of passion's full-tide height.

SAPPHO (*singing again*)

'Weary are they, sorrowful are their dreamings
Whom the high Gods stricken with perfect vision
Making soul-will infinite, and the senses
Mortal and weakling.'

MEGARA

The measure of thy days is meted out,
Thy sweet young life is taken as a prey,
And strangest loves are knelt to and adored
At Lesbian shrine with thee for sacrifice.
These lips will give delight to maiden mouth
No more; thine eyes will never long
And look with lingering fancies filled of love
Again; no girl will ever pass her hands and hold
Unto her languid lips this heavy hair,
Laying her head caressingly against
This cheek. Ay, thou art verily too sweet
For death. Just here, beneath this red breast-fruit
The heart lies trembling like a fluttering bird.
Poor heart! that ne'er was mine, the dagger's point
Down-turned lies over like a hawk above
A brooding dove, thine eyes must never ope
To look on me . . . I would not see thine eyes . . .
And I will veil mine own, lest sudden fear
Death . . .
The steel's sharp point should turn aside from
Why wilt thou not look up? Could those sweet eyes

Avert thy doom! The dagger trembles, quick.
Courage . . . Poor heart of mine!

(*She kills him.*)

He shuddered once.
Yea, it is done! I can now turn my head;
He started not, no groan slipped from his lips:
Yea, he is dead; I can unveil my face,
He cannot see me now, for he is dead.

SAPPHO (*heard outside singing*)

'Through the twilight shadows of fading evening,
By the shore-strand, glimmering in the rays of
Purple sunset, purpling all the ocean
Cliffs and headlands.

'Women dream there, sorrowful women, dreaming,
Gazing sunward whispering sweetest secrets,
Hands on hands laid, shivering with the languors
Born of their passion.

'Others white-robed, sister-like, wander slowly
Through the dark woods filled with the apparitions,
Mixing fearful frothing of pleasure unto
Weeping of torments.'

George Moore, 1881

SAPPHO: PARISIAN MANNERS

. . . As soon as the young man was seated, Caoudal, pointing to him with a comical transport, exclaimed:

'Isn't he handsome, that creature there? To think that I was once his age, and curly like that. Oh! youth, youth.'

'Still on the same subject?' said Déchelette, greeting his friend's hobby with a smile.

'My dear fellow, don't joke. All that I have, that I am, medals, crosses, the Institute, the whole bag of tricks, I would give them all for that hair and sunburnt face.' Then, turning to Gaussin, with his abrupt manner:

James Pradier's marble statue, *Sapho* (1852), said to have been modelled on either the famous tragic actress Rachel, or the writer Louise Colet, mistress of Gustave Flaubert and many other well known men. It inspired the plot of Alphonse Daudet's novel *Sappho*. Musée d'Orsay, Paris.

'And Sappho, what have you done with her? One never sees her now.'

Jean opened his eyes, not understanding.

'Are you no longer with her?' And, seeing his astonishment, Caoudal added impatiently: 'Sappho, come – Fanny Legrand – Ville d'Avray.'

'Oh! that's all over long ago.'

How came he to tell this lie! From a kind of shame, of uneasiness at this name of Sappho given to his mistress; a distaste for talking about her with other men; perhaps, too, a desire to hear things that one would otherwise not have mentioned before him.

'What! Sappho! She is still on the go?' asked Déchelette carelessly, full of the intoxication of again seeing the steps of the Madeleine, the flower market, the long line of boulevards between two rows of green.

'Don't you remember her at your place last year? She looked superb in her Egyptian peasant's costume. And one morning that autumn, when I found her breakfasting at Langlois's with this pretty boy, you would have thought her a fifteen days' bride.'

'How old is she then? From the time one has known her – '

Caoudal threw up his head to calculate: 'How old? How old? Let's see, seventeen in '53, when she sat to me for my statue, it's now '73. So count for yourself.' All at once his eyes sparkled: 'Ah! if you had seen her twenty years ago, tall, slender, with arched lip, fine forehead. Such arms, shoulders still a trifle thin – but that suited the ardent Sappho. And as a woman, a mistress! What rapture to be drawn from that fleshy form, what sparks from that flint; a keyboard where never a note was wanting. The whole gamut! as La Gournerie used to say.'

Jean deadly pale, asked: 'Was he too one of her lovers?'

'La Gournerie? I should think so; I suffered enough through him. Four years we lived together as man and wife, four years I tended her, slaved to satisfy her every caprice; singing-masters, music-masters, riding-masters, masters for everything. And when I had got her well-polished, licked into shape, cut like a precious stone, emerged from the gutter out of which I had lifted her one night, in front of the Bal Ragache, that infernal botcher of rhymes came and took her from under my nose, at the hospitable table where he dined every Sunday!'

He breathed hard as if to drive away this old love sore, which vibrated still in his voice: then he resumed more calmly:

'After all, his rascality profited him nothing. Their three years of life together were like hell. This poet with the insinuating manners was mean, vicious, mad. They used to comb one another, you should have seen! When one went to see them, one found her with a bandage over her eye, he with his face scratched and clawed. But the beauty of it was when he wanted to leave her. She stuck to him like a teazle, followed him, hammered at his door, waited for him stretched on his mat. One night in the middle of winter, she waited five hours for him outside the Farcy's where the whole troop of them had gone up. A pitiful tale! But the elegiac poet remained implacable up to the day when, to get rid of her, he put the matter in the hands of the police. Ah! a nice gentleman; and as a final wind-up, a thank-offering to this beautiful girl who had given him the best of her youth, her intelligence and her flesh, he poured out on her head a volume of spiteful drivelling verses, curses, lamentations, "The Book of Love," his best work.'

Motionless, his back stiff, Gaussin listened, sipping through a long straw the iced drink before him. Some poison, surely, they had given him which froze his heart and stomach.

He shivered in spite of the glorious weather, he saw a pale vision of shadows which came and went, a water-cart standing in front of the Madeleine, and the crossing and recrossing of carriages rolling over the soft roadway, silently as if upon cotton wool. No longer a sound in Paris, nothing beyond what was being said at this table. Now Déchelette was speaking; it was he who was pouring out the poison:

'What fearful things are these ruptures!' and his quiet and scoffing voice assumed an expression of gentleness, of infinite pity. 'Two persons have lived together for years, slept together, mingled their dreams, their sweat. They have had no secrets, no possessions apart from one another. They have assumed the same habits of living, of speaking, the same features even. They are bound together hand and foot, regular glutination in fact! Then suddenly they leave one another, are torn apart. How do they do it? How have they the courage? For myself I could never do so. Yes, deceived, insulted, befouled, with ridicule and filth, if the woman wept and said to me: "Stay," I should not go. And that is the reason why, when I take one, it is always by the night. No morrow, as they used to say in old France, or else, marriage. It is decisive and fitter.'

'No morrow, no morrow – it is very fine for you to talk. There are women one cannot keep only for a night. That one for instance.'

'I did not give her a minute's grace,' said Déchelette with a placid smile which the poor lover thought revolting.

'Then that was because you were not her fancy, otherwise – She is a girl who, when she loves, sticks tight. She has domestic tastes. But then, no luck in that line. She takes up with Dejoie, the novelist; he dies. She is passed on to Ezano; he marries. Then appears on the scene handsome Flamant, the engraver, formerly a model, for she has always had a rage for talent or beauty, and you know his dreadful story.'

'What story?' asked Gaussin in a choking voice, and he set himself to draw at his straw again, whilst listening to the love-drama which was one of the sensations of Paris a few years ago.

'The engraver was poor, madly in love with this woman: and, from fear of dismissal, to keep her in luxury he forged some bank-notes. Discovered almost immediately, arrested with his mistress, he got off with ten years' imprisonment, she with six months at Saint-Lazare, her innocence having been proved.'

And Caoudal reminded Déchelette, who was present at the trial, how pretty she looked in her little prison cap, and cheeky, not snivelling, faithful to her lover to the last. And her answer to the old owl of a judge, and the kiss which she threw to Flamant over the cocked hats of the gendarmes, calling out to him in a voice which would have melted a stone, 'Keep up your spirits, deary; the happy days will come back, we shall love one another again!' All the same, it had rather sickened her of her domestic tastes, poor girl.

'Since then, launched into the gay world, she took lovers by the month, the week, and never artists. Oh! artists; she had a horror of them. I was the only one, I really believe, that she continued to see. From time to time she came and smoked a cigarette in my studio. Then months passed without my hearing of her, until the day I found her at breakfast with this pretty child, eating grapes from his lips. I said to myself, "Sappho is bitten again." '

Jean could listen to no more. He felt the steeping poison was killing him. After freezing just before, he now felt flames in his chest, mounting to his head which buzzed and seemed about to split like a metal plate at a white heat. He crossed the road, reeling under the wheels of the vehicles. Coachmen called out. The idiots! who were they shouting at?

Passing along the Madeleine market he was annoyed at the smell of heliotrope, his mistress's favourite scent. He hastened to escape it, and furious, torn by emotion, he thought aloud: 'My mistress! yes, a nice baggage, Sappho, Sappho. To think that I've lived a year with a thing like that!' He repeated the name in his fury, remembering having seen it in scurrilous prints, among other prostitutes' nick-names, in the grotesque Court Guide of fast life: Sappho, Cora, Caro, Phryne, Jeanne de Poitiers, Le Phoque.

And with the six letters of her hateful name, all this woman's life passed in disgusting review before his eyes. Caoudal's studio, the scenes with La Gournerie, the night-watches before the dirty lodgings or on the poet's door-mat. Then the handsome engraver, the forgeries, the assizes, and the little prison cap which suited her so well, and the kiss thrown to her forger – 'Keep up your spirits, deary.' Deary! the same name, the same caress she bestowed on him. What a disgrace! Ah! he would sweep away this filth. And always this smell of heliotrope which pursued him in a twilight of the same pale lilac as the tiny flower . . .

. . . And then at the bottom of his heart there reared itself an evil, an unspeakable pride, at sharing her with those great artists, at telling himself that they had found her beautiful. At his age one is never sure, never certain. One loves woman, loves Love; but perception and experience are wanting, and the young lover who shows you the portrait of his mistress seeks a look, an approbation, to reassure him. Sappho's figure seemed magnified, surrounded by a halo, since he knew her sung by La Gournerie, immortalised by Caoudal in marble and bronze.

But suddenly, seized with rage again, he left the seat on the distant boulevard where his meditation had cast him, in the midst of the cries of children, the gossiping of workmen's wives in the dusty June night; and he set off walking again, talking out loud, furiously. A pretty thing, the bronze of Sappho, the bronze of commerce, dragged about everywhere, hackneyed as the tunes on a street organ, like the word itself, Sappho, which, coming down to us through the mist of ages has had its former beauty clogged with obscene legends, and from being the name of a goddess has become that of a disease.

Alphonse Daudet, *Sappho: Parisian Manners: A Realistic Novel*, 1884, English translation 1886

Madame Rizzini as Sapho in Massenet's opera (1897), based on Daudet's novel. In the opening scene, the innocent hero, a provincial youth named Jean Gaussin, meets Fanny Legrand at a party where she sings a scurrilous song about how she got her nickname, 'Sappho'. James Gardiner Collection, Fourth Estate.

HALLUCINATION: I

One petal of a blood-red tulip pressed
Between the pages of a Baudelaire:
No more; and I was suddenly aware
Of the white fragrant apple of a breast
On which my lips were pastured; and I knew
That dreaming I remembered an old dream.
Sweeter than any fruit that fruit did seem,
Which, as my hungry teeth devoured it, grew
Ever again, and tantalised my taste.
So, vainly hungering, I seemed to see
Eve and the serpent and the apple-tree,
And Adam in the garden, and God laying waste
Innocent Eden, because man's desire,
Godlike before, now for a woman's sake
Descended through the woman to the snake.
Then as my mouth grew parched, stung as with fire
By that white fragrant apple, once so fair,
That seemed to shrink and spire into a flame,
I cried, and wakened, crying on your name:
One blood-red petal stained the Baudelaire.

Arthur Symons, 1902

'SAPPHO'; OR, LOOK BEFORE YOU LEAP!

AN ORIGINAL DRAMA, IN TWO ACTS,
FOUR SCENES, AND EIGHT TABLEAUX
Discovered in an Attic Story, and adapted to the Drawing-Room Floor

TABLEAU III

ACT I – SCENE II

[*Music School-room in* SAPPHO'S *Academy for Young Musicians.* SAPPHO *is discovered directing a class of several young ladies who, headed by* CLEOMENE, *are sitting before* SAPPHO, *each having a harp in her hand.*]

Sappho (directing their attention to a slate) Now the first note that's on this slate by me

Is known as C. D'ye see?

Young Ladies We see

Cleo (in very excellent French) Oui

An Italian Young Lady (in her own native tongue) Si

Sappho Now let's attend at once to what's before us;
I'll sing, and you, as usual, join in chorus.
The key that I will take it in is sharp E;
Your *harp* (*rapping* CLEOMENE'S *knuckles, who is looking out of the window*).

Cleo Yes, Missis; (*aside*) bother the old *harpy.*

[SAPPHO *looks up, as if inspired, and then commences.*]

'Happy Land.'

Harp in hand! harp in hand!
Music of old Greece or Rome;
In the Strand! in the Strand!
Mem'ry of my Attic home.

(*Pauses, strikes her forehead; then, as if suddenly inspired with an original idea*), –

Tra la la la la!
Tra la la la la!
Tra la la la la!
Trallalallalal – LA!

[*All pupils in raptures except* CLEOMENE, *who tries to get a peep out of window.* SAPPHO *raises her hand and harp; all pupils do the same, then altogether striking the strings of their harps.*]

CHORUS

CHARITY-SCHOOL AIR – '*This is the way we wash our hands.*'

This is the way we use our hands!
This is the way we use our hands!
This is the way we use our hands!
On a musical lesson morning.

[*They all join hands and dance round* SAPPHO, *who stands statuesquely in the centre.*]

Round and round our Gouvernante,
our Gouvernante,
our Gouvernante,
Round and round our Gouvernante,
On a musical-lesson morning.

[*They finish their dance, and all strike their attitudes and their harps at the conclusion.*]

Cleo Please, Sappho, I have come to ask you; may
Your pupils have a holiday to-day?
There is a boat-race coming off, and we
Would very much the contest like to see.

1st Young Lady Yes, on the meadows we can run,

Sappho (*serenely*) Ah, that's
Leaving the *sharps* to scamper o'er the *flats*.

Cleo And yet, 'tis *natural* that these pretty faces
Should wish to early go, and get good places.

Sappho By mixing in these crowds yourselves you lower, –

Cleo (*rapturously*) In the first *row* we'll welcome the first *rower*.

(*Shout without*)

Sappho, the match already has begun;

Sappho (*youthfully*) Then from my windows, girls, you'll see the fun.

[*All go up to back of stage and look anxiously out of the windows, which open down to the ground, and command a view of the river, or not, as the state of the drawing-room stage may require; a landscape view of the river and the opposite banks, and a few little cardboard boats, may be drawn across the scene from one side to the other, and then disappear.*]

[SAPPHO *stops* CLEOMENE, *who is kissing a letter, as she is following the other girls.*]

Sappho Ah! why so anxious? What is in that letter?
You've got a *bet* of gloves, –

Cleo Oh, no! much *better*.
'If from the *glove* you take the letter G,
'Then Glove' –

Sappho (*sharply*) 'Spells love' –

Cleo An' love's the spell for me.

Sappho Rash girl! the meaning, then, of that epistle.
Cleo For the contents of this, ma'am, you may –
(*whistle heard without*)
Sappho (*starting*) Whistle!
Cleo (*aside*) My lover's signal! now I know –
Sappho (*severely observing her*) What, miss?
Cleo (*not attending to her*)
Going by that, that he is going by this.
(*runs to window and waves her handkerchief*)
Sappho The slowest eyes her secret might discover:
She loves – and – oh, my heart! has got a lover!
While I, who care for everybody, see
With pain that nobody will care for me.
Oh! in these many lonely years, how often
I've longed for some one my hard fate to soften,
And in my lone old age, dry and unsappy,
This *wretched maid* will never be *made happy!*
Cleo (*waving her handkerchief, and crying to the rowers out of window*)
Now then you're winning! Oh, what skill he's shown
(*to girls*)
1st Y. Lady Now, Yellow!
2nd Y. Lady Red!
3rd Y. Lady Blue!
Cleo (*excitedly*) Oh, the *Blue* is *blown*.
Billitalōros in the scarlet coat
Spurts forward with *his purly* little boat.
Sappho (*listening*) Billitalōros – Ha! I understand.
Cleo (*wildly to her*)
Yes, if he wins this race, he claims my hand.
Sappho (*to herself*) And why should I say no?
I am her guardian.
Cleo (*at window*) See how he flies!
2nd Y. Lady Indeed, he's not a tardy 'un.
None of success have of a chance the ghost.
Cleo Like a stamp'd note he's going by the post;
The winning post.
(*Cheers without*)
Yes, he is drawing near. Oh (*to* SAPPHO *imploringly*)
He's *coming here – Oh!*
Sappho (*majestically*) Then the coming *Hero*
We will receive and place him by our side.

Cleo (*bashfully*) And if he asks –

Sappho Yes, you shall be his bride,

MUSIC – '*See, the Conquering Hero Comes.*'

[*The Maidens prepare to receive the Winner in line. Flourish. Tune changes to the Charity-School Chorus sung by the Maidens.*]

CHORUS

This is the way to strike our harps,
to strike our harps,
to strike our harps;
This is the way to strike our harps,
The Glorious Victor crowning!

[*Repeat as* BILLITALŌROS, *accompanied by Greek Watermen, and friends, and crowned with a wreath of flowers, enters triumphantly.*]

Sappho Welcome, thrice welcome, youthful victor, now's
The time to drop your *oar* and make your *bows*.

Francis Cowley Burnand, 1870

TEN

The New Woman

Two Pupils in Greek Dress, Thomas Eakins (c. 1883). The dress, the bare feet, the artist's palettes and the frieze over the desk, add to the subtle permissions in the poses taken up by these two 'pupils'. Metropolitan Museum of Art, New York.

In Francis Cowley Burnand's 1870 burlesque his heroine was a 'strong-minded woman' and a schoolmistress, offering to give Phaon 'private lessons'. In Harry Lobb's classical burlesque, which ends this section, Sappho sets out the terms of 'woman's mission':

what a foolish thing is a man!
Masterful in conceit, fretful under constraint, ever unwilling!
But, mark me, it is woman's mission to make him tame!
We find him like the wild steed of the mountain!
Kicking his heels in the air!
Gently – cautiously, with the sly lasso –
We make him captive – hold him fast –
Teach him to curvet and to prance –
Slip in his mouth the peremptory bit!
Saddle and bridle him with dexterous hands,
Then, laughing, mount upon his back,
And lo! he is our slave!

Sappho's trite conclusion is that it is love that makes all this possible, but the terms that Lobb and Burnand use, 'the strong-minded woman' versus the imperative of 'woman's mission', positioned even these trifles within the long-running argument that the Victorians called 'the woman question'.

This was, to put it at its simplest, a moral and social question about women's roles in public and in private, and a series of entirely practical questions about the character of women's education, women's right to financial independence and to the possession of their own property after marriage, their rights in marriage, divorce, the custody of their children and – in the end especially – women's right to vote. It was an argument that had raged since about the 1840s and went on to the end of the century. And it was not an argument that simply polarised into men versus women: some men, like the philosopher John Stuart Mill, were proponents of women's rights; some women, like the reactionary advice writer Sarah Stickney Ellis, author of *The Women of England* (1838) and any number of bestselling sequels, were against them.

The 'woman question', though primarily a social and political issue, spilled over into the literature of the period and gets discussed in works like Tennyson's *The Princess* (1846), Elizabeth Barrett Browning's *Aurora Leigh* (1857), George Meredith's *Diana of Crossways* (1885), and even feeds into novels such as Thomas Hardy's *Tess of the D'Urbervilles* (1891) and, especially, his *Jude the Obscure* (1895). And, as so often in her history, Sappho – though alien in time and place – was pressed into service for this contemporary cause, by writers such as Caroline Norton, an early campaigner for women's legal independence.

By about the 1880s, however, the whole 'woman question' had moved on to a new stage. Agitators had drawn up petitions over the Married Women's Property Act (in nineteenth-century English law, a married woman's property belonged to her husband); they had set up women-only journals and promoted the possibilities of work for middle-class women; they had begun the process of establishing schools and colleges for women. A younger generation of girls was growing up in this more radical atmosphere, with a more extensive agenda that included sexual autonomy, social freedoms, separatism and certain kinds of 'fast' behaviour: smoking, riding bicycles, cropping your hair, drinking, swearing and practising birth control. This new breed was associated by her critics with the many ills of the late nineteenth century: the Decadence, a fashionable mannishness, promiscuity or (if, unlike Queen Victoria, they had heard of such a thing) lesbianism, and feminism. She was called the 'New Woman', and Sappho was one.

As so often in Sappho's story, she was co-opted into New Womanhood because she offered a model of female achievement in the past. In November 1888 the *Pall Mall Gazette* published the results of a questionnaire sent out to a number of prominent people asking whom they considered to be the world's twelve greatest women. Olive Schreiner (1855–1920), the South African feminist and author of *The Story of an African Farm* (1883), replied with this list:

George Sand
Monica (mother of St Augustine)
Sappho
George Eliot
Emily Brontë
Joan of Arc
St Catherine of Siena
Charlotte Brontë

Elizabeth Browning
Mary Wollstonecraft
Margaret Fuller
Madame Roland.

Schreiner was very specific about the criteria for her selection: 'Many definitions of the word *great* being equally true, I have chosen one for myself which excludes those whose greatness has been the result of circumstances and not of inherent qualities.' Pictures and lists of 'great women' were popular at this time of burgeoning feminism. The Grolier Club in New York held an exhibition in 1895 of engraved portraits of 'Women Writers from Sappho to George Eliot'. Just as at the end of the eighteenth century when Greek scholarship, archaeological finds and political movements came together to make Sappho an ideal for the age, so at the end of the nineteenth century issues in sexual politics coincided with other events to make Sappho a fashionable name.

But there was a specific reason why a Sappho fashion came into being at around this time, and it was to do with the fact that she is Greek.

For centuries, but especially from the late eighteenth century on and during the rise of the great public schools in the nineteenth century, Greek and Latin were the province of the educated man. Women's weak intellect, so they were given to understand, was not capable of grappling with the mysteries of Latin declensions, or the secrets of Greek accents. Those bold women who did manage it, like Elizabeth Barrett Browning and George Eliot, complained about this exclusion in books such as *Aurora Leigh* (1857) and *Middlemarch* (1871–2). Jealously regarding the privileges reserved for her brothers, the New Woman wanted to become one of the initiates. Learning to read Greek, it seemed, was her first step. After that she would drink whisky and adopt 'aesthetic' or 'reformed' dress.

John Addington Symonds (1840–93) was an Oxford don and a Classics scholar who was not averse to explaining the niceties of Greek poetry to young ladies. He was friendly with Katharine Bradley (1846–1914) and Edith Cooper (1862–1913), who wrote together under the name of 'Michael Field'. William Cory was Classics master at Eton, and he taught Mary Coleridge (1861–1907) whose poem 'Marriage' mimics a Sapphic metre and takes on a Sapphic subject borrowed from Fragment 114. Both men were interested in, and wrote on, Sappho, and both – as it happened –

were homosexual. Symonds was in fact an early champion of homosexual rights and the author of two important pamphlets on the subject, *A Problem in Greek Ethics* (1883) and *A Problem in Modern Ethics* (1891). His poem 'Accentual Sapphics' is particularly interesting because it is, on the one hand, authentic, in that he does reproduce a Sapphic metre; at the same time it is contemporary, for its clear purpose is to return an answer to the Decadent Sapphos of Baudelaire and Swinburne, restoring Lesbos as an ideal state, where poetry, love and art can live without the soiling innuendo of nineteenth-century prudes.

It was in the second half of the nineteenth century that the idea of Sappho-as-schoolmistress started to take hold. That she was satirised and ridiculed as such in popular burlesques, like those by Burnand and Lobb, had very little to do with classical history and everything to do with the educational ambitions of contemporary Victorian women. Campaigners and reformers like Bessie Rayner Parkes and Barbara Bodichon, Miss Buss and Miss Beale, were their real targets. In a more serious vein, there were paintings of 'Sappho's School', such as Hector Le Roux's of around the 1860s (Musée de la Princerie, Verdun). Lawrence Alma-Tadema's well-known 1881 painting of 'Sappho' (Walters Art Gallery, Baltimore) shows her listening to Alcaeus singing, surrounded by her own school of girls whose names (though some of them are boys' names, as Oscar Wilde pointed out to the artist) are engraved on the seats of the marble amphitheatre. The American Estelle Lewis, who wrote under the name of 'Stella', opens her tragedy of *Sappho* in her school at Mitylene, where she is surrounded by envious and disgruntled pupils.

Catherine Amy Dawson's Sappho is altogether more independent and successful. She is a true New Woman, or even 'a girl of the period' – 'breezy, plucky, quick to enjoy, and ready to stand by her sex . . . intensely alive . . . and brimming over with hopes and aims' (Lynn Linton, 'A Chat with the Girl of the Period', *Girl's Realm* 1, December 1898). The character and upbringing of Dawson's Sappho are clearly modelled on that given to Elizabeth Barrett Browning's earlier proto-feminist heroine in *Aurora Leigh* (1857). Like Aurora, Sappho's mother dies early, so she is mainly influenced by men – in this case, her older brother Cleon – and allowed to grow up a tomboy, leading a healthy outdoor life and hearing her brother's stories of inspiring 'hero-deeds'. Published at her own expense when she was only twenty-four, Dawson's *Sappho* became so well known that she was ever afterwards called 'Mrs Sappho'. By the time her biography was published by her daughter, Marjorie Watts, in 1987 the name had become a bit of an embarrassment, and a preface had to explain that Dawson's interest in the Greek poet had nothing to do with sex or sexuality.

But for other late nineteenth-century women writers there was a very strong connection between Sappho, the classical poet, a scholarly education, and the expression of their sexuality. One such writer was Amy Levy (1861–1889), the first Jewish student at the recently founded Newnham College, Cambridge, whose intense and moving poems to other women are often quietly grounded in a matter-of-fact everyday life, while a remote classical past beckons seductively.

Amy Levy committed suicide in 1889, unable to find support and encouragement even from the 'aesthetic' set that preached freedom of living for women, whether in small things like dress and manners or large things like work opportunity and sexual equality.

The 'Michael Fields' did rather better, but perhaps only because they kept out of the eye of the world, and because they did, at least, have each other. They were Katharine Bradley and Edith Cooper, aunt and niece, who wrote poetry together under the pseudonym of 'Michael Field' and were lovers. As classicists and as poets, they were intrigued by Sappho, and their peculiar situation made her still more appealing. Learning and love came together for the Fields, and sometimes the connection was explicit and revealing, as in their poem 'An Invitation' (1893):

Come and sing, my room is south;
Come with thy sun-governed mouth,
  Thou wilt never suffer drouth,
    Long as dwelling
In my chamber of the south . . .

There's a lavender settee,
Cushioned for my love and me;
  Ah, what secrets there will be
    For love-telling,
When her head leans on my knee!

Books I have of long ago
And today; I shall not know

Some, unless thou read them, so
    Their excelling
Music needs thy voice's flow . . .

All the Latins *thou* dost prize!
Cynthia's lover by thee lies,
Note Catullus, type and size
    Least repelling
To thy weariable eyes.

And for Greek! Too sluggishly
Thou dost toil; but Sappho, see!
  And the dear Anthology
    For thy spelling.
Come, it shall be well with thee.

When Henry Thornton Wharton published his *Sappho: Memoir, Text, Selected Renderings and a Literal Translation* in 1885, the Michael Fields were among the first to make imaginative use of it. Wharton gave all the known Fragments of Sappho in Greek, in his own literal translation and in selections from other English translations. Following Wharton, the Michael Fields were inspired to create *Long Ago* (1887), a volume of verse based on Sappho's Fragments and coded with the seductions of 'An Invitation'. The title of their volume refers to Sappho's Fragment 49, 'I loved you once, Atthis, long ago . . .', and each new Field poem – for these are not translations, but interpretations – is preceded with a Greek quotation. Field, already a persona created by a partnership, makes Sappho her collaborator, just as Sappho herself, in her Fragment 1, appealed to Aphrodite to make herself her ally.

There were many other, much less authentic Sapphos abroad by the end of the nineteenth century. Robert Dalton's *Lesbia Newman* (1889) – as you might guess from her name – is very much a New Woman, whose future reforms are supposed to include the wholesale remaking of Church and state. Bret Harte's *A Sappho of Green Springs* (1891), on the other hand, is a failure, an aspiring poet who, in the end, is forced to give up her romantic dreams and her poetry, and settle for marriage to the only man who will have her. Robert Appleton's *Violet: The American Sappho* (1894) has no pretensions to art of any kind, but she is certainly fast and loose, for she begins as the mistress of at least three men and ends, in effect, as a murderess. Along similar lines, Anna C. Steele's *Lesbia: A Study* (1896, not included here) is a ninny and a flirt, interested only in her clothes and her looks, until the love of a good man and the prospect of a baby bring her to her senses.

Once again, the punitive element in these fictions of Sappho is clear. Just as her name was taken in vain by pornographers at the end of the eighteenth century in order to put aspiring women in their places, so at the end of the nineteenth century the ambitions of the New Woman were tempered by the regulations of the Old Man (and woman) who turned her into a Young Airhead or – as Burnand puts it – an Old Harpy.

Based on Alma Tadema's 1881 painting, the frontispiece to Henry Thornton Wharton's *Sappho: Memoir, Text, Selected Renderings* (London, 1885).

SAPPHO: A TRAGEDY

ACT I

SCENE I

A room in SAPPHO'S *house at Mitylene. Busts of Homer, Apollo and the Muses in niches. Lyres, harps and lutes around a table, centre. Enter* ERINNA, ATHIS, UNICA, GONGYLA, ANACTORIA, *and* NASIDICA, *right, with flowers, and take their places at the table.*

SAPPHO (*entering, left, with a branch of myrtle in her hand*)
Good morn, dear pupils, each a sweet good morn,
And many sweet thanks for these smiles of Flora,
Which put to flight unwelcome melancholy,
And shrive my heart.
Ye have been to the concerts of the birds –
Sweetest sopranos, tenors, and contraltos –
Essay to weave their melody in verse
For this day's lesson:
Bring me the soul of song in chastest garb,
And not a corpse bedecked with gaudy tinsel:
Now court the Muses with the poet's ardour,
Whilst I go forth to watch the eagle's flight.
[*She pauses at* HOMER'S *bust, at left door.*]

ATHIS
These lessons are not worth the time they kill.

UNICA
My thoughts are not obedient to my will.

GONGYLA
Before I came to Sappho's school my thoughts
Ran into poetry as naturally
As music flows from lark's mellifluent throat;
Now with a hesitating step they come,
Like curbless coursers to receive the bit.

ANACTORIA
Song never was and never can be taught.
Think'st if Alcæus had been Homer's pupil
He could create a second Iliad?
No more than I can write an Odyssey
Because I'm pupil of the Sapphic Muse.

ATHIS

If Sappho be a Muse, I am a goddess.

ANACTORIA

Tenth Muse the poets of the time have styled her.

ATHIS

Her gold, and not her genius, bought that title.
Before she wed the merchant prince of Andros
The critics could not bear the Lesbian's lyre;
It's golden strings then made such wondrous music,
All Greece got drunk on joy, and cried 'Tenth Muse!'

ANACTORIA

Alcæus always praised the Lesbian's song

ATHIS

Alcæus is a hoary doting fool,
As old men always are when they're in love.
'Tis known when Sappho wedded Cercolas
For gold – not love – Alcæus went stark mad.
Upset the tables, beat to death his servants,
Spurred on his steeds till they fell dead beneath him,
And played the devil till her husband left her,
And Pittacus, to save her reputation,
Sent him to Egypt.

ERINNA

Silence! her name is written on the stars
In letters that will live as long as they.

ATHIS

List to the champion of the Lesbian's fame!
She pleads her cause like lawyer double-fee'd.
All Mitylene swear that Sappho's mad:
What good can rumour of a woman say
Who writes more love-songs than Anacreon;
Spends half her nights in babbling with the stars,
And gives the other half to clamorous lovers?

ERINNA

I'll hear no more against our noble Sappho.
Who is as chaste as Dian – great as Homer

ATHIS

  As great as Homer!
  Of poetry she knows no more than I:
  She writes no better poetry than I;
Yet, yesterday, she cut and slashed my poem
Until beginning had it none, nor ending.

NASIDICA

So slashed she mine.

UNICA

She tore mine into pieces.

GONGYLA

She struck mine out with one dash of her pen.

ANACTORIA

A day agone I wrote an ode to Love
The which she ground to powder 'twixt her fingers.

ATHIS

She is an envious pedagogue. I hate her.

ERINNA (*rising*)

Silence, ungrateful maids! Poor half-fledged bardlings,
Whose lyres will ne'er be heard in Fame's proud temple.
Posterity will only know you as
The pupils Lesbian Sappho loved and taught.
Doth she not shelter, feed you, teach you gratis?
Toil like a slave to purge your minds of darkness,
And fill them with th' eternal night of Zeus?
Great, high-souled Sappho! envied, slandered, and
Misunderstood by those who ought to know
Thee best, and prize thee more than wealth of Crœsus,
I love thee with a reverential love
That I can only feel for one who wears
The mantle of Divinity.

SAPPHO (*rushing forward*)

Erinna, guardian angel of my fame,
I honour, love thee for thy sense of justice!

[*To her pupils.*]

My generous pupils, I will not detain you,
Retire, and bring me each an ode on slander.

[*Exeunt pupils.*]

Estelle Lewis, 1875

SAPPHO'S CHILDHOOD

Oh, happy day! when first across the hills
We went together, he in quest of game,
And I content with little running steps
To follow on his stride. He taught my hand
All hunter's craft – to bend and string the bow,
To load the feathered weapon with a death
For fleeting quarry, with ensample wise
Of self-control and patience, till I toiled
In chase of deer across the wilderness
With even step that hid its flagging strength.
So would he give endurance, courage, craft,
Such qualities as other women lose
By a close labour behind sheltering walls,
A fear of sunshine and the beat of rain,
A greater fear of liberty. At eve –
If; resting on the brooklet's brink, I marked
The blue of peeping iris or the fronds
Of maidenhair reflected in the stream,
And questioned of their growth, he would unroll
The varied book of nature, till I knew
Each songster's note and every nodding flower
Which scents the honey-laden breath of spring.
But in our graver moments, when the moon
Had risen, silver-clouded, from the brim
Of turgid waters, and the arms of night
Relaxed their darkness from a dreamer's world,
He spake of hero-deeds, as though the souls
Of heroes listened, and from feats of strength
Rose to portray the wondrous sympathy
Which woman scatters through surrounding lives,
Contrasting the protecting love of man
With that strong patience of unswerving faith
She gives with her affection. Oftentimes
He sought to take our mother for his theme,
But ever faltering, could only bid
Me ripen her image. And the dim,
Faint recollection of the mother-face
Awoke to life of memory, until
I heard her voice in sleep and Cleon's words,

Sank deeper as the visioned mother-tones
Repeated them in dreams.

Catherine Amy Dawson, *Sappho: A Verse Novel*, Book I, 1889

ACCENTUAL SAPPHICS

When like dawn our Lady of Love, the deathless,
Rose from waves that whisper around Cythera,
She with both hands gave to the race of mortals
Joy for a guerdon.

Stretching arms ambrosial, she divided
All her realm of beauty to be partaken;
This way marriage, help, and the hope of children
Born in the homestead.

Then she bent dim eyes of diviner yearning
That way o'er foam-fretted and eager ocean,
Till from darkness, yea and the earth's foundations,
Came a green island.

Ringed with uncontrollable storms that threaten
Ringed with envious shoals and a tide rebellious,
Fair it sleeps, and sirens around it alway
Sing to the sunlight.

Here the goddess set for the souls of poets
Their abiding place to be won with danger,
Where for aye, unshaken and uncorrupted,
Shines the ideal.

John Addington Symonds, 1880

TO LALLIE
(Outside the British Museum)

Up those Museum steps you came,
And straightaway all my blood was flame,
    Oh Lallie, Lallie!

The world (I had been feeling low)
In one short moment's space did grow
    A happy valley.

There was a friend, my friend, with you;
A meagre dame, in peacock blue
    Apparelled quaintly:

This poet-heart went pit-a-pat;
I bowed and smiled and raised my hat;
    You nodded – faintly.

My heart was full as full could be;
You had not got a word for me,
    Not one short greeting;

That nonchalant small nod you gave
(The tyrant's motion to the slave)
    Sole mark'd our meeting.

Is it so long? Do you forget
That first and last time that we met?
    The time was summer;

The trees were green; the sky was blue;
Our host presented me to you –
    A tardy comer.

You look'd demure, but when you spoke
You made a little, funny joke,
    Yet half pathetic.

Your gown was grey, I recollect,
I think you patronised the sect
    They call 'aesthetic'.

I brought you strawberries and cream,
I plied you long about a stream
    With duckweed laden;

We solemnly discussed the – heat.
I found you shy and very sweet,
    A rosebud maiden.

Ah me, to-day! You passed inside
To where the marble gods abide:
    Hermes, Apollo,

Sweet Aphrodite, Pan; and where,
For aye reclined, a headless fair
    Beats all fairs hollow.

And I, I went upon my way,
Well – rather sadder, let us say;
    The world looked flatter.

I had been sad enough before,
A little less, a little more,
    What *does* it matter?

Amy Levy, 1884

ATTHIS, MY DARLING

Τὸ μίλημα τόυρον

Atthis, my darling, thou did'st stray
A few feet to the rushy bed,
When a great fear and passion shook
My heart lest haply thou wert dead;
It grew so still about the brook,
As if a soul were drawn away.

Anon thy clear eyes, silver-blue,
Shone through the tamarisk-branches fine;
To pluck me iris thou had'st sprung
Through galingale and celandine;
Away, away, the flowers I flung
And thee down to my breast I drew.

My darling! Nay, our very breath
Nor light nor darkness shall divide;
Queen Dawn shall find us on one bed,
Nor must thou flutter from my side
An instant, lest I feel the dread,
Atthis, the immanence of death.

Michael Field (Katharine Bradley and Edith Cooper), 1889

Just as Michael Field's poems returned to the Greek fragments for inspiration, so the Fields included illustrations based on authentic artefacts, with a frontispiece that copies the fifth century B.C. *hydria* at Athens. Michael Field, *Long Ago* (London, 1889).

'WHY ARE WOMEN SILENT? IS IT TRUE'

Why are women silent? Is it true,
As he thinks, they are not poets just because they dare not woo?
Let them sing themselves their passions Nature resonant all through!

O Christina, by thy cry of pain,
Sappho by thy deadly sweat, I answer women can attain
The great measures of the masters only if they love in vain.

Michael Field (Katharine Bradley and Edith Cooper), 1889

MARRIAGE

No more alone sleeping, no more alone waking,
  Thy dreams divided, thy prayers in twain;
Thy merry sisters to-night forsaking,
  Never shall we see thee, maiden, again.

Never shall we see thee, thine eyes glancing,
  Flashing with laughter and wild in glee,
Under the miseltoe kissing and dancing,
  Wantonly free.

There shall come a matron walking sedately,
  Low-voiced, gentle, wise in reply.
Tell me, O tell me, can I love her greatly?
  All for her sake must the maiden die!

Mary Coleridge, 1900

A PARTY AT HOME

Set in the future (1900), Dalton's novel has as its heroine a New Woman (hence her name, Lesbia Newman), who assists in establishing a new church that recognises women's rights and promotes their active role in society.

It has not been mentioned that our heroine had matriculated at Ousebridge, and become an undergraduate of New College, the first college erected after the original one, which was called Foundation College. She enjoyed the life thoroughly, and was the leading spirit of the place in all things that savoured of its principal purpose, the eradication of the old ideas and standards of feminine vocation. Undoubtedly, before the days of Ousebridge, Girton and Newnham and other institutions had been praiseworthy moves in the right direction, but the authorities in those places had been content with the improvement in studies, and had been willing to compromise with the old regimen in other matters; whereas at Ousebridge the object was to obliterate every artificial distinction between the sexes which had been in the past, or might be in the future, used to the detriment of the female sex. And it was in aiding such a purpose that our heroine's strength lay. She was no abnormal genius; she was simply a healthily developed girl, strong physically, mentally, and spiritually; a pattern for girls in general, so soon as society shall have been led – or driven – to do women justice.

Robert S. Dalton, *Lesbia Newman*, 1889

A SAPPHO OF GREEN SPRINGS

'Come in,' said the editor.

The door of the editorial room of the 'Excelsior Magazine' began to creak painfully under the hesitating pressure of an uncertain and unfamiliar hand. This continued until with a start of irritation the editor faced directly about, throwing his leg over the arm of his chair with a certain youthful dexterity. With one hand gripping its back, the other still grasping a proof-slip, and his pencil in his mouth, he stared at the intruder.

The stranger, despite his hesitating entrance, did not seem in the least disconcerted. He was a tall man, looking even taller by reason of the long formless overcoat he wore, known as a 'duster', and by a long straight beard that depended from his chin, which he combed with two reflective fingers as he contemplated the editor. The red dust which still lay in the creases of his garment and in the curves of his soft felt hat, and left a dusty circle like a precipitated halo around his feet, proclaimed him, if not a countryman, a recent inland importation by coach. 'Busy?' he said, in a grave but pleasant voice. 'I kin wait. Don't mind *me*. Go on.'

The editor indicated a chair with his disengaged hand and plunged again into his proof-slips. The stranger surveyed the scant furniture and appointments of the office with a look of grave curiosity, and then, taking a chair, fixed an earnest, penetrating gaze on the editor's profile. The editor felt it, and, without looking up, said: –

'Well, go on.'

'But you're busy. I kin wait.'

'I shall not be less busy this morning. I can listen.'

'I want you to give me the name of a certain person who writes in your magazine.'

The editor's eye glanced at the second right-hand drawer of his desk. It did not contain the names of his contributors, but what in the traditions of his office was accepted as an equivalent, – a revolver . . . 'What do you want to know for? . . .

'. . . As we make ourselves responsible for the conduct of the magazine,' continued the young editor, with mature severity, 'we do not give up the names of our contributors. If you do not agree with their opinions – '

'But I *do*,' said the stranger, with his former composure, 'and I reckon that's why I want to know who wrote those verses called "Underbrush", signed "White Violet", in your last number. They're pow'ful pretty.'

The editor flushed slightly, and glanced instinctively around for any unexpected witness of his ludicrous mistake. The fear of ridicule was uppermost in his mind, and he was more relieved at his mistake not being overheard than at its groundlessness.

'The verses *are* pretty,' he said, recovering himself, with a critical air, 'and I am glad you like them. But even then, you know, I could not give you the lady's name without her permission. I will write to her and ask it, if you like.'

The actual fact was that the verses had been sent to him anonymously from a remote village in the Coast Range, – the address being the post office and the signature initials.

The stranger looked disturbed. 'Then she ain't about here anywhere?' he said, with a vague gesture. 'She don't belong to the office?'

The young editor beamed with tolerant superiority: 'No, I am sorry to say.'

'I should like to have got to see her and kinder asked her a few questions,' continued the stranger, with the same reflective seriousness. 'You see, it wasn't just the rhymin' o' them verses, – and they kinder sing themselves to ye, don't they? – it wasn't the chyce o' words, – and I reckon they allus hit the idee in the centre shot every time, – it wasn't the idees and moral she sort o' drew out o' what she was tellin', – but it was the straight thing itself, – the truth?'

'The truth?' repeated the editor.

'Yes, sir. I've bin there. I've seen all that she's seen in the brush – the little flicks and checkers o' light and shadder down in the brown dust that you wonder how it ever got through the dark of the woods, and that allus seems to slip away like a snake or a lizard if you grope. I've heard all that she's heard there – the creepin', the sighin', and the whisperin' through the bracken and the ground-vines of all that lives there.'

'You seem to be a poet yourself,' said the editor, with a patronising smile.

'I'm a lumberman, up in Mendocino,' returned the stranger, with sublime *naïveté*. 'Got a mill there. You see, sightin' standin' timber and selectin' from the gen'ral show of the trees in the ground and the lay of roots hez sorter made me take notice.' He paused. 'Then,' he added, somewhat despondingly, 'you don't know who she is?'

'No,' said the editor reflectively; 'not even if it is really a *woman* who writes.'

'Eh?'

'Well, you see, "White Violet" may as well be the *nom-de-plume* of a man as of a woman – especially if adopted for the purpose of mystification. The handwriting, I remember, was more boyish than feminine.'

'No,' returned the stranger doggedly, 'it wasn't no *man*. There's ideas and words there that only come from a woman; baby-talk to the birds, you know, and a kind of fearsome keer of bugs and creepin' things that don't come to a man who wears boots and trousers. Well,' he added, with a return to his previous air of resigned disappointment, 'I suppose you don't even know what she's like?'

'No,' responded the editor, cheerfully. Then, following an idea suggested by the odd mingling of sentiment and shrewd perception in the man before him, he added: 'Probably not at all like anything you imagine. She may be a mother with three or four children; or an old maid who keeps a boarding-house; or a wrinkled school-mistress; or a chit of a school-girl. I've had some fair verses from a red-haired girl of fourteen at the Seminary,' he concluded, with professional coolness.

The stranger regarded him with the *naïve* wonder of an inexperienced man. Having paid this tribute to his superior knowledge, he regained his previous air of grave perception. 'I reckon she ain't none of them. But I'm keepin' you from your work. Good-bye. My name's Bowers – Jim Bowers, of Mendocino. If you're up my way, give me a call. And if you do write to this yer "White Violet", and she's willin', send me her address.'

He shook the editor's hand warmly – even in its literal significance of imparting a good deal of his own earnest caloric to the editor's fingers – and left the room. His foot-fall echoed along the passage and died out, and with it, I fear, all impression of his visit from the editor's mind, as he plunged again into the silent task before him.

Presently he was conscious of a melodious humming and a light leisurely step at the entrance of the hall. They continued on in an easy harmony and unaffected as the passage of a bird. Both were pleasant and both familiar to the editor. They belonged to Jack Hamlin, by vocation a gambler, by taste a musician, on his way from his apartments on the upper floor, where he had just risen, to drop into his friend's editorial room and glance over the exchanges, as was his habit before breakfast.

The door opened lightly. The editor was conscious of a faint odour of scented soap, a sensation of freshness and cleanliness, the impression of a soft hand like a woman's on his shoulder and, like a woman's, momentarily and playfully caressing, the passage of a graceful shadow across his desk, and the next moment Jack Hamlin was ostentatiously dusting a chair with an open newspaper preparatory to sitting down.

'You ought to ship that office-boy of yours if he can't keep things cleaner,' he said, suspending his melody to eye grimly the dust which Mr Bowers had shaken from his departing feet.

The editor did not look up until he had finished revising a difficult paragraph. By that time Mr Hamlin had comfortably settled himself on a cane sofa, and, possibly out of deference to his surroundings, had subdued his song to a peculiarly low, soft, and heart-breaking whistle as he unfolded a newspaper. Clean and faultless in his appearance, he had the rare gift of being able to get up at two in the afternoon with much of the dewy freshness and all of the moral superiority of an early riser.

'You ought to have been here just now, Jack,' said the editor.

* * *

Intrigued by the editor's story, Jack Hamlin decides to go to Green Springs to try to find 'White Violet'. He does not manage to find her, or even to see her, but he does get close, and – most importantly, as it turns out – she sees him. 'White Violet' is Mrs Delatour, a middle-aged widow, disappointed in life and struggling to bring up her five children on a poverty-stricken farm. It was one of these children, a boy on the make, who sent her manuscripts to the magazine, and this child convinces Hamlin that the poet is his sister Cynthia, and not his mother.

Jim Bowers, on the other hand, makes the same journey and succeeds in finding out who the true author of the poems is. Then one day Bowers reappears in the editor's office, insisting that he has come to return a gift of money, sent by Jack Hamlin to 'White Violet'. Bowers begins by assuming that the gift has come from the editor . . .

'One moment, Mr Bowers,' he said, hurriedly. 'This is the most dreadful blunder of all. The gift is not mine. It was the spontaneous offering of another who really admired our friend's work, – a gentleman who – ' He stopped suddenly.

The sound of a familiar voice, lightly humming, was borne along the passage; the light tread of a familiar foot was approaching. The editor turned quickly towards the open door, – so quickly that Mr Bowers was fain to turn also.

For a charming instant the figure of Jack Hamlin, handsome, careless and confident, was framed in the door-way. His dark eyes, with their habitual scorn of his average fellow-man, swept superciliously over Mr Bowers and rested for an instant with caressing familiarity on the editor.

'Well, sonny, any news from the old girl at the Summit?'

'No-o' hastily stammered the editor, with a half-hysterical laugh. 'No, Jack. Excuse me a moment.'

'All right; busy, I see. *Hasta mañana*.'

The picture vanished, the frame was empty.

'You see,' continued the editor, turning to Mr Bowers, 'there has been a mistake. I – ' but he stopped suddenly at the ashen face of Mr Bowers, still fixed in the direction of the vanished figure.

'Are you ill?'

Mr Bowers did not reply, but slowly withdrew his eyes and turned them heavily on the editor. Then, drawing a longer, deeper breath, he picked up his soft felt hat, and, moulding it into shape in his hands as if preparing to put it on, he moistened his dry, grayish lips, and said, gently –

'Friend o' yours?'

'Yes,' said the editor – 'Jack Hamlin. Of course, you know him?'

'Yes.'

Mr Bowers here put his hat on his head, and, after a pause, turned round slowly once or twice, as if he had forgotten it and was still seeking it. Finally he succeeded in finding the editor's hand, and shook it, albeit his own trembled slightly. Then he said –

'I reckon you're right. There's bin a mistake. I see it now. Good-bye. If you're ever up my way, drop in and see me.' He then walked to the doorway, passed out, and seemed to melt into the afternoon shadows of the hall.

He never again entered the office of the 'Excelsior Magazine,' neither was any further contribution ever received from White Violet. To a polite entreaty from the editor, addressed first to 'White Violet' and then to Mrs Delatour, there was no response. The thought of Mr Hamlin's cynical prophecy disturbed him, but that gentleman, preoccupied in filling some professional engagements in Sacramento, gave him no chance to acquire further explanations as to the past or the future. The youthful editor was at first in despair and filled with a vague remorse of some unfulfilled duty. But, to his surprise, the readers of the magazine seemed to survive their talented contributor, and the feverish life that had been thrilled by her song in two months had apparently forgotten her. Nor was her voice lifted from any alien quarter; the domestic and foreign press that had echoed her lays seemed to respond no longer to her utterance.

It is possible that some readers of these pages may remember a previous chronicle by the same historian wherein it was recorded that the volatile spirit of Mr Jack Hamlin, slightly assisted by circumstances, passed beyond these voices at the Ranch of the Blessed Fisherman, some two years later. As the editor stood beside the body of his friend on the morning of the funeral, he noticed among the flowers laid upon his bier by loving hands a wreath of white violets. Touched and disturbed by a memory long since forgotten, he was further embarrassed, as the *cortège* dispersed in the Mission graveyard, by the apparition of the tall figure of Mr James Bowers from behind a monumental column. The editor turned to him quickly.

'I am glad to see you here,' he said, awkwardly, and he knew not why; then, after a pause, 'I trust you can give me some news of Mrs Delatour. I wrote to her nearly two years ago, but had no response.'

'Thar's bin no Mrs Delatour for two years,' said Mr Bowers, contemplatively stroking his beard; 'and mebbe that's why. She's bin for two years Mrs Bowers.'

'I congratulate you,' said the editor; 'but I hope there still remains a White Violet, and that, for the sake of literature, she has not given up – '

'Mrs Bowers,' interrupted Mr Bowers, with singular deliberation, 'found that makin' po'try and tendin' to the cares of a growin'-up famerly was irritatin' to the narves. They didn't jibe, so to speak. What Mrs Bowers wanted – and what, po'try or no po'try, I've bin tryin' to give her – was Rest! She's bin havin' it comfor'bly up at my ranch at Mendocino, with her children and me. Yes, sir' – his eye wandered accidentally to the new-made grave – 'you'll excuse my sayin' it to a man in your profession, but it's what most folks will find is a heap better than readin' or writin' or actin' po'try – and that's – Rest!'

Bret Harte, 1891

Lawrence Alma Tadema's entirely fanciful *Sappho* (1881). The marble benches and other 'authentic' antique paraphernalia appear in many of Alma Tadema's paintings including *A Reading from Homer*, (1885). The poet, in his view, is clearly always male: in spite of the title, Alcaeus performs here, not Sappho. Walters Art Gallery, Baltimore.

SAPPHO: A LYRIC ROMANCE

DRAMATIS PERSONAE

SAPPHO	(*The Poetess, Age 28*)
PHAON }	{ (*Age 40*) *Tenor or*
PHAON }	{ (*Age 20*) *Baritone*
APHRODITE	
VENUS	
IRENE	(*Soprano*)
DAPHNE	(*Contralto*)
ERINNA	(*A Girl Dancer*)
CHORUS	(*24 or more young girls*)

Period 600 BC *Dress – Classic Greek*

SCENE

A rocky hill, with Temple of Apollo P. overlooking the sea. On the Stage O. P. a built double row of seats, (Alma Tadema) – surrounded by rocky pines, blue sky. A lovely bright morning. Overture. Curtain rises.

(CHORUS *grouped – some are playing instruments*)

Chorus The light waves are breaking,
O'er the sands, as we, shaking,
Our locks, toilet-making –
In the sea – our bath taking –
Sisters dear – hand-in-hand –

(*Some join hands and dance*)

Let us dance on the strand,
Tripping lightly, our band,
Leave no marks on the sand –

(IRENE *comes forward*)

Irene Blow gentle gale! sweetly and tenderly o'er the green sea
Laden with sighs –
With sighs heavy-laden!
Each youth to his maiden –
There is one who is thinking of me.
And my bright eyes.

Chorus And of me – and of me – and my bright eyes!

Daphne From Thrace and Aegina – Chios and Lesbia

Come the sweet breeze –
Wrung by soft showers, from grasses and flowers,
And sweet-scented trees.
Love bringing to me.
Chorus And to me – And to me!
Irene But why so dismal – let us all be jolly!
No more sadness – away with melancholy.
(*All come forward dancing. Repeat 1st Chorus*)
Irene We're Attic and Dorian ladies
Roman Phoenician ladies,
We're Gallo-Hispano – *Angli non Angeli*
Neo-Carthaginian ladies –
We're Mediterranean ladies
Chian and Lesbian ladies
We're Alpine Cisalpine – Asian Levantine,
Greek Archipelago ladies.
Daphne Stay. A sound! Some one approaches!
(*Enter* PHAON *in boat R. lands*)
Irene Oh, it's only old Phaon, we don't
Mind him! Come along, old man,
We'll make you feel young again,
Shake up your old bones for you!
(*dance round, singing and laughing 'We're Alpine &c'*)
Poor old Phaon! Did they tease him! Did 'em have rheumatism in his back – shall we rub it for him?

Daphne Do not tease him, dear, he's a good old boy! Besides, Sappho leads him such a life.

Phaon Ah me! she does, indeed! My life I have given her – my prized youth gone in her service, and now, mid-aged, I toil and sweat in her behalf. Dear maids, this warning take by me – live for yourselves – throw not away your love – on one who values it not.

Chorus Ha! Ha! Ha!

Irene Professor Phaon with a Lecture on 'Love combined with boating as an athletic art.'

Chorus Ha! Ha! Ha!

(SAPPHO, *from Temple above, witnesses a portion of this scene – now descends*)

Sappho Maidens! the cause of these riotous proceedings – Irene – speak!

Irene Oh! Sappho! Know that it was this old man, Phaon, who interrupted us – as we sang thy ode to Aphrodite.

Phaon Great Zeus!
Sappho Silence, old man! Proceed, Irene!
Irene And, as we sang those beautiful lines – Girls, you remember –
Daphne and Chorus
What gentle youth – I would allure –
Whom in my artful toils secure,
Who does thy tender heart subdue –
Tell me, Sappho? Tell me who?
Sappho (*Beating time*) Yes, dear. Very good! Proceed!
Daphne and Chorus
Though now he shuns thy loving arms,
He soon shall court thy slighted charms,
Though now thy offerings he despise,
He soon to thee shall sacrifice!
Though now he freezes, he soon shall burn,
And be thy victim in his turn.
Sappho Thank you, dear girls! Very good – and this wretched Phaon interrupted you in this?
Irene He said – What did *you* know about love!
Phaon Oh, Irene! How glibly to thy tongue the lie doth come!
Sappho Silence! He said that, did he? You shall be sorry for this, old man! I, who am the high priestess of love – I, who have composed more odes to all-powerful Aphrodite than all other poets combined! Oh, I'll be revenged! Come, hither, culprit, you doubt my power of loving, and of writing odes to Love – See what I can do, *to hate!*

(SAPPHO *in centre with lyre.* PHAON *kneeling at her feet.* CHORUS *semicircle behind.* SAPPHO *intones through* MUSIC)

Sappho Ugly old Phaon – given up to lying,
Grey is thy hair – hideous thy features –
Ragged thy raiment – worn out thy chlamys
So is thy spirit!
Chorus Ha! ha! ha! So are thy feelings!
Sappho Come, let us hear thee, what hast thou to tell us!
Hast caught any fish? Courted fair young mermaid?
Has she thee flouted? Or flirted with another?
Speak – ere we beat thee!
Chorus Ha! ha! ha! Speak – ere we beat thee!
Phaon (*Rising in anger*) Fair young mermaid! I hate the whole lot of you!

Fair sex you're called? – More foul than fair to me!
But I'll be revenged – if I wait till I'm a hundred!
Curse you all – Harpies!
(*Exit* PHAON *in a rage*)
Chorus Ha! Ha! Ha! Calls us all harpies!
Sappho Maidens, what a lesson can be learnt from this exhibition of temper in an old man!
O what a foolish thing is a man!
Masterful in conceit, fretful under constraint, ever unwilling!
But, mark me, it is woman's mission to make him tame!
We find him like the wild steed of the mountain!
Kicking his heels in the air!
Gently – cautiously, with the sly lasso –
We make him captive – hold him fast –
Teach him to curvet and to prance –
Slip in his mouth the peremptory bit!
Saddle and bridle him with dexterous hands,
Then, laughing, mount upon his back,
And lo! he is our slave!
Ask me the spell by which this change is wrought,
I answer, it is Love!
Love rules the world, and, thanks to Love alone,
We women reign supreme! but still remember,
We are as men's proud conquerors – not their slaves,
The privilege of Love, and Loveliness!
From the wise woman passion falls away
Like sunlight from a flower, not scorching it,
But playing gently round with ambient beams!
By never yielding, never granting,
By ever tempting, never acquiescing,
She keeps her throne, the feverish heart of man!

Music by Walter Slaughter, libretto by Harry Lobb, 1886

A couch and (almost) bare breast are the only recognisable Sapphic attributes for Violet. But note the spider's web window, and the bear skin – upon which to sin? Illustration to Robert Appleton's *Violet: The American Sappho* (Boston, 1893).

VIOLET: THE AMERICAN SAPPHO

Violet Whitney is one of a 'series of pictures of the different types of men and women that go to compose "American society"'. An actress with a 'past', she is beautiful, confident and predatory. As the novel opens, she is the mistress of the wealthy Fred, whom she eventually marries, although she has also become involved with the artist Harry Latouche. Latouche paints Violet as 'The Beautiful Witch' and, later, secretes himself in her bedroom to declare his passion. At the end of the novel Fred overdoses on chloroform and Violet decides to let him conveniently die . . .

There she lay, Violet, in all her radiant beauty, looking coquettishly from under her long eyelashes, a scarce perceptible smile hovering on her exquisitely cut features, in which tenderness mingled with gayety, and helped to accentuate the purity and smoothness of her skin. A luminous background and a graceful drapery threw in relief the dazzling whiteness of her bust which seemed instinct with voluptuous life, and her attitude of lying on a divan, one of her feet carelessly hanging over its edge, contained an abandon, a grace that was ravishingly fascinating in expression. The back of her head rested on one of her hands and the other upheld, in a poise of exquisite grace, a magic wand, the end of which was shaped into a heart.

Latouche looked on, lost in admiration of the painting before him. He was almost dazed with joy, and was incredulous of the effect. He rubbed his eyes to assure himself that his sight was not deceiving him. He approached nearer, stared at it, – no, there was no doubting it! Was it possible that Violet had bewitched his senses? He looked at her closer, more scrutinisingly. She lay there, her figure almost breathing passionate tenderness; a woman whose beauty would bewitch the senses of mankind, an expression pervading her features and body which would kindle a delirium in men's breasts and heads; a woman whose love was instinct with transports of devotion and self-abnegation; a woman who had only to move the magic wand and man would know of no existence, outside her smiles and charms . . . 'Shall I move the wand?' her eyes seemed to say. Oh, no, it was impossible for this treasure to be his, – his own work, his own possession!

The tumult of joy was overcoming him; tears started to his eyes, and he sank on his knees, his heart surcharged with love, crying: –

'Oh, Violet! My own beautiful Violet!'

Robert Appleton, *Violet: The American Sappho . . . A Realistic Novel of Bohemia*, 1894

"Things are as they are."

Lori Belilove

First visit greece 1903

"Sheer excitement and tradegy of her life, have tended to dim our awareness of the originality, depth and boldness of her thought"

ELEVEN

Return to Mytilene

A drawing of Isadora Duncan by her secretary Christine Dallies (1920). The spirit of a fantasy Greece that inspired so many of Sappho's early twentieth century admirers is in this image of Isadora's dance. Christine Dallies Collection.

In January 1907 the French writer Colette and her lover, Missy, the Marquise de Belboeuf, were very nearly arrested for indecency and breach of the peace. In a mood of exuberant defiance, Colette was asserting her independence and displaying her body on the stage of the Moulin Rouge. Her (soon-to-be-ex) husband Willy, always a showman, had devised a mimed tableau for Colette and Missy called 'Rêve d'Égypte'. Colette was a beautiful Egyptian mummy dressed in a jewelled bra, see-through skirt and snake bracelets under her transparent wrappings. Missy, under her stage name of 'Yssim', which concealed nothing at all from the cognoscenti of Paris, was to play the besuited archaeologist who discovers her. As the mummy came back to life, Colette began a seductive dance, slowly peeling off her wrappings until the scholar took the mummy in 'his' arms and kissed her at the climax of the scene. At this point the audience, already whistling and cat-calling, hissed and booed, or cheered and clapped. A fracas broke out and the police were called. There was, as a result, one performance only of this version. The next night the scene was called 'Songe d'Orient', and Georges Wague played the part of the archaeologist. But, in the context of the time, Colette's pantomime hints both at the Egyptian Sappho, newly alive in Oxyrhynchus, and at a contemporary Sappho, newly awakening to the possibilities of feminine sexuality.

Henry Thornton Wharton's influential *Sappho* went into a second (1887) and third edition (1895, with a new cover designed by Aubrey Beardsley), but by then the map of Sappho scholarship was already being redrawn. 'Last spring', wrote Wharton in the Preface to his second edition, 'a telegram from the Vienna correspondent of the *Times* announced that some new verses of Sappho had been found among the Fayum papyri in the possession of the Archduke Renier'. In fact, these verses were not that new, the Fragment (now in the Egyptian Museum in Berlin) having been brought from Egypt in 1879 and edited in 1880. But the discovery of an eighth-century parchment at Medinet-el-Fayum in central Egypt inspired hopes of further finds. By the time of Wharton's third edition he was aware of the Egypt Exploration Fund, and he was still waiting: 'I would fain have enriched this edition . . . with some new words of the poetess . . . but, to the world's sorrow, that pleasure has been denied me.'

This was 1895, the very year that Bernard Grenfell and Arthur

Hunt set out on their first expedition to Egypt. Two years later they had settled at Oxyrhynchus and the papyri were beginning to pile up. They found Fragment 5, 'To the Nereids', in 1897 and nine years after that came across the remains of two ancient libraries. As they wrote to *The Times* on 14 May 1906:

> The evidence of documents found below the literary texts shows that the latter must have been thrown away in the fifth century; but the manuscripts themselves are chiefly of the second or third century . . . It is doubtful whether continuous sheets of much length can be built up out of the innumerable fragments, which range in size from some lines to a few letters. This is the more regrettable because the owner of the library was much interested in the lyric poets. His collection included two or three manuscripts apparently of Sappho.

Even before these new poems began to appear in public reports and scholarly journals, Sappho's popularity was on the increase. In 1895 Wharton had remarked on the fact: 'To enumerate the pictures that have been painted, the articles and books and plays that have been written . . . in the last ten years, would be an almost impossible task.' He pointed to the efforts of James Dryden Hosken, 'the postman poet' and author of *Phaon and Sappho* (1891); to a thesis on 'Sappho the Mitylenean' by Joachim Paulidos, a native of Lesbos (1885); to the work of Michael Field; and to a recent citation from Tennyson in 'Locksley Hall Sixty Years After' ('Hesper, whom the poet called the Bringer home of all good things', 1886). He might also have mentioned the work of the poet's brother Frederick, who published a volume of poems *The Isles of Greece* (1890); or J. Easby-Smith's translation (1891); or A. Cipollini's Italian book on Sappho and her 'curiosities' (1890; none included here); or any number of other works. On the brink of the twentieth century, just as she was being resuscitated in Egypt, Sappho was experiencing a revival in Europe.

But this revenant was coming back as a lesbian, and she was living in Paris.

The central figure in the circle that incarnated the early twentieth-century Sappho was Natalie Barney (1876–1972). She was an American, beautiful, blonde, rich, independent, clever. She settled in Paris in 1902 after she inherited half her father's fortune, and there she created a 'salon', first in Neuilly, and then at 20 Rue Jacob.

Natalie studied Greek, wrote poetry, gave parties and seduced women.

Olive Custance (1874–1944) was one of her lovers. Barney wrote to her when Olive first published *Opals* (1897) suggesting that, with her other longtime lover Renée Vivien (1877–1909) – another English girl, whose real name was Pauline Tarn – they should form a Sapphic circle. Olive replied with a poem:

For I would dance to make you smile and sing
Of those who with some sweet mad sin have played
And how Love walks with delicate feet afraid
Twixt maid and maid.

When Olive came to Paris (with chaperone) in 1901, she and Natalie set off romantically for Venice, until they both came down with malaria. Olive later married Lord Alfred Douglas, but Renée Vivien was still on the scene, just as the courtesan Liane de Pougy, had been, and the painter Romaine Brooks would be. And over it all, at least in the early days, Sappho presided.

In the garden at the Rue Jacob, Barney had a Greek-style *Temple à l'Amitié*, adorned outside with four columns and a triangular pediment, and inside with an altar, a bust of Sappho and a *chaise-longue*. It was reminiscent of the garden room where Théophile Gautier's cross-dressing Mademoiselle de Maupin almost seduced Rosette; of Marie Antoinette's Petit Trianon; of the secret Salon of the Anandrynes; but, most of all, it evoked Lesbos, transcending time and space and translated to a Parisian setting.

'So long as I live,' wrote Barney, 'the love of Beauty will be my guide.' In her home she set about creating an island – *the* women's island – in the modern city. It was to be a nostalgic re-creation of Sappho's ancient home, and a celebration of the modern woman: free, independent, sensually loving, self-sufficient. Colette (also one of Barney's lovers) was seen sliding naked through the greenery. The Temple was lit up with candles and perfumed with incense. Poetry was read, music was played. Barney, Vivien and the rest dressed up as ladies and pages, as wood nymphs and shepherds, as the Loves and the Graces. In June 1906 Barney's play *Équivoque* – a rewriting of the Sappho story – was presented in her garden, with Marguerite Moreno playing Sappho and Eva Palmer (another lover) playing the girl who leaves her for marriage.

Palmer had first introduced Barney to Greek, to Greek culture, to

Sappho and (so it appears) to sapphism. She was another American heiress, this time to the Huntley and Palmer biscuit empire – whose profits at this time were being bolstered by the Egypt Exploration Fund. Eva eventually married a Greek national (related to Isadora Duncan through her brother) and settled in Athens, to become a passionate advocate of Greece and Greek art. Barney also studied Greek more systematically with Professor Charles Brun, but to her Sappho was much more than a dead letter. When Liane de Pougy published an account of her liaison with Barney (with Natalie's active encouragement) it was called *Idylle saphique* (1901). Barney's own *Équivoque* was based on Sappho's story, as was her earlier *Cinq Petits Dialogues Grecs: (Antithèses et Parallèles) par Tryphe* (1902), detailing imagined discussions and conversations between Sappho's Lesbians. It began with a poem (in French):

Sister of Aphrodite, Lesbos, daughter of the wave
Strangely known, too disturbing and divine
To remain unexplored . . . isolated androgyne
In your perversity, knowingly infertile.

. . . . . .

Lesbos, beautiful Lesbos, with your bruised lips
Revive the beauty of your celebrated amours,
Their lost fleshliness and their outlandish glory.

For you I want to sing, lover among friends.
Listen to my song from your blue bed in the Aegean
And smile for me, Sapho, in the depth of your darkness.

The story of the complicated uses to which Barney and her circle put their image of Sappho is told in Elyse Blankley's essay 'Return to Mytilene: Renée Vivien and the City of Women' in *Women Writers and the City* (1984), and in Shari Benstock's *Women of the Left Bank, Paris 1900–1940* (1986).

One of the more curious episodes in this sapphic Sapphic history has to do with *Cinq Petits Dialogues Grecs*. Barney dedicated the volume *'à Monsieur Pierre Louys par "une jeune fille de la Société future"'*. He was one of the numerous older men whom she cultivated, asking for advice on her writings (which she rarely took).

The reference was to Louys' own dedication to his *Chansons de Bilitis* (1894), which went: 'This little book of antique love is respectfully dedicated to the young daughters of a future society.' In their time the *Chansons* had created something of a scandal, because they were frankly erotic and explicitly lesbian. And yet this famous piece of *fin-de-siècle* soft porn also drew its framework from current events in the real world of Greek scholarship. Like those of Lantier and others in this story, Louys' *Chansons* were supposed to be 'translated from the Greek' and based on a found manuscript by 'Bilitis', a contemporary of Sappho, whose 'life' he supplied at the beginning of the volume along with a hoax bibliography and scholarly notes.

For Barney, for Vivien and for other women, the search for authenticity took them back to Sappho's words and to Sappho's home. 'Let us go to Mytilene,' wrote Renée Vivien, and 're-sing to an intoxicated earth/The hymn of Lesbos'. Not content with translating Sappho (1903), not content with a temple in the garden, she took a villa on Lesbos from 1904 and travelled there with Natalie Barney, whom she saw as 'the incarnation of my Destiny', as she put it in her short prose piece of that same year, 'Sappho Enchants the Sirens'. Vivien returned to Lesbos several times over the following years, but the Sappho in her poems was a Decadent, descended from Baudelaire and Swinburne, sadistic and obsessive. So too with Vivien herself. Barney tried to bring her into the sunlight, but Natalie's faithlessness – as Vivien saw it; Barney saw it as faith-through-sexual-freedom – contributed to her melancholy. She relied more and more on drink and drugs, and by 1910 when *Dans un coin de violettes* – one of her most Sapphic collections of poems, was published – she was dead of starvation and self-abuse.

Sappho was a heroine for many other, more successfully independent young women. The American poet Sara Teasdale (1884–1933) published a collection of soliloquies supposed to be by Sappho, Beatrice and other sexually non-conforming women, in her *Helen of Troy and Other Poems* (1911). As early as 1901 the artist William Rothenstein gave a copy of Sappho's poems to Kathleen Bruce, a sculptor who came to Paris to study with Rodin (who called her '*un petit morceau grec d'un chef d'oeuvre*'). Bruce (who later married Robert Falcon Scott of the Antarctic) became very friendly with the dancer Isadora Duncan, helping her through the lonely birth of her illegitimate daughter Deirdre. They also had Greece in common, and

Duncan too travelled to Athens, tried to build herself a house there and was much influenced in her work by the (fantasised) simplicity and freedoms of ancient Greek culture. Sappho scholars too were drawn there, along with the lesbians, the poets, the dancers and the artists: the American Mary Mills Patrick paid a lengthy visit to Greece, recorded in her *Sappho and the Island of Lesbos* (1912). Radclyffe Hall (1880–1943), so far as I know, did not visit Lesbos. But Winnaretta Singer, the Princesse de Polignac (and Isadora Duncan's sister-in-law) did go there, and in July 1913 she read the manuscript account of her travels aloud to 'John' and 'Ladye', Radclyffe Hall's first serious lover, Mabel Batten. Hall's first collection of poems, *A Sheaf of Verses* (1908), had been dedicated to Mabel Batten and included the 'Ode to Sappho' that Ladye set to music. In her biography *The Trials of Radclyffe Hall* (1998), Diana Souhami tells how John and Ladye heard a performance of this song in a 1910 concert held in the Albert Hall, no less.

Sappho was also a 'sister' to other women who identified themselves as lesbian, albeit less publicly. The Australian poet Lesbia Harford (1891–1927) was one of those who made Sappho a private icon:

> Would that I were Sappho,
> Greece my land, not this!
> There the noblest women,
> When they loved, would kiss.

A little later, Sylvia Townsend Warner (1893–1978) and Valentine Ackland (1906–68), a couple who wrote both independently and together, used a reminiscence of Sappho's attributed Fragment 168B, mixed with allusions to Tennyson's 'Mariana' and 'Fatima', to make their poem 'The clock plods on – '. In England, in Australia, in Paris Sappho became a patron saint for lesbians, and that is how she appeared in a recipe for 'Spring Fevers, Love Philters and Winter Feasts' from Djuna Barnes' arcane calendar-à-clef, the *Ladies Almanack* (1928), which includes 'a peep of No-Doubting-Sappho blinked from the Stews of Secret Greek Broth, and some Rennet of Lesbos'.

At the same time as this saucy Sappho reigned in Paris and elsewhere, there were those who were much exercised in defending her honour.

If Sappho did hang out with girls, so their arguments went, then there must have been a reason for it. Critics – Wharton among them – dusted down the frowsy image of the burlesques that had made Sappho a schoolmistress and turned this into their explanation:

> Sappho seems to have been the centre of a society in Mytilene, a kind of aesthetic club, devoted to the service of the Muses. Around her gathered maidens from even comparatively distant places, attracted by her fame, to study under her guidance all that related to poetry and music; much as at a later age students resorted to the philosophers of Athens.

The most important and influential champion of the clean-up-Sappho brigade in the early twentieth century was the German scholar Ulrich von Wilamowitz-Moellendorf. He revived Friedrich Welcker's 1816 theory of her chastity to defend Sappho from accusations of homosexuality in general, and from the imputations of Pierre Louys' *Chansons de Bilitis* in particular. Wilamowitz's *Sappho und Simonides: Untersuchungen über griechische Lyriker* (1913) argued that Sappho was only interested in girls because she ran a school. When he had occasion in 1902 to explain his theory to the British composer (and lesbian) Ethel Smyth, she was not convinced: 'I dismissed this depressing view of "burning Sappho" from my mind'. All the same, as Holt Parker shows in his essay 'Sappho Schoolmistress', in *Re-Reading Sappho* (1996) edited by Ellen Greene, Wilamowitz-Moellendorf's picture has retained its place in the popular imagination, as well as finding its way into more scholarly articles and books. In Algiers J.-M.-F. Bascoul, a medical doctor and amateur scholar, published two pamphlets – one on Fragment 31 (1911) and the other on Fragment 1 (1913) – both with the overall title of *La Chaste Sappho* and designed to show that it was only the calumny of centuries that made these poems about love. They were in fact, said Bascoul, records of Sappho's passionate defence of her position as the leading poet of the day in the face of a challenge by a rival, Stesichore.

While this tussle between gentlemen-scholars and lady-lesbians was going on, Sappho was being made available to a still wider public. New translations were published, including those by Percy Osborn (1909), Henry de Vere Stacpoole (c. 1919) and J.R. Tutin (1903), as well as Bliss Carmen's in *One Hundred Lyrics* (1911).

Educated men and dedicated poets read Sappho. In 1886 Gerard Manley Hopkins sent his friend Robert Bridges some music for the Greek of Fragment 1. Bridges himself later composed an English translation of the 'Ode to Aphrodite', while the German poet Rainer Maria Rilke (1875–1926) was inspired to create his own new versions in a series of terse exchanges between Sappho and Eranna.

Then there were books about Sappho written for a general audience, as there were on the classical heritage in general. In the early twentieth century the development of the 'science' of archaeology meant that studies in the Classics were becoming less the province of the educated amateur and more the realm of career academics. But at the same time a popularising movement arose, taking the Classics out to readers who would not necessarily have studied Latin and Greek at school, with books like J.C. Stobart's companion volumes *The Glory That was Greece* (1911) and *The Grandeur That was Rome* (1912).

John A.T. Lloyd's *Sappho: Life and Work* (1910) was part of this pattern, retelling for a general readership the old stories about the actress Rachel modelling for Pradier's sculpture of Sappho; about Clesinger's polychrome statue; about the brilliance and the decadence of Sappho's island. Other similar volumes followed, including Arthur S. Way's introduction to *Sappho* (1920), which tried to reassure his readers about her morals. It was only the 'foul imaginings' of those who 'cast the filth engendered by their own souls upon the robes of Sappho' that suggested lubricious tendencies on her part. In reality, all was boarding-school innocence (again):

> Readers who know something of the passionate attachments between girls at school and college, of their adoration for each other and their teachers, will not think it strange that we find evidence in these poems of similar links of love between Sappho and some of her girl-students, that we find records of rapturous happiness, of adoring worship, of burning reproaches, passioning and thrilling through these immortal lines.

Another book for a popular audience, David M. Robinson's *Sappho and Her Influence* (1925), took a similar line. His third chapter includes a section on 'the vice idea':

> The moral purity of Sappho shines in its own light . . . [she] is

> never erotic. There is no language to be found in her songs which a pure woman might not use, and it would be practically impossible for a bad woman to subject her expressions to the marvellous niceties of rhythm, accent and meaning which Sappho everywhere exhibits. Immorality and loss of self-control never subject themselves to perfect literary and artistic taste ... Sappho's love for flowers, moreover, affords another luminous testimony. A bad woman as well as a pure woman might love roses, but a bad woman does not love the small and hidden wild flowers of the field, the dainty anthrysc and the clover, as Sappho did. There is, moreover, in a life of vice something narrowing as well as coarsening ...

Robinson's flowery Sappho found expression in a collection of musical settings from the early part of the century. This was a cycle of songs created from Wharton's edition of Sappho's Fragments by Helen von Schweitzer, and set to music by her husband Sir Granville Bantock. His 'Sappho Songs' were published in 1906, remained in the concert repertoire for some time and have recently been reissued, along with Bantock's 'Sapphic Poem' for cello and orchestra (1906), performed by Julian Lloyd Webber. The modern sleeve-notes continue the old legends: 'It is said she was short and dark and unattractive and she may well have had the role of older teacher, a sort of Aeolic Jean Brodie.'

Schoolmistress, vamp, singer, lady-lover: the early twentieth-century Sappho had plenty of 'star-quality', even if she had missed her true vocation, according to the anonymous author of a poem published in a newspaper in the early 1920s and quoted by David Robinson:

THEY LIVED TOO SOON

I fear Cleopatra was wasted
Way back in her misty old realm.
As matters befell, she did fairly well
But she'd have been great in a film.
If Dido and Sappho were with us –
They're advertised widely, you see –
And Helen of Troy – good gracious
My boy, what movie successes they'd be.

LOVE'S FIRSTFRUITS

'As the sweet-apple blushes on the end of bough, the very end of the bough, which the gatherers overlooked, nay overlooked not, but could not reach.' – SAPPHO

I bring to thee the fruitage of first love!
The flower but faintly touched with passion's pink
Pushed forth, untended, t'was a fragile thing
To fight alone with all the fears of life!
And yet it grew expanding day by day,
Each petal pure as sun-soft summer air
Pressed forward to the perfect Fane of Love
That fronted it. For Love was king and light –
The only king that fair faint blossom knew!
And so it flourished – till at last it fell
And the fruit framed in girlhood's life of leaves
Hung warm and sweet, flushed crimson from the sun
Of girlhood's Summer, so the Autumn came
And with it came a Gatherer strong and bold
Who raised a longing hand to reach it down,
That little fruit of love – but it out-soared
That long lithe arm, and so the Gatherer shook
The slender green-girt stem until at last
Loosed from its hold Love's firstfruit dropped to him.
. . . So my heart's harvest has been yielded up
A rapturous, speechless sacrifice to thee!

Olive Custance, 1897

WORDS IN THE NIGHT

We sleep with eyes closed. The silence is great around our bed. Ineffable nights of summer! But she, believing me asleep, places her warm hand on my arm. She murmurs: 'Bilitis, are you asleep?' My heart beats, but without replying I breathe as regularly as a woman wrapt in dreams. Then she begins to talk. 'Since you cannot hear me,' she says, 'oh, how I love you!' And she repeats my name: 'Bilitis . . . Bilitis . . .' And she touches me with the tips of her trembling fingers. 'It is mine, that mouth, mine alone! Is there a more beautiful one in the world? Oh my joy, my joy! Those naked arms are mine, that neck and this hair . . .'

Pierre Louys, *The Songs of Bilitis*, 1894

SAPPHO ENCHANTS THE SIRENS

The incarnation of my Destiny, She who was the first to reveal me to myself, took me by the hand. She took me by the hand and led me towards the grotto where Sappho's songs enchant the Sirens themselves.

Just as once the Goddess hid herself in the depths of Venusberg and reigned there despite the turning centuries and the changing universe, so the Musicians took refuge in a Mediterranean grotto. There the blue stalactites glittered distantly like the frozen stars. The sea whispered round the rocks, rocks whose green-algae hair was bejewelled with anemones. A wisp of foam broke over a rock wall which was more polished than marble.

'Come,' the virgin who was the incarnation of my Destiny said to

Natalie Barney as a troubadour Sappho, with lute and pageboy Cupid, flower wreath and book, and all accessories at the ready for performing poetry. Photo by Meryle Beveridge.

me. 'But remember that those who enter this grotto may never return again among the mob of those who live.'

'Like these women here, you will be eternally under the spell of the Past. For you, the waves will muffle the distant bawling of the multitude. The bluish-grey of evening will cause you to scorn the broad light of day. You will become estranged from the race of men. Their joys will be strange to you; you will be indifferent to their rebukes. You will remain apart till the end of your earthly existence. You will become more dead than the gleaming phantoms which surround you and who guard the uncertain survival of the Illustrious Ones. Sappho will extend to you the flower of her graces.'

'Eranna will tell you of Agartharchis and Myro. Nossis will braid her mauve irises for you. Telesilla will sing the praises of valiant heroines for you. In her pastoral strophes, Anyta will evoke for you the coolness of the fountains and the shadows of orchards. Moiro will disturb you with her enigmatic Byzantine expression. The Past, more alive than the Present, and more resonant, will catch you in its silvery nets. You will be held captive by dreams and by long-vanished harmonies. But you will inhale the violets of Sappho and the crocuses of Eranna of Telos. You will observe the white peplos worn by the virgins who bend to gather the shellfish which are as delicately mysterious as half-glimpsed genitals. At times, while seated on a rock, they hear the sea-soul of the conches. Towards evening, the Kitharedes will sing for them the songs of their native lands. Come!'

And I heard a harmonious sound like the whispering of the breeze at sunset across the pines of evening . . .

My singular companion took me by the hand, and I followed her into the grotto where Psappha enchants the Sirens.

Renée Vivien, *The Woman of the Wolf, and Other Stories*, 1904,
trans. Karla Jay and Yvonne M. Klein, 1983

ODE TO SAPPHO

If not from Phaon I must hope for ease,
Ah! let me seek it from the raging seas:
To raging seas unpitied I'll remove;
And either cease to live or cease to love.
Ovid's *Heroic Epistle*, XV

Immortal Lesbian! canst thou still behold
  From some far sphere wherein thy soul doth sing
This earth, that once was thine, while glimmered gold
  The joyous beams of youth's forgotten spring?

Can thine unfathomed eyes embrace this sea,
  Whose ebb and flow once echoed in thy brain?
Whose tides bear record of thine ecstasy
  And thy despair, that in its arms hath lain?

Those love-burnt lips! Can death have quenched their fire?
  Whose words oft stir our senses to unrest?
Whose eager ardour caught and held desire,
  A searing flame against thy living breast?

Passion-wan Lesbian, in that awful place
  Where spirits wander lost without a name
Thou still art Sappho, and thine ardent face
  Lights up the gloom with love's enduring flame.

Oh! Goddess, woman, lover, all divine
  And yet divinely mortal, where thou art
Comes not as cadence from some song of thine
  Each throbbing beat that stirs the human heart?

Canst thou forget us who are still thy friends,
  Thy lovers, o'er the cloudy gulf of years?
Who live, and love, and dying make amends
  For life's short pleasures thro' death's endless fears?

Once thou didst seek the solace of thy kind,
  The madness of a kiss was more to thee
Than Heaven or Hell, the greatness of thy mind
  Could not conceive more potent ecstasy!

Life was thy slave, and gave thee of her store
  Rich gifts and many, yet with all the pain
Of hopeless longing made thy spirit sore,
  E'en *thou* didst yearn, and couldest not attain.

Oh! Sappho, sister, by that agony
  Of soul and body hast thou gained a place

Within each age that shines majestic'ly
  Across the world from out the dusk of space.

Not thy deep pleasures, nor thy swiftest joys,
  Have made thee thus, immortal and yet dear
To mortal hearts, but that which naught destroys,
  The sacred image of thy falling tear.

Beloved Lesbian! we would dare to claim
  By that same fear fond union with thy lot;
Yet 'tis enough, if when we breathe thy name
  Thy soul but listens, and forgets us not.

Radclyffe Hall, 1908

'I CAN'T FEEL THE SUNSHINE'

I can't feel the sunshine
Or see the stars aright
For thinking of her beauty
And her kisses bright.

She would let me kiss her
Once and not again.
Deeming soul essential,
Sense doth she disdain.

If I should once kiss her,
I would never rest
Till I had lain hour long
Pillowed on her breast.

Lying so, I'd tell her
Many a secret thing
God has whispered to me
When my soul took wing.

Would that I were Sappho,
Greece my land, not this!

There the noblest women,
When they loved, would kiss.

Lesbia Harford, 1915, published 1985

'THE CLOCK PLODS ON – '

The clock plods on –
'She comes not, she comes not – '
(A stutter between words)
'She c-comes not – '
Under the hill the wind lurks for weather,
I sit alone.
The gulls driven inshore fly over and thither,
Hide they and hide I.
The clock plods onwards,
'She comes not, c-comes not – '
But now I am glad.
If I heard her step I should go like the birds,
Inshore and away –
At night and when storm-clouds are high
It is no time for play.
I know I am glad that she comes not –
If she came, and love's storm should arise –
What then –
With the gale outside, and within
A fiercer wind blowing?
If she came with the storm in her eyes
There's no knowing.

Sylvia Townsend Warner and Valentine Ackland, 1934

SAPPHO AND THE GODDESS

A very beautiful young Jewess, driven by poverty, was compelled to become an artists' model. She arrived one morning at the studio of Pradier some little time before the famous sculptor. Sitting down in front of the fire to wait for him she abandoned herself to morose thoughts as she reviewed her pitiful destiny. Her head sank upon her breast, as though weighed down by the sorrow of memory; her hair fell loose in rich, heavy waves. Unconsciously she stretched her arms out in a gesture of appeal and her hands met convulsively between her knees. Her cloak had fallen away from her lovely shoulders and hung in deep folds from her arms, exactly as the drapery enfolds the great Greek statues. Pradier found her in this unstudied attitude and signed to her not to move, and there and then he commenced to sketch her. This sketch, when the necessary dress and other details had been added to it, became 'Sappho pensive on the Leucadian Rock'. The graceful statue interpreted the sorrow and mystery, the fantasy of legend, the passion and the despair of that extraordinary poetess who was called by Plato the Tenth Muse. It is the poetess musing on the despair of life in the instant of death. It is the lover flying from love towards the terrible unknown. It is the consummation of a legend which for more than two thousand years has haunted mankind.

In bust, on coin and medal, on canvas and in frescoes, the figure of Sappho challenges us with its appealing beauty. Clesinger, too, carved her in marble and expressed his own appreciation of that fatality of beauty and genius which Pradier caught so suddenly in that unstudied pose of his Jewish model. 'Clesinger,' says Perrier, 'has caressed with a poet's love the voluptuous hips and gleaming torso of the Lesbian who feels that death is nigh.' Who was she? What was her enigmatic secret? What is the spell which, through a few disjointed fragments of poetry, she has been able to cast upon posterity? . . .

. . . The atmosphere of Lesbos at the time of the development of lyric poetry was essentially charged with the electricity of passion. The Æolians of Lesbos lived out their brief artistic life with fierce intensity. For a little while they were, as lyric poets, supreme in Greek literature but their very brilliance had in it the seeds of decadence. The Ionians expressed their energies in a hundred different directions, but the Æolians excelled only in the interpretation of personal emotion . . .

. . . But before this period of decadence the Lesbian ladies applied themselves with intense energy to literature, to poetry and to music. Clubs were formed in which everything that appealed to their artistic sensibilities was studied eagerly.

John A.T. Lloyd, *Sappho: Life and Work*, 1910

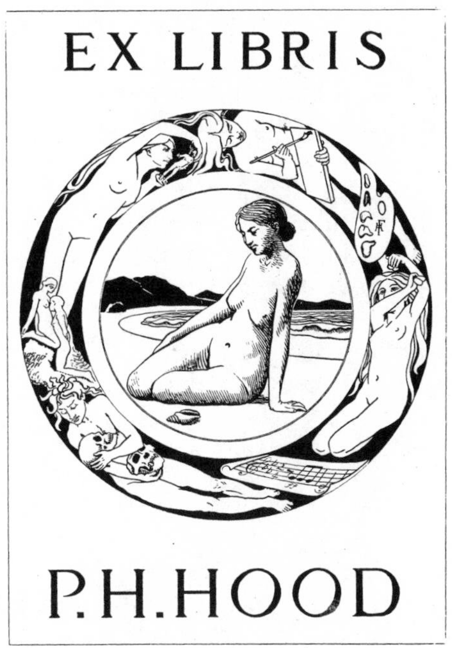

A bookplate, designed by Emery Walker, conjures up a modern Sappho, artistically active and sexually explicit. (c. 1920's)

TO CLEÏS

(The daughter of Sappho)

When the dusk was wet with dew,
  Cleïs, did the muses nine
  Listen in a silent line
While your mother sang to you?

Did they weep or did they smile
  When she crooned to still your cries,
  She, a muse in human guise,
Who forsook her lyre awhile?

Did you feel her wild heart beat?
  Did the warmth of all the sun
  Through your little body run
When she kissed your hands and feet?

Did your fingers, babywise,
  Touch her face and touch her hair,
  Did you think your mother fair,
Could you bear her burning eyes?

Are the songs that soothed your fears
  Vanished like a vanished flame,
  Save the line where shines your name
Starlike down the greying years? . . .

Cleïs speaks no word to me,
  For the land where she has gone
  Lies as still at dusk and dawn
As a windless, tideless sea.

Sara Teasdale, 1911

SAPPHO TO ERANNA

I want to flood you with unrest,
want to brandish you, you vine-clasped staff.
Like dying I want to pierce through you
and pass you on like the grave
to the All: to all these waiting things.

Rainer Maria Rilke, 1907, trans. Edward Snow, 1984

TWELVE

Modernist Sappho

Symbolist Sappho, where hat, fan and flower replace lyre and laurel wreath. Illustration by Sylvain Sauvage to a translation by Mario Meunier, *Poésies de Sappho, suivies des Odes d'Anacreon et de Anacreontiques* (Paris, 1941).

When the English novelist and poet Thomas Hardy bought Wharton's edition of *Sappho* in 1895 he wrote to a friend, '. . . a delightful book. How I love her – how many men have loved her! – more than they have Christ I fear!'

One of the younger people who read Wharton and who loved Sappho was Ezra Pound (1885–1972). He was born in Idaho, the son of Quaker parents. He had piercing green eyes, a brilliant shock of red-gold hair, formidable physical energy and an eagerness for life and learning that made him shout snatches of poems in the street by day and read voraciously by night. When he was only sixteen, and studying at Hamilton College in Pennsylvania, he went to a Hallowe'en party wearing a bright-green robe to set off his hair and there met a girl, a year younger, who was his match, though they never married.

Hilda Doolittle (1886–1961) was the daughter of an academic father and a mother whose family was part of the Moravian brotherhood. Though Hilda's parents were of a liberal turn of mind, they were not at all sure about Pound – or about any of the other boys who frequented the house, drawn there because Hilda was exceptionally beautiful. The poet William Carlos Williams was one of them:

> In early spring there was frequently a crowd of young bucks led by Ezra of a Saturday afternoon or a Sunday for a walk across the beautiful countryside, rolling grassy hills crowded with violets, I remember especially the grape hyacinths that were to be found everywhere. Hilda was always at the head of the procession – I don't remember any other girls . . .

As passionate as Pound, as physically commanding and as impulsively romantic, Hilda would sit down in the middle of field, raise her arms to the thunderstorm and cry, 'Come, beautiful rain.' Pound set himself to educate her, so she read William Morris and Balzac, William Blake, Ibsen and Bernard Shaw, Whistler and Swedenborg, and the legends of King Arthur. And Sappho.

In 1905 Hilda and Ezra became engaged, but Hilda's parents were anxious, and three years later Pound set out for Europe with nothing settled about their marriage. There he set about establishing a name for himself as a poet and prominent intellectual. In 1911 Hilda followed, travelling with her friend (and lover) Frances Gregg, but settling in London by herself. There she learned that Ezra was engaged to an English girl, Dorothy Shakespear. 'I felt bleak, a chasm opened,' she wrote. But there was no going back, and Hilda stayed.

Then into this young and ambitious circle came one still younger, Richard Aldington (1892–1962). Pound introduced Hilda to the nineteen-year-old poet, and soon all three were sharing books, poems and cakes in London's teashops. Aldington also read Greek, and in the pages of the *Classical Review* he had seen a series of articles by John Maxwell Edmonds about the new Fragments of Sappho being brought to light in Berlin and unearthed in Egypt. Working from these articles, Aldington composed a poem out of Fragment 96, which he titled 'To Atthis (After the Manuscript of Sappho now in Berlin)'. This he showed to Pound, who tried to get it published in Harriet Monroe's new magazine *Poetry*. She refused it on the grounds that the head of the Greek department at the University of Chicago was suspicious about its authenticity and 'wouldn't stand for it'.

By now both Pound and Doolittle were also hooked on Sappho's shards. Aldington was too young to get a ticket for the British Museum Reading Room, so Hilda would sit in the library copying out scholarly articles and references from the *Classical Review*, and all three (and others) would meet in the refreshment room to divide up the results along with the buttered toast and cream puffs. One day in the tearoom Hilda fetched out a typewritten sheet – not library notes, but two poems with Greek themes and a Sapphic style, 'Priapus' and 'Hermes of the Ways'. Pound took Hilda's typescript, 'slashed' it (as Hilda said) – 'Cut this out, shorten this line' – and at the bottom 'scratched' (Hilda again) 'H.D. Imagiste'. It was the birth of a poet and a movement. 'Ezra,' wrote Aldington, 'was so much worked up by these poems of H.D.'s that he removed his *pince-nez* and informed us that we were Imagists.'

The principles of 'Imagism' come close to what Pound and H.D. had made of Sappho's speaking spaces. When Pound produced the first issue of *Des Imagistes: An Anthology* in 1914 he included Aldington's 'To Atthis', and in 1916 he set out the ground-rules:

a. concision, or style, or saying what you mean in the fewest and clearest words.
b. the actual necessity for creating or constructing something; of

> presenting an image, or enough images of concrete things arranged to stir the reader.

These were the concepts realised in Pound's collection *Lustra* published in 1916. Seeing how Sappho's silences spoke volumes, Pound stripped down to the essentials. One of the poems in *Lustra* was 'Papyrus',

> Spring . . .
> Too long . . .
> Gongula . . .

It should have been preceded by the poem 'Ιμερρω', which drew on Sappho, and Aldington's version of Sappho, but Pound's publisher and printer objected that the poem was too sexually explicit. After 'Papyrus' came ' "Ione, Dead the Long Year" ', which is pure Sappho, and 'Shop Girl', which transposes her to the modern age as Pound recognises his predecessors in the Sapphic mode, Baudelaire and Swinburne. Other poems in *Lustra*, like 'To Καλαν', and 'Ladies' or 'Alba' and the well-known 'In a Station of the Metro', also acknowledge Pound's debt. In his later work his sources became ever more eclectic and diverse, but Sappho references came and went, appearing in Pound's *Canto 5* (1920) and *Pisan Cantos* (1948) for instance.

Sappho also continued to figure in the work of Richard Aldington and, most especially, in the work of H.D. After a trip when they travelled, together with Pound, to Paris and Venice, H.D. and Aldington married in 1913 in a fit of 'sudden mutual attraction' – which is suspicious, under the circumstances. When he went into the army, H.D. had to take over many of his literary and editorial commitments, including assisting with the 'Poet's Translation Series', published in association with *The Egoist* magazine, which produced *The Poems of Anyte of Tegea and Poems and Fragments of Sappho* (1919), with Anyte translated by Aldington and Sappho translated by Edward Storer.

At the same time H.D. worked on her own poems. She published 'Sea Rose', 'Sea Lily' and 'Sea Iris' in *Some Imagist Poems* (1915), while many others that were Sapphic in style, theme or content appeared in her collections *Sea Garden* (1916), *Hymen* (1921) and *Heliodora* (1924). Her poem 'Fragment Forty' was one of a group that specifically invoked Sappho by quoting her from Wharton's edition, using his numbering. (Wharton's Fragment 40 is Fragment 130, 'Love once again . . . limb loosening . . . bitter sweet', in modern editions and in this anthology.) H.D. also kept up her Sappho scholarship, reviewing Edwin Marion Cox's new edition of *The Poems of Sappho* (1925) and writing a prose meditation 'The Wise Sappho' during the 1920s.

Meanwhile the world and the war had intruded. In 1915 H.D. gave birth to a stillborn child when, according to her own account, Aldington in a brutal and jingoistic mood told her about the sinking of the *Lusitania*. The hasty marriage was soon over. After a chaotic period – an affair with D. H. Lawrence, then with the composer Cecil Gray – H.D. became pregnant again. A woman now appeared to take care of her. This was Winifred Ellerman, or 'Bryher', who stood to inherit a fortune from her father's shipbuilding industry and who had fallen in love with H.D. In 1920 Bryher took H.D. and her daughter Perdita to Greece – possibly even to Lesbos on that trip or later – and the two women remained more or less constant companions (with other affairs and interludes) for the rest of their lives. It is often supposed that H.D.'s allegiance to Sappho grew out of her gratitude to Bryher, but Sappho had long been in her life and would continue in her work.

And Aldington? It was he who produced one of the strangest Sappho-oriented volumes to come out of this triangle. While he was in the trenches, waiting in lorry convoys or confined to barracks, Aldington wrote. On the one hand he wrote angry, ugly, colloquial poems about war – some militaristic, others protesting against the pain and the stench and the waste. On the other hand he wrote poems about girls, specifically about lesbians. *The Love of Myrrhine and Konallis* was published in 1926 and tells, in flowery but explicit detail, of how Konallis the goat-girl was loved by Myrrhine the *hetaira* ('courtesan'), who taught her 'strange/ burning caresses':

> Hierocleia, weave white-violet crowns
>   and spread mountain-haunting lilies
>   upon my couch,
> For Konallis comes! And shut the door
>   against the young men for this is a
>   sharper love.

Aldington's Sapphic sequence was a private escapist strategy, but he shared his Sapphic model with other poets and other Imagists. The

American poet Amy Lowell (1874–1925), though older than the others, had been inspired by her readings of H.D.'s work published in *Poetry*. Pound included one of Lowell's poems in *Des Imagistes: An Anthology* and after he broke with the movement Lowell edited the three annual anthologies for 1915–17. Sappho allusions figured in much of her work, especially in the volume *Pictures of the Floating World* (1919), where Fragment 2 is suggested in 'A Shower' and where Fragment 168B underlies 'The Letter':

> I am tired, Beloved, of chafing my heart against
> The want of you;
> Of squeezing it into little inkdrops,
> And posting it.
> And I scald alone, here, under the fire
> Of the great moon.

Sappho also appears, along with others, as a model for the woman poet in Lowell's 'The Sisters' from *What's O'Clock* (1925):

> Taking us by and large, we're a queer lot
> We women who write poetry. And when you think
> How few of us there've been, it's queerer still . . .
> There's Sapho, now I wonder what was Sapho.
> I know a single slender thing about her:
> That, loving, she was like a burning birch-tree
> All tall and glittering fire, and that she wrote
> Like the same fire caught up to Heaven and held there,
> A frozen blaze before it broke and fell . . .
> And she is Sapho – Sapho – not Miss or Mrs,
> A leaping fire we call so for convenience . . .

Edna St Vincent Millay (1892–1950) was another American poet who exploited Sappho's possibilities. Her 'Evening on Lesbos' is teasingly suggestive and distinctively understated, translating Sappho's girls to the 1920s and turning them into flappers who drink cocktails and crop their hair. By contrast, in another poem, 'Sappho Crosses the Dark River into Hades', her poet is heterosexual and hoping for a respite from her desire for Phaon: 'A peace whereon may not encroach/ That supple back, that strong brown arm,/ That curving mouth, the sunburned curls . . .'

It is an unusual return to the older legends, for with the newly

discovered Fragments in Egypt, with the increased professionalism of Greek scholarship and perhaps, above all, with new ideas about sex and sexology, Phaon had almost completely disappeared, and Sappho's girls had taken over.

Which is what they do in Virginia Woolf's satirical short story 'A Society', published in 1921 in *Monday or Tuesday*. Here it is not Atthis and Erinna and Gorgo, but Cassandra (the narrator), Jane and Poll (who 'has always been queer'), Clorinda and Fanny, Rose, Helen, Sue, Moll, Judith, Jill, Eleanor, Ruth and Liz. Virginia Woolf (1882–1941), in spite of her self-deprecating essay 'On not knowing Greek', was knowledgeable about the Classics and well up on her Sappho, both academic and popular. When Eleanor quotes a review from a weekly newspaper, ' "Since Sappho there has been no female of first rate – " ', Woolf is citing her own public arguments with Desmond MacCarthy, who said exactly this in his journalistic persona 'Affable Hawk'. When Castalia, in pursuit of the Society's stated aim to prove the great worth of men and their works, goes to Cambridge to observe the scholars, she comes across Professor Hobkin, whose life work is to prove that Sappho was chaste – a skit on the real endeavours of classicists like Welcker, Wilamowitz-Moellendorf and Bascoul. And the conclusion to the story plays with Pierre Louys' dedication to the *Chansons de Bilitis*, as Castalia's little girl Ann bursts into tears upon being told that she has been chosen to be 'President of the Society of the future'. Woolf knew her Sappho, and could play with all her legends, all her many shapes, leaving hints and spaces to speak louder than words.

With Woolf, H.D. and Pound, Sappho moved into the twentieth century. She became a Modernist, parading modern anxieties, inhabiting urban isolation, and the tatters of her work were pieced seamlessly even into that classic of Modernism, T.S. Eliot's *The Waste Land* (1922), where her Fragment 104 'on the evening star' turns into 'the violet hour, the evening hour that strives/ Homeward, and brings the sailor home from sea,/ The typist home at teatime . . .'

Ιμέρρω

Thy soul
Grown delicate with satieties,
Atthis.

O Atthis,
I long for thy lips.
I long for thy narrow breasts,
Thou restless, ungathered.

Ezra Pound, 1915

SHOP GIRL

For a moment she rested against me
Like a swallow half blown to the wall,
And they talk of Swinburne's women,
And the shepherdess meeting with Guido.
And the harlots of Baudelaire.

Ezra Pound, 1915

FRAGMENT FORTY

Love . . . bitter-sweet.
SAPPHO

Keep love and he wings
with his bow,
up, mocking us,
keep love and he taunts us
and escapes.

Keep love and he sways apart
in another world,
outdistancing us.

Keep love and he mocks,
ah, bitter and sweet,
your sweetness is more cruel
than your hurt.

Honey and salt,
fire burst from the rocks
to meet fire
spilt from Hesperus.

Fire darted aloft and met fire:
in that moment
love entered us.

Could Eros be kept?
he were prisoned long since
and sick with imprisonment;
could Eros be kept?
others would have broken
and crushed out his life.

Could Eros be kept?
we too sinning, by Kypris,
might have prisoned him outright.

Could Eros be kept?
nay, thank him and the bright goddess
that he left us.

Ah, love is bitter and sweet,
but which is more sweet,
the sweetness
or the bitterness?
none has spoken it.

Love is bitter,
but can salt taint sea-flowers,
grief, happiness?

Is it bitter to give back
love to your lover
if he crave it?

Is it bitter to give back
love to your lover
if he wish it

for a new favourite?
who can say,
or is it sweet?

Is it sweet
to possess utterly?
or is it bitter,
bitter as ash?

I had thought myself frail;
a petal,
with light equal
on leaf and under-leaf.

I had thought myself frail;
a lamp,
shell, ivory or crust of pearl,
about to fall shattered,
with flame spent.

I cried:
'I must perish,
I am deserted,
an outcast, desperate
in this darkness,'
(such fire rent me with Hesperus,)
then the day broke.

What need of a lamp
when day lightens us,
what need to bind love
when love stands
with such radiant wings
over us?

What need –
yet to sing love,
love must first shatter us.

H.D., 1924

Cocktail glass in hand, this thoroughly modern greek girl is both vestal and vamp. Endpaper design by Frank Mechau for Richard Aldington's *The Love of Myrrhine and Konallis* (Chicago, 1926).

THE SINGER

Sappho, Sappho, long ago the dust of
  earth mingled with the dust of your
  dear limbs,
And only little clay figures, painted
  with Tyrian red, with crocus, and
  with Lydian gold,
Remain to show your beauty; but your
  wild lovely songs shall last forever.
Soon we shall join Anaktoria and Kudno
  and kiss your pale shadowy fingers.

Richard Aldington, 1926

A SHOWER

That sputter of rain, flipping the hedgerows
And making the highways hiss,
How I love it!
And the touch of you upon my arm
As you press against me that my umbrella
May cover you.
Tinkle of drops on stretched silk.
Wet murmur through green branches.

Amy Lowell, 1919

EVENING ON LESBOS

Twice having seen your shingled heads adorable
Side by side, the onyx and the gold,
I know that I have had what I could not hold.

Twice have I entered the room, not knowing she was here.
Two agate eyes, two eyes of malachite,
Twice have been turned upon me, hard and bright.

Whereby I know my loss.
Oh, not restorable
Sweet incense, mounting in the windless night!

Edna St Vincent Millay, 1928

A SOCIETY

This is how it all came about. Six or seven of us were sitting one day after tea. Some were gazing across the street into the windows of a milliners shop where the light still shone brightly upon scarlet feathers and golden slippers. Others were idly occupied in building little towers of sugar upon the edge of the tea tray. After a time, so far as I can remember, we drew round the fire and began as usual to praise men – how strong, how noble, how brilliant, how courageous how beautiful they were – how we envied those who by hook or by crook managed to get attached to one for life – when Poll, who had said nothing, burst into tears. Poll, I must tell you, has always been queer. For one thing her father was a strange man. He left her a fortune in his will, but on condition that she read all the books in the London Library. We comforted her as best we could; but we knew in our hearts how vain it was. For though we like her, Poll is no beauty; leaves her shoe laces untied; and must have been thinking, while we praised men, that not one of them would ever wish to marry her. At last she dried her tears. For some time we could make nothing of what she said. Strange enough it was in all conscience. She told us that, as we knew, she spent most of her time in the London Library, reading. She had begun, she said, with English literature on the top floor; and was steadily working her way down to the *Times* on the bottom. And now half, or perhaps only a quarter, way through a terrible thing had happened. She could read no more. Books were not what we thought them. 'Books' she cried, rising to her feet and speaking with an intensity of desolation which I shall never forget, 'are for the most part unutterably bad!'

Of course we cried out that Shakespeare wrote books, and Milton and Shelley.

'Oh yes,' she interrupted us. 'You've been well taught, I can see. But you are not members of the London Library.' Here her sobs broke forth anew. At length, recovering a little, she opened one of the pile of books which she always carried about with her – 'From a Window' or 'In a Garden' or some such name as that it was called, and it was written by a man called Benton or Henson or something

Three women and three books. Woodcut illustration by Vanessa Bell for Virginia Woolf's short story 'A Society'; *Monday or Tuesday* (London, 1921).

of that kind. She read the first few pages. We listened in silence. 'But that's not a book,' someone said. So she chose another. This time it was a history, but I have forgotten the writer's name. Our trepidation increased as she went on. Not a word of it seemed to be true, and the style in which it was written was execrable.

'Poetry! Poetry!' we cried, impatiently. 'Read us poetry!' I cannot describe the desolation which fell upon us as she opened a little volume and mouthed out the verbose, sentimental foolery which it contained.

'It must have been written by a woman' one of us urged. But no. She told us that it was written by a young man, one of the most famous poets of the day. I leave you to imagine what the shock of the discovery was. Though we all cried and begged her to read no more she persisted and read us extracts from the Lives of the Lord Chancellors. When she had finished, Jane, the eldest and wisest of us, rose to her feet and said that she for one was not convinced.

'Why' she asked 'if men write such rubbish as this, should our mothers have wasted their youth in bringing them into the world?'

We were all silent; and in the silence, poor Poll could be heard sobbing out, 'Why, why did my father teach me to read?'

Clorinda was the first to come to her senses. 'It's all our fault' she said. 'Every one of us knows how to read. But no one, save Poll, has ever taken the trouble to do it. I, for one, have taken it for granted that it was a woman's duty to spend her youth in bearing children. I venerated my mother for bearing ten; still more my grandmother for bearing fifteen; it was, I confess, my own ambition to bear twenty. We have gone on all these ages supposing that men were equally industrious, and that their works were of equal merit. While we have borne the children, they, we supposed, have borne the books and the pictures. We have populated the world. They have civilised it. But now that we can read, what prevents us from judging the results? Before we bring another child into the world we must swear that we will find out what the world is like.'

So we made ourselves into a society for asking questions. One of us was to visit a man-of-war; another was to hide herself in a scholar's study; another was to attend a meeting of business men; while all were to read books, look at pictures, go to concerts, keep our eyes open in the streets, and ask questions perpetually. We were very young. You can judge of our simplicity when I tell you that before parting that night we agreed that the objects of life were to produce good people and good books. Our questions were to be directed to finding out how far these objects were now attained by men. We vowed solemnly that we would not bear a single child until we were satisfied.

Off we went then, some to the British Museum; others to the King's Navy; some to Oxford; others to Cambridge; we visited the Royal Academy and the Tate; heard modern music in concert rooms, went to the Law Courts, and saw new plays. No one dined out without asking her partner certain questions and carefully noting his replies. At intervals we met together and compared our observations. Oh, those were merry meetings! Never have I laughed so much as I did when Rose read her notes upon 'Honour' and described how she had dressed herself as an Æthiopian Prince and gone aboard one of His Majesty's ships. Discovering the hoax, the Captain visited her (now disguised as a private gentleman) and demanded that honour should be satisfied. 'But how?' she asked. 'How?' he bellowed. 'With the cane of course!' Seeing that he was beside himself with rage and expecting that her last moment had come, she bent over and received, to her amazement, six light taps upon the behind. 'The honour of the British Navy is avenged!' he cried, and, raising herself, she saw him with the sweat pouring down his face holding out a trembling right hand. 'Away!' she exclaimed, striking an attitude and imitating the ferocity of his own expression, 'My honour has still to be satisfied!' 'Spoken like a gentleman!' he returned, and fell into profound thought. 'If six strokes avenge the honour of the King's Navy' he mused, 'how many avenge the honour of a private gentleman?' He said he would prefer to lay the case before his brother officers. She replied haughtily that she could not wait. He praised her sensibility. 'Let me see,' he cried suddenly, 'did your father keep a carriage?' 'No' she said. 'Or a riding horse?' 'We had a donkey,' she bethought her, 'which drew the mowing machine.' At this his face lightened. 'My mother's name – ' she added. 'For God's sake, man, don't mention your mother's name!' he shrieked, trembling like an aspen and flushing to the roots of his hair, and it was ten minutes at least before she could induce him to proceed. At length he decreed that if she gave him four strokes and a half in the small of the back at a spot indicated by himself (the half conceded, he said, in recognition of the fact that her great grandmother's uncle was killed at Trafalgar) it was his opinion that her honour would be as good as new. This was done; they retired to a restaurant; drank two bottles of wine for which he insisted upon paying; and parted with protestations of eternal friendship.

Then we had Fanny's account of her visit to the Law Courts. At her first visit she had come to the conclusion that the Judges were either made of wood or were impersonated by large animals resembling man who had been trained to move with extreme dignity, mumble and nod their heads. To test her theory she had liberated a handkerchief of bluebottles at the critical moment of a trial, but was unable to judge whether the creatures gave signs of humanity for the buzzing of the flies induced so sound a sleep that she only woke in time to see the prisoners led into the cells below. But from the evidence she brought we voted that it is unfair to suppose that the Judges are men.

Helen went to the Royal Academy, but when asked to deliver her report upon the pictures she began to recite from a pale blue volume 'O for the touch of a vanished hand and the sound of a voice that is still. Home is the hunter, home from the hill. He gave his bridle reins a shake. Love is sweet, love is brief. Spring, the fair spring, is the year's pleasant King. O! to be in England now that April's there. Men must work and women must weep. The path of duty is the way to glory – ' We could listen to no more of this gibberish.

'We want no more poetry!' we cried.

'Daughters of England!' she began, but here we pulled her down, a vase of water getting spilt over her in the scuffle.

'Thank God!' she exclaimed, shaking herself like a dog. 'Now I'll roll on the carpet and see if I can't brush off what remains of the Union Jack. Then perhaps – ' here she rolled energetically. Getting up she began to explain to us what modern pictures are like when Castalia stopped her.

'What is the average size of a picture?' she asked. 'Perhaps two feet by two and a half,' she said. Castalia made notes while Helen spoke, and when she had done, and we were trying not to meet each others eyes, rose and said, 'At your wish I spent last week at Oxbridge, disguised as a charwoman. I thus had access to the rooms of several Professors and will now attempt to give you some idea – only,' she broke off, 'I can't think how to do it. It's all so queer. These Professors,' she went on, 'live in large houses built round grass plots each in a kind of cell by himself. Yet they have every convenience and comfort. You have only to press a button or light a little lamp. Their papers are beautifully filed. Books abound. There are no children or animals, save half a dozen stray cats and one aged bullfinch – a cock. I remember,' she broke off, 'an Aunt of mine who lived at Dulwich and kept cactuses. You reached the conservatory through the double drawing-room, and there, on the hot pipes, were dozens of them, ugly, squat, bristly little plants each in a separate pot. Once in a hundred years the Aloe flowered, so my Aunt said. But she died before that happened – ' We told her to keep to the point. 'Well,' she resumed, 'when Professor Hobkin was out I examined his life work, an edition of Sappho. It's a queer looking book, six or seven inches thick, not all by Sappho. Oh no. Most of it is a defence of Sappho's chastity, which some German had denied, and I can assure you the passion with which these two gentlemen argued, the learning they displayed, the prodigious ingenuity with which they disputed the use of some implement which looked to me for all the world like a hairpin astounded me; especially when the door opened and Professor Hobkin himself appeared. A very nice, mild, old gentleman, but what could *he* know about chastity?' We misunderstood her.

'No, no,' she protested, 'he's the soul of honour I'm sure – not that he resembles Rose's sea captain in the least. I was thinking rather of my Aunt's cactuses. What could *they* know about chastity?'

Again we told her not to wander from the point, – did the Oxbridge professors help to produce good people and good books? – the objects of life.

'There!' she exclaimed. 'It never struck me to ask. It never occurred to me that they could possibly produce anything.'

'I believe,' said Sue, 'that you made some mistake. Probably Professor Hobkin was a gynæcologist. A scholar is a very different sort of man. A scholar is overflowing with humour and invention – perhaps addicted to wine, but what of that? – a delightful companion, generous, subtle, imaginative – as stands to reason. For he spends his life in company with the finest human beings that have ever existed.'

'Hum,' said Castalia. 'Perhaps I'd better go back and try again.'

Some three months later it happened that I was sitting alone when Castalia entered. I don't know what it was in the look of her that so moved me; but I could not restrain myself, and dashing across the room, I clasped her in my arms. Not only was she very beautiful; she seemed also in the highest spirits. 'How happy you look!' I exclaimed, as she sat down.

'I've been at Oxbridge' she said.

'Asking questions?'

'Answering them' she replied.

'You have not broken our vow?' I said anxiously, noticing something about her figure.

'Oh, the vow' she said casually. 'I'm going to have a baby if that's what you mean. You can't imagine,' she burst out, 'how exciting, how beautiful, how satisfying – '

'What is?' I asked.

'To – to – answer questions,' she replied in some confusion. Whereupon she told me the whole of her story. But in the middle of an account which interested and excited me more than anything I had ever heard, she gave the strangest cry, half whoop, half holloa –

'Chastity! Chastity! Where's my chastity!' she cried. 'Help Ho! The scent bottle!'

There was nothing in the room but a cruet containing mustard, which I was about to administer when she recovered her composure.

'You should have thought of that three months ago' I said severely.

'True' she replied. 'There's not much good in thinking of it now. It was unfortunate, by the way, that my mother had me called Castalia.'

'Oh Castalia, your mother – ' I was beginning when she reached for the mustard pot.

'No, no, no,' she said, shaking her head. 'If you'd been a chaste woman yourself you would have screamed at the sight of me – instead of which you rushed across the room and took me in your arms. No, Cassandra. We are neither of us chaste.' So we went on talking.

Meanwhile the room was filling up, for it was the day appointed to discuss the results of our observations. Everyone, I thought, felt as I did about Castalia. They kissed her and said how glad they were to see her again. At length, when we were all assembled, Jane rose and said that it was time to begin. She began by saying that we had now asked questions for over five years, and that though the results were bound to be inconclusive – here Castalia nudged me and whispered that she was not so sure about that. Then she got up, and, interrupting Jane in the middle of a sentence, said,

'Before you say any more, I want to know – am I to stay in the room? Because,' she added 'I have to confess that I am an impure woman.'

Everyone looked at her in astonishment.

'You are going to have a baby?' asked Jane.

She nodded her head.

It was extraordinary to see the different expressions on their faces.

A sort of hum went through the room, in which I could catch the words 'impure', 'baby', 'Castalia', and so on. Jane, who was herself considerably moved, put it to us,

'Shall she go? Is she impure?'

Such a roar filled the room as might have been heard in the street outside.

'No! No! No! Let her stay! Impure? Fiddlesticks!' Yet I fancied that some of the youngest, girls of nineteen or twenty, held back as if overcome with shyness. Then we all came about her and began asking questions, and at last I saw one of the youngest, who had kept in the background, approach shyly and say to her:

'What is chastity then? I mean is it good, or is it bad, or is it nothing at all?' She replied so low that I could not catch what she said.

'You know I was shocked,' said another, 'for at least ten minutes.'

'In my opinion,' said Poll, who was growing crusty from always reading in the London Library, 'chastity is nothing but ignorance – a most discreditable state of mind. We should admit only the unchaste to our society. I vote that Castalia shall be our President.'

This was violently disputed.

'It is as unfair to brand women with chastity as with unchastity,' said Moll. 'Some of us haven't the opportunity either. Moreover, I don't believe Cassy herself maintains that she acted as she did from a pure love of knowledge.'

'He is only twenty one and divinely beautiful' said Cassy, with a ravishing gesture.

'I move,' said Helen, 'that no one be allowed to talk of chastity or unchastity save those who are in love.'

'Oh bother,' said Judith, who had been enquiring into scientific matters, 'I'm not in love and I'm longing to explain my measures for dispensing with prostitutes and fertilising virgins by Act of Parliament.'

She went on to tell us of an invention of hers to be erected at Tube stations and other public resorts, which, upon payment of a small fee would safeguard the nation's health, accommodate its sons, and relieve its daughters. Then she had contrived a method of preserving in sealed tubes the germs of future Lord Chancellors 'or poets or painters or musicians' she went on, 'supposing, that is to say, that these breeds are not extinct, and that women still wish to bear children – '

'Of course we wish to bear children!' cried Castalia impatiently. Jane rapped the table.

'That is the very point we are met to consider,' she said. 'For five years we have been trying to find out whether we are justified in continuing the human race. Castalia has anticipated our decision. But it remains for the rest of us to make up our minds.'

Here one after another of our messengers rose and delivered their reports. The marvels of civilisation far exceeded our expectations, and as we learnt for the first time how man flies in the air, talks across space, penetrates to the heart of the atom, and embraces the universe in his speculations a murmur of admiration burst from our lips.

'We are proud,' we cried, 'that our mothers sacrificed their youth in such a cause as this!' Castalia, who had been listening intently, looked prouder than all the rest. Then Jane reminded us that we had still much to learn, and Castalia begged us to make haste. On we went through a vast tangle of statistics. We learnt that England has a population of so many millions, and that such and such a proportion of them is constantly hungry and in prison; that the average size of a working man's family is such, and that so great a percentage of women die from maladies incident to childbirth. Reports were read of visits to factories, shops, slums and dockyards. Descriptions were given of the Stock Exchange, of a gigantic house of business in the City, and of a Government Office. The British Colonies were now discussed, and some account was given of our rule in India, Africa and Ireland. I was sitting by Castalia and I noticed her uneasiness.

'We shall never come to any conclusion at all at this rate,' she said. 'As it appears that civilisation is so much more complex than we had any notion, would it not be better to confine ourselves to our original enquiry? We agreed that it was the object of life to produce good people and good books. All this time we have been talking of aeroplanes, factories and money. Let us talk about men themselves, and their arts, for that is the heart of the matter.'

So the diners out stepped forward with long slips of paper containing answers to their questions. These had been framed after much consideration. A good man, we had agreed, must at any rate be honest, passionate and unworldly. But whether or not a particular man possessed those qualities could only be discovered by asking questions, often beginning at a remote distance from the centre. Is Kensington a nice place to live in? Where is your son being educated – and your daughter? Now please tell me, what do you pay for your cigars? By the way, is Sir Joseph a baronet or only a knight? Often it seemed that we learnt more from trivial questions of this kind than from more direct ones. 'I accepted my peerage,' said Lord Bunkum 'because my wife wished it.' I forget how many titles were accepted for the same reason. 'Working fifteen hours out the twenty four as I do – ' ten thousand professional men began.

'No, no, of course you can neither read nor write. But why do you work so hard?' 'My dear lady, with a growing family – ' 'but *why* does your family grow?' Their wives wished that too, or perhaps it was the British Empire. But more significant than the answers were the refusals to answer. Very few would reply at all to questions about morality and religion, and such answers as were given were not serious. Questions as to the value of money and power were almost invariably brushed aside, or pressed at extreme risk to the asker. 'I'm sure,' said Jill, 'that if Sir Harley Tightboots hadn't been carving the mutton when I asked him about the capitalist system he would have cut my throat. The only reason why we escaped with our lives over and over again is that men are at once so hungry and so chivalrous. They despise us too much to mind what we say.'

'Of course they despise us' said Eleanor. 'At the same time how do you account for this – I made enquiries among the artists. Now no woman has ever been an artist, has she Poll?'

'Jane-Austen-Charlotte-Brontë-George-Eliot,' cried Poll, like a man crying muffins in a back street.

'Damn the woman!' someone exclaimed. 'What a bore she is!'

'Since Sappho there has been no female of first rate – ' Eleanor began, quoting from a weekly newspaper.

'It's now well known that Sappho was the somewhat lewd invention of Professor Hobkin,' Ruth interrupted.

'Anyhow, there is no reason to suppose that any woman ever has been able to write or ever will be able to write' Eleanor continued. 'And yet, whenever I go among authors they never cease to talk to me about their books. Masterly! I say, or Shakespeare himself! (for one must say something) and I assure you, they believe me.'

'That proves nothing,' said Jane. 'They all do it. Only,' she sighed, 'it doesn't seem to help *us* much. Perhaps we had better examine modern literature next. Liz, it's your turn.'

Elizabeth rose and said that in order to prosecute her enquiry she had dressed as a man and been taken for a reviewer.

'I have read new books pretty steadily for the past five years,' said she. 'Mr Wells is the most popular living writer; then comes Mr

Arnold Bennett; then Mr Compton Makenzie; Mr McKenna and Mr Walpole may be bracketed together.' She sat down.

'But you've told us nothing!' we expostulated. 'Or do you mean that these gentlemen have greatly surpassed Jane-Eliot and that English fiction is – where's that review of yours? Oh, yes, "safe in their hands".'

'Safe, quite safe' she said, shifting uneasily from foot to foot. 'And I'm sure that they give away even more than they receive.'

We were all sure of that. 'But,' we pressed her, 'do they write good books?'

'Good books?' she said, looking at the ceiling. 'You must remember,' she began, speaking with extreme rapidity, 'that fiction is the mirror of life. And you can't deny that education is of the highest importance, and that it would be extremely annoying, if you found yourself alone at Brighton late at night, not to know which was the best boarding house to stay at, and suppose it was a dripping Sunday evening – wouldn't it be nice to go to the Movies?'

'But what has that got to do with it?' we asked.

'Nothing – nothing – nothing whatever' she replied.

'Well, tell us the truth' we bade her.

'The truth? But isn't it wonderful,' she broke off – 'Mr Chitter, has written a weekly article for the past thirty years upon love or hot buttered toast and has sent all his sons to Eton – '

'The truth!' we demanded.

'Oh the truth,' she stammered – 'the truth has nothing to do with literature,' and sitting down she refused to say another word.

It all seemed to us very inconclusive.

'Ladies, we must try to sum up the results' Jane was beginning, when a hum, which had been heard for some time through the open window, drowned her voice.

'War! War! War! Declaration of War!' men were shouting in the street.

We looked at each other in horror.

'What war?' we cried. 'What war?' We remembered, too late, that we had never thought of sending anyone to the House of Commons. We had forgotten all about it. We turned to Poll, who had reached the history shelves in the London Library, and asked her to enlighten us.

'Why,' we cried 'do men go to war?'

'Sometimes for one reason, sometimes for another' she replied calmly. 'In 1760, for example – ' The shouts outside drowned her words. 'Again in 1797 – in 1804 – It was the Austrians in 1866 – 1870 was the Franco-Prussian – In 1900 on the other hand – '

'But it's now 1914!' we cut her short.

'Ah, I don't know what they're going to war for now,' she admitted.

The war was over and peace was in process of being signed when I once more found myself with Castalia in the room where our meetings used to be held. We began idly turning over the pages of our old minute books. 'Queer,' I mused, 'to see what we were thinking five years ago.' 'We are agreed,' Castalia quoted, reading over my shoulder, 'that it is the object of life to produce good people and good books.' We made no comment upon that. 'A good man is at anyrate honest, passionate and unworldly.' 'What a woman's language' I observed. 'Oh dear,' cried Castalia, pushing the book away from her, 'What fools we were! It was all Poll's father's fault,' she went on. 'I believe he did it on purpose – that ridiculous will, I mean, forcing Poll to read all the books in the London Library. If we hadn't learnt to read,' she said bitterly, 'we might still have been bearing children in ignorance and that I believe was the happiest life after all. I know what you're going to say about war,' she checked me, 'and the horror of bearing children to see them killed, but our mothers did it, and their mothers, and their mothers before them. And *they* didn't complain. They couldn't read. I've done my best,' she sighed, 'to prevent my little girl from learning to read, but what's the use? I caught Ann only yesterday with a newspaper in her hand and she was beginning to ask me if it was "true". Next she'll ask me whether Mr Lloyd George is a good man, then whether Mr Arnold Bennett is a good novelist, and finally whether I believe in God. How can I bring my daughter up to believe in nothing?' she demanded.

'Surely you could teach her to believe that a man's intellect is, and always will be, fundamentally superior to a woman's?' I suggested. She brightened at this and began to turn over our old minutes again. 'Yes,' she said, 'think of their discoveries, their mathematics, their science, their philosophy, their scholarship – ' and then she began to laugh, 'I shall never forget old Hobkin and the hairpin,' she said, and went on reading and laughing and I thought she was quite happy, when suddenly she threw the book from her and burst out, 'Oh, Cassandra why do you torment me? Don't you know that our belief in man's intellect is the greatest fallacy of them all?' 'What?' I exclaimed. 'Ask any journalist, schoolmaster, politician or public house keeper in the land and they will all tell you that men are much cleverer than women.' 'As if I doubted it,' she said scornfully. 'How could they help it? Haven't we bred them and fed and kept them in comfort since the beginning of time so that they may be clever even if they're nothing else? It's all our doing!' she cried. 'We insisted upon having intellect and now we've got it. And it's intellect,' she continued, 'that's at the bottom of it. What could be more charming than a boy before he has begun to cultivate his intellect? He is beautiful to look at; he gives himself no airs; he understands the meaning of art and literature instinctively; he goes about enjoying his life and making other people enjoy theirs. Then they teach him to cultivate his intellect. He becomes a barrister, a civil servant, a general, an author, a professor. Every day he goes to an office. Every year he produces a book. He maintains a whole family by the products of his brain – poor devil! Soon he cannot come into a room without making us all feel uncomfortable; he condescends to every woman he meets, and dares not tell the truth even to his own wife; instead of rejoicing our eyes we have to shut them if we are to take him in our arms. True, they console themselves with stars of all shapes, ribbons of all shades, and incomes of all sizes – but what is to console us? That we shall be able in ten years' time to spend a week-end at Lahore? Or that the least insect in Japan has a name twice the length of its body? Oh, Cassandra, for Heaven's sake let us devise a method by which men may bear children! It is our only chance. For unless we provide them with some innocent occupation we shall get neither good people nor good books; we shall perish beneath the fruits of their unbridled activity; and not a human being will survive to know that there once was Shakespeare!'

'It is too late' I said. 'We cannot provide even for the children that we have.'

'And then you ask me to believe in intellect' she said.

While we spoke, men were crying hoarsely and wearily in the street, and listening, we heard that the Treaty of Peace had just been signed. The voices died away. The rain was falling and interfered no doubt with the proper explosion of the fireworks.

'My cook will have bought the Evening News' said Castalia 'and Ann will be spelling it out over her tea. I must go home.'

'It's no good – not a bit of good' I said. 'Once she knows how to read there's only one thing you can teach her to believe in – and that is herself.'

'Well that would be a change,' said Castalia.

So we swept up the papers of our Society, and though Ann was playing with her doll very happily, we solemnly made her a present of the lot and told her we had chosen her to be President of the Society of the future – upon which she burst into tears, poor little girl.

Virginia Woolf, *Monday or Tuesday*, 1921

THIRTEEN

Sapphistories

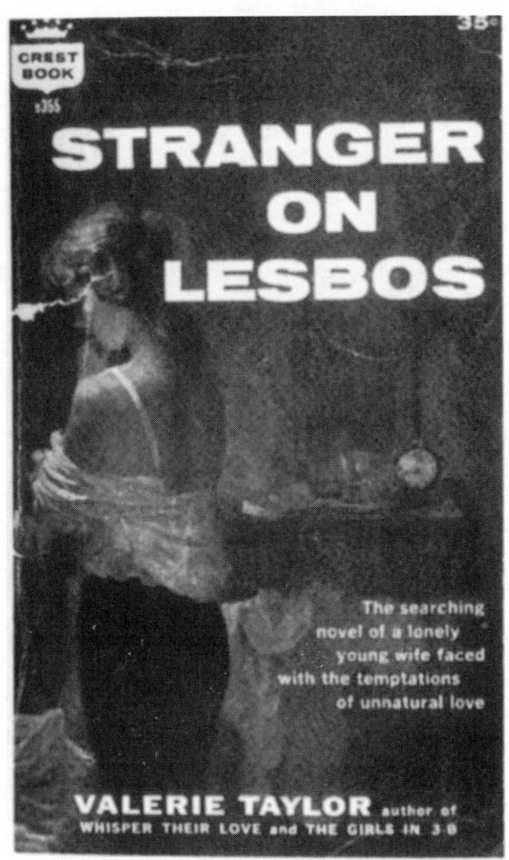

'The searching novel of a lonely young wife faced with the temptations of unnatural love'. The title and the cover illustration for Valerie Taylor's popular pulp novel told eager readers all they wanted to know. Valerie Taylor, *Stanger on Lesbos* (New York, 1961)

Virginia Woolf's Professor Hobkin, worrying about the uses of an ancient implement that looked to a woman's eye 'for all the world like a hairpin' – and I take it that it *is* a hairpin – is foreshadowed by Ronald Firbank's Professor Inglepin in his *Vainglory*. Sappho appears many times in Firbank's work, and here, in a knowledgeable send-up that reflects on the whole of Sappho's fragmentary history, Firbank (1886–1926) gives us a dinner party, complete with wine from Lesbos procured in Pall Mall and violets scattered artistically across the table, all designed to frame the professor's revelation of a new Fragment of Sappho. The story is a tease, just as Sappho is a tease; always almost there, just glimpsed behind gossip about the hotels in Mytilene or broken pots seen at Tanagra, and in the end we – and the guests at Mrs Henedge's party – never quite get what we have been promised. The 'imperishable lines' turn out to be 'Could not, for the fury of her feet'. 'Oh, delicious,' as Lady Listless says.

When Firbank wrote *Vainglory* in 1915 classical scholarship was beginning to consolidate the new finds and was systematising Sappho. Edwin Marion Cox's edition appeared in 1925; C.R. Haines' *Sappho: The Poems and Fragments* in 1926; John Maxwell Edmonds edited three volumes of *Lyra Graeca* for the Loeb Classical Library (1927); Jean Larnac published an account of Sappho's work and life (1934); Edgar Lobel and Denys Page published their edition of *Poetarum Lesbiorum Fragmenta* (1955); and Page produced his important commentary on *Sappho and Alcaeus* in the same year.

While all this textual activity was going on between and immediately after the two world wars, the particular social and cultural moods of the period were not conducive to the promotion of Sappho's fictions. Just as Phaon had disappeared from her scene, so Sappho herself was thoroughly taken over by Natalie Barney's circle and taken in by the furore surrounding the obscenity trial brought against Radclyffe Hall's *The Well of Loneliness* (1928). Now Sappho became resolutely homosexual. 'Our thoughts centre upon Sapphism,' wrote Virginia Woolf, 'we have to uphold the morality of that Well of all that's stagnant and luke warm and neither one thing or the other.'

For literary reasons Woolf did not like the book, but neither did she like the opprobrium that gathered around women-loving-women as a result of the attention focused on the trial. The magistrate dealing with the case spoke of 'unnatural tendencies' and 'horrible practices'. Compton Mackenzie wrote a nasty lampoon, *Extraordinary Women* (1928). In England these were not happy times for lesbians. Even in Paris the days of lesbian chic were fading, and the smoky nightclubs run by husky-voiced Amazons were disappearing, while in America, as Lilian Fadermann says in her *Odd Girls and Twilight Lovers* (1991), lesbians were turned into 'sickos'.

But they were still there, of course, and in the 1950s two women, Phyllis Lyon and Del Martin, formed a support group called 'Daughters of Bilitis'. The reference to Louys' Sapphic fiction guaranteed anonymity, except for those in the know, and often that was exactly what was required by married lesbians, by lesbians in the Forces or in the public eye. Private reading, however, was quite another matter, and there were lesbian novels to be had, such as Sheila Donnisthorpe's *Loveliest of Friends* (1931), Carol Hales' *Such is My Beloved* (1953), Kay Addams' *Warped Desire* (1960) and Vicky Spain's *Trouble in Skirts* (1965). This 'pulp Sappho' – and there were some titles that included the allusion, like Valerie Taylor's *Stranger on Lesbos* (1956) – invariably ended more or less unhappily, and that is what they also made of the original voyager along the 'strange and guilty bypaths of Lesbianism'. In Ann Aldrich's well-known 1955 novel *We Walk Alone* she comes to the conclusion that Sappho was 'as ill adjusted to her plight as any female homosexual and at the same time unwilling to change'.

In these days Sappho was mainly to be found not in Britain or America, but abroad. In Greece, Stratis Myrivilis set his novel *The Schoolmistress with the Golden Eyes* (1954) in the towns of his native Lesbos. Although his modern-day heroine, the widowed Sappho Vranas, had been unable to respond to her husband and wondered about her womanly credentials, by the end of the novel all is resolved in a happy scene of heterosexual consummation. The English writer Lawrence Durrell (1912–90), who was born in India and lived in Cyprus, Rhodes and Greece, as well as in countries around the eastern Mediterranean, produced a verse-play *Sappho* in 1950. Durrell's Sappho, famous, discontented, vain, unable to work and – in an interesting play on the fragmentation of her works – with a stammer, is a very twentieth-century woman, a politician, forced to give up her children and racked by the results of that choice. It was on this verse-drama that Peggy Glanville-Hicks based her opera *Sappho* (1960). Norman Douglas (1868–1952), another expatriate British writer, this time living in Italy, wrote extensively about sun, sea and boys and other hedonistic pleasures, so that the predilections of 'that naughty old Sappho of Greece' come as no surprise, even if his lady informant is unable to enlighten him on their significance.

Such fictions of Sappho as there were from the 1930s to the 1950s were rather tamer. Margaret Goldsmith's *Sappho of Lesbos: A Psychological Reconstruction of her Life* (1938, not included here) read the Fragments as a story, turning the real-life classical poet Erinna into one of Sappho's girls, but making her a disciple and a pupil who refused Sappho's offer of a closer relationship. Peter Green's *The Laughter of Aphrodite: A Novel About Sappho of Lesbos* (1957) puts the sex back in, but retraces that old Ovidian story where Sappho tires of girls and desires the stronger meat of a man.

Sylvia Plath's extraordinary poem 'Lesbos' (1962) in many ways looks forward to what was to come in the later 1960s. 'Viciousness in the kitchen!' . . . it's only the beginning. The violent imagery of the poem, the angry terms, the psychedelically wild phrases and stabbing rhythms make it a difficult read. Men come off badly, babies are disgusting, all the ordinary daily jobs are degrading and vile, domestic life is a concentration camp governed by stink and shit – only somewhere else might women have a better time:

> I should sit on a rock off Cornwall and comb my hair.
> I should wear tiger pants, I should have an affair.
> We should meet in another life, we should meet in air,
> Me and you.

But that better time was a long way off, and far too late for Sylvia Plath.

VAINGLORY

Mrs Henedge lived in a small house with killing stairs just off Chesham Place.

'If I were to die here,' she had often said, 'they would never be able to twist the coffin outside my door; they would have to cremate me in my room.' For such a cottage, the sitting-rooms, nevertheless, were astonishingly large. The drawing-room, for instance, was a complete surprise, in spite of its dimensions, being ocularly curtailed by a somewhat trying brocade of drooping lilac orchids on a yellow ground.

But to-day, to make as much space as possible to receive her guests, all the household heirlooms – a faded photograph of the Pope, a bust of *poor dear Leslie*, some most Oriental cushions, and a quantity of whimsies, had been carried away to the top of the house. Never before had she seen the room so bare, or so austere.

As her maid exclaimed: 'It was like a church.' If an entire Ode of Sappho's had been discovered instead of a single line she could have done no more.

In the centre of the room, a number of fragile gilt chairs had been waiting patiently all day to be placed, heedless, happily, of the lamentations of Thérèse, who, while rolling her eyes, kept exclaiming, 'Such wild herds of chairs; such herds of wild chairs!'

In her arrangements, Mrs Henedge had disobeyed the Professor in everything.

Professor Inglepin had looked in during the week to ask that severity might be the key. 'No flowers,' he had begged, 'or, at most, placed beside the fragment (which I shall bring), a handful, perhaps, of – '

'Of course,' Mrs Henedge had replied, 'you can rely upon me.' And now the house was full of rambler roses and of blue sweet-peas.

A buffet, too, had arisen altar-like in her own particular sanctum, an apology to those whom she was unable to dine; nor, for toothsome curiosities, had she scoured a pagan cookery-book in vain . . .

Glancing over the dinner list whilst she dressed it seemed to her that the names of her guests, in neat rotation, resembled the cast of a play. 'A comedy, with possible dynamics!' she murmured as she went downstairs.

With a tiara well over her nose, and dressed in oyster satin and pearls, she wished that Sappho could have seen her then . . . On entering the drawing-room she found her beautiful Mrs Shamefoot as well as her radiant Lady Castleyard (pronounced Castleyud) had already arrived, and were entertaining lazily her Monsignor Parr . . .

. . . Lady Castleyard was a pretty woman, with magnificently bold shoulders and a tiny head, she was, as a rule, quite fearlessly made up. It was courageous of her, her hostess thought, to flaunt such carnational cheeks. Only in a Reynolds or in a Romney did one expect to see *such a dab*.

'Tell me! Tell me!' she exclaimed airily, taking hold of Mrs Henedge. 'I feel I must hear the line before everyone else.'

Mrs Henedge, who did not know it, pressed to her lips her fan.

'Patience!' she murmured, with her subtlest smile.

Monsignor Parr gazed at her with heavy opaque eyes.

Something between a butterfly and a misanthrope, he was temperamental, when not otherwise . . . employed.

'I must confess,' he observed, 'that Sappho's love affairs fail to stir me.'

'Ah, for shame!' Mrs Henedge scolded, turning from him to welcome an elaborate young man, who, in some bewildering way of his own, seemed to find charming the fashions of 1860.

'Drecoll?' she enquired.

'Vienna,' he nodded.

'This is Mr Harvester,' she said. She had nearly said 'Poor Mr Harvester,' for she could not endure his wife.

* * *

The guests at Mrs Henedge's party carry on their own conversations, forgetting the purpose of their gathering. Then the Professor arrives to reveal his new-found fragment of Sappho . . .

A flattering silence greeted the Professor.

'I'm afraid you must feel exhausted from your field day at the British Museum,' Mrs Henedge said to him half hysterically, as they went downstairs.

The success of the dinner-table, however, restored her nerve. To create a slight atmosphere she had made a circuit of the table earlier in the evening, scattering violets indiscriminately into the glasses and over the plates.

For a moment her guests forgot to chatter of themselves. They remembered Sappho.

The Lesbian wine (from Samos. Procured, perhaps, in Pall Mall) produced a hush.

Claud Harvester bethought him then that he had spent a Saturday-to-Monday once, in Mitylene, at 'a funny little broken-down hotel upon the seashore.'

It had been in the spring, he said.

'In the spring the violets in Athens are wonderful, are they not?' Mrs Calvally enquired.

'Indeed, yes.'

She spoke to him of Greece, but all he could remember of Corinth, for instance, was the many drowned lambs he had seen lying upon the beach.

'*Ah! Don't speak to me of Corinth!*'

'What a pity – and in Tanagra, tell me, what did you see?'

'In Tanagra. . . ?' he said, 'there was a kitten sunning himself in the Museum, beside a pile of broken earthenware – handles of amphoræ, arms and legs of figurines, and an old man seated in the doorway mending a jar!'

'How extraordinary!' she marvelled, removing with extreme precaution an atom of cork that had fallen into her glass. 'Really! Is that all?' . . .

. . . As Mrs Henedge had explained, it was only a fragile little dinner. She was obliged to return to the drawing-room again as soon as possible to receive her later guests. It occurred to her as she trailed away with the ladies that after the Professor's Sapphic postscript they might, perhaps, arrange some music. It would bring the evening to a harmonious close . . .

. . . An unwarrantable rush for places, however, announced that the critical moment had come.

'Well, darling,' Mrs Thumbler, triumphant, explained to her daughter, excusing herself for a sharp little skirmish with Monsignor Parr, 'I was scarcely going to have him on my knee!' And with emotion she fluttered a somewhat frantic fan.

'I think your *young musician* so handsome,' Mrs Asp whispered to Mrs Henedge, giving a few deft touches to a bandeau and some audacious violet paste. 'With a little trouble, really, he could look quite Greek.'

'Is your serial in *The Star*, my dear Rose, ever to be discontinued?' Mr Sophax, who stood close behind her, stooped to enquire.

'Don't question me,' she replied, without turning round. 'I make it a rule never to be interviewed at night.'

Next her, Lady Listless, perched uncomfortably on Claud Harvester's *New Poems*, sat eyeing the Professor with her most complacent smile. She knew hardly anything of Sappho, except that her brother, she believed, had been a wine merchant – which, in those times, was probably even better than being a brewer.

'But if they had meant to murder me,' the camel-lady was mysteriously murmuring to Monsignor Parr, 'they would not have put chocolate in the luncheon-basket; my courage returned to me at that!' when a marvellous hiss from Mrs Asp stimulated Miss Compostella to expand.

'My dear, *when an angel* like Sabine Watson . . .' she was heard to exclaim vaguely above everyone else.

Julia, just then, was in high feather. George Calvally had promised to design for her a beautiful poster, by the time that Eysoldt should arrive, with cypress-trees and handfuls of stars . . .

But the Professor was becoming impatient.

It would be utterly disgusting, Mrs Henedge reflected, if he should get desperate and retire. It was *like* Julia to expatiate at such a time upon the heavenliness of Sabine Watson, who was only *one*, it seemed, of quite a troop of angels.

To conceal her misgivings she waved a sultry yellow fan. There was a forest painted upon it of Arden, in indigo, in violet, in sapphire, in turquoise, and in common blue. The fan, by Conder, was known perversely as *The Pink Woods*.

'I'm not going to inflict upon you a speech,' the Professor said, breaking in like a piccolo to Miss Compostella's harp.

'Hear, hear!' Mr Sophax approved.

'You have heard, of course, how, while surveying the ruins of Crocodileopolis Arsinoë, my donkey having – '

And then, after what may have become an anguishing obbligato, the Professor declaimed impressively the imperishable lines.

'Oh, delicious!' Lady Listless exclaimed, looking quite perplexed. 'Very charming indeed!'

'Will anyone tell me what it means,' Mrs Thumbler queried, 'in plain English? Unfortunately, my Greek – '

'In plain English,' the Professor said, with some reluctance, 'it means: "Could not" [he wagged a finger] "Could not, for the fury of her feet!" '

'Do you mean she ran away?'

'Apparently!'

'O-h!' Mrs Thumbler seemed inclined to faint.

The Professor riveted her with his curious nut-coloured eyes.

'Could not . . .' she murmured helplessly, as though clinging to an alpenstock, and not quite sure of her guide. Below her, so to speak, were the rooftops, pots and pans: Chamonix twinkling in the snow.

'But no doubt there is a *sous-entendu*?' Monsignor Parr suspiciously enquired.

'Indeed, no!' the Professor answered. 'It is probable, indeed, that Sappho did not even mean to be caustic! Here is an adventurous line, separated (alas!) from its full context. Decorative, useless, as you will; a water-colour on silk!'

'Just such a Sapphic piece,' Mrs Asp observed, with authority, 'just such a Sapphic piece as the *And down I set the cushion*, or the Γέῳ̣ς παιδο φιλώτερυς, or again the *Foolish woman, pride not thyself on a ring*.'

'I don't know why,' Lady Georgia confessed, 'it thrills me, but it does!'

'Do you suppose she refers to – '

'Nothing of the kind!' the Professor interrupted. 'As Mrs Asp explains, we have, at most, a broken piece, a rarity of phrase . . . as the poet's *With Golden Ankles*, for instance, or *Vines trailed on lofty poles*, or *With water dripped the napkin*, or *Scythian Wood* . . . or the (I fear me, spurious) *Carrying long rods, capped with the Pods of Poppies*.'

'And isn't there just one little tiny wee word of hers which says: '*A tortoise-shell*?' Mrs Calvally murmured, fingering the huge winged pin in the back of her hair.

'I should say that Sappho's powers were decidedly in declension when she wrote the Professor's "water-colour",' Mrs Steeple said disparagingly.

'I'm sure I don't see why!'

'Do you remember the divine Ode to Aphrodite?' she asked, and rapidly, occult, archaic, before anybody could stop her, she began to declaim:

'Zeus-begotten, weaver of arts deceitful,
From thy throne of various hues behold me,
Queen immortal, spare me relentless anguish;
        Spare, I beseech thee.

Hither haste, if ever of old my sighing
Moved thy soul, O Goddess, awhile to hear me,
From thy Father's house to repair with golden
        Chariot harnessed.

Lovely birds fleet-winged from Olympus holy
Fluttering multitudinous o'er the darksome
Breast of Earth their heavenly mistress hastened
        Through the mid ether;

Soon they brought the beautiful Aphrodite;
Softly beamed celestial eyes upon me;
And I heard her ask with a smile my trouble,
Wherefore I called her.

What of all things most may appease thy frenzy?
Whom (she said) would Sappho beguile to love her?
Whom by suasion bring to heart adoring?
Who hath aggrieved her?

Whoso flies thee, soon shall he turn to woo thee;
Who receives no gifts shall anon bestow them;
If he love not, soon shall he love, tho' Sappho
Turneth against him!

– Lady now too come, to allay my torment;
All my soul desireth, I prithee grant me;
Be thyself my champion and my helper,
Lovely Dione!'

'Exquisite, dear; thanks.'

'Christianity, no doubt,' the Professor observed, with some ferocity, to Monsignor Parr, 'has invented many admirable things, but it has destroyed more than it has created!' The old pagan in him was moved.

Ronald Firbank, 1915

THE SCHOOLMISTRESS WITH THE GOLDEN EYES

Leonis Drivas returns to Lesbos after the Second World War. His mind is full of the atrocities he has witnessed, the bitter hatred between enemy and friend, between Greek and Turk, and nothing of the horror of war is left out of this novel. Its author, Stratis Myrivilis, was a noted journalist, as well as a soldier during the First World War and an activist in the Greek underground during the Second.

As a painter, Leon tries to take up his work again, and to find peace in the landscape of his native island and in the love of his only remaining family, his younger sister Adriani. But the war has left him one duty: he must take back to the widow of a fellow soldier his wallet and its contents. The widow, Sappho Vranas, is remote, beautiful, clever and the reluctant mother of a crippled and incapacitated child. Though both Leon and Adriani are drawn to her, there is a coolness that sets Sappho apart. Here, towards the end of the novel and the surprise revision of her namesake's history, Leon, Adriani and Sappho enjoy an outing in the luxuriant countryside of Lesbos before the appointed day of their separation . . .

They set off early in the morning. It was to be an all-day excursion. Leon was conscious of a nagging sense of melancholy at the thought of the next day's separation. It preoccupied them all, but they didn't talk about it. At the same time he felt as though a weight had been lifted off his chest. The way ahead lay clear now: his conscience had triumphed.

The sun was just rising, burning hot, rose-coloured. The air was full of the murmuring sounds of morning: an occasional shout, a shrill whistle, the braying of a donkey, the rustling of birds in the trees.

They travelled light, having decided to eat whatever they found when they reached their destination. On the heights above the Sentinel they stopped to admire the view of the sea below. Her eyes glistening, Adriani gazed at the landscape which she loved so much and would now be leaving so soon. In the east the sun was already beginning to shimmer on the sea.

'If only you'd let me bring our bathing things,' she told Leon, 'we'd have had a heavenly swim.'

It was just that contingency that he had foreseen and wished to avoid.

'It would have taken up too much time,' he said casually. 'The sea's so lovely that we'd have dawdled for hours. And then we'd have had to climb up in the heat . . .'

Sappho didn't say anything. But she was glad she wouldn't have to appear before him undressed. Adriani's suggestion had a curious effect on her: she felt as though she'd been through a kind of test.

The most bucolic imagination couldn't have dreamt of a more attractive stretch of country than the one through which the track led up to Anerragi. The rough stairway soon gave way to a path with large flat stones placed at intervals so as to serve as steps and reduce the effort demanded of the climber. It wound through olive orchards and echoing gorges, shady with plane trees and agnus castus. Everywhere there was a smell of crushed sweet-smelling herbs which they trod underfoot and the air was full of the swishing sound made by Leon's walking-stick as he slashed a way through the giant nettles.

Adriani was so moved that she stopped for a moment.

'Isn't it beautiful?' she said slowly. 'I wonder if there's a landscape to equal it anywhere else in the world.'

Leon felt like saying that this soil had exhaled an atmosphere of eroticism ever since the days of Sappho; that for centuries the island's poets had sung of nothing but love and desire. But he didn't. Sappho might have read some other meaning into his words. He slowly approached the stout trunk of an olive tree and cupped a cicada, which was shrilling dementedly, in the hollow of his hand. For a moment he thought of placing it on the back of Adriani's neck. He might, with equal innocence, have slipped it into Sappho's bosom. Exactly as in *Daphnis and Chloe*. He thought of reminding Adriani that this was the scene of Longius's idyll – the most erotic countryside in the world. But all he said was:

'The peasants here have a curious superstition, you know. They say it brings good luck to bite the first cicada of the year. Quite gently, of course. Then you let it hop away. Funny, isn't it?'

They saw a pear tree. Almost all its fruit had been plucked, but as Leon gazed at it his eye fell on a pear, a single pear, the colour of gold, hanging from one of the topmost branches. He began to climb up. The rustling leaves felt cool and fresh. With the crook of his walking-stick he caught the branch on which the fruit hung and pulled it gently down towards him.

He was reciting the old Lesbian lines in a loud voice which echoed across the valley:

> 'As the sweet apple is found at the top of the branch,
> at the top-most tip, overlooked by the reapers!'

Down below Sappho replied in her deep vibrating voice, which seemed to have acquired a strangely boyish tone, with the line:

> 'No, not overlooked: they were not able to reach it!'

They all laughed.

Stratis Myrivilis, 1954, trans. Philip Sherrard, 1964

SAPPHO: A PLAY IN VERSE

A headland overlooking the fine bay of Eresos in Lesbos. Minos, the old tutor of Sappho, is seated upon a block of fallen marble gazing out to sea. It is dawn.

[*Enter* SAPPHO *from door right. She is expensively dressed and wears a golden wig. She looks haggard and sleepy.* MINOS *rises, but she takes no notice of him and advances to the sunlit courtyard where she stretches and yawns.* MINOS *sits and watches her.*]

MINOS

And so last you are here, as always,
Towards the ending of your element, the summer,
Lovely, famous and discontented, Sappho . . .

SAPPHO

Discontented . . .

MINOS

Now as the year declines austerely on itself
Leading from autumn into winter,
Sappho, Sappho, you must climb out of bed
To patronise the morning with your beauty,
A creditor to work, to joy an ignoramus.

SAPPHO

Dear Minos, I am late again. I know it!

MINOS

Three epigrams and two enigmas . . .

SAPPHO

And the m-marriage song for Alcaeus. I know it.

MINOS

The stylus must have broken in the middle,
Your writing was so bad. Some of it I doubted
Altogether. I made some notes for you to see.
Remember that you promised to be early?

SAPPHO

I remember . . .

MINOS

The image of the swallow seemed too trite.

SAPPHO

Very well. If you s-say so.
[*She goes indifferently to the table and starts to eat.*]

MINOS

But from its triteness we might make
An image of more force. Why not let's say
'The trite midsummer swallow.'

SAPPHO

The s-sparrow would be better.
There was a swallow in the eaves all spring.
I wonder if its house is still there.
[*She crosses suddenly and looks up at the roof of the courtyard.*]
No. It has t-tumbled down.

MINOS

O dear! And I had hoped to do some work.
It is so fine a day, the sea like glass.
Too fine a working-day for sophistries.
[SAPPHO *turns towards him and sighs.*]

SAPPHO

O . . . Minos! I am b-bored with it all to-day!

MINOS

And yesterday you were bored.

SAPPHO

And yesterday I was bored.

Lawrence Durrell, 1950

THE LAUGHTER OF APHRODITE

So, last night, I sat between the candlesticks and stared at my shadowy, flame-tinted image in the great bronze mirror. Night was kind to me, hiding the grey streaks in my thick, wiry-springing black curls, smoothing out the lines from nostril to mouth, the fine web of laughter-wrinkles round my eyes. *What unimaginable blood runs in my veins, what history has gone to make up this I, this time-bound self?* The robe scorched my flesh, as though it were Deianira's. Too-swarthy skin, irregular features in a wedge-shaped face, small bird-boned body. I smiled bitterly. *How could this two-cubit I ever touch the heavens?* The question – and the answers I had sought to it – echoed mockingly in my mind . . .

. . . I loosened the girdle of my robe, and let it fall in a heap at my feet as I stood up between the candlesticks, naked and burning. *Changed*, the voice whispered, *all changed. No*, I cried silently, *no: I am what I was* – and my hands flew up, touched my breasts, seeking reassurance, knowing them high and firm as they had always been, seeing the nipples dark and neat in the mirror before me, my hands moving as though of themselves, as though they were the hands of some other person, over my still-slender hips and firm, smooth, gently curving belly. The fire raged in me, I was quicklime. *Tonight. It must be tonight*, I thought.

I remembered, hot with shame, the words I had scratched on a scrap of papyrus a week before. *Come now. Quickly. Quickly* – buying love-charms like any village girl, humiliating myself to that filthy old hag – oh yes, she knew, she knew too well who I was – intriguing with contemptuous, moon-faced sluts for nail-parings and scraps of hair, open utterly now in my extremity of desire, a scandal to put my brother's in the shade. *Wryneck, wryneck, draw that man to my house* – the crucified bird flickering on its wheel in the firelight, the spells and burnt herbs and small, obscene sacrifices, there is nothing I have left untried, no shameful trick to which I have not stooped. But if the Goddess has betrayed my devotion and my trust, where else can I turn? She is cold and capricious as the foam from which she was born, and her eternally renewed virginity the cruellest deception of all.

The moon was at the full now. My skin prickled: I knew, without looking, that the slave girl – Thalia, yes, I remembered: how could I have forgotten? – had come softly through to the curtained archway from the bath-house, and was standing there in the shadows, watching me. Perhaps that is the answer, I thought: to drive out fire with fire. I sat down again and called softly: 'Thalia.'

She caught her breath, startled. 'My lady,' she whispered. She was behind me now: I heard the crisp rustle of her skirts, and the sound of her sandals padding across the floor. In the bronze mirror I glimpsed a young, nervous face, eyes two great questioning smudges, hair braided in a heavy coil. She had no idea what to do with her hands: she either clasped them frantically, as though in agony, or else let them hang, awkward and inert, at her sides. I picked up the pot of lanolin and began to wipe off my make-up.

'Is the bath ready?' I said.

'Yes, my lady.' The same choked, breathy whisper. What was she feeling? Shyness? Fear? Embarrassment?

'Shall I bring your bath-robe, my lady?'

I paused, stretched luxuriously, and yawned like a cat: I could feel a quiver run through her as I did so, like the ripple moving over a field of green barley, the spring breeze that sets leaves dancing and stipples a calm sea with fugitive shadows.

Desire? Surely not. And yet –

'Thank you,' I said, and turned to watch her move across the candle-lit room, picking her way with neat, short steps to the big press in the corner, beside my bed. She was slighter than I had thought: there was a touching fragility about her movements. She had to reach up on tip-toe to fetch down the saffron-and-green striped robe, and memory stirred uneasily in me as I watched. *Atthis*, I thought: *of course*; yet the realisation came without surprise, or indeed any violence of emotion. Atthis as an awkward schoolgirl, eyes starred with tears, waving good-bye to me on the quayside at Mytilene; Atthis, a chrysalis no longer, but the small, brilliant butterfly who burst on my senses when I came back from my five years of Sicilian exile. Even the coil of hair – and then I stopped short, remembering the miniature that hung in my study alcove, seeing the pathetic imitation of it that Thalia had achieved.

She came back with the robe, smiling shyly, her great brown eyes anxious and adoring at once. I turned back to the mirror and let her wait while, very slowly and meticulously, I wiped the last traces of make-up from my face. Then our eyes met in the mirror and I nodded, leaning back as she slipped the robe over my arms and wrapped it about me. Her hands – how well I knew the symptoms! – hesitated at each physical contact, in an agony of uncertainty. I smiled to myself, and then thought, disconcerted: It is not only the Goddess who is cruel. So many years her votary, and can I hope to have escaped her nature?

I walked through to the bath-house, beckoning Thalia after me. The water was steaming, fragrant with pine-resin. I lay back in it, letting the heat work through me, watching Thalia as she stood there, fingers unconsciously stroking out the folds in the heavy linen robe. I smiled at her, feeling nothing except the blessed warmth of the water, conscious of my power.

'Now,' I said, 'you may wash me.'

She came to the side of the marble bath – slowly, very slowly – and I saw her tense her muscles to hide the trembling of her hands. She washed my back, and all the time her breath was coming faster and shallower. I felt nothing, nothing, nothing. Then I lay back again, and waited, smiling, still. As she touched my breasts the tremors ran faster and faster through her till she could hardly stand, and she snatched her hand away as though the water had suddenly become scalding hot.

Not yet. Wait. Be cruel.

She wrapped me in a heavy warm towel, and we went back to the bedroom again. I sat on the side of my bed, still in the towel, while she unpinned and brushed out my hair.

'Now the powder,' I said, and almost purred as she dusted my shoulders and feet with the fine-smelling talc Iadmon had given me in Samos.

Time enough, I thought, and took her hand in mind, and shook a little talc over my breasts, and guided her fingers to smooth it out. She was sobbing silently now, the tears streaming down from wide eyes, and I slipped my other hand inside her robe, caressing the high young breasts till they rose under my touch and her lips reached out to me blindly, and I tasted the salt of her tears. Nothing still. Nothing. You cannot drive out fire with dead ashes. Suddenly I felt active disgust surging up through the emptiness and the boredom – disgust with myself, with her, with the whole absurd situation. I flung her off me violently: she lay on the floor with hurt, bewildered eyes, staring up at me, terrified by this sudden change of mood. I wrapped the robe round me again, and found, to my astonishment, that I was shivering.

'Get out,' I said. 'Out of my sight.'

Peter Green, *The Laughter of Aphrodite: A Novel About Sappho of Lesbos*, 1965

NAUGHTY OLD SAPPHO

That naughty old Sappho of Greece
Said: 'What I prefer to a piece
  Is to have my pudenda

Rubbed hard by the enda
The little pink nose of my niece.'

American.

These lines being unintelligible to me, I sent them to my lady-specialist for comment and elucidation. Her reply, I confess, leaves me where I was – in complete ignorance of what the poem is about. She writes: 'I learnt no Greek at school, but have of course heard of Sappho's poems. They must be fifth-rate stuff, if she knew no more about poetry than she did about other things. The nose: what next? Be sure, dear Sir, there is some mistake here. The suggestion is too absurd. No woman is ever so much of a fool, not even under the influence of drink.'

I will leave it there, and wait for enlightenment from some other quarter, merely noting that Sappho was not born in Greece (though a good many other people were) and that tradition fails to record whether she had a niece or not.

Norman Douglas, *Limericks*, 1969

LESBOS

Viciousness in the kitchen!
The potatoes hiss.
It is all Hollywood, windowless,
The fluorescent light wincing on and off like a terrible
  migraine,
Coy paper strips for doors –
Stage curtains, a widow's frizz.
And I, love, am a pathological liar,
And my child – look at her, face down on the floor,
Little unstrung puppet, kicking to disappear –
Why she is schizophrenic,
Her face red and white, a panic,
You have stuck her kittens outside your window
In a sort of cement well
Where they crap and puke and cry and she can't hear.
You say you can't stand her,
The bastard's a girl.
You who have blown your tubes like a bad radio

Clear of voices and history, the staticky
Noise of the new.
You say I should drown the kittens. Their smell!
You say I should drown my girl.
She'll cut her throat at ten if she's mad at two.
The baby smiles, fat snail,
From the polished lozenges of orange linoleum.
You could eat him. He's a boy.
You say your husband is just no good to you.
His Jew-Mama guards his sweet sex like a pearl.
You have one baby, I have two.
I should sit on a rock off Cornwall and comb my hair.
I should wear tiger pants, I should have an affair.
We should meet in another life, we should meet in air,
Me and you.

Meanwhile there's a stink of fat and baby crap.
I'm doped and thick from my last sleeping pill.
The smog of cooking, the smog of hell
Floats our heads, two venomous opposites,
Our bones, our hair.
I call you Orphan, orphan. You are ill.
The sun gives you ulcers, the wind gives you TB
Once you were beautiful.
In New York, in Hollywood, the men said: 'Through?
Gee baby, you are rare.'
You acted, acted, acted for the thrill.
The impotent husband slumps out for a coffee.
I try to keep him in,
An old pole for the lightning,
The acid baths, the skyfuls off of you.
He lumps it down the plastic cobbled hill,
Flogged trolley. The sparks are blue.
The blue sparks spill,
Splitting like quartz into a million bits.

O jewel! O valuable!
That night the moon
Dragged its blood bag, sick
Animal
Up over the harbour lights.

And then grew normal,
Hard and apart and white.
The scale-sheen on the sand scared me to death.
We kept picking up handfuls, loving it,
Working it like dough, a mulatto body,
The silk grits.
A dog picked up your doggy husband. He went on.

Now I am silent, hate
Up to my neck,
Thick, thick.
I do not speak.
I am packing the hard potatoes like good clothes,
I am packing the babies,
I am packing the sick cats.
O vase of acid,
It is love you are full of. You know who you hate.
He is hugging his ball and chain down by the gate
That opens to the sea
Where it drives in, white and black,
Then spews it back.
Every day you fill him with soul-stuff, like a pitcher.
You are so exhausted.
Your voice my ear-ring,
Flapping and sucking, blood-loving bat.
That is that. That is that.
You peer from the door,
Sad hag. 'Every woman's a whore.
I can't communicate.'

I see your cute décor
Close on you like the fist of a baby
Or an anemone, that sea
Sweetheart, that kleptomaniac.
I am still raw.
I say I may be back.
You know what lies are for.

Even in your Zen heaven we shan't meet.

Sylvia Plath, 1962

FOURTEEN

Swingers and Sisters

Sappho in seventies soft porn; heavy eye make-up and velvet suits. From *Sappho, the Art of Loving Women*, J. Frederick Smith (London and New York, n.d.)

In the 1960s and 1970s Sappho was a split personality. She was a swinger; up for sex (of whatever kind), and drugs and rock 'n' roll. But then she was a sister; turning out for 'take-back-the-night' marches, wearing labrys earrings, eating no meat.

It took time for these cultural images to filter into publications, but there are two in particular that make my case: a picture book by J. Frederick Smith called *Sappho: The Art of Loving Women* and a history and advice book by the activists Sidney Abbott and Barbara Love called *Sappho was a Right-On Woman: A Liberated View of Lesbianism* (1972).

In Smith, Sappho does figure as a poet, because versions of her Fragments are made to function as excuses for 159 soft-porn photographs that range in costume and setting from velvet jackets and embroidered kaftans worn by women laid out on parquet floors to torn bikinis in a pounding surf; from lingerie sported in front of open fires, to naked girls on horseback in green meadows. Fred Smith says (so the jacket tells me) that *Sappho: The Art of Loving Women* 'comes at the right time . . . it is a great chance for women to express their love for each other and a chance for me to document their beauty and excitement'. It is true that Smith's photographs only show women, together and alone, but none the less the sexualised settings and the provocative poses make the pictures much like any Pirelli calendar from the same period, and seem to be aimed at an audience of men.

Sappho was a Right-On Woman, on the other hand, has hardly anything to do with Sappho the poet at all. It is a very practical book for women who have, or are about to, come out. It is politically correct and deeply unsexy, though the British Library still sees fit to catalogue it as a 'private case' book. The dirty words are only in the title, taken from the poem by Sue Schneider called 'Thinking Back Lesbian'. It concludes:

> We weave our minds round your Grecian words
> Of the Mused collective consciousness:
> 'Lesbians Love Now'
>
> Sappho, you must have been a 'Right On' woman.

The 'swinging' side of Sappho's Sixties incarnation is represented here by an extract from John Crosby's novel *Sappho in Absence* (1970). The bemused narrator ends up following his errant wife halfway round the world when she goes off to find herself. This Sappho is a heterosexual, drugged-up and meditating hippy, but she does – in a joke against her namesake – also write poetry. The terror roused in men's minds by the spectacle of female sexuality unleashed is curiously revealed in this novel by an ending where Sappho still escapes her loyal husband and his new girlfriend, Fiona, actually ends up getting eaten in India:

> 'We've had a visiting tiger lately. Or so they say. Actually no one has seen him.'
> 'Her,' I said . . .
> 'A man-eating lady tiger! How romantic.'
> 'A woman-eating lady tiger. She eats only girls.'
> 'A Lesbian tiger? How very with it! . . .'

If this seems misogynistic enough, then George Baxt's novel *Burning Sappho* (1972), is even worse. The opening word is ' "Murderess!" ', and it goes on in pretty much the same vein. His heroine is Belle, a police officer, who just cannot wean herself off girls, even though she really likes Tony, her all-he-man colleague. When her current lover, Willi, gets a job, as secretary to Sappho Yannopoulos, fashionable novelist and ardent feminist, Belle is deeply worried. As the blurb puts it:

> Under the bewitching powers of Sappho (best selling authoress of *Female Slave*) the group known as Sappho's Sisters stages a march and demo, culminating in a bonfire of brassières and an amazing mass denudation . . .

Eventually Sappho Yannopoulos turns out to be none other than one Ilsa Lubin, notorious commandant of a women's concentration camp, who has undergone plastic surgery and made a new life as a pulp-writer with her butch lover, Babe Lustig. She meets her just deserts when she is kidnapped by a group of Nazi-hunters and carried off to Israel for trial. Meanwhile Belle, you will be glad to know, disowns Willi and women, and succeeds in getting it together with lovable, beer-swilling, foul-mouthed Tony Mingus.

Not all Sappho texts were quite as obviously anxious. Patrick

Fetherston's verse narrative *Woman from Child (Sappho)* (1970, not included here) is a happy celebration of feminine sexuality, which uses the Fragments imaginatively to create a biography for a modern woman:

> I love to play.
> I'm ready
> to play now.
> Rataplan! Rataplan!
> Salt and honey pour down together!
> Thighs shudder!
> Feral love's
> shaken me up.

For the most part, however, it was women who responded to Sappho's challenge and made her their own, along with all her many dependants and associates. It was a trend that began in the 1950s with the founding of the lesbian club called 'Daughters of Bilitis', which published a magazine entitled *The Ladder*. For many years it was a discreet group, holding private meetings, promising privacy and discretion along with support and companionship. From the 1960s it took on a more public and politicised role, and the founders, Lyon and Martin, published *Lesbian/Woman* in 1972. It was during this time that many of the characters in Sappho's story also went public.

In America there was a 1969 song by Maxine Feldman called 'Angry Atthis', which complained about the social prejudice that would not let her hold her lover's hand in public. In England a magazine called *Sappho*, founded in 1972, took over from the earlier radical *Arena Three* and worked for women and for gays, helping to found the Lesbian and Gay Switchboard, setting up support groups and advising lesbians on artificial insemination. It was this socially and politically active picture of Sappho that coloured Martha Rofheart's novel *Burning Sappho* (1975), in which Doricha the courtesan, lover of Charaxus (Sappho's brother) and usually portrayed as Sappho's enemy, meditated on the poet's role as spokeswoman for her lowlier sisters, and on the 'scandal' that greeted her defection to the arms of a man.

Christine Bruckner's Sappho in 'Don't Forget the Kingfisher's Name' from *Desdemona, – If Only You had Spoken!* (1983) is one of many women from the past who are given back a voice, just as

Monique Wittig's Sappho is one of many bodies in *The Lesbian Body* (1973). Reclaiming, renaming, revaluing were all part of the political projects undertaken by feminists and lesbians at this time, and Sappho was one historical figure who came in for a refit. She started to appear, both as a positive and a negative image, in works like 'Sappho's Reply' (1981) by Rita Mae Brown, 'A Meeting of the Sapphic Daughters' (1979) by Ann Allen Shockley, 'Pro Femina' (1973) by Carolyn Kizer; in Robin Morgan's *Monster* (1972), in Gillian Hanscombe's 'Fragment' (1987), and in Marilyn Hacker's *Love, Death and the Changing of the Seasons* (1987); and her influence lies also in the work of Judy Grahn, Olga Broumas, Audre Lorde and Sapphire.

But in the second half of the twentieth century Sappho was not the only 'right-on' woman, the only role-model, the only ideal who could be resurrected from the past. The Amazons were invoked too, witches were rehabilitated, matriarchal societies were rediscovered (or invented). All the old names had to be remade in the image of this new present. We were not women (as in '—men'), but *wimmin* or *womon*, as we all learned a new *herstory* about this new *cuntry*. For centuries the word 'Sappho' had been a code among women. Now it was only one of many new names and old names, quite a few of which we have already met in this book. Intellectual women could claim Elizabeth I or Queen Christina, Christine de Pisan or Virginia Woolf; women-identified women could turn to Marie Antoinette or Colette or the Ladies of Llangollen; women-worshipping women could even make heroines of those who portrayed the pantheon, Bette Davis, Marlene Dietrich, Greta Garbo.

At the same time all the old passwords and signals were revisited, complicated, restated – but publicly, as open declarations, rather than as secret symbols. Sappho's violets, for instance, became a clear sign. They are her flower because she mentions them in Fragments 94 and 103, and because she describes the Muses as 'violet-haired'. So a gift of violets spelt out a private message between women in the nineteenth century's language of flowers; so they make an appearance in Robert Appleton's *Violet: The American Sappho* (1894), in Renée Vivien's *Dans un coin de violettes* (1910) and in the mauve-coloured covers of lesbian pulp novels such as *Imitation of Sappho* (1930) and *Diana* (1939). Lavender showed lesbians in their true colour. It is there in Monique Wittig, in the lesbian film company Lavender Blue Productions, in Alix Dobkin's 1971 album 'Lavender Jane Loves Women'.

Here was a new world, and Sappho and all her attributes held an honourable place in it. And if there was something rather earnest about Sappho's descendants in the Sixties and Seventies, if there was more social work than sex on their agendas, then that was soon to change. In 1980 the lesbian-feminist, leather-clad, sadomasochist writer Pat Califia called her explicit book on lesbian sexuality . . . *Sapphistries*. Sappho, after all, had turned into a swinger *and* a sister, and in Honor Moore's poem her daughter Cleis has everything, every way.

SAPPHO IN ABSENCE

We were discussing nymphomania on Leolia Heathcote's lawn at four o'clock Sunday afternoon one miserably warm October day and I was saying that nymphomania was getting to be as fashionable with contemporary authors as virginity with the Victorians and that neither contemporary nor Victorian authors knew what they were talking about.

'Yes, but do *you* know what you're talking about, darling?' said my wife, Sappho. 'How can you say with assurance that all Victorian girls were not virgins and all girls today aren't nymphomaniacs? How can you be sure?' . . .

* * *

Gerald can't, of course be sure, and when Sappho, the barrister hero's wife, suddenly disappears he is convinced that she is having an affair with an actor friend. With his own new paramour Fiona, he sets off in pursuit around the world, first of all to New York, where he has heard that Sappho is performing a hippie revue called 'The Bloody End', then to Turkey, where he ends up in prison on a charge of drug smuggling, and finally to Katmandu and then Bahpindar, where he finds Sappho again . . .

Then we'd smoke smoke a little hash and think about the Infinite. Prison is a great place to think about the infinite. You have lots of time. Once in a while I'd spare a moment to think about Fiona and Deep Down, but I was unworried. They were very close. I could feel their vibrations. If there's one thing hippies know above all others, it's unspoken communication. They have spent hours, days, years, communicating without saying anything and, after a while, it comes easy.

Soon Charlie Che had me standing on my head and the other yoga exercises. As I say, we had lots of time. After yoga, he'd continue my education, telling me about the history of outcasts everywhere in all periods of history – the Tooklats in the tenth century in Sweden, the Roussenon heretics in ninth-century France, he knew about them all. 'How did you get so wise?' I asked him one day.

'I studied under Leary at Harvard,' he said. 'I'm one of the greybeards of the movement.'

'How can you have served two-year sentences in so many jails and still be so young?'

'You don't serve the whole sentence. I have been sentenced to a total of forty-two years for possession. I am still only twenty-eight.'

Every day he'd tell me something new. I was the young Count of Monte Cristo and he was the Abbé and we were in the Château d'If and he'd rap on for hours, drawing parallels between today and history. The great weakness of our time was the total failure of the Church. Christianity, as far as the young were concerned, was an outworn superstition and that's why the young were grasping at every last wisp of mysticism – flying saucers, lines of force in the Glastonbury hills and all that. 'The same religious vacuum existed in the Roman empire. Its God was the state – Rome itself – and that's what started Christianity because people needed a better God than that. And today's children need better Gods than the Pentagon or the Kremlin. The magic has gone out of Christianity and so now kids are discovering Merlin or Buddha or Camelot or Katmandu.'

After a week, I told him about Sappho. 'Oh,' he said, 'Sappho.' He looked at me thoughtfully through those dark spectacles. I should have suspected that he knew Nik because everyone like him seemed to know Nik. He'd seen them both a month earlier at Peshawar.

'Sappho read me some of her poetry.'

'Her poetry?'

'You didn't know she was writing poetry?'

I sighed. 'She's taken up a good many new activities since I saw her last.'

Charlie Che contemplated me a long while. Then he said: 'She told me she takes a picture of a poem in her mind and then writes it down as fast as she can to preserve the truth of it.'

'Can you remember any of her poetry?' I was poring over every last scrap about the girl, like someone analysing Gladstone's letters for clues to his Irish policy.

Charlie wrinkled his forehead with a monstrous effort of recollection. ' "There are red peacocks under my eyelids da da da".' He shook his head. 'That's all I can remember. Something about *red* peacocks. Crazy.'

John Crosby, 1970

THE CORPORI CAVERNOSA THE
VAGINAL BULBS THE SKELETON
THE VERTEBRAL COLUMN THE
CLAVICLES THE RIBS THE
STERNUM THE HUMERI THE RADII
THE ULNAE THE CARPALS THE
METACARPALS THE PHALANGES
THE ILIAC BONES THE PELVIS THE
SACRUM THE COCCYX THE
FEMORA THE PATELLAE THE
FIBULAE THE TIBIAE THE TARSALS
THE METATARSALS THE CRURALS
THE MASTOIDS THE ORBITS THE
PATELLAE THE MONS PUBIS THE
VULVA THE WOMB THE BLADDER
THE INTESTINES THE KIDNEYS
THE SPLEEN THE LIVER THE GALL-
BLADDER THE STOMACH THE
LUNGS THE HEART

Sappho when *I* beseech her causes a violet lilac-smelling rain to fall over the island. *I* do not seek the shelter of the trees under pretext of escaping the moisture or to contemplate the divers signs multiplying between earth and sky. *I* stand head erect, mouth open, *I* thank Sappho the very tender goddess while you m / y very radiant one hold m / y hands. The clouds are hardly any darker than the water dripping from them, the sun lights them transparently, the hills are their exact replica the other way round violet rounded, the olive-trees seem paler by contrast more silver than green. You release m / y hands to undo my girdle, you remove m / y clothes, *I* watch you doing this, you too are naked, your skin is white in the violet light, your lips are mauve, the chestnut of your eyes is mauve your hair is brown mauve, you raise your arms, you begin to stir singing, you whistle between your teeth, you sing, loudly *I* praise Sappho the all-attentive, you recapitulate m / y phrases in your song, you spin them out, you modulate them interminably, you rotate on yourself, the water strikes your cheeks your shoulders your breasts your belly your back your buttocks your thighs your calves, violet rings appear on your skin, they enlarge progressively, immense circles cover your entire body, m / y fingers touch them while you laugh, you lift your feet so that their soles may be stained in their turn, you fall backwards on the sand all violet, the inward of your arms and thighs is involved, *I* inhale you m / y very odoriferous one, you smell very headily of lilac, Sappho could have done no better by clasping you against her violet breasts, now *I* lick you, you roll over and over, thousands of grains of violet sand sting your body, you are aglow with all your fires, your hair your pubic fleece that of your armpits is definitively violet and when as they say *I* look deep into your violet eyes m / y adored one *I* do not recognise them, you take hold of m / y fingers so they may touch your body so *I* may familiarise m / yself with your new appearance so *I* may interpret you m / y mauve one, glory to Sappho over centuries of centuries.

Monique Wittig, *The Lesbian Body*, 1973, trans. David LeVay, 1986

THE WISE

Sappho began, about the time of becoming a councilwoman, to write small treatises, very moral. It earned her another nickname, a new one, 'The Wise'. I cannot remember them all, or even a few, only scraps remain in the mind; they are not melodic, after all, and do not stir the emotions, as her songs had done. Of course, they were all quite true, but very dull; also, she did not practise what she urged on others! But then the artist cannot be held accountable for his work; the god, or goddess, speaks through him – or her, of course. In this case, it must have been the grave Athene!

One treatise in particular I well recall: 'When anger rises in the breast, restrain the idly yelping tongue.' I thought of those horrid letters she had sent to Charaxus, reviling me. Did Mars speak, too? Never mind, I had grown to love her well, this fascinating, wild, self-centred being. I had not forgotten, either, that all her life she had worked to improve the lot of women.

Indeed, though I travelled much with my husband, to near and far places, only on Lesbos did I see, ever, women and girls (outside of the hetaerae, another thing entirely) taught letters and sums, music and singing. Only on Lesbos did respectable women walk free in the agora, protected by the law. Even the poor hill wives enjoyed a few privileges; for instance, their parents, in famine time, might hire them out to work in some fine house, but there was no more selling into slavery, as had happened to me. As for the prostitutes, they gave only

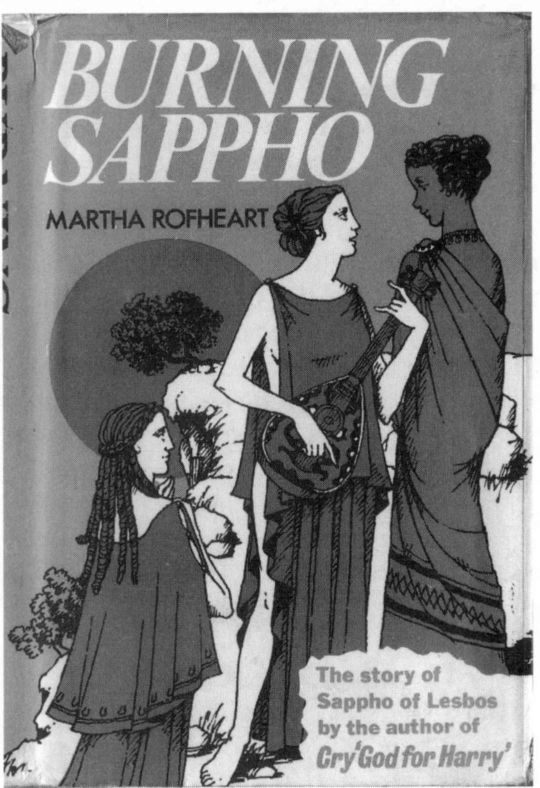

The cliff, the robes and the lyre turned guitar . . . otherwise Sappho is unrecognisable. Cover illustration by Sumiko for Martha Rofheart's historical novel *Burning Sappho* (London, 1974).

a token sum to the temple, and might leave at any time. This was true, also, of those who lived in brothels; they could not be kept against their will. As for the procurer, he was considered an outlaw; if he was discovered at it, the crime was punishable by death. Of course, all these laws were broken every day, in small ways, and the authorities, being men, winked at it. But one such case was not small, and one of the authorities was not a man – one was Sappho. The story, at the time, rocked the world.

Martha Rofheart, *Burning Sappho*, Book V, 1975

DON'T FORGET THE KINGFISHER'S NAME

Sappho bids farewell to the
young girls leaving Lesbos

How lovely you are – my girls! I taught you how to weave the crowns of flowers that adorn your hair today. Dancing with feet as light as gossamer to do the Goddess honour. Your voices ring out as bright and clear as the song of the lark rising in the morning. Don't look back! I taught you to be happy and to make others happy. I stand in the shadows – all the light is falling on you. You are my work, I sacrifice you to the Goddess Aphrodite – I give you up. I have prepared you ill for your roles as wives. Forgive me. By this evening a man's hand will already be tangled in Dika's hair. This very day your husbands will be undoing the ribbons which I taught you how to tie with such artistry; and you will minister to their raging desires, obey their exigent voices. Happy the man who will call you his own; unhappy, she whom you are forsaking.

I loved you all. Loved all of you in one of you; loved in you – and honoured – Aphrodite, the Goddess of Love, of Youth, of Beauty. Come! Gather around me once again, place me in your midst, conceal my ageing body from the eyes of the Goddess. Girls – Oh do not weep! I can see your arms stretching out towards the man to whom henceforward you will belong. But do not forget the Gardens of Mytelene; do not forget Sappho! You have been used to freedom – to days passed in play and in dancing. You have been told that this day, today, is the most beautiful and most important day of your life – you believed it, because everyone believes it. I have not taught you the art of suffering and enduring. I have kept from you what it is that awaits you. Sorrows are waiting for you. Duties! No longer will you detect the call of the nightjar, because a man will lie beside you on your couch – snoring, after taking too much wine. And in the mornings it is no longer the call of the finch that will waken you, but your wailing child, whose first tooth is on its way. I forgot to tell you about teething. Our lavishness will be a thing of the past; you will have to learn thrift; the talk will be all of rancid oil, nothing of the deep shade spreading under the olive tree. Take care to see that the water jugs are always full. Send the maids to the spring, but don't forget how you used to look at your own reflections and bathe in the fountain.

Don't forget the kingfisher's name! You spoke the words in chorus and the words turned into songs. Aphrodite passed among you and leaned, smiling, against the trunk of the flowering pomegranate tree. Everything was blossom and springtime and desire. I never told you that it all passes. You lived a today that had no end. The days were gifts that we gave away. Naked and barefoot you walked over the grass with steps so light they seemed to skim each blade. You learned to destroy nothing of all that the Gods let grow. With what tender solicitude you lifted up the snails and set them down again on the edges of the paths! Not one of you ever did any harm to the little lizard. Now you will have to take the quail's warm little body in your hands and wring its neck, pluck off its feathers, tear out its entrails. I have kept that from you. Your husband's mother is only waiting for the moment when she can teach you how to kill with a steady hand.

Christine Bruckner, *Desdemona, – If Only You Had Spoken!: Eleven Uncensored Speeches by Incensed Women*, 1983, trans. Eleanor Bron, 1992

CLEIS

She was young. The jeep was yellow. She
cruised past; her style was studied – a white
shirt crisply collared: a visitation, or
an extrapolation, from Sappho's
grove. Invitations had prevented our day
in bed, and we were suffering. Flowers, sun –

we had left brunch. A young woman in a sun
chariot, eyes burning beneath blond bangs, she
drove slowly towards us, a clean car. 'Good day,'
she said. You noted the greeting. The white
pelargonium were still in bloom. Sappho's
girls would be weaving them into garlands, or

dancing, singing what the scent inspired, or
quilling lyres. She leaned out the window, sun
glinting off her tousled brow. Sappho
would have applauded her approach, how she
directed her gaze without guile, whites
of her eyes cosseting blue irises. 'Good day'

was perhaps not all she said. It was Sunday
in California, weather like paradise or
Lesbos, clouds seductively adrift, white
as if to reassert cloud, reflecting sunlight. Our music had begun, our swoon, when she
drove down the hill and hovered. Was she Sappho's

gold-dressed daughter Cleis? Or Sappho's
dapple-throned Aphrodite, girl for a day,
oaring down from heaven in a gold car? She
slowed nonetheless, as if she expected us, or
had perhaps conjured us. We wore sun-
glasses, so she was not an attack of white

blindness, or any blindness. She was a white-
kirtled vision to tease us back to Sappho's –
dare I speak it? – bower; a trenchant, sun-
drenched mirage to accentuate a day
we were taken transcendentally, or
at least fervently, with one another. She

accelerated. White wheels whirled into day,
and, as Sappho's jeep, emblazoned NO NUKES OR
WIFE ABUSE flashed in the sun and vanished, so did she.

Honor Moore, 1984

FIFTEEN

Fragments

Rebellious daughter, complete with dreadlocks and found jewellery, Sarah Baylis's Sappho is a modern image, part shadowed, part self portrait. Cover illustration to *Sappho: Poems and Fragments,* translated by Josephine Balmer (London, 1984).

The National Art Library in London's Victoria and Albert Museum holds an artist's book called 'Sappho Fragments' by Rose Frain. It is one of only two copies in existence, and although it was only made in 1989, it is ephemeral, fleeting, evanescent, here-today-gone-tomorrow. It is hardly an art work at all, in the way that we have come to understand the form. Who will see it? Who will care? How, unless you have handled these pages – and few have – can you see what is here? And yet it is an art work: precious, rare, strange, full of meaning. When I wrote to the V & A about it, Elizabeth James, one of the curators of the Special Collections, wrote back to me: '(A personal aside: this is I think a remarkable work, both subtle and passionate; specifically responsive to texts without being in the slightest illustrational).'

Here is what happens.

You are presented with an ordinary grey, acid-free box. (*I think of Grenfell and Hunt, and the biscuit tins from Huntley and Palmer.*) Inside is an ordinary linen pillow case. (*I think of the Michael Fields, of the Ladies of Llangollen.*) Inside is another box; this time it is gauze-covered, with an embossed label, where you read on the cover, 'SAPPHO FRAGMENTS', white on white. (*I think of blank pages, empty spaces, writing in white ink.*) Inside the lid of the box it is signed with 'Rose Frain, 1989, 1/2', and 'SAPPHO FRAGMENTS' is printed in pale pink. There is a pair of white gloves labelled 'Minette 100% cotton'. (*Everything seems significant by now.*) And then another parcel wrapped (*like Colette's reviving mummy?*) in transparent gauze. 'Should I wear the gloves?' I ask the invigilator at the desk. She does not know. Solemnly we inspect the box. I really do not know what to do. I am so steeped in Sappho-symbols that the gauze, the pink, the pillow case, the acid-free box speak to me much more than they mean. I hesitate. The invigilator is robustly practical: 'If you were meant to wear gloves, it would say so,' she decides. But this does not really help me. The gloves, in that case, are a sign. I note them down. Or write them up.

Then, another layer. Another white gauze wrapping around twenty leaves of paper. The first of these is handmade, thick, white with pinkish hues just discernible, and across the centre a frail fault-line, where the paper is thin, about to tear, marked with fine silver thread. Then another piece of handmade paper, smaller this time, printed with the words:

now I shall sing these delightful songs
beautifully,
to my girls.

And so it goes on for twenty pages. Some with words on them (from Suzy Groden's 1964 translation), some just blank pieces of paper with traces . . . of paint, of pulped paper marked by texture and colour, feathers, silver thread, muslin, tatters of silk, human hair. Page 4 is a sheet of handmade paper, black in colour, with a short vertical fault-line, a tear or a wound, and a pale triangle three-quarters of the way down the page stuck with the finest traces of hair. Human hair. Red hair.

It says so much. It says nothing at all.

After the 1960s, after the 1970s, after 2,600 years, Sappho has been around. At the end of the eighteenth century women who made themselves in her image thought they would have education and power. At the end of the nineteenth century women who invoked her image thought they would be free. At the end of the twentieth century – for the first time – reforms became effective, social change took place and cultural visibility let strong women take their place in the world. Sappho, as a result, has become less unique than she once was. Now any number of historical icons is available, just as there is no shortage of contemporary idols – k.d.lang, Elizabeth Bishop, Sylvia Plath, Martina Navratilova, Madonna, Jodie Foster, Adrienne Rich – who could take over Sappho's social and cultural roles, allowing her to go back to being a poet who . . . writes poetry.

In Tony Harrison's 1990s play *The Trackers of Oxyrhynchus* one of the themes was the rediscovery of papyri bearing Sappho's verses. Of course it makes a good story, but all the same it had been disregarded (except by scholars) for a good century. In the years leading up to a new millennium the past assumes even greater significance than that usually lavished upon it, and in an age that values at once 'heritage' and 'political correctness' then the story of Sappho's re-emergence was bound to provide good copy. Of course Harrison's play is about so much more, but it was his pithy verses on poetry-as-compost – 'Spinach now flourishes from the pulped-up roll/ that held still hidden secrets of Sappho's soul' – that made the headlines when the play was introduced at London's National Theatre.

Text, papyri, solidity, earth, water, 'mulch' . . . the bits and pieces of what Eavan Boland calls 'love's archaeology' are what lie behind many of the pieces in this section. Harrison's is directly about the discovery of the papyri; Anne Carson's poem centres on the body represented (and misrepresented); Robert Chandler's poem is the story of a journey in/on the Underground; Boland's too. Many of these poems and stories are, quite literally, journeys – Chandler, Boland, Winterson, Padel, – into another place, into the past. In Boland's poem this is complicated by her multiple frame of reference, so that Sappho becomes a poet mother and a guide through the scenes of the past, just as Virgil appeared to Dante to guide him through heaven and hell. With good reason Hermes, god of travelling, god of communication, makes his appearance more than once in this selection. We are always moving on. And yet one thing here remains solid. The poem. Especially the Sapphic poem.

Chandler and Boland write with a Sapphic metre, and both use her technique of *enjambement*. Then the Fragments themselves are vividly present. Carson rewrites Sappho's Fragment 31 in her lines 2, 4, 6, 8, 10, 12, where broken words mark out the traces of the poem. Boland in 'The Journey' (1990) rewrites Fragment 1, with Sappho appearing to her in much the same way as Aphrodite once manifested herself to Sappho. In Jeanette Winterson's short story – and even more so in the larger fiction that it led to, *Art & Lies* (1994) – Sappho's Fragments are hinted at, recalled, quoted, misremembered. We are even offered a new Fragment, forged by Handel's Cardinal:

> Then rose the white moon.
> My love is whiter.
> White as salt
> Drawn from bitter pools.

In *Art & Lies*, as in 'The Poetics of Sex', Winterson's twentieth-century Sappho has a long memory. She re-incarnates, yet again, to recall all things that have been done under her name, in her name, to her name, for her name:

> I have a lot of questions, not least WHAT HAVE YOU DONE WITH MY POEMS? when I turn the pages of my manuscripts my fingers crumple the paper, the paper breaks up in burnt folds, the paper

> colours my palms yellow. I look like a nicotine junkie. I can no longer read my own writing . . .

Sappho cannot read her own writing because the writing is not hers. As Winterson says in *Art & Lies*:

> Her body is an apocrypha. She has become a book of tall stories, none of them written by herself. Her name has passed into history. Her work has not. Her island is known to millions now, her work is not.

Sappho escapes us. 'What you have seen,' says Boland's guide, 'is beyond speech,/ beyond song, only not beyond love.' The tall stories are in this book, the Fragments are in this book, her remains are in this book, but Sappho is not. And yet we reach for her, across what Ruth Padel's poem calls 'That whole impossible/ Space between her – between her and us.'

Sappho's poems, composed 2,600 years ago, are with us still. Sappho's name is with us still. From the past she glimmers, and we remember. In the future she beckons, and we respond.

THE TRACKERS

GRENFELL

Here at Oxyrhynchus where there's never been much rain
are rubbish heaps of riches. All these mounds contain
preserved papyri from the distant past.
These mounds need excavating fast . . . fast . . . fast.

(FELLAHEEN *activity increases.*)

Rubbish heaps of riches! Quite a paradox
there are priceless papyri in every crate and box,
from mundane wage bills for labour on a road
to fragments of a long-lost Sapphic Ode.
These chaps, our fellaheen, can't see what's unique
about scraps of old papyrus in ancient Greek.
We ship back papyri to decipher them at Queen's
but they'd use them, if we let them, as compost for their
greens.
Bits of Sappho, Sophocles and Plato
used as compost for the carrot and potato!

Papyri! Insects gnaw them. Time corrodes
and native plants get potted in a mulch of Pindar's Odes!
Horrible to contemplate! How can a person sleep
while Sophocles is rotting on an ancient rubbish heap?
Our fellaheen, though, are not entirely sure
if Menander's not more use to them as manure!
They ferret for fertiliser, and Hunt and I track
for philosophy and drama in nitrogenous *sebakh*.
Spinach now flourishes from the pulped-up roll
that held still hidden secrets of Sappho's soul.

Tony Harrison, *The Trackers of Oxyrhynchus*, 1990

SAPPHO FRAGMENT 31

(from the unfinished sequence *TV Men*)

TV makes things disappear. Oddly the world comes from Latin *videre* 'to see'. Longinus *de Sublimitate* 5.3

Sappho is smearing on her makeup at 5 AM in the woods by the TV studio.
He She Me You Thou disappears

Now resembling a Beijing concubine Sappho makes her way onto the set.
Laugh Breathe Look Speak Is disappears

The lighting men are setting up huge white paper moons here and there on the grass.
Tongue Flesh Fire Eyes Sound disappears

Behind these, a lamp humming with a thousand broken wasps.
Cold Shaking Green Little Death disappears

Places everyone, calls the director.
Nearness When Down In I disappears

Toes to the line please, says the assistant camera man.
But All And Must To disappears

Action!
Disappear disappears

Sappho stares into the camera and begins, *Since I am a poor man-*
Cut

Anne Carson, 1990

POEM ON THE UNDERGROUND

A prayer to Hermes

Guide me safely down into Pluto's kingdom,
Make the escalator run swift and smooth, and
Spare me never-ending delays beside the
Banks of the Northern

Line. And find me, swiftly, an empty carriage,
One that's just been hung with the latest poems;
May I taste each word between lips and tongue as I
Jolt towards Hendon.

May some young and heterosexual Sappho
See me mouthing sensuous rhymes – and catch my
Eye – and join me whispering verses during
Stops between stations.

May our two hearts beat to a long-lost measure,
May immortal goddesses smile from posters,
As we quietly float up the moving stairs into
Brightening sunlight.

Robert Chandler, 1998

THE JOURNEY

For Elizabeth Ryle

Immediately cries were heard. These were the loud wailing of infant souls weeping at the very entranceway; never had they had their share of life's sweetness for the dark day had stolen them from their mother's breasts and plunged them to a death before their time.

– Virgil, *The Aeneid*, Book 6

And then the dark fell and 'there has never'
I said 'been a poem to an antibiotic:
never a word to compare with the odes on
the flower of the raw sloe for fever

'or the devious Africa-seeking tern
or the protein treasures of the sea-bed.
Depend on it, somewhere a poet is wasting
his sweet uncluttered metres on the obvious

'emblem instead of the real thing.
Instead of sulpha we shall have hyssop dipped
in the wild blood of the unblemished lamb,
so every day the language gets less

'for the task and we are less with the language.'
I finished speaking and the anger faded
and dark fell and the book beside me
lay open at the page Aphrodite

comforts Sappho in her love's duress.
The poplars shifted their music in the garden,
a child started in a dream,
my room was a mess –

the usual hardcovers, half-finished cups,
clothes piled up on an old chair –
and I was listening out but in my head was
a loosening and sweetening heaviness,

not sleep, but nearly sleep, not dreaming really
but as ready to believe and still
unfevered, calm and unsurprised
when she came and stood beside me

and I would have known her anywhere
and I would have gone with her anywhere
and she came wordlessly
and without a word I went with her

down down down without so much as
ever touching down but always, always
with a sense of mulch between us,
the way of stairs winding down to a river

and as we went on the light went on
failing and I looked sideways to be certain
it was she, misshapen, musical –
Sappho – the scholiast's nightingale

and down we went, again down
until we came to a sudden rest
beside a river in what seemed to be
an oppressive suburb of the dawn.

My eyes got slowly used to the bad light.
At first I saw shadows, only shadows.
Then I could make out women and children
and, in the way they were, the grace of love.

'Cholera, typhus, croup, diptheria,'
she said, 'in those days they racketed
in every backstreet and alley of old Europe.
Behold the children of the plague.'

Then to my horror I could see to each
nipple some had clipped a limpet shape –
suckling darknesses – while others had their arms
weighed down, making terrible pietàs.

She took my sleeve and said to me, 'be careful.
Do not define these women by their work:
not as washerwomen trussed in dust and sweating,
muscling water into linen by the river's edge

'nor as court ladies brailled in silk
on wool and woven with an ivory unicorn

and hung, nor as laundresses tossing cotton,
brisking daylight with lavender and gossip.

'But these are women who went out like you
when dusk became a dark sweet with leaves,
recovering the day, stooping, picking up
teddy bears and rag dolls and tricycles and buckets –

'love's archaeology – and they too like you
stood boot deep in flowers once in summer
or saw winter come in with a single magpie
in a caul of haws, a solo harlequin.'

I stood fixed. I could not reach or speak to them.
Between us was the melancholy river,
the dream water, the narcotic crossing
and they had passed over it, its cold persuasions.

I whispered, 'let me be
let me at least be their witness,' but she said
'What you have seen is beyond speech,
beyond song, only not beyond love;

'remember it, you will remember it'
and I heard her say but she was fading fast
as we emerged under the stars of heaven,
'there are not many of us; you are dear

'and stand beside me as my own daughter.
I have brought you here so you will know forever
the silences in which are our beginnings
in which we have an origin like water,'

and the wind shifted and the window clasp
opened, banged and I woke up to find
the poetry books stacked higgledy piggledy,
my skirt spread out where I had laid it –

nothing was changed; nothing was more clear
but it was wet and the year was late.
The rain was grief in arrears; my children
slept the last dark out safely and I wept.

Eavan Boland, 1990

WHY DO YOU SLEEP WITH GIRLS?

My lover Picasso is going through her Blue Period. In the past her periods have always been red. Radish red, bull red, red like rose hips bursting seed. Lava red when she was called Pompeii and in her Destructive Period. The stench of her, the brack of her, the rolling splitting cunt of her. Squat like a Sumo, ham thighs, loins of pork, beefy upper cuts and breasts of lamb. I can steal her heart like a bird's egg.

She rushes for me bull-subtle, butching at the gate as if she's come to stud. She bellows at the window, bloods the pavement with desire. She says, 'You don't need to be Rapunzel to let down your hair.' I know the game. I know enough to flick my hind-quarters and skip away. I'm not a flirt. She can smell the dirt on me and that makes her swell. That's what makes my lithe lover bulrush-thin fat me. How she fats me. She plumps me, pats me, squeezes and feeds me. Feeds me up with lust till I'm as fat as she is. We're fat for each other we sapling girls. We neat clean branching girls get thick with sex. You are wide enough for my hips like roses, I will cover you with my petals, cover you with the scent of me. Cover girl wide for the weight of my cargo. My bull-lover makes a matador out of me. She circles me and in her rough-made ring I am complete. I like the dressing up, the little jackets, the silk tights, I like her shiny hide, the deep tanned leather of her. It is she who gives me the power of the sword. I used it once but when I cut at her it was my close fit flesh that frilled into a hem of blood. She lay beside me slender as a horn. Her little jacket and silk tights impeccable. I sweated muck and couldn't speak in my broken ring. We are quick change artists we girls.

WHICH ONE OF YOU IS THE MAN?

Picasso's veins are Kingfisher blue and Kingfisher shy. The first time I slept with her I couldn't see through the marble columns of her legs or beyond the opaque density of each arm. A sculptor by trade, Picasso is her own model.

The blue that runs through her is sanguine. One stroke of the knife and she changes colour. Every month and she changes colour. Deep pools of blue silk drop from her. I know her by the lakes she leaves on the way to the bedroom. Her braces cascade over the stair-rail, she wears earrings of lapis lazuli which I have caught cup-handed, chasing her *deshabillée*.

When she sheds she sheds it all. Her skin comes away with her clothes. On those days I have been able to see the blood-depot of her heart. On those days it was possible to record the patience of her digestive juices and the relentlessness of her lungs. Her breath is blue in the cold air. She breathes into the blue winter like a Madonna of the Frost. I think it right to kneel and the view is good.

She does perform miracles but they are of the physical kind and ordered by her Rule of Thumb to the lower regions. She goes among the poor with every kind of salve unmindful of reward. She dresses in blue she tells me so that they will know she is a saint and it is saintly to taste the waters of so many untried wells.

I have been jealous of course. I have punished her good deeds with some alms-giving of my own. It's not the answer, I can't catch her by copying her, I can't draw her with a borrowed stencil. She is all the things a lover should be and quite a few a lover should not. Pin her down? She's not a butterfly. I'm not a wrestler. She's not a target. I'm not a gun. Tell you what she is? She's not Lot no. 27 and I'm not one to brag.

We were by the sea yesterday and the sea was heavy with salt so that our hair was braided with it. There was salt on our hands and in our wounds where we'd been fighting. 'Don't hurt me,' I said and I unbuttoned my shirt so that she could look at my breasts if she wanted to. 'I'm no saint,' she said and that was true, true too that our feet are the same size. The rocks were reptile blue and the sky that balanced on the top of the cliffs was sheer blue. Picasso made me put on her jersey and drink dark tea from a fifties flask.

'It's winter,' she said. 'Let's go.'

We did go, leaving the summer behind, leaving a trail of footprints two by two in identical four. I don't know that anyone behind could have told you which was which and if they had there would have been no trace by morning.

WHAT DO LESBIANS DO IN BED?

Under cover of the sheets the tabloid world of lust and vice is useful only in so much as Picasso can wipe her brushes on it. Beneath the sheets we practise Montparnasse, that is Picasso offers to paint me but we have sex instead.

We met at Art School on a shiny corridor. She came towards me so swiftly that the linoleum dissolved under her feet. I thought, 'A woman who can do that to an oil cloth can certainly do something for me.' I made the first move. I took her by her pony tail the way a hero grabs a runaway horse. She was taken aback. When she turned round I kissed her ruby mouth and took a sample of her sea blue eyes. She was salty, well preserved, well made and curved like a wave. I thought, 'This is the place to go surfing.'

We went back to her studio, where naturally enough, there was a small easel and a big bed. 'My work comes first,' she said. 'Would you mind?' and not waiting for an answer she mixed an ochre wash before taking me like a dog my breasts hanging over the pillow.

Not so fast Picasso, I too can rumple you like a farm hand, roll you like good tobacco leaf against my thighs. I can take that arrogant throat and cut it with desire. I can make you dumb with longing, tease you like a doxy on a date.

Slowly now Picasso, where the falling light hits the floor. Lie with me in the bruised light that leaves dark patches on your chest. You look tubercular, so thin and mottled, quiescent now. I picked you up and carried you to the bed dusty with ill-use. I found a newspaper under the sheets advertising rationing.

The girl on the canvas was sulky. She hadn't come to be painted. I'd heard all about you my tear-away tiger, so fierce, so unruly. But the truth is other as truth always is. What holds the small space between my legs is not your artistic tongue nor any of the other parts you play at will but the universe beneath the sheets that we make together.

We are in our igloo and it couldn't be snugger. White on white on white on white. Sheet Picasso me sheet. Who's on top depends on where you're standing but as we're lying down it doesn't matter. What an Eskimo I am, breaking her seductive ice and putting in my hand for fish. How she wriggles, slithers, twists to resist me but I can bait her and I do. A fine catch, one in each hand and one in my mouth. Impressive for a winter afternoon and the stove gone out and the rent to pay. We are warm and rich and white. I have so much enjoyed my visit.

'Come again?' she asked. Yes tomorrow, under the sodium street lights, under the tick of the clock. Under my obligations, my history, my fears, this now. This fizzy, giddy all consuming now. I will not let time lie to me. I will not listen to dead voices or unborn pain. 'What if?' has no power against 'What if not?' The not of you is unbearable. I must have you. Let them prate, those scorn-eyed anti-romantics.

Love is not the oil and I am not the machine. Love is you and here I am. Now.

WERE YOU BORN A LESBIAN?

Picasso is an unlikely mother but I owe myself to her. We are honour-bound, love-bound, bound by cords too robust for those healthy hospital scissors. She baptised me from her own font and said, 'I name thee Sappho.' People often ask if we are mother and child.

I could say yes, I could say no, both statements would be true, the way that lesbians are true, at least to one another if not to the world. I am no stranger to the truth but very uncomfortable about the lies that have dogged me since my birth. It is no surprise that we do not always remember our name.

I am proud to be Picasso's lover in spite of the queer looks we get when holding hands on busy streets. 'Mummy, why is that man staring at us?' I said when only one month old. 'Don't worry dear, he can't help it, he's got something wrong with his eyes.'

We need more Labradors. The world is full of blind people. They don't see Picasso and me dignified in our love. They see perverts, inverts, tribades, homosexuals. They see circus freaks and Satan worshippers, girl-catchers and porno turn-ons. Picasso says they don't know how to look at pictures either.

WERE YOU BORN A LESBIAN?

A fairy in a pink tutu came to Picasso and said, 'I bring you tidings of great joy. All by yourself with no one to help you you will give birth to a sex toy who has a way with words. You will call her Sappho and she will be a pain in the ass to all men.'

'Can't you see I've got a picture to finish?' said Picasso.

'Take a break,' said the fairy. 'There's more to life than Art.'

'Where?' said Picasso, whose first name wasn't Mary.

'Between your legs,' said Gabriel.

'Forget it. Don't you know I paint with my clit?'

'Here, try a brush,' said the fairy offering her a fat one.

'I've had all the brushes I need,' said Picasso.

'Too Late,' said the fairy. 'Here she comes.'

Picasso slammed the door on her studio and ran across to the Art College where she had to give a class. She was angry so that her

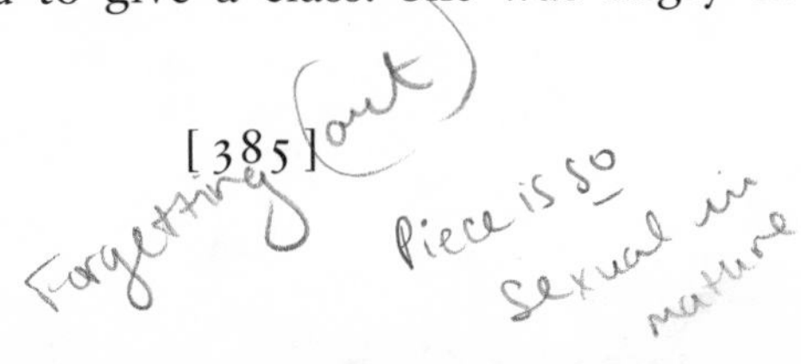

breath burnt the air. She was angry so that her feet dissolved the thin lino tiles already scuffed to ruin by generations of brogues. There was no one in the corridor or if there was she was no one. Picasso didn't recognise her, she had her eyes on the door and the door looked away. Picasso, running down the clean corridor, was suddenly tripwired, badly thrown, her hair came away from her glorious head. She was being scalped. She was being mugged. She was detonated on a long fuse of sex. Her body was half way out of the third floor window and there was a demon against her mouth. A poker-red pushing babe crying, 'Feed me, Feed me now.'

Picasso took her home, what else could she do? She took her home to straighten her out and had her kinky side up. She mated with this creature she had borne and began to feel that maybe the Greek gods knew a thing or two. Flesh of her flesh she fucked her.

They were quiet then because Sappho hadn't learned a language. She was still two greedy hands and an open mouth. She throbbed like an outboard motor, she was as sophisticated as a ham sandwich. She had nothing to offer but herself, and Picasso, who thought she had seen it all before, smiled like a child and fell in love.

WHY DO YOU HATE MEN?

Here comes Sappho, scorching the history books with tongues of flame. Never mind the poetry feel the erection. Oh yes, women get erect, today my body is stiff with sex. When I see a word held hostage to manhood I have to rescue it. Sweet trembling word, locked in a tower, tired of your Prince coming and coming. I will scale you and discover that size is no object especially when we're talking inches.

I like to be a hero, like to come back to my island full of girls carrying a net of words forbidden them. Poor girls, they are locked outside their words just as the words are locked into meaning. Such a lot of locking up goes on on the Mainland but here the doors are always open.

Stay inside, don't walk the streets, bar the windows, keep your mouth shut, keep your legs together, strap your purse around your neck, don't wear valuables, don't look up, don't talk to strangers, don't risk it, don't try it. He means she except when it means Men. This is a Private Club.

That's all right boys, so is this. This delicious unacknowledged island where we are naked with each other. The boat that brings us

here will crack beneath your weight. This is territory you cannot invade. We lay on the bed, Picasso and I, listening to the terrible bawling of Salami. Salami is a male artist who wants to be a Lesbian.

'I'll pay you twice the rent,' he cries, fingering his greasy wallet. 'I'll paint you for posterity. I love women, don't you know? Oh God I wish I was a woman, wafer-thin like you, I could circle you with one hand.' He belches.

Picasso is unimpressed. She says, 'The world is full of heterosexuals, go and find one, half a dozen, swallow them like oysters, but get out.'

'Oh whip me,' says Salami getting moist.

We know the pattern. In half an hour he'll be violent and when he's threatened us enough, he'll go to the sleaze pit and watch two girls for the price of a steak.

As soon as he left we forgot about him. Making love we made a dictionary of forbidden words. We are words, sentences, stories, books. You are my New Testament. We are a gospel to each other, I am your annunciation, revelation. You are my St Mark, winged lion at your feet. I'll have you, and the lion too, buck under you till you learn how to saddle me. Don't dig those spurs too deep. It's not so simple this lexographic love. When you have sunk me to the pit I'll mine you in return and we shall be husbands to each other as well as wives.

I'll tell you something Salami, a woman can get hard and keep it there all night and when she's not required to stand she knows how to roll. She can do it any way up and her lover always comes. There are no frigid lesbians, think of that.

On this island where we live, keeping what we do not tell, we have found the infinite variety of Woman. On the Mainland, Woman is largely extinct in all but a couple of obvious forms. She is still cultivated as a cash crop but is nowhere to be found growing wild.

Salami hates to hear us fuck. He bangs on the wall like a zealot at an orgy. 'Go home,' we say, but he doesn't. He'd rather lie against the skirting board complaining that we stop him painting. The real trouble is that we have rescued a word not allowed to our kind.

He hears it pounding through the wall day and night. He smells it on our clothes and sees it smeared on our faces. We are happy Picasso and I. Happy.

I thought I had lost Picasso. I thought the bright form that shapes my days had left me. I was loose at the edges, liquid with uncertainty. The taut lines of love slackened. I felt myself unravelling backwards, away from her. Would the thinning thread snap?

For seven years she and I had been in love. Love between lovers, love between mother and child. Love between man and wife. Love between friends. I had been all of those things to her and she had been all of those things to me. What we were we were in equal parts, and twin souls to one another. We like to play roles but we know who we are. You are beauty to me Picasso. Not only sensuous beauty that pleases the eye but artistic beauty that challenges it. Sometimes you are ugly in your beauty, magnificently ugly and you frighten me for all the right reasons.

I did not tell you this yesterday or the day before. Habit had silenced me the way habit does. So used to a thing no need to speak it, so well known the action no need to describe it. But I know that speech is freedom which is not the same as freedom of speech. I have no right to say what I please when I please but I have the gift of words with which to bless you. Bless you Picasso. Bless you for your straight body like a spire. You are the landmark that leads me through the streets of the everyday. You take me past the little houses towards the church where we worship. I do worship you because you are worthy of praise. Bless you Picasso for your able hands that carry the paint to the unbirthed canvas. Your fingers were red when you fucked me and my body striped with joy. I miss the weals of our passion just as I miss the daily tenderness of choosing you. Choosing you above all others, my pearl of great price.

My feelings for you are biblical; that is they are intense, reckless, arrogant, risky and unconcerned with the way of the world. I flaunt my bleeding wounds, madden with my certainty. The Kingdom of Heaven is within you Picasso. Bless you.

There is something missing and that is you. Your clothes were gone yesterday, your easel was packed flat and silent against the wall. When I got up and left our unmade bed there was the smell of coffee in the house but not the smell of you. I looked in the mirror and I knew who was to blame. Why take the perfect thing and smash it? Some goods are smashed that cannot be replaced.

It has been difficult this last year. Love is difficult. Love gets harder which is not the same as to say that it gets harder to love. You are not hard to love. You are hard to love well. Your standards are high, you won't settle for the quick way out which is why you made for the door. If I am honest I will admit that I have always wanted to avoid love. Yes give me romance, give me sex, give me fights, give me all the parts of love but not the simple single word which is so complex and demands the best of me this hour this minute this forever.

Picasso won't paint the same picture twice. She says develop or die. She won't let yesterday's love suffice for today. She makes it new, she remixes her colours and stretches her canvas until it sighs. My mother was glad when she heard we'd split up. She said, 'Now you can come back to the Mainland. I'll send Phaeon to pick you up.' Phaeon runs a little business called LESBIAN TOURS. He drives his motor-boat round and round the island, just outside the one mile exclusion zone. He points out famous lesbians to sight-seers who always say, 'But she's so attractive!' or 'She's so ugly!'

'Yeah,' says Phaeon, 'and you know what? They're all in love with me.' One sight-seer shakes his head like a collecting box for a good cause. 'Can't you just ask one of 'em?' he says. 'I can ask them anything,' says Phaeon who never waits to hear the answer.

WHY DO YOU SLEEP WITH GIRLS?

Picasso has loved me for fifty years and she loves me still. We got through the charcoal tunnel where the sun stopped rising. We no longer dress in grey.

On that day I told you about I took my coat and followed her footprints across the ice. As she walked the world froze up behind her. There was nothing for me to return to, if I failed, I failed alone. Despair made it too dark to see, I had to travel by radar, tracking her warmth in front of me. It's fashionable now to say that any mistake is made by both of you. That's not always true. One person can easily kill another.

Hang on me my darling like rubies round my neck. Slip onto my finger like a ring. Give me your rose for my buttonhole. Let me leaf through you before I read you out loud.

Picasso warms my freezing heart on the furnace of her belly. Her belly is stoked to blazing with love of me. I have learned to feed her every day, to feed her full of fuel that I gladly find. I have unlocked the storehouses of love. On the Mainland they teach you to save for a rainy day. The truth is that love needs no saving. It is fresh or not at all. We are fresh and plentiful. She is my harvest and I am hers. She seeds me and reaps me, we fall into one another's laps. Her seas are thick with fish for my rod. I have rodded her through and through.

She is painting today. The room is orange with effort. She is painting today and I have written this.

Jeanette Winterson, 1993

SOS

She's in Persia now, but she's remembering us
As we used to be
When you were her goddess. When your songs
Were the songs she loved best. She's new –
Minted, I know, in the East among Lydian girls –
A new moon, a full moon, no less, while dew licks
The earth and the slick sky curls up its trousseau
Of sunset and rose; turning on
All available stars, scattering electric

Largesse, her well-loved razzle of gold, on the skin
Of that shivering ocean
Plus meadows of soft-eye hibiscus –
But it's a dead cert,
Darling, she's anxious and restless.
Soft belly, soft navel
Tattooed with her longing, she's pacing
Those plum-scented avenues thinking of you,
Your face

Through the twilight. Listen:
She's crying for us.
The rude-petalled night has airwaved an alert,
ONE WETSILK BODY ON FIRE, distress signals racing
Through sea-spray and air, the fanfare and cirrhus
Of all the hurt
Cities in their complicated dusk,
That whole impossible
Space between her – between her and us.

Ruth Padel, 1999

Someone, I say to you,
will think of us
in some future time

Sappho, Fragment 147

ACKNOWLEDGEMENTS

A project of this kind results in many debts both professional and personal. I would like to thank the President and Fellows of Clare Hall, Cambridge, where this work was completed, and my colleagues in the English departments at Birmingham University and Queen Mary and Westfield College, University of London for their support and encouragement. For their unfailing courtesy and interest I thank the staffs of the British Library, the Bodleian, the Cambridge University Library, the National Art Library at the Victoria and Albert Museum, the Department of Prints and Drawings at the British Museum, the Warburg Institute, the University of London Library at Senate House, the London Library, the New York Public Library, the Bridgeman Art Library and the Reunion des Musées Nationales in Paris. Thanks also to the bookdealers who have sought titles for me and supplied me with rarieties especially Rick Gekoski, Ulysses, Maggs, Jarndyce, Bell, Book and Radmall, Clearwater Books and the Fortune Green bookshop.

I would like to thank especially those of my colleagues, students and friends who have made contributions which they may, or may not, remember but which have all found their place in this book: Gillian Beer, Dinah Birch, Philippa Brewster, Elisabeth Bronfen, John Carey, Kate Challis, David Constantine, Helen Cooper, Dan Cruikshank, Tony Davies, Maud Ellmann, Inga-Stina Ewbank, David Fairer, Stephanie Forward, Lilian and Karl Fredricksson, Kate Flint, Heather Glen, Edith Hall, Clare Harman, Lesley Howard, James Howett, Vivien Jones, Katy Kabitoglou, Angela Leighton, Jerome McGann, Catherine Maxwell, Leonée Ormond, Ruth Padel, Emma Parker, Mizzi van der Pluijm, Ruth Rendell, Beaty Rubens, Andrew Sanders, Gill Saunders, Marion Shaw, Michael Slater, Ian Small, Mark Storey, Oliver Taplin, Marion Thain, Kelsey Thornton, Sophie Tomlinson, Erica Wagner, Margaret Williamson, and Caroline Zilboorg. Grateful thanks go to my colleagues at the BBC with whom I have made Sappho programmes and especially to those whose musical expertise has provided me with treasures: Kevin Bee, Christopher Cook, Piers Burton Page, Anthony Sellers, Fiona Shelmerdine and Sally Marmion. Thanks also to Jonathan Burnham who first commissioned the book, to Alison Samuel at Chatto and Caroline Michel at Vintage, to Mandy Greenfield, Nick Wetton, and, especially, to Jenny Uglow who saw how to make it into a story and did make it into a picture.

The author and publishers are grateful for permission to reproduce the following copyright material: RICHARD ALDINGTON: 'The Singer' from *The Love of Myrrhine and Konallis* (Pascal-Covici, 1926), © Estate of Richard Aldington, reprinted by permission of Rosica Colin Ltd; LUDOVICO ARIOSTO: an extract from *Orlando Furioso*, translated by Guido Waldman (Oxford University Press, 1983) reprinted by permission of the publisher; JOSEPHINE BALMER: '[From our love]' and 'Leave Crete and come to me now, to that holy temple' from *Sappho* (Bloodaxe Books, 1984) reprinted by permision of the publisher; MARY BARNARD: 'Must I remind you, Cleis', 'Bridesmaids'carol II', 'Pain penetrates', 'It is clear now:', 'Sleep, darling' and 'Prayer to my lady of Paphos' from *Sappho: A New Translation* (University of California Press, 1958), © 1958 The Regents of the University of California, © renewed 1986 Mary Barnard, reprinted by permission of the publisher; ROLAND BARTHES: an extract from *A Lover's Discourse: Fragments,* translated by Richard Howard (Jonathan Cape, 1979) reprinted by permission of The Random House Archive Library; EAVAN BOLAND: 'The Journey' from *Outside History: Selected Poems 1980–1990* (Carcanet Press, 1990), reprinted by permission of the publisher; CHRISTINE BRUCKNER: an extract from "Don't forget the kingfisher's name' from *Desdemona, If Only You had Spoken!: Eleven Uncensored Speeches by Incensed Women*, translated by Eleanor Bron (Virago, 1992), © 1983 by Hoffmann und Campe Verlag, Hamburg, reprinted by permission of Faith Evans Associates and Hoffmann und Campe Verlag; ANNE CARSON: 'Sappho Fragment 31' from "Just for the Thrill: Sycophantizing Aristotle's Poetry" in *Arion*, 1.1 (1990); ROBERT CHANDLER: 'Poem on the Underground' from *Sappho* (Everyman's Poetry/J. M. Dent, 1998), © Robert Chandler, reprinted by permission of the author; WILLIAM CHRISTIE: 'Moonset' from *Pancae Micae (A Few Crumbs)* (The Castlelaw Press, 1971); DAVID CONSTANTINE: 'Some say nothing on earth excels in beauty' from *Waiting for Dolphins* (Bloodaxe Books, 1983); JOHN CROSBY: an extract from *Sappho in Absence* (William Collins, 1970); GUY DAVENPORT: 'Percussion, salt and honey' from *Sappho: Poems and Fragments* (University of Michigan Press, 1965); 'called you' from *Seven Circles* (New Directions, 1995); CHRISTINE DE PIZAN: an extract from *The Book of the City of Ladies*, translated by Earl Jeffrey Richards (Picador, 1983); HILDA DOOLITTLE: 'Fragment Forty' from *Collected Poems, 1912–1944* (Carcanet Press, 1984), © 1982 by the Estate of Hilda Doolittle, reprinted by permission of New Directions Publishing Corporation; GEORGE NORMAN DOUGLAS: 'That naughty old Sappho of Greece' from *The Norman Douglas Limerick Book* (Anthony Blond, 1969); LAWRENCE DURRELL: an extract from *Sappho: A Play in Verse* (Faber & Faber, 1950); RONALD FIRBANK: extracts from *Vainglory* (Grant Richards, 1915); PETER GREEN: extracts from *The Laughter of Aphrodite: a Novel About Sappho of Lesbos* (John Murray, 1965), reprinted by permission of David Higham Associates; SUZY GRODEN: 'Eternal Aphrodite' from *Epigrams from the Palatine Anthology Ascribed to Sappho* in *Arion*, 3.3 (Autumn, 1964); TONY HARRISON: an extract from *The Trackers of Oxyrhynchus* (Faber & Faber, 1990); A.E. HOUSMAN: 'The weeping Pleiads wester' from *Collected Poems and Selected Prose* (Penguin Twentieth Century Classics, 1989); ROBERT LOWELL: from 'Three Letters to Anaktoria' from *Imitations* (Farrar, Straus & Giroux/Faber & Faber, 1962), ©1959 by Robert Lowell, © renewed 1987 by Harriet, Sheridan, and Caroline Lowell, reprinted by permission of the publishers; EDNA ST VINCENT MILLAY: 'Evening on Lesbos' from *Collected Poems* (Harper & Row), © 1928, 1955 by Edna St Vincent Millay and Norma Millay Ellis; HONOR MOORE: 'Cleis' from *Memoir* (Chicory Blue Press, 1988); THOMAS MORE: 'Musas esse noem referunt' from *Complete Works: Volume 3* (Yale University Press, 1984); JOHN FREDERICK NIMS: 'Stars around the luminous moon' from *Poems in Translation: Sappho to Valéry* (University of Arkansas Press, 1990), reprinted by permission of the publisher; RICHARD O'CONNELL: 'Undistinguished you'll lie' and 'like a cyclone' from *Sappho*, translated by Richard O'Connell (Atlantis Editions, 1975), reprinted by permission of Richard O'Connell; RUTH PADEL: 'S.O.S.', reprinted by permission of the author; SYLVIA PLATH: 'Lesbos' from *Collected Poems*, edited by Ted Hughes (Faber & Faber, 1981); EZRA POUND: 'Thy soul' and 'Shop Girl' from *Lustra of Ezra Pound* (Elkin Mathews, 1916); JIM POWELL: 'Most beautiful of all the stars' from *Sappho: A Garland* (Farrar, Straus & Giroux, 1993), © 1993 by Jim Powell, reprinted by permission of Farrar, Straus & Giroux, LLC; DIANE RAYOR (editor.): 'the herald came . . .' from

Sappho's Lyre: Archaic Lyric and Women Poets of Ancient Greece (University of California Press, 1991); RAINER MARIA RILKE: 'Eranna to Sappho' and 'Sappho to Eranna' from *New Poems* [1907], a bilingual edition translated by Edward Snow (North Point Press, 1984), translation © 1984 by Edward Snow, reprinted by permission of North Point Press, a division of Farrar, Straus & Giroux, LLC; MARTHA ROFHEART: an extract from *Burning Sappho* (Talmy Franklin, 1975); SARA TEASDALE: 'To Clës' from *The Collected Poems of Sara Teasdale* (Macmillan, 1937); SYLVIA TOWNSEND WARNER and VALENTINE ACKLAND: 'The clock plods on –' from *Whether a Dove or a Seagull* (Chatto & Windus, 1934); PETER WHIGHAM: 'Children's Song', 'The Apple' and 'Girlhood' from *Things Common, Properly: Selected Poems 1942–1980* (Anvil Press Poetry, 1984), reprinted by permission of the publisher; WILLIAM CARLOS WILLIAMS: 'Peer of the gods is that man' from *Paterson, V* (New Directions, 1958/Carcanet Press, 1992), reprinted by permission of Carcanet Press; JEANETTE WINTERSON: 'The Poetics of Sex', from The World and Other Places (Jonathan Cape, 1997), reprinted by permission of the author; MONIQUE WITTIG: an extract from *The Lesbian Body*, translated by David Le Vay (Peter Owen, 1975), reprinted by permission of the publisher; VIRGINIA WOOLF: "A Society" from *Monday or Tuesday* (The Hogarth Press, 1921); DOUGLAS YOUNG: 'Caller rain frae abune', 'Deid sall ye ligg . . .', 'Thon Time We Aa Wonned' and 'Minnie, I canna caa my wheel' from *Auntran Blads. An Outwale o Verses* (William MacLennan, 1943.)
Every effort has been made to trace or contact all copyright holders. The publishers would be pleased to rectify any errors or omissions brought to their notice at the earliest opportunity.

SELECT BIBLIOGRAPHY

Editions and translations of Sappho

John Addison, *The Works of Anacreon translated into English Verse; with Notes explanatory and poetical. To which are added the Odes, Fragments, and Epigrams of Sappho* (London, 1735)

Richard Aldington, *Des Imagistes* ed. Ezra Pound (The Egoist Press, London, 1914)

Anon. (D.K. Sandford?) 'Greek Authoresses' in *The Edinburgh Review* (January–July 1832), pp. 182–208

Josephine Balmer, trans., *Sappho: Poems and Fragments* (Brilliance Books, London, 1984) reissued (Bloodaxe, Newcastle upon Tyne, 1992)

Mary Barnard, trans., *Sappho* (University of California Press, Berkeley and Los Angelos, 1958), reissued (Shambhala Press, Boston and London, 1994)

Yves Battistini, trans., *Poétesses grecques: Sappho, Corinne, Anyte etc* . . . (Imprimerie Nationale Éditions, Paris, 1998)

George Gordon Byron, *Don Juan*, Canto 3.107 (London, 1820)

David A. Campbell, ed., *Greek Lyric 1: Sappho and Alcaeus* (Loeb Classical Library, Harvard University Press, Cambridge Massachusetts, 1982)

Robert Chandler, ed. and trans., *Sappho* (J.M. Dent, London, 1998)

William Christie, *Paucae Micae (A Few Crumbs)* (The Castlelaw Press, West Linton Peebleshire, 1971)

David Constantine, *Watching for Dolphins* (Bloodaxe, Newcastle-upon-Tyne, 1983)

William Cory, *Ionica* (George Allen, London, 1891)

Edwin Marion Cox, *The Poems of Sappho* (Williams and Norgate Ltd., London, 1925)

Edwin Marion Cox, *Sappho: The Text Arranged with Translations an Introduction and Notes* (The Boar's Head Press, Manaton Devon, 1932)

Guy Davenport, *Seven Greeks* (New Directions Publishing Corporation, 1995)

Anne Finch, Countess of Winchilsea, *Miscellany Poems on Several Occasions* (London, 1713)

E. Burnaby Greene, *The Works of Anacreon and Sappho* (London, 1768)
Suzy Q. Groden, *Arion* Volume 3, part 3 (Autumn, 1964)
C.R. Haines, *Sappho: The Poems and Fragments* (George Routledge and Sons, London, 1926)
John Hall, trans. Longinus *Peri Hypsous*, 'On the Sublime' (1652)
Thomas Hardy, *The Complete Poems* (Macmillan, London, 1981)
A.E. Housman, *More Poems* (London, 1936)
Anne Hunter, *Poems* (London, 1802)
Peter Jay and Caroline Lewis, eds., *Sappho Through English Poetry* (Anvil Press, London, 1996)
Walter Savage Landor, *Pericles and Aspasia* (London, 1836)
Walter Savage Landor, *The Hellenics* (London, 1847)
Edgar Lobel and Denys Page, eds., *Poetarum Lesbiorum Fragmenta* (Clarendon, Oxford University Press, Oxford, 1955)
Robert Lowell, 'Three Letters to Anaktoria' from *Imitations* (Faber and Faber, London, 1962)
John Herman Merivale, *Collections from the Greek Anthology*, by the late Rev. Robert Bland and others (London, 1833)
Marion Mills Miller, trans, and David M. Robinson ed., *The Songs of Sappho: Including the Recent Egyptian Discoveries* (Frank-Maurice, New York, 1925)
Thomas Moore, *Odes of Anacreon translated into English verse* (London, 1800)
John Frederick Nims, *Poems in Translation: Sappho to Valery* (University of Arkansas Press, Arkansas, 1990)
Richard O'Connell, *Sappho* (Atlantis Editions, Philadelphia, 1975)
Percy Osborn, *The Poems of Sappho* (Elkin Matthews, London, 1909)
Ambrose Phillips, translations of Fragment 1 and Fragment 31 (1711), *The Works of Anacreon and Sappho, Done from the Greek, by several hands* (London, 1715)
Jim Powell, *Sappho: A Garland* (Farrar Straus Giroux, New York, 1993)
Diane Rayor, *Sappho's Lyre: Archaic Lyric and Women Poets of Ancient Greece* (University of California Press, Berkeley and Los Angeles, 1991)
Dante Gabriel Rossetti, *The Collected Works of Dante Gabriel Rossetti* (Ellis and Elvey, London, 1888)
Philip Sidney, version of Fragment 31, in *The Old Arcadia* (1598)

Tobias Smollett, version of Fragment 31 in *The Adventures of Roderick Random*, chapter XL (1748)
H. de Vere Stacpoole, *Sappho: A New Rendering* (Hutchinson and Co., London, n.d.)
Edward Storer, *The Poems and Fragments of Sappho* (with *The Poems of Anyte of Tegea* translated by Richard Aldington), (The Egoist Press, London, 1919)
John Addington Symonds, translations published in Henry Thornton Wharton's *Sappho: Memoir, Text, Selected Renderings and a Literal Translation* (David Stott, London, 1885)
Alfred Tennyson, 'Elegiacs' in *Poems, Chiefly Lyrical* (1830)
Eva-Maria Voigt, ed. *Sappho et Alcaeus: Fragmenta* (Amsterdam-Polak and Van Gennep, Amsterdam, 1971)
Moreton John Walhouse, 'The Nine Greek Lyric Poets' in the *Gentleman's Magazine* (April 1877), pp. 433–51
M.L., West, trans., *Greek Lyric Poetry* (World's Classics, Oxford University Press, Oxford, 1993)
Henry Thornton Wharton, *Sappho: Memoir, Text, Selected Renderings and a Literal Translation* (London, 1885)
Peter Whigham, *Things Common, Properly* (Anvil Press Poetry Ltd., London, 1984)
William Carlos Williams, *Paterson*, Book V (New Directions Publishing Corporation, 1958)
Douglas Young, *Auntran Ballads: An Outwale o Verses* (William McLellan, 1943)

Critical works on the classical Sappho

Robert Bagg, 'Love, Ceremony and Daydream in Sappho's Lyrics' in *Arion* 3 (1964), 44–82.
Anne Pippin Burnett, 'Desire and Memory (Sappho Fragment 94)' in *Classical Philology* 74 (1979), 16–27
Anne Pippin Burnett, *Three Archaic Poets: Archilochus, Alcaeus, Sappho* (Harvard University Press, Cambridge Massachusetts, 1983)
Anne Carson, *Eros the Bittersweet: An Essay* (Princeton University Press, Princeton New Jersey, 1986)
Jeffrey M. Duban, *Ancient and Modern Images of Sappho: Translations and Studies in Archaic Greek Love Lyric* (University Press of America, Washington D.C., 1983)
Page DuBois, *Sappho is Burning* (University of Chicago Press, Chicago and London, 1995)

Ellen Greene, 'Apostrophe and Women's Erotics in the Poetry of Sappho', *Transactions of the American Philological Association* 124 (1994), 41–56.

Ellen Greene, ed. *Reading Sappho* (University of California Press, Berkeley and Los Angeles, 1996)

Judith P. Hallett, 'Sappho and her Social Context: Sense and Sensuality' in *Signs* 4 (1979), pp. 447–64.

Judith P. Hallett, 'Beloved Cleis' in *Quaderni Urbinati di Cultura Classica* 10 (1982), pp. 21–31.

Richard Jenkyns, *Three Classical Poets: Sappho, Catullus and Juvenal* (Harvard University Press, Cambridge Massachusetts, 1982)

André Lardinois, 'Lesbian Sappho and Sappho of Lesbos' in ed. Jan Bremmer, *From Sappho to de Sade: Moments in the History of Sexuality* (Routledge, London and New York, 1989), pp. 15–35.

Mary Leftkowitz, 'Critical Stereotypes and the Poetry of Sappho' in *Greek, Roman and Byzantine Studies* 14 (1973), pp. 113–23.

Edith Mora, *Sappho: Histoire d'un Poete* (Flammarion, Paris, 1966)

Denys Page, *Sappho and Alcaeus* (Clarendon Press, Oxford, 1955)

H. Rudiger, *Sappho: Ihr Ruf und Ruhm bei der Nachwelt* (Dieterich, Leipzig, 1933)

Helmut Saake, *Sapphostudien: Forschungsgeschichte, biografische und literarische Untersuchungen* (Schoningh, Munich, 1972)

Marilyn B. Skinner, 'Woman and Language in Archaic Greece, or, Why is Sappho a Woman?' in ed. Nancy Sorkin Rabinowitz and Amy Richlin, *Feminist Theory and the Classics* (Routledge, London and New York, 1993), pp. 125–44

Jane McIntosh Snyder, *Lesbian Desire in the Lyrics of Sappho* (Columbia University Press, New York, 1997)

Margaret Williamson, *Sappho's Immortal Daughters* (Harvard University Press, Cambridge Massachusetts, 1995)

Lyn Hatherly Wilson, *Sappho's Sweet Bitter Songs: Configurations of Female and Male in Ancient Greek Lyric* (Routledge, London and New York, 1996)

John J. Winkler, *The Constraints of Desire: The Anthropology of Sex and Gender in Ancient Greece* (Routledge, New York and London, 1990)

Critical works on the reception of Sappho

Joseph Addison, *The Spectator*, No. 223, November 15, 1711 and No. 233, November 27 (London, 1711)

Shari Benstock, *Women of the Left Bank, Paris 1900–1940* (University of Texas Press, Austin Texas, 1986).

Elyse Blankley, 'Return to Mytilene: Renée Vivien and the City of Women' in ed. Susan Merrill Squier, *Women Writers and the City* (University of Tennessee Press, Knoxville Tennessee, 1984), pp. 45–67

Susan Brown, 'A Victorian Sappho: Agency, Identity, and the Politics of Poetics', *English Studies in Canada* 20.2 (June 1994), pp. 205–25.

Rae Dalven, *Daughters of Sappho: Contemporary Greek Women Poets* (Fairleigh Dickinson University Press, Rutherford, 1994)

Joan DeJean, *Fictions of Sappho, 1546–1937* (University of Chicago Press, Chicago, 1989)

Judy Grahn, *The Highest Apple: Sappho and the Lesbian Poetic Tradition* (Spinsters Ink, San Francisco, 1985)

Ellen Greene, ed. *Re-Reading Sappho: Reception and Transmission* (University of California Press, Berkeley and Los Angeles, 1996)

Germaine Greer, 'The Enigma of Sappho' in *Slipshod Sibyls: Recognition, Rejection and the Woman Poet* (Viking Penguin, London, 1995)

Susan Gubar, 'Sapphistries' in *Signs* 10 (Autumn, 1984), pp. 43–62

Elizabeth Harvey, 'Ventriloquizing Sappho, or the Lesbian Muse' in *Ventriloquized Voices: Feminist Theory and English Renaissance Texts* (Routledge, London and New York, 1992), pp. 116–39

Angela Leighton, *Victorian Women Poets: Writing Against the Heart* (Harvester Wheatsheaf, Hemel Hempstead, 1992)

Lawrence Lipking, *Abandoned Women and Poetic Tradition* (Chicago University Press, Chicago, 1988)

Jane Marcus, 'Sapphistory: The Woolf and the Well' in *Lesbian Texts and Contexts: Radical Revisions* (Onlywomen, London, 1992), pp. 164–80

Catherine Maxwell, 'Engendering Vision in the Victorian Male Poet' in ed. J.B. Bullen, *Writing and Victorianism* (Longman, London and New York, 1997), pp. 73–103

Holt Parker, 'Sappho Schoolmistress' in *Transactions of the American Philological Association* 123 (1993), pp. 309–351

Yopie Prins, *Victorian Sappho* (Princeton University Press, Princeton New Jersey, 1999)

Yopie Prins and Maeera Schreiber, eds. *Dwelling in Possibility: Women Poets and Critics on Poetry* (Cornell University Press, Ithaca and London, 1997)

Margaret Reynolds, 'The Woman Poet Sings Sappho's Last Song' in ed. Angela Leighton, *Victorian Women Poets: A Critical Reader* (Blackwell, Oxford, 1996)

David M. Robinson, *Sappho and Her Influence* (George Harrap and Co. Ltd, London, 1925)

Peter Tomory, 'The Fortunes of Sappho, 1770–1850' in ed. G.W. Clarke with J.C. Eade, *Rediscovering Hellenism: The Hellenic Inheritance and the English Imagination* (Cambridge University Press, Cambridge, 1989), pp. 121–35

Ruth Vanita, *Sappho and the Virgin Mary: Same-Sex Love and the English Literary Imagination* (Columbia University Press, New York, 1996)

Chris White, 'The One Woman (in virgin haunts of poesie): Michael Field's Sapphic symbolism' in ed. Suzanne Raitt, *Volcanoes and Pearl Divers: Essays in Lesbian Feminist Studies* (Onlywomen Press, London, 1995)

Joyce Zonana, 'Swinburne's Sappho: The Muse as Sister-Goddess' *Victorian Poetry* 28 (1990), pp. 39–50

COMPLETE LIST OF EXTRACTS

I The Fragments of Sappho
Fragment 1, 'The Ode to Aphrodite'
Ambrose Phillips (1711)
John Addison (1735)
John Addington Symonds (1883)
Edward Storer (1915)
Mary Barnard (1958)
Suzy Q. Groden (1964)
Fragment 2, 'Hither to me from Crete'
Percy Osborn (1909)
Douglas Young (1943)
Josephine Balmer (1984)
Fragment 5, 'To the Nereids'
C.R. Haines (1926)
Jane McIntosh Snyder (1997)
Fragment 16, 'Some say a host of cavalry'
David Constantine (1983)
Margaret Williamson (1995
Fragment 31, 'That man seems to me . . .'
Sir Philip Sidney (1554–86)
John Hall (1652)
Ambrose Phillips (1711)
John Addison (1735)
Tobias Smollett (1741)
E. Burnaby Greene (1768)
John Addington Symonds (1883)
William Carlos Williams (1958)
Robert Lowell (1962)
Fragment 34, '. . . the stars and the shining moon . . .'
Percy Osborn (1909)
John Frederick Nims (1990)
Fragment 44, 'The wedding of Hector and Andromache'
Diane Rayor (1991)
Fragment 47, 'Love shook my heart . . .'
Richard O'Connell (1975)

M.L. West (1993)
Fragment 49, 'I loved you once Atthis . . .'
T.H. Wharton (1885)
Fragement 55, 'Dead you shall lie there . . .'
Anne Finch, Countess of Winchelsea (1661–1720)
Francis Fawkes (1760)
William Cory (1891)
Thomas Hardy (1901)
Percy Osborn (1909)
Douglas Young (1943)
Richard O'Connell (1975)
Fragment 58, '. . . love has got for me the brightness and beauty of the sun'
Guy Davenport (1995)
Fragment 94, 'Frankly I wish I were dead . . .'
Edward Storer (1915)
Fragment 96, '. . . now she shines among Lydian ladies . . .'
Richard Aldington (1914)
Douglas Young (1943)
Fragment 102, 'Truly sweet mother I cannot weave my web . . .'
Thomas Creech (1659–1700)
Francis Fawkes (1760)
Anne Hunter (1794)
Thomas Moore (1779–1852)
Walter Savage Landor (1775–1864)
Moreton John Walhouse (1877)
Douglas Young (1943)
Fragment 104, '. . . to the Evening star . . .'
George Gordon, Lord Byron (1821)
Alfred Tennyson (1830)
Jim Powell (1993)
Fragment 105 a) and b), . . . the sweet apple . . . and the hyacinth
Dante Gabriel Rossetti (1870)
H. Vere de Stacpoole (1863–1951)
Edward Storer (1915)
Fragment 114, '. . . where are you virginity . . . ?
Edwin Marion Cox (1925)
Mary Barnard (1958)
Peter Whigham (1984)
Fragment 130, '. . . Love once again . . . limb-loosening . . . bitter sweet . . .'

John Addington Symonds (1883)
Guy Davenport (1965)

Fragment 131, 'But to you Atthis, the thought of me is hateful . . .'
H. Vere de Stacpoole (1863–1951)

Fragment 132, 'I have a golden child . . .'
John Herman Merivale (1833)
Mary Barnard (1958)

Fragment 137, Sappho to Alcaeus: 'I wish to say something . . .'
Anon, (D.K. Sandford?) (1832)

Fragment 146, '. . . neither honey nor bee . . .'
Mary Barnard (1958)
Josephine Balmer (1984)

Fragment 150, Must I remind you Cleis that there should be no lamentation in the house of the Muses . . .'
Mary Barnard (1958)

Fragment 168B (Ascribed to Sappho, Loeb edition), 'The moon is set and the Pleiades . . .'
Francis Fawkes (1760)
E. Burnaby Greene (1768)
A.E. Houseman (1936)
William Christie (1971)

II The Tenth Muse

Catullus, 'Ille mi par esse', 'That man, to me, seems like a god' (c. 84–54 BC)

Ovid, from 'Sappho to Phaon', Letter XV, *Heroides* (43 BC–AD 18)

III The Learned Lady

Giovanni Boccaccio, 'Sappho, Poetess of Lesbos', from *Of Famous Women* (1313–75), trans. Guido A. Guarino, (1964)

Christine de Pisan, from *The Book of the City of Ladies* (1405), trans. Earle Jeffrey Richards, 1983

Ludovico Ariosto, from *Orlando Furioso* (1516), trans. Guido Waldman, 1974, 1983

Thomas More, Epigram (c. 1477–1535)

John Lyly, from *Sappho and Phao* (1584)

John Donne, 'Sappho to Philaenis' (1573–1631)

IV Nymphs and Satyrs

Anon, 'The Loves of Damon and Sappho' (c. 1680)

Alexander Radcliffe, 'Sapho to Phaon', from *Ovid's Travestie: A Burlesque Upon Ovid's Epistles,* (1681)

William Bosworth, from 'The Story of Sappho and Phaon' from *The Chast and Lost Lovers* (1651)

Aphra Behn, 'To the Fair Clarinda, Who Made Love to Me, Imagin'd More than Woman' (1688)

William Walsh, from *A Dialogue Concerning Women, Being a Defence of the Sex. Written to Eugenia* (1691)

Pierre Bayle, 'Sappho', from *Historical and Critical Dictionary* (1697), English translation (1710)

Nicholas Rowe, 'Song', Extract from Giles Jacob, *Tractatus de Hermaphroditis; or, a Treatise of Hermaphrodites* (1718)

Wanton Sapphoics

Alexander Pope, 'Sappho to Phaon' (1707)

Anon, from *Crooked Sixpence, With a Learned Preface* (1743

William King, extract from Book II, *The Toast. An Heroick Poem in four books originally written in Latin by Frederick Scheffer: now done into English, and illustrated with Notes and Observations by Peregrine O'Donald* (1736)

Anon, from *Lesbia: A Tale in Two Cantos* (1756)

Anon, from *A Sapphick Epistle from Jack Cavendish to the Honourable and most beautiful Mrs. D***** (1782?)

Anon, from *La Nouvelle Sapho, ou Histoire de la Secte Anandryne* (1789)

VI The Sapphic Sublime

Mark Akenside, from 'Ode XIII. On Lyric Poetry' (1721–70)

George Dyer, 'Ode XXVI, The Resolve. Supposed to be Written by Sappho' (1755–1841)

Robert Southey, 'Sappho. A Monodrama' (1793)

Mary Robinson, Sonnet IV, Sonnet VII and Sonnet XXXVI from *Sappho and Phaon* (1796)

Samuel Taylor Coleridge, ''Alcaeus to Sappho' (1800)

Elizabeth Moody (nee Greenly), 'Sappho Burns her Books and Cultivates the Culinary Arts' (1798)

VII Hellenism and Heroes

Alessandro Verri, from *The Adventures of Saffo* (1780), trans. John Nott, 1803

Abbe Barthelemy, from *Travels of Anacharsis the Younger in Greece* (1788), English translation, 1817
Philip Freneau, from 'The Monument of Phaon' (1770)
Etienne Lantier, from *The Travels of Antenor in Greece and Asia* (1797), English translation, 1799
Germaine de Staël, from *Corinne, or Italy* (1807), trans. Isabel Hill, 1833

VIII The Lady with the Lyre
Charles-Louis Didelot, with music by Joseph Mazzinghi; from the abstract to 'Sapho & Phaon: Grand Ballet Erotique' (1797)
William Mason, from *Sappho: A Lyrical Drama* (1797)
Percy Bysshe Shelley, 'To Constantia, Singing' (1822)
Felicia Hemans, 'The Last Song of Sappho' (1793–1835)
L.E.L., (Letitia Elizabeth Landon), 'Sappho's Song', from *The Improvisatrice* (1824)
Alfred, Lord Tennyson, 'Fatima' (1832)
Elizabeth Barrett Browning, 'Song of the Rose' (1850)
Hans Schmidt, 'Sapphische Ode', (1880's), set to music by Johannes Brahms, op. 94 no.4, 1884
Matthew Arnold, 'A Modern Sappho' (1849)
Charles Kingsley, 'Sappho', (1847)
Christina Rossetti, 'Sappho' (1846)
'What Sappho would have said had her leap cured instead of killing her' (1848)
Music by Giovanni Pacini, and libretto by Giuseppe Cammarano: from *Saffo* (1840)
Music by Charles Gounod, and libretto by Emile Augier from *Sapho* (1851)
Caroline Norton, 'The Picture of Sappho' (1808–77)

IX Daughter of de Sade
Charles Baudelaire, 'Lesbos' (1857)
Emily Dickinson, "Heaven" – is what I cannot reach!' (c. 1861, published 1896)
Algernon Charles Swinburne, from 'Anactoria' (1866)
George Moore, from 'Sappho' (1881)
Alphonse Daudet, from *Sappho: Parisian Manners: A Realistic Novel* (1884), English translation, 1886
Arthur Symons, 'Hallucination I' (1902)

Francis Cowley Burnand, from *Sappho: or, Look Before You Leap* (1870)

X The New Woman

Estelle Lewis, from Sappho: A Tragedy (1875)

Catherine Amy Dawson (later Scott), from *Sappho* (1889)

John Addington Symonds, 'Accentual Sapphics' (1880

Amy Levy, 'To Lallie (Outside the British Museum)' (1884)

Michael Field (Katharine Bradley and Edith Cooper), 'Atthis, my darling, thou dids't stray' from *Long Ago* (1889)

Michael Field, 'Why are women silent?' (1889)

Mary Coleridge, 'Marriage' (1900)

Robert S. Dalton, from *Lesbia Newman* (1889)

Bret Harte, From *A Sappho of Green Springs* (1891)

Music by Walter Slaughter, libretto by Harry Lobb; from *Sappho: A Lyric Romance* (1886)

Robert Appleton, from *Violet: The American Sappho, A Realistic Novel of Bohemia* (1894)

XI Return to Mytilene:

Olive Custance, 'Love's Firstfruits' (1897)

Pierre Louys, 'Words in the Night,' from *The Songs of Bilitis* (1894)

Renee Vivien 'Sappho Enchants the Sirens', from *The Woman of the Wolf, and Other Stories* (1904), trans. Karla Jay and Yvonne M. Klein, 1983

Radclyffe Hall, 'Ode to Sappho' (1908)

Lesbia Harford, 'I can't feel the sunshine' (1915), published 1985

Sylvia Townsend Warner and Valentine Ackland, 'The clock plods on –' (1934)

John A.T. Lloyd, from *Sappho: Life and Work* (1910)

Sara Teasdale, 'To Cleis' (1911)

Rainer Maria Rilke, 'Sappho to Eranna' (1907), trans. Edward Snow, 1984

XII Modernist Sappho

Ezra Pound, 'Ιμερρω' and 'Shop Girl', from *Lustra* (1916)

H.D. (Holda Doolittle), 'Fragment Forty', from *Helidora* (1924)

Richard Aldington, 'The Singer', from *The Love of Myrrhine and Konallis* (1926)

Amy Lowell, 'A Shower' (1919)

Edna St Vincent Millay, 'Evening on Lesbos' (1928)

Virginia Woolf, 'A Society', from *Monday or Tuesday* (1921)

XIII Sapphistories
Ronald Firbank, from *Vainglory* (1915)
Stratis Myrivilis, from *The Schoolmistress with the Golden Eyes* (1954), trans. Peter Sherrard, 1964
Lawrence Durrell, from *Sappho: A Play in Verse* (1950)
Peter Green, from *The Laughter of Aphrodite: A Novel about Sappho of Lesbos* (1965)
Norman Douglas, 'That naughty old Sappho of Greece,' from *Limericks* (1969)
Sylvia Plath, 'Lesbos' (1962)

XIV Swingers and Sisters
John Crosby, from *Sappho in Absence* (1970)
Monique Wittig, from *The Lesbian Body* (1973), trans. David Le Vay, 1986.
Martha Rofheart, from 'The Twilight of Lesbos: Told by Doricha, courtesan of Naukratis, later called Rhodopis, "the roselike one", Book V, *Burning Sappho* (1975)
Christine Bruckner, from 'Don't Forget the Kingfisher's Name' from *Desdemona, – If Only You Had Spoken!: Eleven Uncensored Speeches by Incensed Women* (1983), trans. Eleanor Bron, 1992
Honor Moore, 'Cleis' (1984)

XV Fragments
Tony Harrison, from *The Trackers of Oxyrhynchus* (1990)
Anne Carson, 'Sappho Fragment 31, (from the unfinished sequence *TV Men*)' (1990)
Robert Chandler, 'Poem on the Underground' (1998)
Eavan Boland, 'The Journey' (1990)
Jeanette Winterson, 'The Poetics of Sex' (1993)
Ruth Padel, 'S.O.S.' (1999)

INDEX

The main quotations from the Fragments are indicated in bold type.